Religious Liberty
in Western Thought

Emory University Studies in Law and Religion

General Editor
John Witte, Jr.
Emory University

Number 4

Religious Liberty in Western Thought

edited by
Noel B. Reynolds
W. Cole Durham, Jr.

Religious Liberty
in Western Thought

edited by
Noel B. Reynolds
W. Cole Durham, Jr.

SCHOLARS PRESS
Atlanta, Georgia

EMORY UNIVERSITY
STUDIES IN LAW AND RELIGION

Religious Liberty
in Western Thought

edited by
Noel B. Reynolds
W. Cole Durham, Jr.

© 1996
Emory University

Library of Congress Cataloging in Publication Data
Religious liberty in Western thought / edited by Noel B. Reynolds, W.
Cole Durham, Jr.
   p.   cm. — (Emory University studies in law and religion;
no. 4)
   Includes bibliographical references.
   ISBN 0-7885-0319-7 (cloth : alk. paper). — ISBN 0-7885-0320-0
(pbk. : alk. paper)
   1. Freedom of religion—History.   I. Reynolds, Noel B.
II. Durham, W. Cole, 1948   . III. Series.
BV741.R44   1996
322.44'2'09—dc20   96-43774
                                              CIP

Published by Scholars Press
for
Emory University

CONTENTS

ACKNOWLEDGMENTS

This volume has a longer history than its editors would like to admit. At every step it has benefited from the contributions of others which we are glad to acknowledge here.

This inquiry began with a proposal for a 1992 conference entitled "Rethinking Religious Liberty," which received generous funding from Liberty Fund, Inc., of Indianapolis. With the encouragement of the participants and Liberty Fund, we organized a sequel in 1993 entitled "Religious Liberty and Tradition." While Liberty Fund does not encourage published outcomes for conferences, it became clear in the course of discussions that enlarged versions of the papers presented there could make a valuable contribution to one of the most important topics in public discourse today. By the time we undertook to pull these and other supplementary materials together for this volume, a few of the papers had been committed for publication elsewhere, and are included here by special permission, as noted in the first footnote of each relevant chapter.

We are particularly grateful to Liberty Fund for making the conferences, and hence, the volume possible. We also thank each of the authors for their contributions.

We have benefited greatly from the assistance of staff at Brigham Young University. Theresa S. Brown was indefatigable in tracking down publishers' permissions and final drafts of the papers. We express special appreciation to Scott M. Ellsworth for the extraordinary contributions he has made to the editing of this book. As a law student and former English professor, he brought unique talents and abilities to the project. He contributed endless hours to the process of making sure that citations were consistent and conformed to a model that he sometimes had to define for us. He alerted us to countless errors that might otherwise have been made and carried the editing burden to an extent that has been critical to bringing this project to fruition. We also thank his wife, Laura, and his family for putting up with the many demands from us that made him less available to them. Thomas J. Lowery gave valuable assistance in the final writing and editing stages.

Finally, we express appreciation to our own wives, Louise Durham and Sydney Reynolds, for their constant support and tolerance of the academic lifestyle that makes these kinds of efforts possible.

W. Cole Durham, Jr.
Noel B. Reynolds

Brigham Young University
Provo, Utah
June 1996

INTRODUCTION

W. Cole Durham, Jr.* and Noel B. Reynolds**

Religious freedom is arguably the oldest and the deepest of the rights embedded in modern constellations of liberty.[1] And yet, as events in Bosnia, Chechnya, the Near East, Ireland, and all too many other places remind us,[2] it is a freedom permanently at risk. It is jeopardized not only by the dramatic collisions of cultural difference, but also by mundane insensitivities in schools, in the workplace, and in countless other social settings. Intolerance, it seems, is a poverty of spirit we are destined to have with us always.

The seemingly endless unattainability of full religious freedom is in large part, of course, a reflection of human imperfection. But it is also part of a deeper set of problems about the relationship of religion and politics in human society. Which of these should be the ultimate arbiter of the structure of individual and social life? To what extent are political and legal ordering

---

* Professor of Law, J. Reuben Clark Law School at Brigham Young University. A.B., Harvard College (1972); J.D., Harvard Law School (1975).

** Professor of Political Science, Brigham Young University. B.A., Brigham Young University (1967); Ph.D., Harvard University (1971).

[1] See W. Cole Durham, Jr., "Perspectives on Religious Liberty: A Comparative Framework," in Johan D. van der Vyver & John Witte, *Religious Human Rights in Global Perspective: Legal Perspectives* (The Hague: Martinus Nijhoff Publishers, 1996), 1.

[2] See, e.g., Arcot Krishnaswami, *Study of Discrimination in the Matter of Religious Rights and Practices* (United Nations, 1960 (Sales no. 60, XIV.2)); Elizabeth Odio Benito, *Study of the Current Dimensions of the Problems of Intolerance and Discrimination Based on Religion or Belief* (UN Doc. E/CN.4/Sub.2/1987/26).

schemes dependent on religion both for legitimacy and for effective implementation? (No society can be ruled by coercion alone.) To what extent should the dictates of individual conscience be respected? When should the state be allowed to intervene to limit the darker emanations of superstition and religious intolerance? How can a society best accommodate a multiplicity of religious beliefs?

Questions of this nature are taking on a renewed urgency following the end of the cold war. With the collapse of communism, ancient cultural divides are resurfacing in what Samuel Huntington has called "The Clash of Civilizations."[3] The world has taken on a renewed polycentricity. Religious intolerance, especially when reinforced by cultural and ethnic diversity, generates tensions that pose grave risks to social peace and order at every level of society, from disputes before local school boards and city councils to the threat of global war.

Moreover, as democratic constitutionalism becomes an ever more prevalent form of government, questions remain about precisely how religion and religious freedom should best be actualized in each country. In the United States, the public discussion of these issues focuses on the Supreme Court and First Amendment cases that it addresses. During the twentieth century, the Court has narrowed the terms of discourse radically, relying principally on concepts and categories derived from nineteenth century liberalism and ignoring an older and much richer tradition. Despite broad consensus on certain fundamental principles of religious freedom as articulated in various international instruments[4] and constitutional documents,[5] significant variation exists in the ways regimes structure the

---

[3] Samuel P. Huntington, "The Clash of Civilizations," *Foreign Affairs* 72 (1993): 24–49.

[4] See, e.g., International Covenant on Civil and Political Rights (1966), art. 18, G.A. Res. 2200A, U.N. GAOR, 21st Session, Supp. No. 16, p. 52, U.N. Doc. A/6316, *United Nations Treaty Series* 999: 171; European Convention for the Protection of Human Rights and Fundamental Freedoms (1950), art. 9, *United Nations Treaty Series* 312: 221, *European Treaty Series* 5, as amended by Protocol nos. 3, 5, and 8; American Convention of Human Rights (1978), O.A.S. *Treaty Series* No. 36: 1, OEA/ser. L./V/II.23, doc. rev. 2; Concluding Document of the Vienna Meeting 1986 of Representatives of the Participating States of the Conference on Security and Co-Operation in Europe, Held on the Basis of the Provisions of the Final Act Relating to the Follow-Up to the Conference (1989), *International Legal Materials* 28: 527, 534.

[5] See, e.g., Constitución arts. 14, 19, & 20 (Argentina); Australian Constitution § 116; Bundes-Verfassungsgesetz art. 7, § 1 (Austria); Constituição Federal art. 5 (Brazil); Canadian Constitution pt. I, § 2 (Constitution Act of 1982) (Canadian Charter of Rights and Freedoms); Constitución Política arts. 13, 18, & 19 (Colombia); Suomi Hallitu Smuoto arts. 9 & 83 (Finland); Constitution arts. 2 & 77 (France); Grundgesetz art. 4 (Germany); India Constitution arts. 15, 16, 25, & 26; Israel Constitution §§ 7 & 22; Constituzione arts. 8, 19, & 20 (Italy); Kenpō arts. 19 & 20 (Japan); Kenya Constitution

relations between religious and political institutions. Within constitutional systems, questions constantly emerge about the precise limits of religious freedom and about the relationship (or separation) of church and state institutions.

All of these issues pose deep theoretical questions, but too often they are approached as if these were uniquely twentieth century phenomena. In fact, of course, these issues have attracted the attention of many of the greatest philosophers and political theorists throughout history. Yet their reflections on issues of religious freedom and the relationship of religion, law, and politics are often forgotten or at least neglected, in part because their writings on such issues are often scattered throughout their works, and in part because subsequent commentators tend to pay greater attention to other aspects of their thought.

It was against this background that we convened two conferences to consider the contributions of a series of major Western thinkers on these issues. The first focused on late medieval and early modern thought, Martin Luther, John Locke, the American Founders, and Alexis de Tocqueville; the second addressed Marsilius of Padua, John Calvin, Thomas Hobbes, Jean Jacques Rousseau, and Edmund Burke. We were fortunate to be able to attract an outstanding group of scholars who could prepare papers on each of these thinkers and help us select readings appropriate to our topic. The present volume is the outgrowth of the initial papers presented, the rich discussions that took place at the two conferences, and subsequent revisions to the papers. We hope this volume will facilitate inclusion of these great thinkers and their insights in contemporary discussions of these vital issues.

The Medieval Background.— Professor Brian Professor Tierney provided the late medieval and early modern foundation for each of the conferences. In chapter one he traces the remarkable evolution of religious liberty in the West from the early persecution of heretics and infidels to modern acceptance of freedom of conscience as a well-nigh universally accepted basic human right. The universal love preached by Jesus and the toleration espoused in Constantine's Edict of Milan and by Christian apologists, Professor Tierney explains, was eventually supplanted by less tolerant notions such as Augustine's contention that scripture requires that heretics be compelled to

---

art. 78; Malta Constitution art. 40; Constitution art. 23 (Monaco); Statuut voor het Koninkrijk der Nederlanden art. 6 (Netherlands); Constitución arts. 34 & 35 (Panama); Constitución art. 70 (Paraguay); Constituição Federal art. 41 (Portugal); Constitución art. 16 (Spain); Bundesverfassung arts. 27, 49, & 50 (Switzerland); Turkey Constitution art. 24; Constitution art. 17 (Zaire).

repent—a doctrine which dominated Western religious thought for nearly a thousand years.

Yet, despite this darker side of religious history, two important aspects of the medieval Catholic regime ultimately contributed to the development of the modern concept of religious liberty: (1) the independence of the church from secular authority provided the seed from which doctrines of disestablishment ultimately grew, and (2) the belief that the individual conscience is the proper guide to behavior militated against coerced conversion with eventual success. As Professor Tierney points out, these doctrines were not sufficient, even in conjunction with the gradually developing notion of inherent natural rights, to inspire full-fledged freedom of religion. In the medieval era, dissent was labeled heresy, and likened to treason—even to the point of imposing the death penalty. It was the age of the Inquisition and anti-heresy crusades. In the medieval mind, the notion of reasonable disagreement had no place: Even so moderate a medieval scholar as Thomas Aquinas saw dissent as an act of willful rebellion; and persecution was considered a necessary remedy to prevent others from following such renegades to hell.

Tierney traces the growth of religious liberty from the self-interested toleration that characterized a Europe that was increasingly fractured along religious lines, through the growing rejection of intolerance in light of humanist skepticism, political expediency, and most importantly, interpretations of the doctrine of Christian love. The new post-medieval religious philosophy blended its increasing emphasis on toleration, the growing separation of church from state (Roger Williams' "wall of separation"), and the primacy of the individual conscience with the old doctrine of natural rights, to provide the foundations for an inalienable right to the freedom of religion. But Professor Tierney looks to neither commerce, constitutionalism's pragmatic rule of law, skeptical secularization of the state, nor natural rights idealism for the ultimately compelling argument for religious liberty. Rather, he finds "the best antidote for all the false fundamentalisms of our age" in the general creed of respect and compassion, advanced by the original founders of the western religious tradition (p. 56).

Marsilius of Padua.— But the immediate effect of Catholic hegemony was not so beneficial for competing points of view. In the fourteenth century Marsilius spoke for many who were troubled by the Church's exclusive control of spiritual and temporal matters. In chapter two, Professor Tierney analyzes the *Defensor Pacis,* which foreshadows Hobbes and other early modern writers by advancing a wholly secular theory of the state based on the consent of the governed. Legislative power belonged to the majority or their designated ruler, who therefore wielded the coercive authority of the law. The church lacked the temporal powers of the duly appointed civil magistrate, having been given authority only in a "kingdom not of this world." Indeed, according to Marsilius, the civil magistrate had power over all things temporal, including property and appointment in the church. Heretics, it followed, could only be punished or coerced by civilly enacted law enforced by civil officials. The church, in Marsilius' view, had no right to compel any "through pain or punishment to observe the commands of the evangelic law" (p. 68). However, he would allow the civil authority to wield lawful coercive power against heretics and infidels if it saw fit. With the benefit of centuries of hindsight, we can see that Marsilius may have gone further than necessary in his drive to limit ecclesiastical authority. He accepted "the papalists' view that one power must be superior to the other; but he stood their argument on its head by giving the superior position to the emperor" (ibid.). He wrote perhaps too early to be able to see a regime of separation of church and state as an intermediate stopping point, but he did see the need for limiting the power of the sword to the preservation of peace.

Martin Luther.— Professor Steven Ozment continues the discussion in chapter three, showing the important contributions Luther made to modern conceptions of freedom of conscience. Like Marsilius a century earlier, Luther believed the individual conscience to be the seat of Christian freedom. That conscience, however, could not be allowed to become a basis for spiritual anarchy, but must be informed by a proper understanding of scripture. Religious freedom was the right to disagree with Rome, but it was not a right to depart from religious truth as found in the Bible, particularly by Lutheran clerics. Religious liberty so conceived was a limited freedom, to be sure, but it was a freedom never before enjoyed.

Luther's concept of "inward," "exclusively spiritual" Christian liberty, faith that sets one free from all control save God's alone (p. 64), may have insulated him from any great need to develop a political doctrine of religious liberty. This Christian "self-consciousness" had nothing to do with political realms, since these had nothing to do with the liberation of the soul. But there is an unavoidable political implication. Christian freedom gives the believer the right to resist coercion of his conscience, since God's law restricts civil government to the temporal sphere. However, Luther gave his full support to his prince's suppression of doctrines opposed to Lutheranism. Nevertheless, Luther's "inner conscience" anticipated the elevation of religious liberty to an inalienable right. Luther also argued that Christians have a God-given responsibility to obey legitimate political authority to protect the well-being of their neighbors. In effect, Luther helped to confirm the freedom of internal conscience as an absolute right,[6] but the emanations of this right into the outer world of politics remained sharply constrained.

John Calvin.—In chapter four, Professor John Witte draws together scattered elements in Calvin's thought to document a coherent and surprisingly moderate theory of religious liberty. As with Luther and Marsilius, historians are often ambivalent about Calvin, some hailing him as a "pioneer of the freedom of conscience"—others branding him "notoriously rigid," "oppressive," and fanatically dogmatic (pp. 83–85). Arguing that both judgments derive from biased readings, Witte contends that a balanced reading of the numerous passages strewn throughout Calvin's theological writings yields a more moderate interpretation.

Professor Witte distinguishes two distinct phases in Calvin's thoughts on the subject of religious liberty: an early period characterized by a focus on the nature of individual, spiritual, and political liberty, and a later "mature" period, reflecting the benefit of more extensive practical experience and focusing on the respective jurisdictions of church and state. Both phases, however, are marked by an emphasis on moderation—a balance between liberty and law, tolerance and discipline.

Walking the fine line between the quasi-anarchy of Anabaptist liberalism and the reactionary Catholic legalism of the canon law, Calvin advocated Luther's conciliatory doctrine of the "two kingdoms"—the heavenly or spiritual and the earthly or civil—to both of which the Christian is subject. Witte explores Calvin's middle-of-the-road views of individual freedom and duty in both kingdoms. While the church had no authority to impose laws upon the conscience in areas unrelated to spiritual salvation, civil leaders had a God-given obligation to protect religion. Political liberty and political

---

6 Luther's notion of the freedom of conscience can thus be viewed as a historical antecedent of the distinction in modern international religious freedom norms between freedom of conscience, which is absolute and non-regulable, and manifestations of religion, which may be subjected to certain types of limitations under when "necessary in a democratic society." See Article 9 of the European Convention for the Protection of Human Rights and Fundamental Freedoms (1950), *United Nations Treaty Series* 312: 221, *European Treaty Series* 5, as amended by Protocol nos. 3, 5, and 8; Article 18 of the International Covenant on Civil and Political Rights (1966), *United Nations Treaty Series* 999: 171. The same can be said with regard to the belief-action distinction emphasized in *Cantwell v. Connecticut,* 310 U.S. 296, 303–04 (1940) (declaring that freedom of belief is by nature absolute, but freedom of action cannot be); *Reynolds v. United States,* 98 U.S. 145 (1879).

authority, in Calvin's view, "are constituted together,"[7] based on written laws embodying biblical principles of love of God and neighbor and applied to believer and non-believer alike.

Calvin's later work expands on the notion of positive moral law in both the civil and the ecclesiastical spheres. Witte discusses Calvin's theory of the "three uses" of moral law: theological, civil, and educational. Calvin began to see both church and state as legal entities, each helping to delimit and define religious liberty in the "enforcement of Godly government"—that is, upholding minimal standards of Christian morality, including freeing the community of heresy, idolatry, and blasphemy. In this connection, Professor Witte recounts and discusses one of Calvin's most controversial acts—his role in the execution of the dissident Michael Servetus.

Calvin's views gradually shifted toward legalism and a re-creation of consistory courts to enforce ecclesiastical law. In this setting, Professor Witte lauds Calvin's respect for the rule of law, democratic process, and liberty of conscience (pp. 105–07), noting that it was Calvin's particular genius "to integrate these three cardinal principles of ecclesiology" (121). While acknowledging excesses in Calvin's actions with respect to Servetus and in his "undue empowerment of the consistory courts in his later years," Witte notes that Calvin "urged respect for *liberty* with the church" and "provided an indispensable impetus to the realization and integration of individual and corporate religious liberty" (ibid.).

Thomas Hobbes.—In complete contradistinction to the Lutheran ideal of the "two kingdoms" espoused by Luther and Calvin is the theocratic monism of Thomas Hobbes, as interpreted by Professor Joshua Mitchell in chapter five. Mitchell shares the approach growing among historians that reads Hobbes's commentary on religion and freedom of conscience not as satirical atheism, but as a sincere attempt from within a biblical tradition to comprehend religious liberty within the categories of thought inherited from the Reformation.

Unlike his predecessors, Hobbes understood the "kingdom of God" literally, with rights both sovereign and spiritual. In Moses, Hobbes argued, God unified religious and political sovereignty. It follows then, according to Hobbes, that Christ—the "personator" of God in history—would hardly undo that unity.

---

[7] Page 93, Citing Josef Bohatec, *Calvins Lehre von Staat und Kirche mit besonderer Berücksichtigung des Organismusgedankens*, 2. Ausgabe (Aalen: Scientia Verlag, 1968), 109–116.

Professor Mitchell traces Hobbes' "genealogy of authority" from Moses and the priests of Israel, in unified sovereignty, until the subjects' forgetfulness of their duty to the sovereign stripped them of the covenant. Christ prepared the way for the renewal of the covenant, when men would no longer contest the will of the sovereign. This renewal took place, according to Hobbes, in Reformation England, where the sovereign heads both church and state, and, in contrast to earlier epochs in history, the excessive power of Roman Catholicism could not usurp the rightful unity of authority of the secular sovereign.

According to Hobbes, Professor Mitchell explains, the state exists to protect all the people, not just particular persons. Moreover, argued Hobbes, the scripture ordains that "the powers that be are ordained of God." Society may accordingly punish the creation of factions as inimical to the common good and violative of the divine covenant. Thus, interpretation of scripture (necessary since the cessation of prophecy) belongs to the legitimate sovereign, the personator of God, as were Moses and Christ, not to the individual reason, conscience or the church. Men are not capable of determining good and evil, thought Hobbes. This power belongs to the sovereign—Hobbes' "Leviathan," the "mortal god," who represents God to the people.

Mitchell concludes with a discussion of Hobbes' assertion that monarchy, rather than democracy, is the proper form for the religio-political state. Democracy, according to Hobbes, is inherently unstable, always leading to factions, civil war, and the death of the commonwealth. Monarchy, the submission of individual pride to the will of the Sovereign, is the only road to genuine liberty and equality of the subjects, because it is only "by resisting their pridefulness, by obeying the One Sovereign and not believing in the sufficiency of their own efforts, . . . [that] their undertakings [can] be fruitful. Obedience is the precondition of *genuine* human liberty" (p. 138).

In general, Professor Mitchell suggests that Hobbes stands closer to Reformation thought than many of his secular interpreters have understood. Focusing primarily on Hobbes's work about the Christian commonwealth, he finds ground for Hobbes's views on religious liberty not in the ancient political tradition, medieval nominalism, or the legal pragmatism of the modern social contract, but in the biblical tradition. Hobbes wrestles with a fundamental Reformation "quandary about authority, interpretation, and liberty" (p. 140). While he relies much more heavily on secular authority to resolve this central riddle of emerging pluralism than more religious thinkers, his justification remains at least partially religious. He turns to the power of reason, but also calls for man "to *defer* to a powerful one [the secular sovereign] who stands over all at that place where reason's light grows dim: where God's word must be deciphered" (p. 141).

John Locke.—Locke has long been recognized as a seminal figure not only in the emergence of liberalism and social contract theory, but also in the framing of modern conceptions of religious freedom. Many of his most fundamental arguments have become so axiomatic that their provenance is almost forgotten. In this regard one thinks, for example, of the Lockean argument that one cannot coerce religious belief [8] (the attempt results at best in hypocrisy), or arguments against letting the secular prince choose his subjects' religion (because the prince might choose wrong), or the argument that by respecting dissenters, one actually promotes social stability (by winning their gratitude) rather than social disintegration. Against this background, Joshua Mitchell focuses in chapter six primarily on Locke's religious works, *A Letter Concerning Toleration* and *The Reasonableness of Christianity*, providing a fresh perspective by suggesting that Locke's doctrine of toleration constitutes a theological argument about the dialectic of biblical history—and hence informs and serves as the basis for the historical dialectic of Hegel and Kant. As with his interpretation of Hobbes, Professor Mitchell suggests that the Lockean argumentation is more pervasively religious than many of his secular commentators have been willing to acknowledge, although the success of his argument is enhanced by the absence of Locke's science found in his *Essay Concerning Human Understanding*.

Since Locke's position cannot be properly understood without a thorough consideration of the "fulfillment offered by Christ" (p. 145), Mitchell begins with a discussion of Lockean dualism—the external (political) realm of power and the internal (religious) realm of faith where "reasoned conviction is the judge" (ibid.) Unlike Hobbes, Mitchell explains, Locke held that compulsion has no place in the internal realm; such power violates the convictions of conscience, extinguishing the light of reason which is the way of salvation. The argument against coerced belief thus constitutes not only a general counsel of reason, but also a rejection of Hobbesian secularism that is nested within a theological argument. Locke believed that prior to the first coming of Christ (which revealed to human reason the proper foundation of religious duty), there had been no separation of the realms. In that setting, theocracy was necessary to prevent the straying of unenlightened reason. But once "the New Dispensation revealed to reason the true foundation of duty"

---

[8] See generally John Locke, *A Letter Concerning Toleration* (First published 1689; Buffalo, N.Y., 1990): 19–22, 35, 40–41.

(p. 146), coercion subverts rather than supports the course of enlightened reason.

In this context, Mitchell contends that a theological account helps explain Locke's perceptions of heterodoxy and heresy. A tolerant response to these phenomena is required by Locke's interpretation of the first coming of Christ. For Locke, the universality of the Christian message can (and eventually will) take hold only if individual reason is left free to discover it. Thus, toleration is the only proper course. The use of the coercive power of the state to eliminate heterodoxy, Locke believed, tends to ossify "otherness" rather than to remove it, and is an entirely improper confusion of the two realms. The tendency toward official persecution and intolerance, which Locke referred to as "the yoke that galls their necks," was in his view the real source of the strife so often attributed to religious difference and pluralism. Consequently, Locke was far less concerned about "heresy" than other theologians. The important thing for Locke was the inevitable universality of inner belief—inevitable, that is, if not disrupted by the state's coercive power. One common form of worship, for example, though giving the appearance of unity, does not demonstrate proper worship. Without the inner belief that each individual will reach if his reason is unconstrained, the outward form is meaningless. Summarizing the paradox embedded in Locke's position (and in modern pluralism), Mitchell states, "the one true God is revealed to and in a heterodox world" (p. 153).

Mitchell next turns to Locke's doctrine of Christ's "unconcealment," the gradual revelation of his truth to the unenlightened reason, which Mitchell calls Locke's "dialectic of biblical history" (p. 158). Prior to the first coming, the natural reason granted men by God had however received no assistance from God and was thus unenlightened. This yielded the reasoning of the philosophers, which was incomplete and nonauthoritative. After the death of Christ, however, reason became "conscious of its authority" (p. 158); the reasonable human being could now apprehend Christianity's universality. Locke's doctrine of toleration, in this view, can best be understood as a doctrine of theology associated with the progressive revelation of truth through the course of biblical history.

The significance of this interpretation of Locke is that it points to a need to rethink political theory about toleration. As Mitchell summarizes the point, "the reasonableness of toleration . . . cannot be reduced to a calculus of interest, nor to purely [secular] political considerations" (ibid.). Further, "the argument for separating religion and politics—for *disenchanting* the political world, as it were—is *itself a theological argument*" (p. 159). Efforts to secularize the discourse of religious liberty, by pretending that the fundamentally religious dimensions of the issues can be bracketed out, are doomed to a fundamental incoherence. This is the dilemma of liberalism. The result, in Mitchell's words, is that "[h]aving renounced the attempt to find a moderate theology . . . condemns to oblivion [the liberal] attempt to find a moderate politics. When the theological center is abandoned religion doesn't go away; it shows itself in immoderate forms. Locke is salutary today because he recognized that religion, though *separable* from politics, undergirds politics" (p. 160).

Jean-Jacques Rousseau.—Professor Durham focuses primarily on Rousseau's chapter on civil religion. Too often, this chapter has been regarded as a throw-away, appended to *The Social Contract* without great thought and with even less coherence. Even as repopularized by writers such as Robert Bellah, the notion of civil religion seems flawed with superficiality—the outer rituals of patriotism, ritual phrases in inaugural addresses, pious mottos on coins, and so forth. A principal aim of chapter seven, therefore, is to suggest that something much deeper is at stake for Rousseau.

From the opening lines, Rousseau's essay seems freighted with ambiguity—ambiguities about whether Rousseau is talking about history or abstract theory, ambiguities about how tolerant Rousseau really was, and ambiguities about the nature of community. The more one reflects on the ambiguities, the more one suspects that they are a central part of the message. Perhaps unwittingly, Rousseau had managed to sense the fundamental tensions of modernity. The ambiguities in his text reflect the deeper ambivalence he felt toward the coming age.

Durham argues that Rousseau saw both religion and politics as fundamental dimensions of social life. The chapter on civil religion develops the essential corollaries to Rousseau's political doctrine of the general will in the religious dimension. What Rousseau recognized is that society needs both politics and religion, and that integration of society demands interaction between these crucial dimensions of human existence.

In working out the structure of this interaction, Rousseau recognized the pull of two rival orientations: transcendence and immanence. In many ways, Rousseau is much more strongly attracted to immanent religiosity—the natural religion of the heart that is not dependent on external authority and that is not corrupted by social decadence. In contrast, Christianity, which is the prototypical religion of transcendence, is criticized because it leads people to care more for a transcendent realm than for the realities of the present community. It leads to split sovereignty, and to a state which is no longer genuinely one. Yet immanence has its own dangers: it can swallow up individuals if the "oneness" of community becomes too strong.

The ultimate ambiguity in Rousseau's civil religion, then, is whether his "religions of man and citizen" reduce in fact to a religion based on the immanent traditions of the community, or whether he argues for some synthesis of transcendence and immanence in the sources of communal values. The notion of conscience, as it appears in the *Emile* and various other works, blends elements of transcendence (something that stands above and apart from the world of actual arrangements) and immanence (an internal center from which core values and meanings emanate). Like the general will, conscience can be authoritative without being coercive. It can legitimize the social bonds that structure individual and communal life. Moreover, it is capable of providing the kind of motivation to obey law that law cannot confer upon itself. This idea of conscience explains how religion can be supportive of politics and law without being corrupted by them. In an age in which politics has grown leery of religion, Professor Durham's reflections on Rousseau's civil religion suggests a variety of ways in which thought concerning the interactions of religious and political dimensions of life can be deepened.

Edmund Burke.—Analysis of fundamental church-state positions takes another turn in chapter eight with Professor Michael McConnell's essay on Edmund Burke's "tolerant establishment." For Americans who have become so separationist that establishment seems to have dropped off the list of plausible candidates for political organization, the essay provides a fascinating exploration by a leading constitutional scholar of the residual allure of establishment. This is because Edmund Burke, with all his passion for tradition, advocated not the separation of church and state that has become axiomatic in the United States, but a "Christian commonwealth" in which "Church and State are one and the same thing . . . integral parts of the same whole" (p. 204). Like Hobbes, Burke was a religio-political monist of sorts, arguing ever in favor of religious establishment; like Locke, however, he was profoundly averse to "persecution for conscientious difference of opinion" (ibid.), and championed tolerance throughout his political career. The puzzle for separationists is how the two can coherently fit together.

Professor McConnell begins with a brief sketch of Burke's life and religious background: his mother's lifelong loyalty to Catholicism; his father's convenient conversion to Anglicanism so that he could practice law; his wife's nominal Anglicanism (she was in fact a devout Catholic); and his own broad experience with pluralism: born a Catholic, baptized an Anglican, student at both Catholic, Anglican and Quaker schools. McConnell sees Burke's father's "apostasy" as a major factor in Burke's own tolerance, arguing that this led Burke rhetorically to minimize the differences between Anglicanism and Catholicism. Burke, however, evinced an independent attitude toward religion, rarely quoting from the Bible, which he called a "multifarious" "collection of treatises" (p. 207). With a single exception, Burke never mentions Christ anywhere in his writings, though he frequently refers to God. Moreover, Burke evidently believed religion to be based on "enthusiasm" ("fanaticism" in eighteenth century English) rather than reason, and found the great doctrinal controversies of his day pointless.

Despite his own nonsectarianism, Burke argued in favor of establishment, specifically of the Church of England. In doing so, however, he never supported the notion that religion should be an instrument of the state on the one hand nor a theocracy on the other. Instead, Burke supported the establishment because he believed the Anglican church best reflected the religious experience of the English people. "Theological correctness," McConnell stresses, "was not the point" (p. 209). But neither was social utility, which rendered religion a political device. The purpose of establishment, according to Burke, is the "consecration of the state" (ibid.). It is a reminder that the state has an obligation to conform to higher principles than itself. Establishment thus performs the double service of restraining democracy's overconfidence in itself and of ensuring the continuity of society's established moral order. It does this at least in part by helping to ensure continuity of the traditions of a society. In sharp contrast to a "social contract," Burke held society to be a divine decree, a partnership between those living, those dead, and those as yet unborn. Significantly, however, Burke saw the establishment not as a means of augmenting political power, but of limiting it in accordance with the traditions of the people. Thus, the imposition of an established church "contrary to the 'genius and desires' of [a] nation" will not only not help the society, but will result in disaffection, mutiny, and rebellion (p. 213).

After briefly contrasting Burke's notion with those of both Rousseau and Madison, Professor McConnell discusses the proper characteristics of the established church. First, "independence": Burke believed (exaggeratedly, McConnell contends) that the Church of England was and ought to be above the law and endowed with sufficient property to require no support from outside. Any other arrangement would render the church subordinate to the state. Disagreeing completely with popular notions of clerical poverty, Burke believed the church's high officials should have wealth sufficient to command the respect of secular powers, and, in addition, that a principal duty of civil magistrates should be to protect and promote the church. Second, Burke believed the church's basis in tradition lent it stability, protecting it and society from rapid and improvident change, "tumults and religious wars." Third and finally, Burke believed the established church should be tolerant, respecting the rights of dissenters to preach and worship as they would. He held compulsion in religious matters to be both wrong and ineffective, since coercion cannot alter conscience.

Burke's tolerant establishment was in fact opposed by three major positions. Evangelical separationists opposed establishment as subservience of the church to the state. Secularists opposed establishment because they believed science should supplant religion. Establishmentarians opposed toleration of dissent. These three camps were united only in their antipathy for the Roman Catholic Church, which antipathy Burke did not share. Not surprisingly, given his background, he was outraged by Protestant oppression of Irish Catholics. In general, Burke pressed for legislation that would extend toleration to Catholics in Ireland, and he advocated toleration for any "serious religion," Christian or not. Like Locke, however, Burke declared that atheists "are never to be supported, never to be tolerated" (p. 232). He therefore opposed the Rational Dissenters (secularists) in Ireland, whom he believed to be the vanguard of atheism, and whom he referred to as "traitors" (ibid.). With this single exception of atheism, Burke believed that the only limit on toleration was political parties masquerading as religion—groups for whom Burke had no respect.

Professor McConnell points out two respects in which Burke's arguments for toleration differed from typical Enlightenment views. First, Burke based religious rights on a people's "peculiar and characteristic situation"—usage and custom—rather than on the abstract notion of natural rights (p. 236). Second, unlike many of his contemporaries who favored "toleration" out of indifference, Burke believed religion is the "glorious and distinguishing prerogative of humanity;" "equal neglect," he said, "is not impartial kindness" (p. 238). True toleration, accordingly, is "the toleration of those who 'think the dogmas of religion . . . are all of moment" (p. 238). In this respect, Burkean establishment has something to teach the smug tolerance of liberalism, which is all too often tolerant of religion as long as it retreats sufficiently into the private margins of society and doesn't get too uppity. Burke spoke the language of toleration, but knew the meaning of genuine respect.

The American Founders.—Professor Ellis Sandoz begins his study of theories of religious liberty in the American founding by contrasting them with twentieth century doctrines. He points out that while it was "self-evident" to the Founders that the United States was a Christian country, modern America's "officially sanctioned ideology" is a "religiously neutral atheism" reducing religion to totemism, positivism, and deconstructionism (pp. 190–92, 195).

Admonishing "those . . . charged with husbanding the American system of ordered liberty" to remember the ancient charge *salus populi suprema lex esto*, Sandoz invokes the Founders' essential premise that "a community unified by fundamental convictions beyond . . . merely material interests" is vital for the success of America's republican experiment" (pp.235–255) Sandoz therefore concludes his syllogism by reiterating Justice Jackson's alarming prognosis that "if the Court does not temper its doctrinaire logic with a little practical wisdom, it will convert the constitutional Bill of Rights into a suicide pact."[9]

Professor Sandoz next examines the theoretical and historical basis of American religious liberty, focusing first on the philosophy of James Madison. Pointing out that at the time of the founding, Americans were virtually unanimous in embracing religion, not as Enlightenment hypothesis, but as living faith, Sandoz adduces the philosophers' insight that reason is to the individual as law is to society. For the founders, therefore, rule of law meant governance by God and by reason. The founders embraced liberty of conscience, not as a political device, but as a recognition of their own mortal imperfections. Citing Hooker ("think ye are men, deem it not impossible for you to err"), Sandoz lauds the founders' zeal for toleration as "the saving doubt essential to any free government that is ineluctably grounded in the consent of heterogeneous communities. . . . plac[ing] reliance upon persuasion as the basis of liberty of conscience for individual persons and of peace for society" (p. 261).

Turning to the actual mechanism of American freedom of conscience, Professor Sandoz addresses the dilemma of "bridg[ing] . . . the philosophical and theological anthropology of classical philosophy and general Christianity . . . without formal institutional support" (p. 261). The bridge, Sandoz argues, was Christianity itself, with its basis in humility, self-denial, and brotherly kindness, the fundamental religion—notwithstanding diversity of creed—of Revolutionary America.

Having said this, Professor Sandoz analyzes the two conventionally accepted models of religious toleration: the political principle, which condemned compulsion of conscience as an infringement of liberty; and the religious principle, which held the church wholly separate from the state, and

---

[9] Page 257, citing *Terminiello v. City of Chicago*, 337 U.S. 1, 37 (1949).

entirely free from its rule. Examining both sides of the question as to which philosophy predominated in Revolutionary America, Sandoz argues that neither was dominant. Instead, the definition of American freedom of conscience lay in various distinct elements: the quest for disestablishment (and freedom from church taxes and punishments for dissenters), the quest for equality, the pietistic manifest destiny by which America saw herself as the eschatological "city set on a hill," and the growth of democratic individualism and laissez-faire philosophy.

The religious perspective, Sandoz suggests, reveals a tripartite evolution in the growth of religious liberty: reluctant toleration, liberty of conscience based on recognition of equality, and perfect freedom of belief and practice seen as essential to truth itself. In a more American and political focus, Sandoz offers evidence that issues of religious toleration, far more than trade and taxation, sparked Madison's political involvement, and he proceeds to examine Madison's religious magnum opus, the "Memorial and Remonstrance," in which Madison argues that civil government should never be allowed to "overleap the great Barrier [of unalienable natural rights and higher law]" and thereby invade the realm of religion—since "[b]efore any man can be considered as a member of Civil Society, he must be considered as a subject of the Governour of the Universe." (pp. 271–273).

Professor Sandoz concludes with a discussion of the union of philosophy and religion which gave rise to the American axiom that freedom of conscience stands above and apart from the legislative power of the state. Thus, argues Sandoz, citing McConnell, the First Amendment represents the "most philosophically interesting and distinctive feature of the American Constitution . . . a new and unprecedented conception of government and its relation to claims of higher truth and authority" (p. 275). This emphasis on higher natural law and its concomitant conclusion that the conscience of the one lies outside the power of the majority, has "served to thwart the worst tendencies of religious zealots to persecute minorities with whom they disagree" (p. 280), and has paradoxically managed to keep apart the spiritual and the secular—though far less than the unfortunate "wall of separation" metaphor might suggest. Nevertheless, Sandoz warns, this American solution as it was originally thought out, seems to stand in stark contrast to the supposedly "neutral" and "politically correct" secular ideologies taught in modern schools which often result in de facto hostility toward religion in a way Madison and the other founders certainly never envisioned.

Alexis de Tocqueville.—In our final chapter, Professor Thomas Pangle uses the insights of Alexis de Tocqueville as a vantage point from which to reconsider the fundamentals of religious liberty that are in flux today in both the United States and Canada. Adopting Tocqueville's perspective that freedom of conscience and its social corollary, the separation of church and state, cannot be properly perceived as ends in themselves, Professor Pangle asks why religious liberty and church-state separation are good. Supporters of religious liberty arise from two surprisingly opposed perspectives. One group believes religious authority is a good thing and that religious liberty will strengthen it. The other believes religious authority is a bad thing, and that religious liberty will erode it. Two groups of opponents to religious liberty mirror these positions (p. 239). For example, Tocqueville thought Enlightenment philosophy support for disestablishment and freedom of conscience in the French Revolution was linked to the belief that implementing these would destroy religious authority. The egalitarian ideology was directed squarely against religious hierarchy, and the Enlightenment outlook recognized no authorities beyond reason and science.

Tocqueville lamented the *philosophes'* failure to grasp the practical realities of tolerance, repression, and democracy. Their rationalism did not allow them to grasp the counter-intuitive character of political life. They failed to see that the spirit of liberty burns brightest in times of repression. And they could never have understood what this observer of American democracy was witnessing—democracy is not self-sustaining. It needs healthy religious institutions to provide moral strength and purpose in the people. Religious liberty must be seen as "the means to the strengthening, within modern democracy, of politically responsible religious authority," which, in turn, will nurture and sustain democratic institutions (p. 298).

Tocqueville's greatest fear for democracy—and especially democracy in America—is majoritarian moral tyranny. American democracy is, according to Tocqueville, formed around a popularized, individualistic, and materialistic philosophy, "profoundly skeptical" of authority. Americans are accordingly indoctrinated from early youth with the belief that they have a moral duty to think for themselves, to consider themselves the intellectual equals of all others, to feel ashamed at bowing to another's authority. This philosophy, however, allows no skepticism as to its own intellectual autonomy; nor does it induce any sympathetic comprehension of hierarchical or more authoritarian societies. This woeful ignorance and "massive moral prejudice" renders citizens of democracy generally (and Americans in particular, apparently) completely unaware of "the herd-like limits on their pretended independence of opinion" (p. 300). For there is no such thing as a non-authoritarian society, according to Tocqueville: the only question is where the dogmatic beliefs and opinions lie which govern the society.

The democratic personality loses touch with the future in a passionate attachment with the present moment. This is the sobering picture which Tocqueville paints of the American mind: a passionate attachment to the trivial, the petty, the evanescent—accompanied by an inescapable anxiety and mad haste of acquisition. This in turn leads to a belief that enough work will result in boundless success, though of course, it is difficult for one to advance very far in a uniform crowd. This ceaseless discontent amid plenty is the cause of the "singular melancholy" of citizens of democracies.

Religion, according to Tocqueville, counteracts this "secret anxiety." Worship and the inspiring doctrine of immortality free the democratic personality from its petty passions and taking note of the future rather than the present. The absence of metaphysical answers raises the democratic anxiety to a paralyzing anomie—and, finally, in their despairing search for stability, they "give themselves" a master (such as "reason"). The greatest advantage of religion to democracy, however, according to Tocqueville, is its direct opposition to materialism and individualism—making religious peoples "strong precisely where democratic peoples are weak" (p. 303).

Indeed, for Tocqueville, religion is a crucial oasis in the domestic life of the democratic personality lost in the wastes of individualism. Tocqueville regarded the piety, chastity, fidelity, submissiveness, and devotion of women as perhaps the single most important factor in the success of the American experiment; for in America, "religion reigns supreme over the soul of woman, and it is woman who makes the mores" (p. 304). American women, therefore, are a decisive influence in political life—for though religion does not directly intervene in American politics, it is still the "first of [American] political institutions" (p. 305). Nevertheless, Tocqueville argued fervently for strict but friendly separation of church and state in American democracy. By tying itself to a political regime, religion loses the universality of the sublime and its power to give moral strength to the people. But the democratic state also needs to find ways to promote religion. And so, Pangle concludes, Tocqueville would have favored the traditional Canadian approach over the radical separation of Church and State recommended by Madison and Jefferson and adopted in contemporary American constitutional law.

Conclusion.—The foregoing overview begins to suggest the range of issues addressed by the thinkers discussed in the pages that follow. Before concluding this introduction, however, one recurrent theme that emerged in discussion of virtually all of the thinkers treated here is worth mentioning: we have managed to recover a rich collection of starting points for discussion of religious liberty issues. While religious human rights are not respected by all governments today, most have ratified basic human rights agreements that affirm basic religious freedom claims. Many of the world's major religious movements have internalized the value of religious freedom. Without necessarily abandoning their traditional truth claims, they nonetheless have come to recognize that part of their own religious truth recognizes the dignity and freedom of human beings, and that this may mean that the religious freedom of others should be respected.

Past achievements for religious liberty have made possible much of today's focus on refinements of law and applications to more subtle problems. While such developments may signal significant progress in this area, a recurrence to past wisdom and theories may enrich our future dialogue and may help us see where present doctrines might have pursued some valid insights at the expense of others equally important. Our hope is that this work will contribute to both the deepening and the extension of discourse concerning religious freedom.

—— ·⊙ 1 ⊙· ——

RELIGIOUS RIGHTS:
A HISTORICAL PERSPECTIVE

Brian Tierney[*]

I n the years since World War II, religious liberty has been proclaimed as a
human right in several United Nations documents, and all the major
Christian churches have affirmed their commitment to the same ideal. It
was not always so. A leading scholar in this field observed recently that "For
several thousand years the history of religion was marked by religious
intolerance and persecution." After mentioning specifically the persecutions
of one another by Christians of various persuasions he added, "Clearly
religion and freedom have not been natural allies."[1] This is the situation we
have to bear in mind when we reflect on the historical background to the
modern idea of religious rights.

The Western experience that I want particularly to consider is in some
ways paradigmatic, since a doctrine of natural rights—or human rights as we
say nowadays—first grew up in the Christian West. Of course, all the great
religious cultures of the world have given expression to ideals of justice and
right order in human affairs; but they have not normally expressed those

---

[*] Bryce and Edith M. Bowmar Professor of Humanistic Studies at Cornell University.
Ph.D. (Pembroke College, Cambridge). Another version of this chapter appears in John
Witte, Jr., and Johan D. van der Vyver, eds., *Religious Human Rights in Global Perspective:
Religious Perspectives* (Dordrecht/Boston/London: Martinus Nijhoff Publishers, 1995), 17–
46, and is duplicated herein with permission from the publisher.

[1] James Wood, "Editorial: Religion and Religious Liberty," *Journal of Church and State*
33 (1991): 226.

ideals in terms of subjective natural rights. (It would be hard, for instance, to imagine a Confucian Hobbes or Locke.) Even in the West, a doctrine of religious rights emerged only painfully and belatedly, out of a tradition that had earlier found it much easier to acknowledge other kinds of rights. Nowadays it has become commonplace to maintain, as Pope John Paul II recently asserted, that religious rights are the "cornerstone" of all other rights. But, viewed in historical perspective, religious rights came last; these rights were the most difficult to conceive of, let alone put into practice.

The Roman Catholic Church was the last of the great Christian denominations to embrace wholeheartedly the principle of religious freedom. This at least had the advantage that its leaders could form a mature and well-considered version of the doctrine. Hence the *Declaration on Religious Liberty* of Vatican Council II, promulgated in 1965, provides an appropriate starting point for our discussion:

> This Vatican Council declares that the human person has a right to religious freedom. This freedom means that all men are to be immune from coercion on the part of individuals or of social groups and of any human power . . . the right to religious freedom has its foundation in the very dignity of the human person as this dignity is known through the revealed word of God and by reason itself.[2]

This passage of the *Declaration* referred, in all-embracing fashion, not only to coercion by the state, but by "any human power." It defined religious freedom specifically as a "right" and a right inherent in the human person, a natural or human right therefore. This natural right, discernible by human reason, was also said to be rooted in divine revelation and so intrinsic to the Christian faith. The *Declaration* contained only a bland and innocuous hint that these affirmations represented a radical reversal of a policy of religious repression that the Catholic church (and the mainstream Protestant churches too) had maintained for centuries. The hint came in an observation that the demands of human dignity "have come to be more fully known to human reason through centuries of experience." How true these words are can be gathered from a decree of another general council, promulgated in 1215, just 750 years before the *Declaration* of Vatican Council II. This is from the Fourth Lateran Council:

> We excommunicate and anathematize every heresy that raises itself against the holy, orthodox, and Catholic faith. . . . Secular authorities, as they wish to be esteemed and numbered among the faithful, ought to take an oath that they will

---

[2] Walter M. Abbot, trans., *The Documents of Vatican II* (New York: G. Chapman, 1966), 678–680.

strive in good faith and to the best of their ability to exterminate all heretics pointed out by the church.[3]

My task as a historian is to try to explain how we got from there to here, from the repression of heretics to a declaration on religious liberty. A skeptic, faced by the two conciliar texts, might observe that the Christian religion evidently meant one thing in 1215 and something quite different in 1965. A more sympathetic observer might acknowledge that the church has indeed modified its teachings in the course of time but that this is only because the "centuries of experience" that Vatican II mentioned have led on to deeper insights into the truths that were originally proclaimed by the church's founder. As Jacques Maritain observed in discussing human rights, our understanding has increased "as man's moral conscience has developed."[4]

This idea of a growth of understanding in time is not a novel concept, based on modern historicism. In the thirteenth century the Franciscan theologian Peter Olivi wrote of the need for "new explication in the holy church of God—more and more through the course of time—of the sublime truths of faith." Olivi's master, St. Bonaventure, wrote of "seeds" of truth in scripture that slowly ripened in the minds of men, and he added that "Scripture and its mysteries cannot be understood unless the course of history is known."[5] Such writers were not arguing that divine revelation changes, but that human understanding of scripture deepens in the course of the centuries. We might add that some kinds of understanding, it seems, can be achieved only by undergoing specific historical experiences, sometimes harsh and bitter ones. This is especially true when we consider the theme of religious rights.

In the following discussion I want first to consider some aspects of early Christian teaching and then explain how, even in the medieval church, there were some developments of Christian thought that might seem favorable to a growth of religious liberty. (We shall find in the medieval period, for instance, vigorous assertions of the church's freedom from control by secular governments, strong affirmations of the value of individual conscience, and a newly emerging doctrine of natural rights.) Next I will try to explain why, for many centuries, such ideas were outweighed by an apparently insuperable body of counterargument favoring coercion of religious dissidents. Finally,

---

3 H. J. Schroeder, trans., *The Disciplinary Decrees of the General Councils* (St. Louis: B. Herder Book Co., 1937), 242.

4 Jacques Maritain, *The Rights of Man and Natural Law* (New York: C. Scribner's Sons, 1943), 65.

5 On the views of Olivi and Bonaventure see Brian Tierney, *Origins of Papal Infallibility*, 2d ed. (Leiden: E.J. Brill, 1988), 72–76, 109–114.

we shall need to consider how a new—or renewed—ideal of religious freedom took root in the early modern era, with a glance at the relevance of all this historical experience for the global problems of our modern age.

The Early Church.—From the beginning of the Christian era there were elements in Christian tradition that could lead on either to a doctrine of religious liberty or to a practice of persecution. Jesus himself taught a doctrine of universal love. "I say to you, love your enemies, do good to those who hate you" (Matt. 5: 44). Jesus disclaimed the role of a political Messiah, relying on coercive force, when he said, "My kingdom is not of this world" (John 18: 36). And he offered a new kind of freedom to his followers: "You shall know the truth and the truth shall make you free" (John 5: 32). Paul too wrote eloquently of "the freedom wherewith Christ has made us free" (Galatians 4: 31). And perhaps an ideal of spiritual liberty was always implicit in the Judeo-Christian understanding of the human person as a morally autonomous individual, endowed with conscience and reason and free will. But if an ideal of religious freedom was always implicit in Christian thought it was certainly not always explicitly asserted. There was always a potentiality for intolerance in the early Christians' disregard for all other religions, their conviction that they alone knew the one true God, that they alone were on the one true path to salvation, that all those outside the church were lost in a world of darkness and sin and error.

Still, a belief in the righteousness of one's own cause does not necessarily imply that one should coerce others into joining it. During the early days of the church Christians generally favored religious toleration if only because they were so often the victims of persecution; but of course the situation changed dramatically after the emperors themselves became Christians. When Constantine issued the "Edict of Milan" in 313 he granted toleration to the Christian church and to all other religions "so that every man may worship according to his own wish." Later, the emperors adopted a more repressive attitude toward nonChristian religions; but, in the fourth century, Christian apologists like Hilary of Poitiers and Lactantius still defended the principle of religious freedom. And toward the end of the century St. Martin of Tours bitterly condemned a group of bishops who persuaded the emperor to execute a supposed heretic, Priscillian. Perhaps the case for religious liberty was expressed most eloquently in the words of Lactantius: "Liberty has chosen to dwell in religion. For nothing is so much a matter of free will as religion, and no one can be required to worship what he does not will to worship."[6]

---

[6] Lactantius, *De divinis institutionibus,* in *Patrologia Latina* (Paris, 1844), 6: col. 1061.

A decisive turning point in patristic thought came in the teaching of Augustine (354–430). In 395, when Augustine became bishop of Hippo in north Africa, he found the church in that region divided by a bitter schism between orthodox Catholics and a dissident group known as Donatists. Religious animosities gave rise to frequent civil disturbances, with riots and street fighting in the cities between the two factions. For years Augustine argued that only peaceful persuasion should be used to end the schism. Finally, however, he accepted the view of his fellow-bishops that the civil power should be called in to repress the dissidents. The works he wrote in defense of this policy seem to contradict his earlier writings where he had emphasized freedom in religious matters. But Augustine always maintained that he was seeking only the salvation of the heretics. "It is better to love with severity than to deceive with indulgence," he wrote. Augustine justified the use of coercion against heretics by citing the parable of Jesus about a rich man who prepared a great feast. When none of the intended guests would accept the invitations he sent out, the master dispatched his servants to bring in alternative guests. But the servants told him that there was still room at the table: "Then the Lord said to the servant, Go out into the highways and hedges and compel them to come in" (Luke 14: 23).

The key words for Augustine were the last ones (*compelle intrare*). In his interpretation, the guests who refused their invitations were the Jewish people; those who accepted voluntarily were the Gentiles who became Christians; and those who were "compelled to enter" were heretics who had left the church and could licitly be coerced into returning.[7] Modern historians who have studied Augustine sympathetically point out that he always preferred discussion and persuasion in religious controversies; that he did not favor the harshest penalties against heretics—he did not advocate the death penalty, for instance; that for him the purpose of coercion was not to punish but to win back the heretic to the true faith and so to ensure his ultimate salvation. Less sympathetic historians have designated Augustine as "the prince and patriarch of persecutors" and as "the first theorist of the Inquisition." Certainly his views remained enormously influential throughout the Middle Ages. For a thousand years the church pursued a policy of suppressing religious dissent. Before turning to that theme, however, we need to consider some aspects of medieval religion that could—and eventually did, though only after centuries of struggles and vicissitudes—contribute to a growth of religious freedom.

---

[7] J. R. King, trans., *Writings on the Donatist Controversy, Library of the Nicene and Post-Nicene Fathers* (New York, 1887), 4: 642.

Church and State.—The most obvious way in which the leaders of the medieval church contributed (unintentionally of course) to the emergence of modern religious liberty was by their insistence on the freedom of the church from control by temporal rulers. In the Middle Ages there was never just one hierarchy of government exercising absolute authority, but always two—church and state as we say nowadays—often contending with one another, each limiting the other's power. This duality of government was a rather unusual development in human history. In societies larger than a tribal unit or a city-state the most common form of rulership has been some form of theocratic absolutism. The Pharaohs of Egypt, the Incas of Peru, the emperors of Japan were all revered as divine figures. The order of society was seen as a part of the divine order of the cosmos; the ruler provided a necessary link between heaven and earth. Typically, in such societies, religious liberty was neither conceived of nor desired.

Christianity was different from the beginning. It grew up in an alien culture, the sophisticated classical civilization of Greece and Rome. To become a Christian or to persist in the religion was a matter of free personal choice, often involving considerable self-sacrifice. For early Christians the emperor was not a divine ruler but a persecutor of the true faith. The tension between Roman state and Christian church was expressed classically in the words of Jesus himself. "Render to Caesar the things that are Caesar's and to God the things that are God's" (Mark 12: 17). In all ages Christians have remembered too the words of Peter, "We ought to obey God rather than man" (Acts 5: 29). After the conversion of Constantine and the establishment of a Christian empire there was indeed a possibility for a time that the church might become merely a sort of department of religious affairs in an imperial theocratic church-state. But, as the imperial power crumbled in the West, the independent role of the church was vigorously reasserted by Pope Gelasius (492–496):

> Two there are, august emperor, by which this world is chiefly ruled, the sacred authority of the priesthood and the royal power . . . in the order of religion, in matters concerning the reception and right administration of the heavenly sacraments, you ought to submit yourself rather than rule.[8]

There were *two* authorities in the world; whole areas of religious thought and practice were excluded from the control of the temporal ruler. The text of Gelasius was assimilated into the medieval corpus of canon law and endlessly quoted and discussed in later disputes.

---

[8] Brian Tierney, trans.,*The Crisis of Church and State 1050–1300* (Englewood Cliffs, N.J.: Prentice-Hall, 1964), 13.

The whole issue of empire and papacy arose again when Charlemagne sought to establish a new theocratic empire (c. 800), and his claims were reiterated by his successors of the Ottonian and Salian dynasties of Germany. Claiming to be vicars of God on earth, the kings assumed the right to control their churches; they regularly appointed bishops in the lands they ruled and invested them with the ring and staff that were the symbols of spiritual office. When, from time to time, a German emperor invaded Italy and occupied Rome, he chose and appointed popes, just as he appointed other bishops.

The church seemed to be drifting into another form of theocratic monism. But a dramatic change came in the pontificate of Gregory VII (1073–1085). Gregory condemned the whole existing order of society as radically contrary to divine justice. He declared himself willing to fight to the death for the "freedom of the church," a phrase he used like a kind of battle-cry. To implement his policy he forbade the prevailing practice of lay investiture (the appointment of bishops by kings) and so inaugurated a struggle that historians used to call the Investiture Contest but that is now often referred to simply as the Papal Revolution. Henry IV, king of Germany and later emperor, denounced Gregory as a pseudo-pope and a heretic; Gregory responded by deposing Henry from his kingship. The fight that ensued between pope and emperor was both a war of propaganda and a real civil war in Germany and Italy. At one point Henry had to humiliate himself before the pope at Canossa and humbly beg his forgiveness; but later his armies occupied Rome and drove Gregory into exile. In the end neither side could prevail and, after both of the original protagonists had died, a compromise peace was patched up in the Concordat of Worms (1122).[9]

The struggle between popes and kings was reenacted over and over again in the following centuries. After denouncing the theocratic pretensions of kings, the popes were often tempted to assert a theocratic role for themselves. Sometimes they put forward extreme claims to a kind of overlordship of Christian society in both spiritual and temporal affairs. The point is, however, that such claims were always resisted and never generally accepted by medieval kings or their peoples. The theocratic claims of the papacy reached a high-water mark in Boniface VIII's Bull, *Unam Sanctam* (1302) with its uncompromising declaration: "It is altogether necessary for every human creature to be subject to the Roman pontiff."[10] But Boniface was defeated and humiliated in the struggle with the king of France that had been the occasion of his pronouncement.

---

[9] Ibid., 53–73.

[10] Ibid., 188.

Because neither side could make good its more extreme claims, a dualism of church and state persisted in medieval society and eventually it was rationalized and justified in many works of political theory. The French theologian John of Paris, for instance, writing in 1302 (the year of *Unam Sanctam*), wrote a treatise *On Royal and Papal Power* which presented a carefully balanced dualism, assigning to each power its proper function. "The priest is greater than the prince in spiritual affairs," John wrote, "and, on the other hand, the prince is greater in temporal affairs."[11]

The persistent dualism in medieval society that we have described was far removed from a modern "wall of separation." In the Middle Ages the powers of church and state constantly overlapped and interacted and impinged on one another; but the church remained committed to a radical limitation of state power in the sphere of religion. By the end of the Middle Ages the Catholic kings had again acquired a large measure of control over church appointments; but, in the Reformation era, the revived theory of royal divine right was challenged by new forms of protest that led to new ways of asserting religious rights.

Freedom of the church from control by the state is one important part of modern religious liberty. But it is only a part. The *libertas ecclesiae* that medieval popes demanded was not freedom of religion for each individual person but the freedom of the church as an institution to direct its own affairs. It left open the possibility, all too fully realized from the twelfth century onward, that the church might organize the persecution of its own dissident members. And, when the interests of church and state happened to coincide, as they often did in dealing with heresy, there was room for a savage suppression of religious dissent. But, even during the centuries of persecution, there were some aspects of medieval thought and practice that could have been conducive to an alternative tradition of religious toleration.

The Claims of Conscience.—For one thing, medieval canonists and moral theologians often upheld the overriding value of the individual conscience as a guide to right conduct. When Paul wrote "Everything that is not from faith is sin" (Romans 14: 23), the Ordinary Gloss to the Bible (the standard medieval commentary on the text) explained that the words "not from faith" meant "all that is contrary to conscience." In the twelfth century Peter Abelard expanded the argument. He taught that to act against one's conscience was always sinful, even if the conscience erred in discerning what

---

[11] Ibid., 209.

was right.[12] A century after Abelard, Thomas Aquinas addressed this same question. It might seem that we are not obliged to follow an erring conscience, he wrote, because we are not obliged to obey the command of a lower authority when it conflicts with that of a higher one; but conscience might favor our acting contrary to the law of God, who was the supreme authority. In reply Thomas quoted the Ordinary Gloss to Romans 14:23 and explained that we are only obliged to follow the command of the higher authority when we know that it conflicts with our present judgment. An erring conscience could be formed in good faith if one were ignorant of the higher law. A person was always obliged to do what his conscience discerned as good even though the conscience might be mistaken.[13]

The same doctrine was taught by the canonists. It was expressed in two judgments of Pope Innocent III (1198–1216), that were incorporated into the corpus of medieval canon law. The Ordinary Gloss to the Decretals, a work studied in law schools throughout Europe, explained their implication. "One ought to endure excommunication rather than sin . . . no one ought to act against his own conscience and he should follow his conscience rather than the judgment of the church when he is certain . . . one ought to suffer any evil rather than sin against conscience."[14]

We are not dealing here with a right to religious liberty but with a duty to obey one's conscience. Still, an emphasis on the primacy of the individual conscience was an important element in later theories of religious rights. The medieval position was that a person was right to follow his conscience but that he might suffer at the hands of the authorities if his conscience led him to illicit behavior. Similarly, in the modern world, individuals may be led by a sincere conscience to violate the law—as in some forms of civil rights or antiwar protest—but the law will hold them responsible for their actions. There is one further point; medieval moralists did not hold that people should act on mere subjective whims. Everyone was required to use the utmost diligence and every resource of knowledge and understanding to form a correct conscience. Failure to do this was sinful. In practice, it was assumed that most cases where an erring conscience led to illicit behavior involved culpable ignorance or culpable negligence.

In one sphere the emphasis on individual conscience did lead to a degree of religious toleration. Medieval doctrine always taught that non-Christians

---

[12] D. E. Luscombe, ed. and trans., *Peter Abelard's Ethics* (Oxford: Clarendon Press, 1971), 55–57, 67, 97.

[13] *Summa theologiae*, pt. 1.2ae., quest. 19, art. 5.

[14] *Decretales Gregorii Papae IX cum glossis* (Lyons, 1624), gloss ad bk. 5, tit. 39, chap. 44.

could not be forcibly converted to Christianity. God's grace was a free gift, and it had to be freely accepted. In practice the only substantial populations of non–Christian people scattered throughout the Western church were Jewish communities, and the principle of toleration was explicitly applied to them. The attitude of the medieval church toward the Jews, as toward heretics, was shaped by the teaching of Augustine, though in this case it had a more benign effect. Augustine held that, although the Jewish people had erred at the time of Christ, still it was God's will that they should always survive. They existed to give permanent independent witness to the divine law revealed in the Old Testament. They could also attest to the words of the prophets which Christians understood as foretelling the coming of Christ. (Infidels could not maintain that the Christians had just made up the prophecies about a coming Messiah when the Jews also affirmed their reality.) And accordingly, to fulfill this role, some of the Jewish people would exist until the end of time. The acceptance of this theology shaped the official attitude of the medieval church toward the Jews. They were indeed discriminated against—made to wear a distinctive dress, excluded from positions of authority in government—but they were allowed to have their own synagogues and to practice their own religion. The attitude of the papacy was one of toleration, grudging toleration no doubt, but still a recognition that Jews had a right to exist in a Christian society. The policy was defined by Gregory I (590–604) in a letter that became a part of the permanent canon law of the church.[15] "Just as the Jews ought not to be allowed more than the law concedes," he wrote, "so too they ought not to suffer harm in those things that the law does concede to them." From the beginning of the twelfth century onward it became customary for the Jewish community of Rome to obtain a restatement of Jewish rights from each new pope at the beginning of his reign. In the real-life world of the Middle Ages, needless to say, savage outrages against Jewish communities occurred all too often; but they were due to outbursts of mob violence or actions of secular rulers. They were contrary to the law and teaching of the church.

The Idea of Natural Rights.—There was one further area in which medieval thinkers began to develop a doctrine that would be important for later theories of religious liberty—the idea that all persons possess natural rights.

No consensus exists among modern scholars about the origin of this doctrine or how it is related to the tradition of Christian thought. Jacques Maritain simply assumed that the idea of human rights was always implicit in

---

[15] *Decretales*, bk. 5, tit. 6, chap. 9.

the Judeo-Christian teaching on the dignity and value of each human person.[16] At the opposite extreme, Leo Strauss focussed on the supposedly atheistic philosophy of Thomas Hobbes, whom he regarded as the founder of modern rights theories, and concluded that the idea of natural rights was alien to the whole preceding classical and Christian tradition.[17] Disciples of Strauss will still maintain that "The very idea of natural rights is incompatible with Christian doctrine."[18] But this view seems untenable if only because there certainly were Christian natural rights theorists before Hobbes—Suarez and Grotius for instance. An intermediate point of view, that has come to be widely accepted, was put forward by Michel Villey. He held that the idea of natural rights was indeed derived from Christianity but from a distorted and aberrant form of Christian thought, specifically from the fourteenth-century, nominalist and voluntarist philosophy of William of Ockham. Villey argued that Ockham inaugurated a "semantic revolution" when he interpreted the Latin word *ius* (right) as meaning a subjective power (*potestas*).[19] But subsequent research has shown that the association of "right" and "power" was quite common in earlier medieval jurisprudence. Before 1200, for instance, the canonist Huguccio wrote, concerning a bishop-elect, "He has the power (*potestas*) of administering, that is the right (*ius*) of administering."[20]

According to the most recent work the origin of the later natural rights theories is to be found in the Christian jurisprudence of the late twelfth century, especially in the works of the canonists of that era.[21] The twelfth century was an age of renewal in many spheres of life and thought. New networks of commerce grew up. There was new art, new architecture, a new literature of courtly romance. Religious thought placed a new emphasis on the individual human person—on individual intention in assessing guilt, on individual consent in marriage, on individual scrutiny of conscience.[22] And in

---

16 Maritain, *The Rights of Man*, 64–66.

17 Leo Strauss, *Natural Right and History* (Chicago: Univ. of Chicago Press, 1950), 166–202.

18 "Walter Berns Comments," *This World* 6 (Fall, 1983): 98.

19 Michael Villey, *La formation de la pensée juridique moderne*, 4th ed. (Paris: Montchrestien, 1975), 252, 261.

20 Robert Louis Benson, *The Bishop-Elect: A Study in Medieval Ecclesiastical Office* (Princeton: Princeton Univ. Press, 1968), 118n.5.

21 Brian Tierney, "Origins of Natural Rights Language: Texts and Contexts, 1150–1250," *History of Political Thought* 10 (1989): 615–646; Charles J. Reid, "The Canonistic Contribution to the Western Rights Tradition: An Historical Inquiry," *Boston College Law Review* 33 (1991): 37–92.

22 On the juristic implications of these attitudes see especially Harold J. Berman, *Law and Revolution: The Formation of the Western Legal Tradition* (Cambridge, Mass.: Harvard Univ. Press, 1983).

the secular sphere, at every level of society we find an intense concern for individual rights and liberties.

Above all, the twelfth century was an age of legal renaissance marked by the recovery of the whole corpus of classical Roman law, and by the first adequate codification of the accumulated canon law of the church in Gratian's *Concord of Discordant Canons*, completed circa 1140. In the following decades a succession of great jurists, inspired by the old texts, found ways to express all the new impulses of their own age in juridical language. For us the crucial development was that the new personalism in religious life, and the everyday concern with rights in secular society, infected the language of the canonists when they came to discuss the concept of *ius naturale* (natural right). Earlier the phrase *ius naturale* had been understood in an objective sense to mean natural law or "what is naturally right." But the canonists who wrote around 1200, reading the old texts in the context of their more humanist, more individualist culture, added another definition. In their writings *ius naturale* was now sometimes defined in a subjective sense as a faculty, power, force, ability inhering in individual persons. From this initial subjective definition the canonists went on to develop a considerable array of natural rights. Around 1250 Pope Innocent IV wrote that ownership of property was a right derived from natural law and that even infidels enjoyed this right, along with a right to form their own governments.[23] Other natural rights that were asserted in the thirteenth century included a right to liberty, a right of self-defense, a right of the poor to support from the surplus wealth of the rich.[24] What was still notably lacking was a developed concept of religious rights.

By around 1300 a sophisticated legal language had grown up in which a doctrine of natural rights could be expressed. The next step was the assimilation of the juristic idea of rights into works of political philosophy. William of Ockham was indeed important here. He drew on the earlier canonistic tradition but went beyond it. One of his major contributions was to reshape the scriptural idea of evangelical liberty into a doctrine of natural rights. When Paul wrote about Christian freedom he meant freedom from the law of the Old Testament or freedom from sin, but Ockham used Paul's texts to argue for freedom from any tyrannical government, especially within the church. Not even the pope, he wrote, could injure "the rights and liberties conceded to the faithful by God and nature."[25] Ockham also developed a concept of "suppositional" or contingent natural rights, related to basic

---

[23] *Commentaria Innocentii . . . super quinque libros decretalium* (Frankfurt: Sigismund Feyerabendt, 1570), ad pt. 1, quest. 2, art. 7, fol. 3v, and pt. 3, quest. 34, art. 8, fol. 429v.

[24] Tierney, "Origins," 638–44.

[25] "An princeps," in *Guillelmi de Ockham opera politica*, ed. H. S. Offler (Manchester: Typis Universitatis Mancunii, 1956–74), 1: 251.

human needs, but applied in different ways in different circumstances.[26] The idea could perhaps have some relevance for modern problems concerning the applicability of general norms in a world of cultural diversity.

Ockham's ideas were developed further by Jean Gerson, an eminent theologian who wrote around 1400. Gerson gave a very influential definition of *ius* as "a power or faculty belonging to each one in accordance with the dictate of right reason" and argued that, even in man's fallen state, humans retained many such rights.[27] Gerson also took up and developed further the idea that Christ's law was a law of liberty. In the existing church this was no longer the case, Gerson complained. On the contrary, Christians were oppressed by an intolerable burden of laws and regulations and obligations imposed by human authority, that is, by the church hierarchy. Such enactments were like snares and nets to trap the soul, he wrote.[28] By fusing Paul's doctrine of Christian liberty with his own idea of natural rights Gerson went on to argue that the essential obligation of a Christian was to accept freely the divinely revealed law of scripture and the natural law that his reason and conscience could discern. In the last resort one could exercise an inherent natural right of self-defense that no human law could take away against any oppressive authority, even an oppressive pope. Gerson's words sometimes have an almost modern sound and his ideas were indeed very important in the growth of later natural rights theories. They were transmitted to the early modern world mainly by the Spanish scholastics of the sixteenth century, especially in the course of their debates about the rights of American Indians. Bartolomée de las Casas in particular tried to defend the Indians against subjugation and forced conversion by appealing to a doctrine of natural rights based on medieval legal and theological sources.[29]

Given all these aspects of medieval thought—an insistence on the primacy of the individual conscience, a rejection of forced conversion, a nascent theory of natural rights—one might reasonably hope that at least some medieval thinkers would have moved on from these premises to assert a full-fledged doctrine of religious liberty. Nothing of the sort happened. Every medieval writer who discussed this question saw heresy as a sin and a

---

[26] H.S. Offler, "The Three Modes of Natural Law in Ockham: A Revision of the Text," *Franciscan Studies* 37 (1977): 207–18.

[27] "De vita spirituali animae," in Jean Gerson, *Oeuvres complètes*, ed., P. Glorieux (Paris: Desclée, 1960–73), 3: 141–42.

[28] Ibid., 129. On these views of Gerson see Brian Tierney, "Conciliarism, Corporatism, and Individualism: The Doctrine of Individual Rights in Gerson," *Cristianesimo nella storia* 9 (1988): 81–111.

[29] Brian Tierney, "Aristotle and the American Indians—Again," *Cristianesimo nella storia* 12 (1991): 295–322.

crime that was properly judged by the church and properly punished by the secular power. Even Gerson had no conception of religious freedom as we understand it; indeed, he participated in the trial and burning of John Hus. Gerson could defend the rights of Christians within the church, but it never occurred to him to assert that heretics had rights against the church. Before we can understand how real religious rights emerged in the early modern world, we need to consider why they were so persistently denied in the preceding centuries.

Heresy and Persecution.—In his classic little book, *The Whig Interpretation of History*, Herbert Butterfield warned historians against "present-mindedness." We should not impose our own ideas on the past, he urged, but rather seek to understand each historical era "in its own terms." The sort of question we ought to ask, Butterfield suggested, is not: How did we get our religious liberty? But rather: Why were people in former ages so given to persecution?[30] It seems to me that both questions are legitimate ones for a historian; but obviously we cannot begin to address the first question until we have considered the second one. And it is not an easy question to answer.

In the late Roman empire, laws against heresy, sometimes imposing the death penalty on offenders, were enacted by imperial authority. But in the centuries after the fall of the empire there was little organized persecution, though heretics or people suspected of heresy were sometimes lynched by fanatic mobs. When cases came before church courts the usual penalty was excommunication. A more systematic repression began from the twelfth century onward, even as new doctrines of natural rights were growing into existence. This was partly because of the spread of new heresies and partly because of the growing institutionalization of the church. As the church became more aware of itself as an ordered society with its own system of law and organs of government, it became less tolerant of those who rejected its authority. In 1199 Pope Innocent III declared, in the decretal *Vergentis*, that heresy was equivalent to treason.[31] Heretics were traitors to God, he wrote, just as others guilty of treason were traitors to the emperor. The most threatening heresy of the time was that of the Cathars or Albigensians who had come to dominate substantial areas of southern France. In 1208 Innocent counterattacked by unleashing the Albigensian Crusade, an invasion of southern France by Catholic forces from the north which perpetrated savage massacres in cities that were strongholds of the heretics and effectively

---

[30] Herbert Butterfield, *The Whig Interpretation of History* (London: G. Bell and Sons, 1931), 18.

[31] *Decretales Gregorii IX*, bk. 5, tit. 7, chap. 10.

destroyed the Cathar civilization in Provence. Then, in 1215, Innocent's Fourth Lateran Council issued the general condemnation of heretics that I have already quoted. Secular governments also enacted harsh penalties against heresy. In 1231 Emperor Frederick II decreed that the appropriate punishment was death by burning; the words of his statute indicate the common attitude toward heretics:

> Heretics try to tear the seamless robe of our God. They are violent wolves. . . . They are sons of depravity. . . . Therefore we draw the sword of vengeance against them. . . . Committed to the judgment of the flames, they should be burned alive in the sight of the people.[32]

Other rulers enacted similar legislation, and burning at the stake became the common punishment for heresy. About this same time, Pope Gregory IX (1227–1241) first began to commission groups of inquisitors, usually Dominican and Franciscan friars, to seek out and punish heretics. By mid-thirteenth century such inquisitors were at work in all parts of the church.

In some areas of political thought, medieval ideas were not so different from our own. Medieval people had quite well-developed concepts of representation and consent and government under law. But, when we turn to the idea of individual religious rights, their whole mindset was so alien to ours that it takes a considerable effort of historical imagination to enter into their world of thought. Perhaps we can find a starting point in a remark of the great legal historian, Frederic Maitland: "In the Middle Ages the church was a state." The church, he pointed out, had its own institutions of government, its own bureaucracy, its own laws and law courts. In the Middle Ages secular political power was fragmented. The old Roman empire had passed away and the attempt to found a medieval Christian empire had failed—partly indeed because of the struggle between popes and emperors that we have considered. National monarchies in France and England were only just beginning to grow into existence. The only bond of unity that held western Christian society together was the bond of a common religion. Nowadays the focus of our loyalty is the state; we look to the state to protect our security and our liberty; to be a "stateless person" in the twentieth century is a most unhappy fate. The other side of the coin is that we do not tolerate people who are perceived as traitors to the state. We charge them with treason; we inflict punishment on them, sometimes capital punishment in extreme cases. A plea of personal sincerity, that the traitor has acted from good motives, in accordance with his own conscience, is not a sufficient defense. Medieval people regarded heretics

---

[32] James M. Powell, trans., *The Constitutions of Melfi* (Syracuse: Syracuse Univ. Press, 1971), 7.

in much the same way; they held them guilty of treason to the church, and they treated them as traitors. When a common religion defined the whole way of life of a society, to reject it was to cut oneself off from the community, to become a sort of outlaw—and a dangerous outlaw from a medieval point of view.

When Thomas Aquinas first discussed the issue of heresy he began by presenting a series of apparently cogent arguments in favor of toleration.[33] In the first place, there was the parable of the wheat and the tares from Matthew 13. In this story the good grain and the weeds were allowed to grow together until the time of harvest lest, in destroying the weeds, some of the wheat be destroyed too. In commenting on this, Aquinas quoted John Chrysostom, an early church father, who had explicitly interpreted the text as meaning that heretics were not to be killed because, if this were permitted, some of the innocent would probably suffer along with the guilty. Again, Aquinas noted, canon law taught that Jews were not to be forcibly converted. Moreover, faith required the free assent of the will; and God himself had said, through the prophet Ezekiel, "I do not will the death of a sinner." Against all this, Aquinas quoted one text of Scripture, the one Augustine had already used, "Compel them to enter." And Aquinas understood it in the same sense as Augustine. The texts in favor of toleration applied to Jews and infidels; it was true that they could not be converted by force. But those who had already accepted the faith could be compelled to return to it if they fell into heresy. To explain this, Aquinas used the analogy of a vow or promise. A man could not be compelled to take a vow but if he chose to do so he was obliged to fulfill it. In a later discussion Aquinas compared heretics to counterfeiters of false money.[34] It was a more serious offense to corrupt the faith than to corrupt the currency he argued. Hence, just as counterfeiters were executed, so too heretics could be put to death. Sometimes the health of the whole body required that a diseased limb be cut away.

John Noonan, discussing these texts from the standpoint of a lawyer rather than a theologian, has pointed out that they are based on a series of legal fictions and unpersuasive analogies. It was a fiction that persons baptized in infancy had freely vowed to accept the faith; the comparison between counterfeiters and heretics confused the material realm of property with the spiritual realm of truth; and the use of the phrase *compelle intrare* transferred the words from the context of a parable about the kingdom of God to a context of law and earthly jurisdiction.[35] However cogent such

---

[33] *Summa theol.*, pt. 2.2ae, quest. 10, chap. 8.

[34] Ibid., pt. 2.2ae, quest. 11, chap. 3.

[35] John T. Noonan, Jr., "Principled or Pragmatic Foundations for the Freedom of Conscience," *Journal of Law and Religion* 5 (1987): 205.

objections may appear to us, one has to add that the arguments of Aquinas seemed entirely convincing to the medieval audience he was addressing.

Medieval people were so convinced of the truth of their religion that they could never see dissent from the accepted faith as arising simply from intellectual error, from a mistake in judgment. They thought that heresy must somehow stem from malice, from a perverted will that deliberately chose evil rather than good, Satan rather than God. Aquinas wrote, "Unfaithfulness is an act of the intellect, but moved by the will."[36] This was the root cause of the medieval hatred of heresy. The heretics were seen, not only as traitors to the church, but as traitors to God. To medieval people it seemed that they had rejected God's truth and God's love out of pride and self-love, the love of their own self-contrived errors. They had set themselves on a path that could lead only to eternal damnation and, unless they were restrained, they would lure countless others to the same terrible fate. Elementary justice and charity, it seemed, required that they be rooted out. The Inquisition that pursued this task with increasingly harsh and cruel measures, including the use of torture to extort confessions, was accepted as a necessary safeguard of Christian society.

Thinking about the Inquisition may remind us of two aphorisms that Lord Acton quoted.[37] The first is the well-known saying of Mme de Staël, "To understand all is to forgive all." The other, less indulgent, is from the Duke de Broglie, "We should beware of too much explaining lest we end up with too much forgiving." Neither aphorism is altogether satisfying for a historian. Our task is surely to understand and explain as fully as possible; but we do not have to condone everything that we have tried to understand; and, when everything possible has been said in mitigation, the medieval theory and practice of religious persecution will seem abhorrent to most modern people. Over a period of centuries thousands of persons were hunted down, tortured, and killed for a crime that, to us, might seem a mere eccentricity of personal belief.

A critical observer, looking back over the history of the West for the past thousand years and at the policies pursued in many parts of the world during the present century, might suppose that persecution is a normal pattern of human conduct. He might think that Butterfield had got his question upside down after all. Perhaps the real question a historian has to answer is not: Why were they so given to persecution? But rather: Why are we so committed to an ideal of religious liberty? This is the final topic that we have to consider.

---

[36] *Summa theol.*, pt. 2.2ae, quest. 10, chap. 2.

[37] "Inaugural Lecture," in *Lectures on Modern History*, ed. J. N. Figgis and R. V. Laurence (London: Macmillan and Co., Ltd., 1906), 27.

The Emergence of Religious Rights.—In the context of medieval life, religious persecution seemed both right and necessary. No one could see that "freedom of the church" could mean freedom of conscience for each individual Christian or that the duty to obey one's conscience might imply a right to act in accordance with it, or that a natural right to liberty was radically incomplete if it did not include a right to freedom of religion. The Reformation of the sixteenth century created a new historical context in which all these matters were reevaluated in the light of new understandings of Christian teaching shaped by new historical experiences in the centuries after Martin Luther's first protests.

The changes that came about were not due to any intangible "spirit of Protestantism" or to the specific teachings of the first great reformers. It would indeed be hard to discern any seeds of religious liberty in Luther's rantings against Catholics and Jews or in Calvin's grim-lipped defense of persecution after the execution of Servetus. Luther, Calvin, Beza, Bullinger, Melanchthon all accepted the entirely conventional view of their time that heretics should be suppressed, just as their Catholic contemporaries did. Moreover Lutheranism gave Europe the doctrine of the "godly Prince" whose duties included the suppression of idolatry and error; and Calvin introduced a new kind of clerical theocracy that could be as intolerant as the medieval church hierarchy. Religious liberty arose out of a play of contingent events that no one had planned and no one had foreseen.

Thomas Carlyle observed that new historical events do not spring from one single cause but from a whole web of causation, from "all other events, prior or contemporaneous."[38] Then, he noted, the new event combines with all the other ones to give birth to further change. This is the sort of situation we have to deal with in considering religious liberty. Between 1500 and 1700 a new web of causation was created. Europe experienced a series of savagely destructive wars of religion that ended in stalemates and a splintering of religious unity into innumerable competing sects. Eventually this led on to a growth of national states that could command the loyalty of subjects who professed a variety of religious beliefs. But before that final outcome was achieved, religious groups who rejected an established faith found themselves persecuted in many countries—Huguenots in France, Roman Catholics and Puritan separatists in England, Lutherans in the Catholic principalities of Germany, and every kind of dissenter from Catholic orthodoxy in Spain.

In each country the groups that were being persecuted sought toleration for their own beliefs; but these demands were not at first based on any

---

[38] Thomas Carlyle, "On History," in *Critical and Miscellaneous Essays: Collected and Republished* (London: Chapman and Hall, 1872), 2: 257.

devotion to religious liberty as such. The right and duty of the ruler to punish religious error was taken for granted; it was just that each group was convinced that it alone held fast to the truth. In England, an anonymous pamphlet of 1615 urged King James I to relax the laws against Puritans but to inflict the death penalty on Catholics.[39] At the other end of the religious spectrum, the Jesuit Robert Parsons protested against an oath of allegiance demanded of Catholics with an eloquent plea against coercion: "For he that should force a Jew or a Turke to sweare, that there were a blessed Trinity ... against their conscience should synne grievously."[40] But Parsons was defending a church that persecuted religious dissidents wherever it had the power to do so. Each religious group believed that it should be tolerated because it was right and, usually, that its adversaries should be persecuted because they were wrong. Oliver Cromwell said, in a moment of exasperation, "Everyone desires to have liberty, but none will give it."[41] Looking back rather disdainfully on the whole situation, J. N. Figgis wrote of the competing sects, "It was . . . the inability of any single one to destroy the others, which finally secured liberty."[42]

There is truth in this, but it is not quite the whole truth. From the middle of the sixteenth century onward a few voices were raised in defense of a genuine religious freedom. Among Protestant groups, the Anabaptists and Baptists always condemned coercion in matters of religion. And the execution of Servetus for heresy in Calvin's Geneva (1553) evoked a response from Sebastian Castellio, *On Heretics, Whether they Should be Persecuted* that provided the first full-scale argument for freedom of conscience.

A century later a volatile and complex situation that arose during the English Civil War made England for a time the principal forcing ground for the ideal of religious freedom. The Parliament that defeated Charles I was controlled by Presbyterians who wanted to impose, by force if necessary, a rigorous Presbyterian discipline on the English church. Their position was summed up in a statement of Thomas Edwards: "A toleration is against the nature of reformation, a reformation and a toleration are diametrically opposite; the commands of God given in his word for reformation do not admit of toleration."[43] But the armies that had won Parliament's victories

---

[39] W. K. Jordan, *The Development of Religious Toleration in England* (Cambridge, Mass.: Harvard Univ. Press, 1932–40), 2: 209.

[40] Ibid., 500.

[41] W. Abbott, ed., *The Writings and Speeches of Oliver Cromwell* (Cambridge: Mass., Harvard Univ. Press, 1937–47), 3: 547.

[42] J. N. Figgis, *Churches in the Modern State* (London: Longmans, Green and Co., 1913), 101.

[43] Thomas Edwards, *Antapologia* (London, 1641), 285.

were filled with members of dissenting sects—Congregationalists, Baptists, Unitarians, Fifth Monarchy Men, Muggletonians, and many others. They all demanded and, under Cromwell, enjoyed for a time a measure of toleration. Moreover, in the vast pamphlet literature that grew up, some spokesmen went further and began to argue for a real religious liberty for all, not just toleration for one group. The Presbyterian Richard Baxter, when serving as a chaplain to one of Cromwell's regiments, noted disapprovingly that among the soldiers, "their most frequent and vehement disputes were for liberty of conscience as they called it; that . . . every man might not only hold, but preach and do in matters of religion what he pleased."[44] Perhaps the most impassioned plea came from Roger Williams who had known persecution both in old England and New England. In *The Bloudy Tenent of Persecution*, Williams wrote: "It is the will and command of God that (since the coming of his Sonne the Lord Jesus) a permission of the most Paganish, Jewish, Turkish, or Antichristian consciences and worships be granted to all men in all Nations and Countries."[45]

It was not unusual for seventeenth-century Protestants to urge toleration for "Jews and Turks." This was just a way of reaffirming the old medieval doctrine against forced conversion. But Williams was exceptional in his willingness to tolerate even Roman Catholics. He wrote that even Catholics had consciences "more or less," and that their consciences were to be respected. A man who converted to Catholicism in good faith might still be a "loving and peaceable" person, according to Williams.[46]

In the early modern world the practice of persecution was attacked by three main lines of argument which we might characterize as based on skepticism, or on expediency, or on an appeal to the underlying principles of the Christian faith itself. The arguments were not all of equal value. The first two could lead on only to a plea for some limited degree of toleration; only the third could provide a basis for a principled commitment to an ideal of religious freedom.

The skeptical approach was rooted in Renaissance humanism. The humanists began by dismissing all the finespun arguments of scholastic philosophy as dreary nonsense; then some of them carried over the same attitude in considering the arcane theological disputes that divided the Christian churches of their own day. This was the underlying attitude of Castellio. (Before writing his treatise on toleration he had composed another

---

[44] A.S.P. Woodhouse, ed., *Puritanism and Liberty: Being the Army Debates (1647–49) from the Clarke Manuscripts* (Chicago: Univ. of Chicago Press, 1951), 388.

[45] *The Complete Writings of Roger Williams* (New York: Russell & Russell, 1963), 3: 3.

[46] Ibid., 4: 317, 508.

work on *The Art of Doubting*.) The skepticism of the humanists was not (at least not at first) a skepticism about the fundamental truths of Christian faith. Castellio wrote confidently, "No one doubts that there is a God, whether He is good and just, whether He should be loved and worshipped. . . ."[47] On the other hand, the things that Christians did not agree about—doctrines concerning predestination, free will, baptism, the eucharist, the Trinity— were matters of controversy precisely because they were not clearly revealed in scripture. The truth about such things could not be known with certainty, Castellio thought. So it was futile and cruel for Christians to persecute one another over these matters. This line of argument was continued by the Italian, Acontius and then, in mid-seventeenth-century England, by writers like William Walwyn and Francis Osborne.

The Huguenot exile, Pierre Bayle, presented a more radically skeptical attack on religious persecution. His work provides a link between the questioning of the Christian humanists and the more thoroughgoing skepticism of the Enlightenment, when a defense of toleration was often associated with indifference or hostility to all religious teaching. We should not underestimate our debt to the Enlightenment. No doubt the skeptical mockery of a Voltaire was needed to expose the lingering cruelties and superstitions of established religion. But perhaps in the end skepticism is not enough. Humans are religious animals, and if their old faiths are worn away by too much doubt they are likely to invent new and more savage substitutes. The Enlightenment did not lead on to a new era of peace and harmony; it led to a reign of terror in revolutionary France and a new round of religious persecution.

The second line of argument in favor of toleration was simple expediency. This attitude was typified in Henry IV of France who changed his religion from Protestant to Catholic in order to gain the French crown but then, as a Catholic king, issued the Edict of Nantes (1598) that granted substantial liberties to Protestants. Henry's contemporary, Queen Elizabeth of England, also pursued a religious policy guided mainly by reason of state. Reasons of economic policy were cited too. The Spanish regent in the Netherlands, Don Juan of Austria, wrote in 1577 "The Prince of Orange has always insisted . . . that freedom of conscience is essential to commercial prosperity."[48] The greatest theoretical exponent of the argument from expediency was the political philosopher Jean Bodin. He acknowledged that

---

[47] Sebastian Castellio, *Concerning Heretics*, trans. Roland H. Bainton, Columbia Records of Civilization, No. 22 (New York: Octagon Books, 1935), 294.

[48] Quoted in Henry Kamen, *The Rise of Toleration* (London: McGraw-Hill, 1967), 149.

religious uniformity was desirable and he did not doubt that the state could lawfully suppress religious dissent; but he argued that, when a new religion had become so entrenched that it could not be suppressed without a danger of civil strife, the most reasonable policy was to tolerate it.[49] A king's duty to maintain the public welfare took precedence over his obligation to uphold religious truth. A problem with the argument from expediency is that, in many circumstances, toleration is not the most obviously expedient course of action. Often it seems that the most effective way to maintain order and unity is to crush dissent. It was a rather unusual set of circumstances in the seventeenth century that made persecution so often ineffective. The argument from expediency left open the likelihood of renewed persecution when circumstances changed again.

The third argument for toleration was ultimately the most important one. Over and over again the idea was asserted—though not indeed generally accepted, for these are still dissident voices—that the practice of persecution was radically contrary to the teaching of Jesus himself. This argument was included in the works of many different thinkers. Castellio wrote of persecution that "Satan could not devise anything more repugnant to the nature and will of Christ." Pierre Bayle argued in a similar fashion. He framed his case for toleration as a commentary on the text, "Compel them to enter," the text that Augustine and Aquinas had used to justify persecution; but Bayle argued in a different spirit that to understand the words of Christ in this way was "contrary to the essential spirit of the Gospel itself."[50] Bayle was a man of skeptical temperament, but the same kind of argument was put forward by writers of fervent religious faith. Roger Williams presented various considerations in favor of religious freedom, but the fundamental one was that persecution was "directly contradicting the spirit and mind and practice of the Prince of Peace."[51]

The awareness that religious liberty needed to be grounded on Christian principles as well as on pragmatic considerations of expediency was well expressed in an English pamphlet of 1614. The author wrote, "A man would think we had been schooled and whipt long enough to it by our calamities." That is to say, recent practical experience had shown the ill-effects of persecution. But the author added at once that "liberty of conscience is no new doctrine." Rather, he declared, it was "as old certainly as the blessed

---

[49] Jean Bodin, *Six Books of the Commonwealth*, trans. M. J. Tooley (Oxford: B. Blackwell, 1955), 4.7, 140–142.

[50] Castellio, *On Heretics*, 123; A. G. Tannenbaum, trans., *Pierre Bayle's Philosophical Commentary* (New York: P. Lang, 1987), 1.3, 42.

[51] "Bloudy Tenent," in Williams, *Writings*, 3: 219.

word of God."[52] The new exigencies of the time led discerning Christians to understand more deeply the implications of their old faith. The more learned authors quoted the early patristic texts in favor of religious freedom. Often the parable of the wheat and tares was cited as an argument for toleration. A Baptist pamphlet of 1661 declared that liberty of conscience was "a part of the Christian religion."[53] In the Netherlands, Dirck Coornhert, arguing against the skeptical views of Justus Lipsius, defended religious freedom as a part of the authentic teachings of Christ, and insisted that the truth of those teachings could be known with certainty.[54] Among the English writers, John Milton took up St. Paul's texts about Christian liberty, the texts that Ockham and Gerson had appealed to earlier, and derived from them an argument that the use of force in matters of faith was contrary to "the very weightiest and inmost reasons of Christian religion."[55]

In this new climate of opinion, when persecution was increasingly condemned as contrary to the teachings of Jesus, all the old medieval strands of argument about the freedom of the church from secular control, the overriding authority of conscience, and the existence of natural rights were taken up again and woven into new patterns. These arguments, I suggested earlier, could all have been conducive to a doctrine of religious liberty, but in the context of medieval life they never led on to that result. In the post-medieval world, in a new historical context, the arguments were carried further to conclusions that perhaps had always been implicit in them but that had never been explicitly affirmed.

The old claim that the church ought not to be controlled by secular rulers was now taken to mean that the civil magistrate had no right to interfere with any person's choice of religion. Protestant dissenters often pointed out that the magistrate was no more infallible than the pope or the bishops. It

---

[52] "Religion's Peace," in E. B. Underhill, ed., *Tracts on Liberty of Conscience and Persecution (1614–1661)* (London: J. Haddon, 1846), 10–11. The anonymous author continued,

> War and its miseries have overspread all lands. Love, meekness, gentleness, mercy, the truest badges of Christianity, have been damned and banished; and, in their room, cruelty, hard-heartedness, respect of persons, prisons, tortures, etc., things that our blessed Lord and Master, and his apostles never (ap)proved . . . have had great sway for these many hundred years.

[53] "Sion's Groan," in Underhill, ed., *Tracts*, 379.

[54] Justus Lipsius argued that, since the truth concerning the matters that divided the Christian sects could not be known anyway, the civil magistrate was justified in punishing dissenters from an established church. Skepticism did not always lead to toleration! On the views of Lipsius and Coornhert see R. Tuck, *Philosophy and Government, 1572–1651* (Cambridge, Eng.: Cambridge Univ. Press, 1993), 58.

[55] Woodhouse, *Puritanism and Liberty*, 227.

followed that, as William Walwyn observed, "he who is in an error may be the constrainer of him who is in the truth."[56] Another argument against government coercion of religion pointed out that progress in the understanding of divine revelation could be achieved only through free and reasoned discourse. When Milton wrote of "the reforming of the Reformation itself" in a coming new age, he was arguing specifically for freedom of the press.[57] Medieval theologians had sometimes envisaged a gradual progress in the understanding of scripture through the course of the centuries. The new insight was that such progress required freedom of thought and expression.[58]

The view that any meaningful freedom of the church required that the civil magistrates refrain from interfering in matters of religion was widespread among members of the separatist groups in England. During the army debates held at Whitehall in 1648 one of them declared, "No man or magistrate on the earth hath power to meddle in these cases."[59] A Leveller pamphlet written in the following year set out the same doctrine that the First Amendment would eventually proclaim for Americans:

[W]e do not impower or entrust our said representatives to . . . compell by penalties or otherwise any person to any thing in or about matters of faith, Religion or God's worship or to restrain any person from the profession of his faith, or exercise of his Religion according to his conscience. . . .[60]

Roger Williams, arguing against any sort of unified church-state, introduced the phrase "wall of separation" when he wrote of a "wall of separation between the Garden of the church and the Wilderness of the world."[61]

Another strand of medieval argumentation that underwent radical development in the early modern era concerned the authority of the individual conscience. In the middle of the seventeenth century the prevailing view was still that religious disagreements sprang "from malice, rooted in sin."[62] But by then alternative opinions were also being expressed. The

---

[56] W. B. Haller, *Tracts on Liberty in the Puritan Revolution, 1638–1647*, Columbia Records of Civilization, No. 18 (New York: Columbia Univ. Press, 1934), 3: 70.

[57] John Wesley Hales, ed., *Milton: Areopagitica* (Oxford: Clarendon Press, 1904), 45.

[58] Milton's contemporary, John Goodwin, also developed the idea of a progressive understanding of scripture. For him, "Revelation was an unfinished but progressive process of indefinite duration." See W. B. Haller, *Liberty and Reformation in the Puritan Revolution* (New York: Columbia Univ. Press, 1955), 252.

[59] Woodhouse, *Puritanism and Liberty*, 141.

[60] "An Agreement of Free People," in W. B. Haller and G. Davies, eds., *The Leveller Tracts, 1647–1653* (New York: Columbia Univ. Press, 1944), 323.

[61] Williams, *Writings*, 1: 392.

[62] Haller, *Liberty and Reformation*, 251. This was the opinion that John Cotton still maintained in his dispute with Roger Williams. See Williams, *Writings*, 3: 42.

Latitudinarian Anglican, Chillingworth, declared in 1638, "An honest man
. . . a true lover of God, and of his truth . . . may embrace errour for truth."[63]
In the subsequent years of civil war it became increasingly difficult for men of
good will and good sense to believe that their neighbors, sometimes men they
had fought with side by side in a common cause, were really inspired by
active malice to do the work of the devil because of a disagreement about
some obscure point of theology. Yet this belief in the malice of the dissenter
had been the essential basis of the medieval abhorrence of heresy. When
differences of religious opinion could be seen as effects of intellectual error
rather than of perverted will, the way was open to reconsider the proper
attitude to a mistaken conscience. William Walwyn took up the text
"Whatever is not of faith is sin," the same text that medieval authors had used
to defend the primacy of conscience, but arrived at a conclusion that no
medieval theologian had reached: ". . . [E]very man ought to have Liberty of
Conscience of what Opinion soever."[64] Walwyn argued that a person's
conscience could be directed only by his own individual reason. A person
could not be compelled to believe as true something that reason and
conscience told him was false. If, under compulsion, he acted against his
conscience, he sinned; but, and this was the new twist to the argument, the
one who compelled him was a party to the sin and was acting like a tyrant.[65]
This became a common argument among those who defended freedom of
conscience. Even an extreme royalist like Michael Hudson argued that a
magistrate who compelled a man to act against his conscience forced him to
commit the sin of hypocrisy, and that the magistrate himself was guilty of
"sacrilegious intrusion upon those sacred prerogatives which God hath
preserved unto himself."[66] The Anglican divine Jeremy Taylor argued at
length that a person who followed an erring conscience did not sin in doing
so and, again, concluded with a plea for religious freedom. "If God will not be
angry at men for being invincibly deceived, why should men be angry one at
another?"[67] Sometimes the forcing of a person's conscience was compared to
physical rape; in the pungent language of Roger Williams it was "spirituall
and soule rape."[68]

The final outcome of all the new argument about conscience was a fusion
of the new ideal of religious liberty with the older doctrine of natural rights.

---

[63] W. Chillingworth, *The Religion of Protestants* (Oxford: Leonard Lichfield, 1638),
21.

[64] Haller, *Tracts on Liberty*, 3: 67.

[65] Ibid., 3: 71, 86.

[66] Hudson's views are discussed in Tuck, *Philosophy and Government*, 270.

[67] Jordan, *Toleration*, 4: 405.

[68] "Bloudy Tenent," in Williams, *Writings*, 3: 219.

Freedom of conscience came to be seen as one of the natural rights of man, guaranteed by natural law and discernable by the "light of reason" or "light of nature." The parliamentary leader, Henry Vane, for instance, asserted that freedom of religion could be claimed "upon the grounds of natural right."[69] Roger Williams has also been called an extreme exponent of natural rights because of his all-embracing argument for freedom of conscience,[70] but this seems to be a misunderstanding of his position. I do not think Williams ever used the language of natural rights.[71] William Penn, however, did so, and with "classic clarity," according to Searle Bates. Penn wrote, "I ever understood an impartial liberty of conscience to be the natural right of all men. . . ."[72] He argued that the people did not and could not give up this natural right to any government formed by the original contract that first established a political society. Hence, subsequently, government could have no lawful power to invade this right of the individual. As one might expect, the constitution of Pennsylvania in due course echoed the words of the founder and proclaimed "a natural and unalienable right" to freedom of worship. As a Quaker, Penn stood outside the mainstream of the religious thought of his age but his eminently respectable contemporary, Bishop Burnet, expressed a similar view. "I have long looked on liberty of conscience as one of the rights of human nature, antecedent to society, which no man could give up . . . ."[73] Going back to the roots of Christian tradition, Burnet also undertook a translation of Lactantius and, in his preface to it, again argued for toleration. John Locke, too, in his influential *Letter Concerning Toleration*, wrote that "liberty of conscience is every man's natural right."[74] Outside England, Pierre Bayle defended the rights of conscience,[75] and Spinoza drew on his own idiosyncratic doctrine of natural rights in asserting an inalienable right to freedom of religion.[76]

---

[69] Henry Vane, *A Healing Question Propounded* (London, 1656), 5.

[70] Haller, *Tracts on Liberty*, 1: 60.

[71] Williams relied on his own idiosyncratic understanding of scripture rather than on any appeal to natural rights in defending religious freedom. He inveighed against the "light of nature" in "The Examiner Defended," in Williams, *Writings*, 7: 242: "Come to the light of nature—and then I ask, if it be not a downright Doctrine of Free-will, in depraved nature?"

[72] M. Searle Bates, *Religious Liberty: An Inquiry* (New York: Harper, 1945), 297, quoting William Penn, *England's Present Interest Discovered* (London, 1675).

[73] G. Burnet, *History of My Own Times*, (Oxford: Clarendon Press, 1823), 5: 107.

[74] J. Locke, *A Letter Concerning Toleration*, ed. M. Montuori (The Hague: M. Nijhoff, 1963), 95.

[75] Bayle, *Philosophical Commentary*, 161, 173, 193.

[76] "A Theologico-Political Treatise," in R.H.M. Elwes, ed., *The Chief Works of Benedict de Spinoza*, (London: G. Bell, 1883), 1: 257.

By the end of the seventeenth century reasonably adequate theories of religious rights had been formulated. Implementing them took much longer. Persecution became more sporadic in the eighteenth century, but it was not until the liberal revolutions of the nineteenth century that freedom of religion became widely established in the constitutions of Western states and not until the twentieth century that the major Christian churches proclaimed religious rights as an essential feature of the Christian faith itself.

Conclusion.—The peoples of Western Europe slowly learned, through centuries of cruel experience, to acknowledge at least the practical necessity of tolerating religious differences among Christians; and, at best, they came to see religious freedom as an ideal inherent in their traditional faith. We need to ask in conclusion what relevance this distinctively Western Christian experience can have for a world of many religions and diverse cultures.

Some critics have suggested that all the brave new pronouncements about human rights, including religious rights, simply inflate Western concepts into universal values and then assume without question that such values are valid for all other societies, regardless of their histories and cultures. Perhaps, it is suggested, this is just another kind of Western chauvinism. On the other hand, it is evident that the whole world has willingly accepted some aspects of Western culture, notably Western technology. And Wolfgang Huber has argued that it would be merely arrogant for the West to export its material culture on a worldwide scale while assuming that other societies are incapable of appreciating Western ideals or learning from Western experience.[77] Technology itself, we may note, is a product of several centuries of distinctively Western cultural evolution; but the fruits of technology—a computer or an internal combustion engine—can easily be replicated in societies with quite different cultural traditions. The situation is evidently more complex when we consider the fruits of Western religious experience; it is easier to export an artifact than to implant an ideal. And certainly, in this sphere, communication could not be along a one-way highway. The West had to learn—or relearn—the practice of nonviolence from India, through Mahatma Ghandi. Modern Western ideas, including religious ideas, on respect for the environment and for all species of life, have been shaped in part by currents of Buddhist thought. Moreover, we should not expect to find Western ways of institutionalizing religious rights duplicated exactly in any African or Asian society (and, indeed, the institutional arrangements vary a great deal in the West from country to country).

---

[77] Wolfgang Huber, "Christianity and Democracy in Europe," *Emory International Law Review* 6 (1992): 35–53.

Yet, for all this, the actual state of the world suggests that the lessons the West learned so painfully may indeed have a universal relevance. Evidently, the global utopia envisaged in the various United Nations pronouncements has not yet arrived. In some countries religious minorities are openly persecuted or at best denied full civic rights. New forms of religious fundamentalism inspire hatred and fear of all those outside the chosen group. In many regions, from Northern Ireland to Sri Lanka—in the republics of the former Soviet Union, in what was once Yugoslavia, in parts of the Islamic world—ancient religious animosities have fused with ethnic rivalries to produce new and explosive socio-religious compounds. The resulting violence ranges from individual assassinations to large-scale massacres to outright civil war. Religious conflict is a major cause of global disorder in the modern world. The recognition of religious rights is a necessity if a more peaceful world-order is ever to be achieved.

Obviously, all societies cannot reenact the specific experiences of early modern Europe that shaped the modern idea of religious rights; and indeed that would be a dismal prospect. But during the present century, people in all parts of the world have experienced for themselves the grievous effects of religious conflict and religious persecution. It would certainly be expedient to end such savageries. One might think that we too should have been "schooled and whipt by our calamities" into recognizing this. And perhaps a certain skepticism might be an appropriate response to the claims of the more fanatical fundamentalists. But modern pragmatism and modern skepticism seem insufficient to assuage the existing conflicts within religions and between religions. Perhaps the only answer for all peoples is the one that Christians discovered so painfully when they compared the words of Jesus with all the hatreds and cruelties of their contemporary world; that is, the need for a return to the original sources of religious tradition and a reconsideration of their implications in the light of our accumulated centuries of experience. Modern Christian pronouncements on religious rights base those rights on the dignity of human beings as children of God. But Mohammed too said, "Verily we have honored every human being." Jesus told us to love those who hate us, but Gautama Buddha also declared, "Hatred does not cease with hatred; hatred ceases only with love." Among all the founders of the great world religions we can find an attitude of respect and compassion for the human person that is the best argument—the only ultimately compelling one—for religious liberty. Often contingent historical circumstances have distorted human understanding of the original revelations and intuitions that lie at the root of our religious traditions. Perhaps the best antidote for all the false fundamentalisms of our age might be a true fundamentalism, a return to the words and spirit and example of the great founders.

—⚬ 2 ⚬—

POLITICAL AND RELIGIOUS FREEDOM
IN MARSILIUS OF PADUA

*Brian Tierney**

Marsilius of Padua is a controversial figure. Some modern scholars see him as "a prophet of modern times." Others find in his work only "the normal judgment and practice of the Middle Ages." For some he is an early champion of democracy, for others an advocate of a totalitarian state. He has also been called a defender of religious freedom and a forerunner of the Reformation. Marsilius was certainly a vehement critic of the fourteenth-century papacy, but he was by no means alone in that. The unusual feature of his work is that the criticisms are set in the framework of a sophisticated political theory that has continued to engage the attention of historians and political philosophers down to the present day.

We know only a few facts about the life of Marsilius. He was born about 1275, the son of a Paduan notary. He may have attended the University of Padua. Certainly, as a young man, he migrated to Paris where he studied philosophy and medicine. In 1313 he served as rector of the university. So far, Marsilius seemed destined for a moderately successful, not particularly distinguished career as a university professor. Then in 1324 his masterwork, the *Defensor Pacis* ("Defender of the Peace") appeared. It was a radical attack on papal authority in general and on the policies of the contemporary pope, John XXII, in particular. The work was soon condemned as heretical and in

---

* Bryce and Edith M. Bowmar Professor of Humanistic Studies at Cornell University. Ph.D. (Pembroke College, Cambridge).

1326 Marsilius fled from Paris to take refuge at court of the emperor-elect, Lewis of Bavaria, who was also engaged in a conflict with John XXII. Marsilius spent the rest of life in the service of the emperor. He died probably in 1342.

Marsilius's political theory was based partly on Aristotelian philosophy and partly on the actual practice of the medieval Italian city communes; but its whole polemical thrust was determined by the ecclesiastical politics of early fourteenth-century Europe. Before considering the argument of the *Defensor Pacis* we need first to look at this background.

Fourteenth-Century Background.—Thomas Hobbes wrote that the Roman church was nothing but "the ghost of the deceased Roman empire sitting crowned on the grave thereof." The saying perhaps applies best of all to the papacy of the fourteenth century, the institution that Marsilius attacked so vigorously. A medieval empire still existed, but its ruler exercised only a tenuous authority over the scattered principalities of Germany and the city-states of Italy. Meanwhile the popes ruled as almost absolute sovereigns over a real ecclesiastical empire, and sometimes claimed temporal jurisdiction too over the secular princes of the world, including the emperor.

At this time the popes had established their court in the pleasant city of Avignon, comfortably remote from the turbulence of central Italy and the faction-fighting of Rome. There they built themselves a great fortress-palace and created the most effetive system of centralized government that the medieval world had thus far known. The pope ruled as supreme judge and legislator, administering a universal system of canon law that prevailed over the whole of Western Christendom. He was served by a complex bureaucracy exercising what we should call executive, judicial, and legislative functions. The popes also reserved to themselves the right of making appointments to church benefices all over Europe and so built up a vast patronage machine. It was conducted primarily as a revenue-raising operation. When a church in England or Sweden or Hungary became vacant the new incumbent would probably have to obtain a confirmation of his appointment from Avignon, which meant paying a set fee to the curia and probably a bribe to a curial official.

In a way it was an efficient system. The community of the church was given order and discipline; individuals could usually be kept happy by the constant stream of appointments, privileges and indulgences that flowed from the curia. An active Inquisition kept heresy in check. The popes of Avignon were not particularly corrupt or wicked persons. They were for the most part very capable administrators who knew how to run a bureaucracy. The best of them might have made good Roman emperors. The trouble was that the system they presided over was becoming moribund. The role of the popes was supposed to be an essentially spiritual one; the more they became engaged in the worldly task of running the church like a vast financial machine the less effective they became in giving moral leadership to the Christian world. The more the church looked like the Roman Empire the less it looked like the humble community that Jesus had founded centuries before.

The abuses of papal government evoked bitter criticisms from many writers more orthodox than Marsilius. Dante kept a place in hell for Pope Boniface VIII; Petrarch referred to Avignon as "the impious Babylon, the hell on earth, the sink of vice, the sewer of the world"; and the great St. Catherine of Siena observed of the curia at Avignon, with greater brevity but equal force, that "it stank like hell." The difference between such critics and Marsilius was that they attacked perceived abuses of papal authority; Marsilius attacked the institution of the papacy as such.

To understand his arguments we need to consider two specific controversies in which the popes of the early fourteenth century became involved. One of them was a dispute between the popes and the Franciscan Order concerning the nature of evangelical poverty. A cherished doctrine of the Franciscans held that Christ and the apostles had lived in absolute poverty, holding no property singly or in common (just like good Franciscans). In 1323, acting from motives that remain obscure, Pope John XXII denounced this doctrine as heretical. The most obvious reason for his decision is that the Franciscan teaching implied a damaging criticism of the whole established church. The church did own property, a great deal of it, and even members of religious orders like the Benedictines, who were vowed to personal poverty, still owned large possessions in common. If the Franciscans were right, it could be argued that the church never had exemplified the perfect way of life that Jesus had originally lived and taught.

Marsilius wrote his *Defensor Pacis* at Paris during the early stages of this controversy and he made use of the Franciscan arguments as part of his onslaught on the papacy. But this was perhaps opportunistic. Marsilius's real animosity against the popes, as he made abundantly clear, arose from another area of papal theory and practice, the popes' assertion of a right to temporal power over the empire, a claim that provoked endless dissension in Italy and Germany. This claim had been developed by earlier popes, especially Gregory VII (1073–1085) and Innocent III (1198–1216). It could be supported by several arguments. The simplest and most sweeping one held that the pope as successor of St. Peter was God's vicar on earth and that, just as God ruled the whole world, so too his representative the pope should rule over all. Another argument was based on the Donation of Constantine. This document, actually a ninth-century forgery, declared that the emperor Constantine had handed over the whole western empire to the pope when he left Rome to found his eastern capital at Constantinople. To harmonize these two arguments, papal apologists sometimes maintained that Constantine had merely acknowledged an authority that had existed *de jure* in the papacy from the beginning. Apart from such fantasies, the popes could point to a more solid historical precedent to justify their claims. Ever since the coronation of Charlemagne at Rome in 800 A.D. it had been generally acknowledged that the ruler chosen by the German princes had to be crowned by the pope in order to advance to the dignity of emperor. So while the popes sometimes asserted a vague supremacy over all secular rulers, their claims as regards the empire were more specific. They maintained that the pope could examine an emperor-elect to determine whether he was worthy of the imperial office; that in case of a disputed election the pope could choose between the rival candidates; and that during an imperial vacancy the pope could administer the affairs of the empire.

During the first years of the fourteenth century the papal claims reached a sort of crescendo. In 1302 Pope Boniface VIII promulgated the famous bull *Unam Sanctam* which stated that "the spiritual power has to institute the earthly power and to judge it." The bull ended with the ringing declaration, "It is altogether necessary to salvation for every human creature to be subject to the Roman pontiff." A little later Pope Clement V (1305–1314) fell into a dispute with Emperor Henry VII and reiterated all the standard claims of the papacy over the empire. The next pope, John XXII (1316–1334), gave added weight to Clement's decrees by incorporating them into a new collection of canon law that he promulgated. Then John himself became involved in a dispute with the empire. In 1314 a majority of the prince-electors had named Ludwig of Bavaria as the next emperor. The pope refused to recognize his claim and the ensuing dispute led to outbreaks of sporadic warfare in Germany and Italy. Finally, in 1324, John XXII excommunicated Ludwig. That was the state of affairs when Marsilius wrote the *Defensor Pacis*.

The Argument of the Defensor Pacis.—The *Defensor Pacis* was divided into three "Discourses." The first dealt with the structure of the state, the second was concerned with the structure of the church and its relation to the state, and the third was a brief summary of conclusions.

Discourse I.—In his introduction, Marsilius stated, in words addressed directly to Ludwig of Bavaria, that his purpose was to promote peace and tranquility by revealing the causes of civil discord. There were several such causes, he wrote, and most of them had been discussed by Aristotle; but there was one "singular and very obscure" cause in the Christian society of his own day that Aristotle could not have known, and this was to be his main concern.[1] Although his central theme was peace rather than freedom, Marsilius noted at the outset that civil strife had subjected the people of Italy to "the harsh yoke of tyranny instead of liberty."[2] He waited until the end of Discourse I before expounding his "singular" cause of discord, but then stated it very plainly. It was "the perverted desire for rulership" of the Roman popes, and especially the recent claims of Clement V and John XXII to jurisdiction over the empire.[3]

The whole purpose of Discourse I can best be understood in the light of this conclusion. Marsilius wanted to show how an adequate theory of the state could be constructed by purely secular arguments, based solely on human reason, without any appeal to the theocratic assumptions of his papalist opponents. He began by defining the state in Aristotelian terms as "a community established for the sake of living and living well."[4] To be self-sufficient such a community needed the services of six parts or offices, defined as "the agricultural, the artisan, the military, the financial, the priestly and the judicial or deliberative."[5] Since this division was taken directly from Aristotle's *Politics*, a work well known to orthodox writers and often quoted by them, it might seem harmless enough; but Marsilius had established at the outset that priesthood was simply one of the offices of the state and later he would show how this assertion could be developed in radical ways.

Marsilius next distinguished between good and bad forms of government. Here he still claimed to be following Aristotle but in fact introduced a doctrine of his own that became the animating principle of all the subsequent argument in Discourse I. Government, he wrote, could be exercised over voluntary or involuntary subjects; the first kind of regime was healthy, the second diseased. A good government was one that ruled according to laws made for the common benefit and with the consent of the subjects; but, according to Marsilius, "absolutely or in the greater degree, it is the consent

---

[1] *Defensor Pacis*, disc. 1, chap. 1, § 3, in Alan Gewirth, *Marsilius of Padua. The Defender of the Peace,* vol. 2. *The Defensor Pacis Translated with an Introduction* (New York: Columbia Univ. Press, 1956).

[2] Ibid., disc. 1, chap. 1, § 2.

[3] Ibid., disc. 1, chap. 19, § 12.

[4] Ibid., disc. 1, chap. 5, § 2.

[5] Ibid., disc. 1, chap. 5, § 1.

of the subjects which is the distinguishing criterion."[6] Marsilius quoted
Aristotle's *Politics* here, but Aristotle always emphasized rule for the common
good as the distinguishing characteristic of healthy government while barely
mentioning consent of the subjects. Marsilius made consent the focal point of
his political theory.

There was a similar shift of emphasis when Marsilius discussed the nature
of law. Marsilius first distinguished between "immanent" and "transient" acts,
the same distinction that John Stuart Mill would make centuries later when
he wrote of "self-regarding" and "other-regarding" actions. Human law,
Marsilius held, was concerned with the regulation of the "transient" acts of
citizens that would affect other human agents.[7] Then he presented a
"positivist" view of law that is often seen as one of the typically modern
elements in the *Defensor*. For Marsilius, law was not in essence a statement of
what is intrinsically just; its essence rather was the coercive command of a
legislator. Human law could be defined as "a command which one is
compelled to observe."[8]

Such a definition raises a key question: Who is the legislator? Who has
the right to issue coercive commands to the citizens? Marsilius's answer
seems clear-cut; "the legislator or the primary and proper efficient cause of
law, is the people or the whole body of citizens, or the weightier part thereof,
through its election or will expressed by words in the general assembly." But
then Marsilius introduced a qualification (to be discussed further at the end
of this section). In determining the weightier part that acted on behalf of the
whole, both the "quantity and quality" of the citizens was to be taken into
account.[9] The whole body or its weightier part, Marsilius argued, was most
likely to make good laws aiming at the common benefit because "no one
knowingly harms himself."[10] Moreover laws made by the whole people were
more likely to be observed than those imposed by one person or a few. Then
Marsilius moved into an argument concerned directly with political freedom.
By definition, he wrote, the state was a community of free men. So the
citizens ought not to be subjected to "despotism or slavish dominion."[11] But if
one person or a few could make laws for the rest they would be despots over
the others. On the other hand, when laws were made by the whole people
each citizen would seem to have set the law on himself and so would not
resent it. The fact that the whole body was likely to make good laws was also

---

6 Ibid., disc. 1, chap. 9, § 5.

7 Ibid., disc. 1, chap. 5, § 4; disc. 2, chap. 8, § 5.

8 Ibid., disc. 1, chap. 10, § 4.

9 Ibid., disc. 1, chap. 12, § 3.

10 Ibid., disc. 1, chap. 12, § 5.

11 Ibid., disc. 1, chap. 12, § 6.

conducive to freedom since "under bad laws there arise unbearable slavery, oppression, and misery."[12]

In this discussion, Marsilius noted that the people did not always exercise its legislative power directly but could entrust it for a time to a ruler who would act on behalf of the whole. His final topic in Discourse I dealt with the installation of such a ruler, and again the core of the argument was the need for popular consent. A good ruler, Marsilius observed, should be outstanding in prudence and moral virtue; but the possession of these qualities did not in itself confer a right to rule. That could come only from the "legislator," the whole body of the citizens or its weightier part. To them too belonged the power to correct a ruler or even depose him if the common good so required.[13] Once installed, it was the duty of the ruler to "establish and determine" the other parts of the state (and one of the "parts," it must be remembered, was the priesthood).[14] Aristotle, Marsilius noted, had said that without careful control some parts of the state would tend to grow disproportionately "like the number of poor in democracies." To this, Marsilius added drily, "and like the priesthood in the law of the Christians."[15] His final political argument emphasized the necessary unity of the state. There had to be one government, and if several levels of government existed, one had to be supreme over the rest. Otherwise civil strife would ensue since some citizens would obey one government, others the other.[16] The implicit point of the argument was that the church could have no claim to temporal jurisdiction, to be a government in its own right. Then, in the concluding section of Discourse I, Marsilius made the point explicit. Returning to his starting point he defined "the singular cause of discord" that afflicted his own age as the papal claim to temporal power.[17]

This sketch of Marsilius's argument leaves open several disputed points of interpretation. In evaluating his ideas on political freedom the doctrine of community consent is obviously of central importance. But modern commentators have differed sharply about the meaning of the "weightier part" that acted on behalf of the whole, and especially about Marsilius's assertion that this *valentior pars* was determined by the "quantity and quality" of the citizens who composed it. The reference to "quality" seems to rule out any simple one-person one-vote democratic system, and it has led some

---

12 Ibid., disc. 1, chap. 12, § 7.
13 Ibid., disc. 1, chap. 15, § 2.
14 Ibid., disc. 1, chap. 15, § 8.
15 Ibid., disc. 1, chap. 15, § 10.
16 Ibid., disc. 1, chap. 17, § 5.
17 Ibid., disc. 1, chap. 19, § 12.

modern writers to argue that Marsilius was really advocating government by a narrow oligarchy. Marsilius himself was not clear or explicit on this point. He wrote that the composition of the weightier part could be determined by reference to Aristotle's *Politics* or to "the honorable custom of polities."[18] But Aristotle provides no clear guidance in this matter, and the customs of Italian polities varied. To understand Marsilius it is useful to remember that he was not presenting a highly original opinion here but rather expressing a common doctrine of medieval corporation law. The medieval canonists always maintained that the acts of a corporation had to be authorized by its *major et sanior pars* ("greater and sounder part"). They thought that a decision approved by a simple numerical majority but opposed by all the more eminent and prudent members of a group was of dubious validity. Marsilius was thinking in the same way. He was also aware of the constant tension in Italian cities between the *populo grasso* and the *populo minuto*, the minority of wealthy eminent citizens and the majority of lesser ones. In Italy the terms "popular" or "democratic" government normally referred to a regime of the common people that excluded the patriciate, the more well-to-do or aristocratic citizens. Marsilius wanted to include all classes in his state. Most probably he did not see his *valentior pars* as a narrow minority imposing its will on the rest of the citizen body, but rather as a majority of the whole that included the more honorable and substantial citizens. Otherwise there would be little sense in his argument that the citizens retained their freedom because they lived under self-imposed laws. A final point, noted by Conal Condren, is that Marsilius's ambiguity here probably arose from the fact that he was not deeply interested in the question at issue.[19] Marsilius argued that political power was derived from the consent of the community primarily in order to prove that it was not derived from the pope or the church. Just how a community expressed its consent was a matter of secondary importance for him.

Another problem for political theorists who want to see Marsilius as an early champion of liberal democracy is the absence in his work of any restraint on the power of the political community. Marsilius insisted on the unity of the state; he identified the weightier part (however determined) with the totality of citizens; and he defined law as essentially the coercive command of the whole. Unusually for a medieval author, he did not develop any theory of natural law as a restraint on human legislators. Nor did he present any doctrine of individual rights against the state or of principled

---

[18] Ibid., disc. 1, chap. 12, § 4.

[19] Conal Condren, "Democracy and the *Defensor Pacis*: On the English Language Tradition of Marsilian Interpretation," *Il pensiero politico* 13 (1980): 301–316.

dissent. Instead he persistently maintained the supremacy of the whole over the parts; he thought this was necessary to control "men of deformed nature" who might disagree with common decisions.[20] This is the aspect of Marsilius's work that might be called totalitarian. As Gewirth noted, "Marsilius's republicanism as to the source of power is coupled with an absolutism as to the extent of power."[21]

Discourse II.—At the beginning of his treatise Marsilius wrote that, in Discourse II, he would confirm by scripture and the writings of church fathers the propositions that he had established by pure reason in Discourse I. That is, he would demonstrate from accepted Christian authorities that, in religious affairs as in civil ones, ultimate authority rested with the whole body of the people, and the exercise of such authority with a ruler to whom the people had entrusted it. As the argument proceeded it became clear that this ruler was not the pope but the civil magistrate, now clearly identified with the emperor (on whose behalf the whole treatise was written).

Marsilius began by distinguishing several senses of the word judge. Anyone could judge in his own area of expertise, a doctor in matters of medicine for instance; but the professional expert had no power to enforce his judgments on others. Also lawyers were sometimes loosely referred to as judges. But the key meaning for Marsilius was a third one, where the word judge referred to a ruler who had the authority to enact sentences and enforce them with coercive power.[22] A central theme of Discourse II was the repeated assertion that ministers of religion—popes, bishops and priests—were not judges in this third sense. They had no coercive authority, no temporal power in this world.

The question at issue, Marsilius explained, was not what powers Christ *could* have given to Peter and the other apostles but what he actually had given them. Then he argued that, by word and example, Jesus persistently disclaimed any temporal authority for himself or his followers. When he was brought before Pilate, Jesus said "My kingdom is not of this world" (John 18.36). When asked to arbitrate a dispute about an inheritance he replied, "Who hath appointed me judge or decider over you?" (Luke 12.14). The evident meaning, Marsilius declared, was that civil disputes had to be settled by secular judges. He also remembered to present here the most famous text of all. When Jesus was asked whether it was lawful to pay tribute to Caesar, he said, "Render unto Caesar the things that are Caesar's . . . ." (Matt. 22.21).

---

[20] *Defensor Pacis*, disc. 1, chap. 12, § 5.

[21] *Marsilius of Padua*, 1: 255–56.

[22] *Defensor Pacis*, disc. 2, chap. 2, § 8.

Finally Jesus submitted his own person to the jurisdiction of the Roman magistrate, Pilate.[23] If Jesus himself thus recognized the power of the secular magistrate to tax and judge, so much the more should his apostles and their successors, the priests and bishops. To all these arguments Marsilius added that coercive power in bishops and priests would in any case be self-defeating since a faith adopted under compulsion could not lead to eternal salvation.[24]

Marsilius returned to these points again and again. Discourse II is endlessly repetitive. It is as though new proof texts kept occurring to Marsilius as he wrote and he could not resist drawing them into his argument. The scriptural and patristic writings that he drew on could be used to support a wide variety of theories about the nature of the church, as the controversies of the Reformation era would demonstrate. Marsilius showed considerable adroitness in deploying all the texts that seemed most destructive of papal authority.

Having proved that the clergy possessed no coercive authority in matters of religion, Marsilius next asked who did have such jurisdiction. Consistently with the argument of Discourse I he asserted that it could only be the "legislator," the whole people, or the ruler established by their authority. Priests could "teach, exhort, censure." They were "judges in the first sense," professional experts who ought to be consulted on questions concerning the Christian faith, but they did not have the coercive jurisdiction of "judges in the third sense."[25] Even the rulers who did possess coercive authority could not punish heresy simply because it was an offense against divine law; such offenses were rather to be punished by God in the next world. Some breaches of divine law, such as fornication, were not civil crimes; but others, such as theft, were offenses against both divine and human law, and so were properly punished by the secular power. Heresy occupied an ambiguous position. It might or might not be forbidden by human law. So heretics could be punished only when a civil law had been enacted prohibiting their heresy, and then only by the civil judge.[26] Returning to an argument from Discourse I, Marsilius added that to attribute coercive jurisdiction to priests would establish a plurality of governments in a society and so disrupt the necessary unity of the state.[27]

At this point the argument veered off into a discussion of the issues raised by the Franciscan poverty dispute. Some critics have seen this as an irrelevant

---

[23] Ibid., disc. 2, chap. 4, §§ 4, 8, 9, 12.

[24] Ibid., disc. 2, chap. 5, § 6.

[25] Ibid., disc. 2, chap. 9, § 7; disc. 2, chap. 10, § 2.

[26] Ibid., disc. 2, chap. 10, § 7.

[27] Ibid., disc. 2, chap. 10, § 8.

interpretation; one modern author called it an "excrescence." But in fact Marsilius's argument was coherent. Having shown that the status of the clergy gave them no claim to temporal power he was now going to argue that it gave them no claim to temporal property. He restated the technical arguments of the Franciscans about ownership and use in order to prove that a person could renounce all legal ownership and all legal rights and still licitly use the goods necessary to sustain life. Then he maintained that Jesus had indeed prescribed such renunciation for the apostles, citing texts like, "Go sell all you have and give it to the poor" (Luke 18.22) and "Take no gold and silver in your purse" (Matt. 10.9) and "Having food and raiment let us be content therewith" (1 Tim. 6.8).[28] Applying these texts to the existing church, Marsilius argued that priests were entitled to receive from their flocks only the necessities that sufficed for day-to-day life; and if the flock was too poor to provide them the priest could work for a living. In the case of revenue-producing property, the clergy could acquire no legal ownership: that belonged to the whole community or remained with the original donor. A bishop or priest could hold such property only with the intention of taking from the income just enough to provide for his food and clothing from day to day while distributing the rest to the poor.[29] Later Marsilius wrote that the distribution of church property among the clergy, that is, appointments to ecclesiastical benefices, rested with the "legislator" or the ruler acting with its authority.[30]

Marsilius then turned back to his central theme of ecclesiastical jurisdiction. He had argued so far that the pope had no temporal power; now he asserted that even within the hierarchy of the church the pope, as successor of Peter, had no authority to rule the other bishops or appoint them to their sees. Christ gave a priestly authority to all the apostles—essentially a power to administer sacraments and preach the gospel—but he did not differentiate between them. When Christ instituted the eucharist with the words "This is my body" (Luke 22.19), he spoke to all the apostles, not Peter alone. Similarly he addressed them all when he said "Receive the Holy Spirit" (John 20.23). The title, "Prince of the apostles," which some had bestowed on Peter was directly opposed to the words of Christ who said, "The princes of the Gentiles lord it over them, but not so you" (Matt. 20.25).[31] Moreover, it could not even be proved that the pope was the successor of Peter in any meaningful sense of the term; there was no specific evidence in scripture that

---

[28] Ibid., disc. 2, chap. 13, §§ 24, 36; disc. 2, chap. 14, § 6.

[29] Ibid., disc. 2, chap. 14, § 9.

[30] Ibid., disc. 2, chap. 17, §§ 8, 9, 10, 11.

[31] Ibid., disc. 2, chap. 16, §§ 2, 10.

Peter was ever in Rome at all.[32] In any case, even if the pope was Peter's successor, this gave him no power to appoint bishops or rule them, for Peter had no such power. When Marsilius asked who then should appoint bishops he gave the expected answer. It was the whole multitude or the ruler acting with its authority.[33]

In similar fashion the popes alone could not decide disputed matters of faith or make laws for the church; that power too belonged to the whole multitude. If it were otherwise, then the decrees of recent popes asserting their jurisdiction over temporal rulers—like Boniface VIII's *Unam Sanctam*— would be valid laws, and for Marsilius that was an outrageous proposition.[34] The proper procedure when a dispute about the faith arose was for the Christian communities to elect representatives, both priests and laity, to meet in a council. The issue would be determined by the weightier part of the council. The decisions reached could be enforced with coercive sanctions by "the faithful legislator" or the ruler.[35]

The treatise ended with some lengthy and fierce invective against current abuses of papal authority and with an historical account of how the popes had come to claim such vast powers for themselves—a process of usurpation accompanied by "cupidity, avarice, pride and ambition" according to Marsilius.[36]

Modern critics of the *Defensor Pacis* have sometimes noticed a shift from popular sovereignty in Discourse I to imperial sovereignty in Discourse II. Marsilius never abandoned the theoretical position that ultimate authority resided with a legislator constituted by the whole people; but in Discourse II there was virtually no distinction between the power of the community and the power of the ruler. The formula used over and over again was "the legislator or the ruler by its authority." Sometimes Marsilius described the ruler as the source of law; a couple of times he forgot himself and referred to the ruler as "legislator."[37] Moreover, in Discourse II, the ruler even has a sort of divine right. "The ruler is judge in this world through the ordination of God, although immediately by institution of the human legislator."[38] The change of emphasis probably arose from the differing subject matter of the two discourses. When Marsilius developed his theory of the state he seems to have always had in mind the Italian city-republics where a citizen assembly

---

[32] Ibid., disc. 2, chap. 16, § 16.

[33] Ibid., disc. 2, chap. 17, § 8.

[34] Ibid., disc. 2, chap. 20, § 8.

[35] Ibid., disc. 2, chap. 20, § 2; disc. 2, chap. 21, § 4.

[36] Ibid., disc. 2, chap. 26, § 2.

[37] Ibid., disc. 2, chap. 21, § 2; disc. 2, chap. 22, § 10.

[38] Ibid., disc. 2, chap. 30, § 4.

could actually meet to enact laws and elect rulers or correct them. But in Discourse II he was concerned with the whole Christian people or the Christian populations of large-scale polities like the German empire or the kingdom of France. In such states the whole people could not assemble together. To say that such-and-such a power belonged to the whole multitude or to the ruler was in effect to attribute it to the ruler.

Conclusion.—At first glance Marsilius seems like a character "born out of due time," a modern secularist thinker suddenly emerging from a religious medieval culture. A closer examination of his work shows that very often he was taking up ideas that were common among his contemporaries but pressing them to unusual extremes. This is especially true in his treatment of government by consent. The idea that all legitimate government must be based on the consent of the governed was becoming rather widespread in the early fourteenth century, and not only among critics of the papacy. Among Marsilius's contemporaries we can find a highly developed consent theory even in a conservative theologian like Hervaeus Natalis, the master-general of the Dominican Order and a friend and supporter of Pope John XXII. Writing a few years before Marsilius, Hervaeus argued that no man could rule over others by natural law, for by nature all men were equal. And power over others that was seized by force was simply illicit. It followed that all licit government must be based on the consent of the governed. This applied even to the pope in that he was elected by the cardinals acting on behalf of the whole church. But at this point Hervaeus introduced a significant reservation. Although each individual pope had to be freely elected, the papal office itself had been established in the first place by Christ. Of course this is precisely what Marsilius denied; and in doing so he pressed the argument about consent over the border between orthodoxy and heresy.

This happened over and over again in the *Defensor Pacis*. It was widely held among the canonists, for instance, that a general council was the highest authority in the church for deciding questions of faith; but the writers who argued in this way usually meant that a pope surrounded by the prelates of the church exercised a weightier authority than a pope acting alone. Marsilius vested the defining power wholly in an elected assembly of clergy and laity. Some reputable theologians held, like Marsilius, that the authority of bishops was not derived from the pope, but they still held that the pope, as Peter's successor, was the divinely established leader of the others. And again Marsilius denied this. Although he often started from orthodox premisses he always succeeded in reaching unorthodox conclusions.

This is true also of a central theme of the *Defensor Pacis*, the relationship between spiritual and temporal power. The more extreme claims of the popes in the temporal sphere were by no means universally accepted by medieval theologians and canonists. They were always contested by "dualists" who maintained that God had established *two* powers to rule the world and that each should respect the role of the other. Back in the days of Innocent III, around 1200, one eminent canonist whose work was still well known in the fourteenth century had written, "I believe that the emperor has the power of the sword and the imperial dignity from election by the princes and people."[39] This seems wholly in accord with Marsilius's view of the question. But the orthodox dualists, having distinguished between spiritual and temporal power, went on to investigate the proper sphere of jurisdiction of each. Marsilius denied that the church had any independent jurisdiction. For him, rendering to God the things that are God's left all power on earth to Caesar. And here again he had passed the bounds of contemporary orthodoxy.

Finally, for the present inquiry, the key question is this: Did Marsilius take up such orthodox ideas as existed concerning toleration in matters of religion and develop them into a new unorthodox doctrine of universal religious liberty? Needless to say, the medieval church was in many ways an extremely intolerant institution; but it did always maintain the principle that no one could be compelled to accept the Christian religion by force. Jews were officially permitted to practise their own religion and so were Muslims in Christian Spain. The work of the Inquisition was directed, not against nonbelievers, but against Christians who had renounced their faith or deviated from it in some unacceptable fashion. Conceivably some medieval author could have developed a thoroughgoing theory of religious freedom from the accepted doctrine that prohibited forced conversion. Marsilius did indeed make use of this doctrine in arguing that the church did not and should not possess any coercive authority.[40] But on the general question of toleration and repression in matters of religion his texts were ambivalent.

Sometimes he wrote like a convinced champion of religious liberty, especially in his repeated insistence that the Christian clergy could exercise no coercive power in matters of faith. Marsilius never denied the reality of divine law or the truth of Christian revelation; to have done so would have deprived his work of all polemical force in a controversy where all parties claimed to be defending Christian positions. But he insisted that divine law

---

[39] B. Tierney, *The Crisis of Church and State, 1050–1300* (Englewood Cliffs, N.J.: Prentice-Hall, 1964), 122, quoting Huguccio of Pisa.

[40] Ibid., disc. 2, chap. 5, § 6; disc. 2, chap. 9, § 2.

imposed no coercive penalties in this present life; the rewards and punishments were to come in the next world. For Marsilius, religious truth as such—or the ability to know and expound religious truth—did not confer any claim to force the truth on others. Priests and bishops were, or ought to be, experts in matters of theology and morality and it was proper to consult them in such matters just as one consulted a physician on matters of bodily health; but, like the physician, the priest had no power to enforce his decisions. At one point Marsilius wrote, "According to the truth and the clear intention of the Apostle and the saints . . . it is not commanded that anyone, whether infidel or believer, be compelled in this world through pain or punishment to observe the commands of the evangelic law, especially by a priest."[41]

This seems a resounding statement in favor of universal toleration. But in another context, discussing this same point, Marsilius wrote, "[W]e do not wish to say that it is inappropriate that heretics or those who are otherwise infidel be coerced, but that the authority for this, if it be lawful to do so, belongs only to the human legislator."[42] It might seem then that Marsilius was simply transferring the function of repressing religious deviance from the church to the state. Moreover his whole scheme of government, in which church personnel and church property were subordinated to the sovereignty of the temporal ruler, could have led to a more repressive authoritarian regime than any that actually existed in the medieval world. We may sympathize with Marsilius's fulminations against the extreme temporal claims of the papacy, but we must also remember that there was no real possibility of those claims being realized in practice. Christian rulers never accepted them, and there is no reason to suppose that any considerable number of their people did. Theologians and canonists were always divided on the issue. In practice, it was the tension between spiritual and temporal authorities that limited the power of each and prevented either from growing into a rigid despotism. Lord Acton once wrote, "To that conflict of four hundred years we owe the rise of civil liberty." But in Marsilius's scheme of government, there would have been no tension. He did not envision any separation of church and state. Rather he accepted the papalists' view that one power must be superior to the other; but he stood their argument on its head by giving the superior position to the emperor.

Marsilius's arguments could then have been applied in such a way as to justify the institutions of an authoritarian, persecuting state. Marsilius himself perhaps had no such intention; but he did not take a clear stance on the issue.

---

[41] Ibid., disc. 2, chap. 9, § 7.

[42] Ibid., disc. 2, chap. 5, § 7.

The whole tone of his work suggests that he was no zealot for religious persecution; but he did not develop any doctrine of an individual right to religious liberty. At one point he wrote that either heresy must be repressed by the emperor or else "individuals must be permitted to teach what they wish concerning the faith."[43] He did not, however, opt for either alternative. The truth may be that, here again, Marsilius was not deeply interested in a question that seems of the first importance to modern people. The important point for him was that the church should have no coercive power; whether the state should coerce religious dissidents was a matter of prudential judgment that Marsilius was apparently content to leave to the "human legislator" and its ruler.

The *Defensor Pacis* had an interesting afterlife. Since it was promptly condemned as heretical it could not achieve a very widespread circulation, but nevertheless French and Italian translations appeared during the fourteenth century. The work was sometimes quoted by Catholic critics of the papacy in the fifteenth century, without acknowledgement of the source. It was translated into German during the Reformation era and, for obvious reasons, was popular with some of the early Protestant controversialists. An English translation appeared in 1535 at the time when Henry VIII was making his break with Rome to establish an autonomous church of England. The *Defensor* was still known to some of the writers of the English Civil War period. In particular, George Lawson made extensive use of it in a work that is now thought to have directly influenced John Locke. Marsilius's book is one of those works that "takes on a life of its own" and is deployed in a variety of contexts for purposes that the author could never have foreseen.

---

[43] Ibid., disc. 2, chap. 28, § 17.

────── ❧ *3* ❧ ──────

MARTIN LUTHER
ON RELIGIOUS LIBERTY
*Steven Ozment**

Christian Freedom.—Martin Luther wrote at length about the freedom of Christians, arguing that government had strict limits on its power to instruct conscience. He also defended the right of Christian congregations to determine the religious teachings and practices by which they lived. Do such freedom and right have anything to do with "religious liberty" as we understand it today? Most modern scholars would answer no; and not a few would argue that in matters of religion and politics, Luther's Reformation contributed far more to bigotry and absolutism than to freedom or liberty. As I hope to demonstrate, Luther's views are in fact more complex than this, both theoretically and in terms of his actual behavior.

In perhaps his most famous treatise, *On the Freedom of a Christian* (1520),[1] Luther describes Christian freedom's first attribute as the right to subject religious custom and church tradition to the authority of Scripture. This was not just a theological argument, but a fundamental principle carried over directly into pamphlet propaganda and Protestant practice. Among the favorite sayings of the Lutheran pamphleteers of the 1520s and 1530s were these: "Christ says, 'I am the Truth,' he does not say, 'I am Custom'" and "The Bible commands us to honor our parents [that is, tradition], *not* to believe

---

* McLean Professor of Ancient and Modern History, Harvard University.

[1] The original German version is entitled *Die Freiheit eines Christenmenschen*, the Latin translation, *De Libertate Christiana*.

and trust in them."[2] In the autobiographies of the first Protestants, we find laymen defending clerical marriage and new liturgies by appeal to the teaching of Scripture, and laywomen in childbirth refusing such traditional aids as rosaries, Masses, and prayers to St. Margaret simply because the Bible makes no mention of such things.[3] Even centuries-old, widely observed canon and imperial laws became mere "Menschensatzungen," when Protestants found them to lack a clear basis in Scripture.

In his preface to *On the Freedom of a Christian*, Luther practiced what he here preached. He invoked Scripture as the great equalizer of Christians, addressing Pope Leo X, who would soon excommunicate him, as if the two were spiritual equals. At the same time, he made it clear that whenever Christian doctrine was debated, the person found to have Scripture on his side must be recognized as the more authoritative spokesman for the church.

Again, such teaching informed the propaganda wars and actual Protestant practice. Lutheran tractarians and playwrights delighted in contrived portrayals of shoemakers, bakers, and peasants so well versed in Scripture that they readily routed learned mendicants and canons in theological discussions. In such works, simple laity define Christian doctrine more authoritatively and exhibit Christian conduct in their secular vocations more consistently than do the church's clergy.

As Protestants understood it, Christian freedom was first and foremost the right and duty of anyone who could understand Scripture to allow it to guide their conscience. Bible-savvy laity might oppose any and all, whether parent or teacher, spouse or employer, emperor or pope, who abused conscience and Scripture by pretending a doctrine or practice was biblical when it manifestly was not, thereby setting pure fabrications in the place of God's Word. In this way, Luther endowed his followers with a divine right to critique and contest whatever was presented to them as the Word of God, assuming only that they did so on the basis of Scripture alone.

In Lutheran territories, such freedom came to be circumscribed in law and practice by the further demand that each layman's interpretation of Scripture agree with Martin Luther's. There is no recognition in Luther's teaching of a *plurality* of *true* biblical interpretations or of different religious confessions based upon them. Luther personally demonstrated the bigotry that might accompany so narrow a concept of Christian freedom during his famous exchange with Erasmus, reputed layer of the egg that Luther hatched, in the mid-1520s, when Luther declared that he would sooner see "the whole

---

[2] Steven Ozment, *Protestants: The Birth of a Revolution* (New York: Doubleday, 1992), chap. 3.

[3] Ibid., chap. 8.

world thrown into turmoil . . . shattered in chaos, and reduced to nothing" than allow Erasmus' views on free will to gain currency; and he treated his Protestant competitors no less harshly.[4]

In practice, then, Luther's notion of Christian freedom circumscribed religious liberty, if by that term we mean toleration of different interpretations of Scripture's teaching on key religious doctrines and practices. In Lutheran lands, not every biblical truth could set one free; only evangelical Lutheran truths might do so. Laity were free to defend and live by the truth as Martin Luther had discovered it in the Bible. Those who attempted to argue religious doctrine apart from Scripture, or, when arguing it properly on the basis of Scripture, defended a point of view deemed unevangelical by the Lutheran creeds, found themselves accused of the wrongful exercise of Christian freedom. When, for example, Anabaptists, with the clearest biblical examples of Jesus and the apostles on their side, rejected the traditional practice of infant baptism, their efforts won them only charges of heresy and treason from Lutheran and Catholic authorities alike. When Luther's great Protestant competitor, the Swiss reformer Ulrich Zwingli, invoked New Testament passages like, "the letter kills, but the spirit makes alive," to portray Christ's presence in the Eucharist as spiritually, but not corporally real in direct challenge of Luther's teaching on the subject, Luther deemed him un-Christian.

In Lutheran lands, Christian freedom in the end meant the right to dissent from Rome and to agree with Wittenberg. By comparison with previous practice, that was for the times a new degree of religious freedom, and it brought about real and lasting change in contemporary religious life. On the other hand, it was also a new bondage to a new dogmatic creed.

Lutherans inculcated this qualified notion of Christian freedom in their young. When twelve- to fourteen-year-olds prepared for confirmation in Lutheran lands, they were not given any genuine religious alternatives. The Nuremberg Catechism or Children's Sermons of 1533, one of the Reformation's most influential, presented children with the only possible reading of the Ten Commandments and the articles of The Lord's Prayer—not with a variety of equally plausible interpretations, or the latest scholarly opinions, from which the young, as they matured, could freely choose in good conscience. Children were not to believe as they reasoned, but as they had been taught. As in the Middle Ages, truth was not something requiring

---

[4] Steven Ozment, *The Age of Reform: 1250-1550* (New Haven: Yale Univ. Press, 1981), 298-99; Mark U. Edwards, *Luther and the False Brethren* (Stanford: Stanford Univ. Press, 1978).

search and discovery; it already existed and needed only to be embraced and memorized.

On the other hand, efforts were made to transform these same youth into vigilant moral and social critics, able to apply what they had learned fearlessly to everyone, from the burgomaster to domestic servants, sparing no one who transgressed biblical precepts in the conduct of their secular life or vocation.[5] The circumscription of religious choice was in this way compensated by an intensification of civic virtue; fired by clear religious truth, youth might exercise their Christian freedom in the pursuit of a godly society with abandon.

In actual practice, then, Christian freedom as Luther conceived it had less to do with determining the eternal truths by which one would live as a religious person than it did with applying the truths other, presumably more knowledgeable people had defined for the community at large. Such freedom gave no one the option to believe as he wished, only the opportunity to serve the true faith. Lay belief, of course, was never a carbon copy of clerical belief; laity put their own stamp on the new faith by stressing or ignoring different aspects of it and by continuing, secretly or openly, to embrace forbidden traditional practices. Luther and his braintrust were the only ones to enjoy the true liberty of actually construing biblical truth at large as they saw it; they had the rare privilege of inventing evangelical truth for a generation. In doing so, they exercised Christian freedom in an original act of religious liberty which the vast majority of their followers neither could nor probably, if the truth were known, wished to emulate. By choice or indifference, the good Lutheran layperson basked in the spiritual wisdom of the founders, which only the most foolhardy dared openly doubt or defy. Still, despite such reduction of the scope of the layman's freedom in determining the content of the faith, there were no limitations on anyone's sacred right to scrutinize others by its standards, or to defy the folkloric customs and Roman traditions with which the new faith had decisively broken.

A second characteristic of Christian freedom, as Luther understood it, is its exclusively spiritual and inward nature. Such freedom makes each Christian a "lord of all," but the realm over which each rules is strictly one of the heart and the soul. Faith sets one free from internal control by all save God, whose word alone possesses the authority to rule over conscience— something denied the entire spectrum of earthly authority, from parents to

---

[5] Ozment, *Protestants*, chap. 5.

princes, who may address this inner realm only by deferring to or confirming God's sovereignty there.

Such inner freedom has little intrinsically to do with religious pluralism, toleration, or liberty in the modern sense of these terms, which would allow individuals to determine absolutely the content of the faith by which they wish to live. Luther's Christian does not create a new religion; the sole practical consequence of his freedom is ethical bondage or moral servitude to his immediate community. Having acquired certitude of salvation by recognition of the truth of a preexisting faith, the freed soul gains the ability to bind its body and control the latter's activities morally. One now becomes able for the first time freely and selflessly to perform the good works one previously ignored, or only grudgingly undertook and always vaingloriously. Such deeds now seemingly become involuntary and irresistible, as the Christian loves and serves his neighbor as naturally as a good tree bears good fruit. In such love and service, the soul's new Christlike innermost nature expresses itself as surely as its previous lack of charity had reflected its selfish fallen nature. Now, as the bride of Christ, the freed soul possesses all the grace, life, and salvation of its bridegroom, in the "happy exchange" with whom, it has lost all fear of sin, death, and damnation and ceased to be the doubting, acquisitive self it was.

Luther describes this new Christian self-consciousness as a "kingship over death, life, and sin" and an "inestimable power and liberty." But he also makes clear that it has nothing to do with social standing or political rights, much less empowers subjects to threaten or coerce their rulers, even tyrannical rulers—behavior Luther dismisses as "madness." Luther's Christian does not derive immediately from his new freedom the right to challenge reigning political authority any more than he does to challenge the ascendant Lutheran creed, although there are circumstances under which he might legitimately do both. On the eve of the Peasants' Revolt in 1525, Luther admonished peasant leaders to "drop the name Christian" from their protest and seek the redress of their grievances as a "natural," not as a "Christian" right.[6] He justified such instruction by describing the "justice" the peasants demanded as a matter only of material equity and political right—not the inner freedom and moral servitude which alone defines Christians. On the one hand, he enthusiastically supported the peasants' campaign for economic and political justice by reminding rulers of their God-given duties to their subjects according to natural law and the Ten Commandments. On the other hand, he made clear his belief that the presence or absence of such justice in

---

[6] Ozment, *Age of Reform*, 282.

people's lives had nothing to do with the liberation of their souls from sin, death, and the devil.

Although Luther describes the consequence of Christian faith and freedom as a moral bondage and servitude to others, its empowering force actually lies in the internal release of conscience from a morally incapacitating sense of sin and guilt, which, ironically, such faith and freedom is said also to awaken in a person for the first time. The unbeliever has no awareness of having transgressed God's law until the first movements of faith apprise him of it and create within him, the desire to be free from it. It is then that one discovers his inability to fulfil God's law, save by abject faith in Christ. For those who experience it, the event is both traumatic and liberating. From it one gains both personal certitude of salvation and the ability to act ethically toward others; once faith fulfills the first commandment (one's obligations to God), all the others (those embracing one's duties toward one's fellow man) are said to become manageable as well.

Political Freedom.—The distinctive faith-love, freedom-servitude dialectic of Luther's theology finds an illuminating complement, even more pertinent to the issue of religious liberty, in his equally famous doctrines of the two kingdoms (*Reiche*), one spiritual and one temporal, and the two governments (*Regiments*), church and state, over both of which Christ and the devil are said to war.[7] Luther elaborated these doctrines in another early treatise entitled *On Temporal Authority* (1523). In the *Freedom of a Christian*, he dealt with faith's ability to give one a sense of inner freedom and security from sin, death, and the devil. Here, too, he intends to inform Christians about their standing and rights before God and in the world, only now with reference to the protection faith gives one from external political coercion and assault.

Again, Luther carves out a sacred and inviolable sphere for the Christian soul. Every Christian is said to have a right to resist the coercion of his conscience by civil authority at least passively, that is, by spoken and written words and acts of protest, even unto death, if required.[8] Such protest is justified because God has confined government to a strictly temporal sphere of power and authority, allowing it to tax subjects in support of public services and to maintain standards of moral behavior. To the latter end, God empowers rulers, Christian and non-Christian alike, to restrain by threat and force the wicked actions of one person or group against another. But God has given government no power or authority within the spiritual sphere, over the

---

[7] See W. D. J. Cargill Thompson, *The Political Thought of Martin Luther* (Sussex: Harvester Press, 1984), 36-44.

[8] *On Temporal Authority*, in *Luther's Works*, ed. W.I. Brandt (Philadelphia: Muhlenberg Press, 1962), 45: 84-85.

Christian's soul or conscience, where the Holy Spirit alone holds sway and, working through the church and the clergy, makes people Christian and righteous by God's word alone.

Luther assumes the reality of an inner world of conscience, faith, and salvation that is distinct from the temporal world and in the light of eternity superior to it. This assumption alone makes "religious liberty" an inalienable right, empowering Christians to resist in good conscience any political attempt to coerce or undermine their religious belief. But Luther also believed that Christians had a very great stake in the quality of life this side of eternity, since it is here that they must live their faith in service to their neighbors, acting as hangmen, constables, and soldiers, if need be, for their neighbor's protection and well-being. Hence, his insistence that disobedience of legitimate political authority acting within its proper sphere is defiance of God, the consequences of which were as terrifying to Luther as later to Thomas Hobbes.

These sentiments were not just theological ideas; they were born of real calamity. When Luther wrote about these matters in 1523, vernacular New Testaments were being confiscated by political authorities in several lands and Luther's own writings banned by rulers determined to suppress the Reformation.[9] Earlier, as it became clear that the church was not going to enact needed reforms, Luther had urged Saxon princes to undertake reforms in lieu of church action. As he now watched Catholic princes meddle in true religion as boldly and improperly as popes had ever done, he regretted his decision. Hence, his new orations on the sovereignty of conscience—only now to magnify the limits God had placed on political authority:

> Temporal authority has laws, which extend no further than to life and property and external affairs on earth, for God cannot and will not permit anyone but himself to rule over the soul. . . . Caesar can neither teach the soul nor guide it, neither kill it nor give it life, neither bind it nor loose it, neither judge it nor condemn it, neither hold it fast nor release it.[10]

When government prescribes laws for the soul, it encroaches on God's government and can even destroy souls by forcing people to believe what is uncertain or untrue. On the other hand, Luther saw no inconsistency in his argument when it was *his* prince, the elector of Saxony, who mandated his (Luther's) teaching and suppressed the views of rival Protestants, something his Swiss rival Zwingli was quick to point out in the wake of the Eucharistic controversy with Luther, when Zwingli's books were burned and thrown into

---

9 Ibid., 112.
10 Ibid., 105, 111.

rivers throughout electoral Saxony. But such behavior was normal for the age; all the reformers at this time, Protestant and Catholic alike, believed faith never to be freer than when their doctrine was being imposed on others.

Conclusion.—The history of Protestantism abounds with examples, both individual and civic, of the exercise of religious conscience. Already in the sixteenth century, the cry of Christian freedom led to new laws that allowed the laity to marry more freely than had been the case in previous centuries under Catholic regimes; the traditional degrees of kinship and affinity that had curtailed and complicated marital choice also now shrank. Also in Protestant territories, genuine divorce and remarriage, in distinction from the traditional separation from bed and table, became possible for the first time among Western Christians. The new clergy gained a long coveted right to marry, which they exercised in large numbers, even playing cupid to one another in a rush to share the newly discovered bliss of married life and to make still another dramatic statement against Rome. To fast or not to fast in certain religious seasons now became a genuine option for the laity, and there were also fewer religious holidays on which the laity had to close their businesses. The religious could break their vow in good conscience and flee their cloisters—although anyone now wishing to make a religious vow, enter a cloister, and live a celibate life had henceforth to move to a Catholic land to do so. Protestants also rewrote inheritance laws to allow endowments previously assigned to cloisters and commemorative masses by then Catholic laity to be secularized, confiscated by government, or turned to familial or community purposes.

——— ❧ 4 ❧ ———

MODERATE RELIGIOUS LIBERTY
IN THE THEOLOGY OF JOHN CALVIN

John Witte, Jr. [*]

[T]here is no kind of government more salutary than one in which liberty is properly exercised with becoming moderation and properly constituted on a durable basis.

— John Calvin, Institutes of the Christian Religion (1543)[1]

John Calvin, the Protestant reformer of Geneva, is a controversial candidate for the honor roll of religious liberty in the West. He is at once valorized and villainized both for his theology and for his politics of religious liberty, particularly his participation in the execution of Michael Servetus. Calvin's champions can be found in many quarters. John Adams urged: "Let not Geneva be forgotten or despised. Religious liberty owes it much respect, Servetus notwithstanding."[2] Jean Jacques Rousseau, for all his anti-religious sentiment, had only praise for his compatriot:

[*] Jonas Robitscher Professor of Law Ethics, and Director of Law and Religion Program, Emory University. B.A. Calvin College (1982); J.D., Harvard Law School (1985). I wish to thank M. Christian Green, J.D. and M.T.S., Emory (1995) and Stephen D. Peterson, J.D., Emory (1994) for their excellent research assistance.

[1] *Instituto christianae religioni. Ioanne Calvino autore* (1543), chap. 20.7, reprinted in G. Baum et al., eds., *Ioannis Calvini opera quae supersunt omnia*, repr. ed. (New York: Johnson Reprint Corp., 1964), vol. 1, col. 1105 (hereafter Calvin's opera cited as "CO").

[2] John Adams, "Discourses on Davilia, XIX," in *The Works of John Adams, Second President of the United States, with a Life of the Author, Notes, and Illustrations* (Boston: Little, Brown & Co., 1850–1856), 6: 313n.

Those who consider Calvin only as a theologian fail to recognize the breadth of his genius. The editing of our wise laws, in which he had a large share, does him as much credit as his Institutes. . . . [S]o long as the love of country and liberty is not extinct among us, the memory of this great man will be held in reverence.[3]

Charles Bourgeaud judged Calvin's Geneva to be "the first stronghold" of religious and political liberty in modern times.[4] Walter Köhler described Calvin as the "pioneer of the freedom of conscience and human rights" that were finally constitutionalized after the French Revolution.[5] Abraham Kuyper declared that "[e]very competent historian will without exception confirm the words of [American historian George] Bancroft: 'The fanatic for Calvinism was a fanatic for liberty; and, in the moral warfare for freedom, his creed was his most faithful counsellor and his never-failing support.' "[6]

Many competent historians, however, have categorically denied such assertions. Ernst Troeltsch described Calvin as "notoriously rigid" and his "personal view as undemocratic and authoritarian as possible."[7] George Sabine believed that Calvinism "lacked all leaning towards liberalism, constitutionalism, or representative principles [and] . . . was, in general, illiberal, oppressive, and reactionary."[8] Stefan Zweig charged Calvin with "fanatical dogmatism" and with "slaughtering freedom of conscience under the Reformation."[9] Roland Bainton declared that "the Reformation at the outset brought no gain for religious liberty. Rather the reverse,"[10] particularly under Calvin, "the arch-inquisitor of Protestantism" and "dictator of Geneva."[11] "If

---

[3] *Du contrat social* (1762), bk. 2, chap. 7n., reprinted in Jean Jacques Rousseau, *The Social Contract and the Discourse on the Origin of Inequality*, ed. Lester G. Crocker (New York: Washington Square Press, 1967), 44n.

[4] Quoted by John T. McNeill, *The History and Character of Calvinism* (Oxford & New York: Oxford Univ. Press, 1954), 196.

[5] Walter Köhler, Book Review, *Theologische Jahrbericht* 24 (1904): 579.

[6] Abraham Kuyper, *Lectures on Calvinism*, repr. ed. (Grand Rapids, Wm. B. Eerdmans Publishing Co., 1981), 78, quoting George Bancroft, *History of the United States of America*, 15th ed. (Boston: Little, Brown & Co., 1853), 1: 319.

[7] Ernst Troeltsch, *The Social Teaching of the Churches*, trans. O. Wyon, 2d. impr. (London: G. Allen & Unwin, 1949), 2: 628.

[8] Quoted by Robert M. Kingdon and Robert D. Linder, eds., *Calvin and Calvinism: Sources of Democracy?* (Lexington, MA: Heath, 1970), xiii.

[9] Stefan Zweig, *Strijd rond een brandstapel. Castellio tegen Calvijn* (Amsterdam: Wein H. Reichner, 1936), 6.

[10] Roland H. Bainton, "The Struggle for Religious Liberty," *Church History* 10 (1941): 96.

[11] Roland H. Bainton, *The Travail of Religious Liberty* (London: Lutterworth Press, 1953), 53. See critical discussion in James K. Cameron, "Scottish Calvinism and the Principle of Intolerance," in B. A. Gerrish, ed., *Reformatio Perennis: Essays on Calvin and the Reformation in Honor of Ford Lewis Battles* (Pittsburg, PA: Pickwick Press, 1981), 113.

Calvin ever wrote anything in favor of religious liberty," said Bainton, "it was a typographical error."[12]

Both these judgments depend on too tendentious a reading of Calvin's writings and too ready a conflation of his views with those of his followers. On matters relating to religious libery, Calvin must be read as a theologian and pastor, not as a political theorist and jurist. To be sure, as a youth in France, he had studied law and the political classics under such masters as Guillaume Budé, Pierre L'Estoile, and Andreas Alciati, and this early training is reflected in the style and substance of some of his early works, particularly his 1532 Commentaries on Seneca's *De Clementia.*[13] And, to be sure, during his pastoral work in Geneva from 1536 to 1538 and again from 1541 till his death in 1564, Calvin frequently addressed legal and political questions— both in Geneva and in many other places in Europe.[14] But Calvin wrote no summa on political theory, no systematic work on religious liberty, no civil code on church-state relations, no letter on religious toleration. His writings were principally theological in character, addressed to the cardinal Christian topics of God and man, sin and salvation, law and Gospel. His discussions of religious liberty were left scattered widely throughout the multiple editions of his *Institutes of the Christian Religion* as well as his biblical commentaries, published sermons, and theological consilia.[15]

---

[12] Roland H. Bainton, *Concerning Heretics. . . . An Anonymous Work Attributed to Sebastian Castellio* (New York: Octagon Books, 1935), 74.

[13] *L'annei Senecae . . . Ioannis Calvini Nouiodunaei comentarijs illustrati* (Paris, 1532), reprinted and translated as *Calvin's Commentary on Seneca's De Clementia,* trans. Ford Lewis Battles and A. M. Hugo (Leiden: E. J. Brill, 1969). On the legal and humanist character of the tract, see the translators' notes in ibid., 72*–99*, 134*–140*, which stress Calvin's preoccupation, inter alia, with questions of equity, the purposes of the law, the problems of parricide, and the structures and limits of political authority. "Calvin's chief legal source" for his Commentary is the *Corpus Juris Civilis,* which he cites 86 times. Ibid., 140*. On Calvin's legal and humanist training in France, see Gisbert Beyerhaus, *Studien zur Staatsanschauung Calvins mit besonderer Berücksichtigung seines Souveränitätsbegriffs,* repr. ed. (Aalen: Darmstadt Scientia Verlag, 1973), 26–47; Josef Bohatec, *Budé und Calvin: Studien zur Gedankenwelt des franzöischen Frühhumanismus* (Graz: H. B. Ohlaus Nachf., 1950), 127–148; Quirinius Breen, *John Calvin: A Study in French Humanism* (Grand Rapids, MI: Wm. B. Eerdmans Publishing Co., 1931), 40–66, 86–99.

[14] See generally John T. McNeill, "John Calvin on Civil Government," in George L. Hunt, ed., *Calvinism and the Political Order* (Philadelphia: Westminster Press, 1965), 23, 24ff., on Calvin's political correspondence.

[15] The best collection is in CO. See also P. Barth and W. Niesel (hrsg.), *Joannis Calvini opera selecta* (München: Chr. Kaiser Verlag, 1926–1936); *Calvin's Commentaries* (Edinburgh, 1843–1859); D.W. Torrance and T.F. Torrance, eds., *Calvin Commentaries* [on the New Testament] (Edinburgh: Oliver & Boyd, 1959–); *Supplementa Calvinia* (Neukirchen: Kreis Moers Neukirchener Verlag der Buchhandlung, 1961–).

It is easy to select from these scattered sentiments quotations to support both positive and negative impressions of Calvin. Calvin often wrote with a strong rhetorical flourish, and in unguarded moments or on particularly controversial subjects, he was not above the bombast and hyperbole that typified sixteenth century humanist literature.[16] Calvin's champions can find many strong statements in his writings on separation of church and state, liberty of conscience, free exercise of religion, and religious toleration, and make Calvin out to be the father of modern religious liberty and political democracy. Calvin's critics can assemble an equally high pile of quotations on religious bigotry, chauvinism, prejudice, repression, and officiousness, and make Calvin out to be a rigid and unbending theocrat.

Neither of these interpretations does justice to Calvin. Viewed as a whole and in sixteenth century theological terms, Calvin's scattered sentiments on religious liberty fall into two distinct phases. In his early writings of the 1530s, Calvin focussed on the spiritual liberty of the individual believer vis-à-vis God's spiritual law and his political liberty vis-à-vis the magistrate's civil law. His principal concern was to distinguish these two forms of religious liberty from each other, and to define the appropriate limitations that the church and the state could impose on them. As his thinking matured after 1540, and he confronted the brute realities of Genevan ecclesiastical and political life, Calvin modified his position considerably. His focus was less on the liberty of the individual, and more on the respective jurisdictions and duties of the church and the state. By the time he had finished dividing up the respective callings and claims of these two jurisdictions, Calvin had created ample room for corporate religious liberty, but less room for individual religious liberty, particular for one so openly heretical as Michael Servetus.

A perennial theme in both phases of Calvin's discussion is that, whatever its form, religious liberty must always be exercised with becoming moderation.[17] Liberty and law, freedom and order, toleration and discipline are created and constituted together, Calvin believed, and must constantly balance each other to achieve the ideal of a "moderate religious liberty." The following sections take up, in turn, Calvin' early formulations and later formulations on religious liberty. The conclusion reflects on the profound

---

[16] See discussion and sources in Don H. Compier, "Denouncing Death: John Calvin's Critique of Sin and Contemporary Rhetorical Theology" (Ph.D. Diss., Emory, 1993); Quirinius Breen, "John Calvin and the Rhetorical Tradition," *Church History* 26 (1957): 14; A. Veerman, *De Stijl van Calvin in de Institutio Christianae Religionis* (Utrecht: Kemink, 1943); Bohatec, *Budé und Calvin*, 257–263.

[17] "Moderation" (*moderatio*) is, for Calvin, a cardinal virtue that he first celebrated in his 1532 *Commentary on Seneca's* De Clementia, and that recurs repeatedly as an ideal throughout his writings. See, e.g., his commentary on bk. 1, chap. 2.

significance of Calvin's views on the evolution of the Western political tradition of religious liberty.

Early Formulations on Religious Liberty.—As a young Protestant neophyte, Calvin naturally came under the influence of the first generation of Protestant leaders. In the years immediately following his conversion circa 1532, Calvin read several writings of Martin Luther, Philip Melanchthon, Martin Bucer, Ulrich Zwingli, Johannes Oecolampadius, and other Protestants, together with a number of Protestant catechisms, confessions, and church laws.[18] His early writings on religious liberty—most notably his long discussion in the 1536 edition of the *Institutes*[19]—reflect a particular affinity for Lutheran lore.

(1) Two Kingdoms.—Like his Lutheran brethren, Calvin sought to formulate a theory of religious liberty that would avoid the extremes of both radical Anabaptist liberalism and radical Catholic legalism. He sought to counter the claims of certain Anabaptists that Christian believers are set free from all law and authority.[20] He sought to counter the claims of certain Catholics that Christian believers can be free only through submission to law and authority.[21] Nowadays, Calvin wrote, "as soon as the term 'Christian liberty' is mentioned, either passions boil or wild tumults rise. . . . On the pretext of this freedom, some men shake off all obedience toward God and break into unbridled license, while others disdain it, thinking such freedom cancels all moderation, order, and choice of things. . . . [T]hese wanton spirits, who otherwise most wickedly corrupt the best things, must be opposed in time."[22]

---

[18] For classic treatments of Calvin's early religious development, and his relations to earlier Protestant reformers, see Emile Doumergue, *Jean Calvin. Les hommes et les choses de son temps* (Lausanne: G. Bridel, 1899–1927); A. Ganoczy, *La jeune Calvin. Genèse et evolution de la vocation réformatorice* (Wiesbaden: F. Steiner, 1966); Harro Höpfl, *The Christian Polity of John Calvin* (Cambridge: Cambridge Univ. Press, 1982), 219–226; Hans Baron, "Calvinist Republicanism and its Historical Roots," *Church History* 8 (1939): 30–42.

[19] *Ioannis Calvini Institutio Religionis Christianae* (Basel: Thomas Platteru & Balthasar Lasius, 1536), reprinted in CO, 1: 1–251, translated as John Calvin, *Institution of the Christian Religion*, trans. Ford Lewis Battles (Atlanta: John Knox Press, 1975). I have generally followed Battles' translation, and his divisions of the text, though I have occasionally provided my own translations.

[20] See generally Willem Balke, *Calvin and the Anabaptist Radicals*, trans. William Heynen (Grand Rapids, MI: Eerdmans, 1981).

[21] See, e.g., *Institutes* (1536), chap. 6.14, where, describing the Catholic magisterium, Calvin writes: "These Solons even fancy that their constitutions are laws of freedom, a gentle yoke, a light burden." See generally Josef Bohatec, *Calvins Lehre von Staat und Kirche*, 2d repr. ed. (Aalen: Scientia Verlag, 1968), 581–633.

[22] *Institutes* (1536), chap. 6.1. See also ibid., chaps. 1.30, 6.35.

Calvin sought to reconcile this dialectic of liberalism and legalism through use of the Lutheran theory of the two kingdoms. According to Lutheran lore, God has ordained two kingdoms or realms in which humanity is destined to live, the earthly or political kingdom and the heavenly or spiritual kingdom. The earthly kingdom is the realm of creation, of natural and civic life, where a person operates primarily by reason, law, and passion. The heavenly kingdom is the realm of redemption, of spiritual and eternal life, where a person operates primarily by faith, hope, and charity. These two kingdoms embrace parallel temporal and spiritual forms of justice and morality, truth and knowledge, order and law, but they remain separate and distinct. The earthly kingdom is fallen, and distorted by sin. The heavenly kingdom is saved, and renewed by grace—and foreshadows the perfect kingdom of Christ to come. A Christian is a citizen of both kingdoms at once, and invariably comes under the structures and strictures of each.[23]

Calvin recited this two kingdoms theory several times in his writings of the 1530s, each time with a breeziness that reflects comfortable acceptance of the doctrine.[24] "[T]here is a twofold government in man," Calvin wrote in summary of his position:

> one aspect is spiritual, whereby the conscience is instructed in piety and in reverencing God; the second is political, whereby man is educated for the duties of humanity and civil life that must be maintained among men. These are usually called the "spiritual" and the "temporal" jurisdictions (not improper terms) by which is meant that the former sort of government pertains to the life of the soul, while the latter has to do with the concerns of the present life—not only with food and clothing but with laying down laws whereby a man may live his life among other men honorably and temperately. For the former resides in the mind within, while the latter regulates only outward behavior. The one we may call the spiritual kingdom, the other the political kingdom. . . . There are in man, so to speak, two worlds, over which different kings and different laws have authority.[25]

---

[23] For discussion and sources, see Harold J. Berman and John Witte, Jr., "The Transformation of Western Legal Philosophy in Lutheran Germany," *Southern California Law Review* 62 (1989): 1573, 1585–1595.

[24] See, e.g., *Institutes* (1536), chap. 6.13, 14, 35. Calvin used multiple terms to describe these two kingdoms: the heavenly kingdom, the Kingdom of Christ, the spiritual kingdom, the spiritual jurisdiction versus the earthly kingdom, the Kingdom of this world, the political kingdom, the civil realm, the temporal jurisdiction. In his later writings, Calvin also described these two kingdoms in more traditional Catholic terms as the inner forum and outer forum, which is a much narrower anthropological conception. See, e.g., *Institutes* (1559), bk. 3, chap. 19.15. For the significance of this narrowing of the two kingdoms for Calvin's understanding of religious liberty, see below note 71 and accompanying text.

[25] Ibid., chap. 6.13.

In a few passages in this early period, Calvin seemed to equate the heavenly kingdom with the church and the earthly kingdom with the state. He states flatly, for example, that "the church is Christ's kingdom"[26] and that the earthly kingdom is "the political order of laws and lawgivers."[27] But such passages must be read in context. Calvin's early two kingdoms theory was not simply a political theory but a theological framework designed to distinguish the realms not only of church and state, but also of soul and body, spirit and flesh, inner life and outer life, conscience and reason, redemption and creation.

Calvin's early views on religious liberty were part of this theological framework.. Calvin distinguished: (1) the "spiritual liberty" or "liberty of conscience" of the believer in the heavenly kingdom; and (2) the "political liberty" or "civil freedom" of the believer in the earthly kingdom. Such terms were commonplace in Catholic and Protestant circles of the day, but Calvin cast them in a distinctive mould. He insisted that these two forms of liberty, like other features of the two kingdoms, are completely separate. He also insisted that these two forms of freedom are perpetually limited by and counterposed to the prevailing laws and orders of the two kingdoms. For Calvin, freedom and order, liberty and law always belong together.

(2) *Spiritual Liberty.*—In the heavenly kingdom, spiritual law and spiritual liberty stand counterposed. God has ordained a "spiritual law" or "law of conscience" to govern citizens of the heavenly kingdom. This law teaches "those things that God either requires of us or forbids us to do, both toward [ourselves] and towards others."[28] Its provisions are written on the heart and conscience of each person, rewritten in the pages of Scripture, and summarized in the Ten Commandments.[29] Obedience of this spiritual law leads to eternal blessings and beatitude in the life hereafter. Disobedience leads to eternal curses and condemnation. Since the fall into sin, Calvin argued, no person has been capable of perfectly obeying this law. The scourge of original sin infects all persons, even the most devout saints. By itself, therefore, the spiritual law becomes "a great accuser, condemning us in our conscience, cursing us to eternal damnation."[30]

Through his grace, God liberates the conscience from such curses and condemnation; he bestows "spiritual liberty" on believers, on citizens of the

---

[26] Ibid., chap. 6.20.

[27] Ibid., chap. 6.14.

[28] Ibid., chap. 1.24. See also ibid., chaps. 1.4, 1.7, 6.47, 6.49.

[29] Ibid., chap. 1.4, 7–23.

[30] Ibid., chaps. 1.4, 1.33.

heavenly kingdom. This liberty has two dimensions. On the one hand, by accepting God's grace in faith, believers are freed from the requirement to earn their salvation by perfect obedience of the law. Faith and grace provide them with an alternative pathway to blessing and beatitude. Believers are made righteous and just despite their inability to obey the law.[31] On the other hand, believers are freed to live by the law, without fear of its condemnation. Although God has cancelled the condemnation of the law, he has not cancelled its commandments. The law remains in place "as an exhortation to believers" to lead a Godly life. It is "not something to bind their consciences with a curse," but it is a means for them "to learn more thoroughly each day what the Lord's will is like."[32] With the sting of the law removed, believers have the liberty of conscience to follow its commandments, albeit imperfectly.[33]

Liberty of conscience stands counterposed not only to God's spiritual law, but also to the Catholic Church's canon law. Like other early Protestants, Calvin had little faith in the vast system of canon law rules and structures by which the Church had come to govern spiritual life and much of temporal life.[34] He issued a bitter broadside against the arguments from Scripture, tradition, and the sacraments which the Church had adduced to support its canon law system.[35] "[T]he power to frame laws was both unknown to the apostles, and many times denied the ministers of the church by God's Word," he argued.[36] And, again, "it is not a church which, passing the bounds of God's Word, wantons and disports itself to frame new laws and dream up new things" for spiritual life.[37]

The church must respect the God-given liberty of conscience of believers. To be sure, said Calvin quoting St. Paul, "all things [must] be done decently and in order."[38] Certain rules and structures "are necessary for internal discipline [and] the maintenance of peace, honesty, and good order in the assembly of Christians."[39] But the church has no authority to impose laws "upon consciences in those matters in which they have been freed by Christ,"

---

[31] Ibid., chap. 6.2.

[32] Ibid., chaps. 1.33, 6.3.

[33] Ibid. See also ibid., chap. 1.30.

[34] See discussion and sources in Harold J. Berman, *Law and Revolution: The Formation of the Western Legal Tradition* (Cambridge, MA: Harvard Univ. Press, 1983).

[35] See *Institutes* (1536), dedicatory epistle, and chap. 6.14–32.

[36] Ibid., chap. 6.17.

[37] Ibid., chap. 6.20.

[38] Ibid., chap. 6.32, quoting I Cor. 14:40.

[39] Geneva Catechism (1536), item 17, "Human Traditions," reprinted in Arthur C. Cochrane, ed., *Reformed Confessions of the Sixteenth Century* (Philadelphia: Westminster Press, 1966), 117ff.; *Institutes* (1536), chap. 6.32.

in the so-called adiaphora—"the outward things of themselves 'indifferent'" to salvation.[40] Though Calvin did not spell them out systematically, such matters included habits of food, drink, dress, holy days, confessions, pilgrimages, marital relations, and the like, which the Catholic Church traditionally governed in copious detail, backed by threats of spiritual sanction and discipline.[41] Canon laws that govern such matters, Calvin regarded as illegitimate "human traditions" that improperly "establish another service of God than that which he demands [in his spiritual law], thus tending to destroy Christian liberty."[42] Such canon laws "tyrannize," "ensnare," confuse," and "destroy the repose" of conscience by all manner of "traps and superstitions." In essential matters of faith and spiritual conduct, of course, Christians are bound to comply with God's spiritual law. But in discretionary matters of spiritual living (the adiaphora), Christian consciences "must be held in no bondage, and bound by no bounds."[43] Christians might voluntarily bind themselves in such discretionary matters, especially to protect the frail consciences of other believers.[44] But such restraint is neither necessary nor subject to the church's regulations.

Calvin's early views on liberty of conscience thus differed markedly both from the rationalist formulations of a Thomas Aquinas and the voluntarist formulations of a Marsilius of Padua. Calvin did not have in mind the freedom of the person to respond either to the dictates of reason or to the impulses of the will. And he certainly did not have in mind the Enlightenment conception of liberty of conscience, defined by James Madison as the liberty to choose "the duty that we owe to our Creator, and the manner of discharging it."[45] Calvin cast this classic concept in much narrower theological terms. Liberty of conscience is "in all its parts, a spiritual thing," he wrote, a liberty to obey the commandments of God with a free conscience. God defines the duties of man, the commandments; man has the liberty to choose to obey them. The "whole force" of liberty of conscience, "consists in quieting frightened consciences before God whether they are disturbed or troubled over forgiveness of sins; or anxious whether unfinished works,

---

[40] Ibid., chap. 6.14.

[41] Ibid.; Geneva Catechism (1536), item 17.

[42] Ibid.

[43] *Institutes* (1536), chap. 6.4.

[44] Ibid., chaps. 6.8–6.13.

[45] James Madison, "To the Honorable the General Assembly of the Commonwealth of Virginia A Memorial and Remonstrance Against Religious Assessments" (1785), para. 1, in *Madison Papers*, eds. William T. Hutchinson and William M.E. Rachael (Chicago, 1962), 8: 298.

corrupted by the faults of the flesh, are pleasing to God; or tormented about the use of things indifferent."[46]

(3) *Political Liberty*.—While God has ordained spiritual liberty to balance the spiritual law of the heavenly kingdom, he has ordained political liberty to balance the political law of the earthly kingdom. These twin forms of spiritual and political liberty and law cannot be conflated, Calvin insisted. "[C]ertain men, when they hear that the Gospel promises liberty . . . think they cannot benefit by their liberty so long as they see any power set up over them. . . . But whoever knows how to distinguish between body and soul, between this present fleeting life and that future eternal life, will without difficulty know that Christ's spiritual kingdom and the civil jurisdiction are things completely distinct."[47] "Spiritual liberty can perfectly well exist along with political bondage."[48] Spiritual bondage can perfectly well exist along with political liberty.

Calvin described the political rulers and laws of the earthly kingdom in largely general and homiletic terms in this early period. God has appointed political rulers to be his "vice-regents," "vicars," and "ministers" in the earthly kingdom. Indeed, says Calvin citing biblical verses, "those who serve as magistrates are called 'gods'."[49] They are vested with God's authority and majesty. They are "called" to an office that is "not only holy and lawful before God, but also the most sacred and by far the most honorable of all callings in the whole life of mortal men."[50] They are commanded to embrace and exemplify clemency, integrity, honesty, mercy, humanity, humility, grace, innocence, continence, and a host of other Godly virtues.[51]

Political rulers must govern the earthly kingdom by written political laws, not by personal fiat. Their laws must encompass the biblical principles of love of God and neighbor, but they must not embrace biblical laws per se.[52] Instead, "equity alone must be the goal and rule and limit of all laws"[53]—a term which Calvin used both in the classic Aristotelian sense of correcting defects in individual rules if they work injustice in a particular case, and in

---

[46] *Institutes* (1536), chap. 6.5.

[47] Ibid., chap. 6.35.

[48] Ibid.

[49] Ibid., chap. 6.38–40. See also Geneva Catechism (1536), item 21 "Magistrates."

[50] *Institutes* (1536), chap. 6.39.

[51] Ibid.; Geneva Catechism (1536), item 21 "Magistrates" and the lengthy discussion in *Calvin's Commentary on Seneca's De Clementia*. See generally McNeill, "John Calvin on Civil Government," 30ff.; Höpfl, *The Christian Polity of John Calvin*, 43ff.

[52] *Institutes* (1536), chap. 6.48.

[53] Ibid., chap. 6.48–6.49.

his own sense of adjusting each legal system to the changing circumstances of the community.[54] Through such written, equitable laws, political rulers must serve to promote peace and order in the earthly kingdom, to punish crime and civil wrongdoing, to protect persons in their lives and properties, "to ensure that men may carry on blameless intercourse among themselves" in the spirit of "civil righteousness."[55] Such laws must also, Calvin said in a pregnant but undelivered aside, "prevent idolatry, sacrilege against God's name, blasphemies against his truth, and other public offenses against religion." But he hastened to add that he did not wish to "commit to civil government the duty of rightly establishing religion, which I put . . . beyond human decision."[56] The political law, said Calvin in summary of his position, serves only to ensure "that a public manifestation of religion may exist among Christians, and that humanity may be maintained among men."[57]

These God-given duties and limits define not only the political office but also the political liberty of Christian believers in the earthly kingdom.[58] Political liberty and political authority "are constituted together," said Calvin.[59] The political liberty of believers is not a subjective right. It does not exist in the abstract; it is a function of the political office. When political officials respect the duties and limits of their office, believers enjoy ample political liberty to give "public manifestation of their faith," or in modern

---

[54] On the classic Aristotelian view of equity as a corrective in the individual case, see Aristotle, *Ethics*, bk. 1, chap. 5; ibid., *The Art of Rhetoric*, bk. 1, chap. 12. See also *Calvin's Commentary on Seneca's De Clementia*, bk. 1, chap. 18 (Latin text, 111; Battles and Hugo trans., 371) and discussion in Beyerhaus, *Studien zur Staatsanschauung Calvins*, 5–8. On Calvin's view of equity as the adjustment of general norms of love to the legal system of particular communities, see *Institutes* (1536), chap. 6.49 where Calvin writes:

every nation is left free to make such laws as it foresees to be profitable for itself. Yet these must be in conformity to that perpetual rule of love, so that they indeed vary in form but have the very same purpose. . . . What I have said will become plain if in all laws we examine (as we should) these two things: the constitution of the law, and the equity on which its constitution itself rests. Equity, because it is natural, cannot but be the same for all and therefore, this same purpose ought to apply to all laws, whatever their object. Constitutions have attendant circumstances upon which they in part depend. It therefore does not matter that they are different, provided all equally press toward the same goal of equity.

[55] *Institutes* (1536), chap. 6.36–6.37. See also ibid., chap. 1.33, where Calvin describes the "civil use of the law."

[56] *Institutes* (1536), chap. 6.37.

[57] Ibid., chap. 6.37.

[58] See esp. Josef Bohatec, *Calvin und das Recht*, 2. Ausgabe (Aalen: Scientia Verlag, 1991), 81–82; id., *Calvins Lehre von Staat und Kirche mits besonderer Berücksichtigung des Organismusgedankens*, 2. Ausgabe (Aalen: Scientia Verlag, 1968), 109–116.

[59] Bohatec, *Calvins Lehre von Staat und Kirche,* 109.

language, to have free exercise of their religion. When political officials betray their office, however, through negligence, injustice, overreaching, or outright tyranny, the political liberty of the believer is abridged or even destroyed.[60]

Calvin insisted that "private individuals" have a Godly duty to obey tyrannical political officials up to the limits of Christian conscience.[61] But this duty of obedience does not preclude believers from petitioning officials to repent of their abuse, to return to their duties, and thus to restore the political freedom of religious believers. Calvin, in fact, opened his 1536 edition of the Institutes with precisely such a petition to King Francis of France, on behalf of the persecuted Protestants within his regime.[62] In his dedicatory epistle to Francis, he stated that, as a believer, he was compelled to "defend the church against [political] furies," to "embrace the common cause of all believers."[63] Against "overbearing tyranny," Calvin later put it, a Christian must "venture boldly to groan for freedom."[64]

Calvin set forth no declaration of religious liberty in his dedicatory epistle; such an act would have been suicide given the political climate of the day. Instead, he cleverly singled out those abuses of Protestants that defied widely-recognized rights and freedoms, particularly criminal procedural

---

[60] Ibid., chap. 6.54.

[61] Ibid., chap. 6.55–56. Calvin did allow for "magistrates, appointed by the people to restrain the willfulness of kings"—a text which became a *locus classicus* for later Calvinist theories of resistance, revolution, and regicide. See generally Julian H. Franklin, *Constitutionalism and Resistance in the Sixteenth Century* (New York: Pegasus, 1969); Michael Walzer, *The Revolution of the Saints: A Study in the Origins of Radical Politics* (Cambridge, MA: Harvard Univ. Press, 1965); Ernst Wolf, "Das Problem des Widerstandsrechts bei Calvin," in Arthur Kaufmann & Leonhard E. Backmann (hrsg.), *Widerstandrecht* (Darmstadt: Wissenschaftliche Buchgesellschaft, 1972), 152–169.

[62] According to some interpreters, this may also have been one of his goals in drafting his *Commentary on Seneca's De Clementia*. See, e.g., Beyerhaus, *Studien zur Staatsanschauung Calvins*, 160ff., calling the tract a *"Tendenzschrift"* addressed to the pressing problems of persecution and political abuse in Calvin's day; Doumergue, *Jean Calvin*, 1:211ff., arguing that Calvin's commentary was a protest against religious persecution, an appeal for royal clemency and restraint, and, as such "a magnificent manifesto on liberty" for persecuted Protestants. But cf. criticisms in Breen, *John Calvin: A Study in French Humanism*, 80ff. Whatever Calvin's actual intent in 1532, he certainly adopted much of the same style of argumentation for political liberty of Christians in his dedicatory letter in the 1536 *Institutes*. Moreover, many of the passages in his *Commentary on Seneca's De Clementia* counselling political magistrates to respect their offices and thereby to protect the liberty of their political subjects have close parallels in various editions of Calvin's *Institutes*. See the convenient table in *Calvin's Commentary on Seneca's De Clementia*, appendix 4, 393–395.

[63] [Dedicatory Epistle] to the Most Mighty and Most Illustrious Monarch Francis, Most Christian King of the French, His Esteemed Prince and Lord, in *Institutes* (1536).

[64] J. Bonnet, ed., *Letters of John Calvin* (Philadelphia: Presbyterian Board of Publication, 1858), 1: 467.

rights. Calvin protested the widespread and unchecked instances of "perjury," "lying slanders," "wicked accusations," and the "fury of evil men" that conspired to incite "public hatred" and "open violence" against believers. He protested that "the case" of the evangelicals "has been handled with no order of law and with violent heat rather than judicial gravity." He protested various forms of false imprisonment and abuses of prisoners. "Some of us are shackled with irons, some beaten with rods, some led about as laughing stocks, some proscribed, some most savagely tortured, some forced to flee." He protested the many procedural inequities. Protestants are "fraudulently and undeservedly charged with treason and villainy." They are convicted for capital offenses, "without confession or sure testimony." "[B]loody sentences are meted out against this doctrine without a hearing." He protested the bias of judges and partiality of the proceedings. "Those who sit in judgment . . . pronounce as sentences the prejudices which they have brought from home." He protested the intrusions on the church's freedoms of assembly and speech. "The poor little church has either been wasted with cruel slaughter or banished into exile, or so overwhelmed by threats and fears that it dare not even open its mouth." All these offenses stood diametrically opposed to basic political freedoms recognized at the time both in the Empire and in France.[65] "[A] very great question is at stake," Calvin declared to King Francis: "how God's glory may be kept safe on earth, how God's truth may retain its place of honor, how Christ's kingdom may be kept in good repair among us."[66]

Calvin sought no absolute political liberty for religious believers. He was fully aware of fraudulent and excessive religious exercises. He urged his fellow believers to "to keep within its own limits all that liberty which is promised and offered to us in Christ."[67] He likewise urged Francis and other political officials to root out the imposter and the impious: "[I]f any persons raise a tumult under the pretext of the gospel, . . . if any depict the license of their own vices as the liberty of God's grace, there are laws and legal penalties by which they may be severely restrained according to their deserts. Only let not the gospel of God be blasphemed," nor those who adhere to it be defamed.[68]

Calvin's early formulations on religious liberty revealed a bold and brilliant young mind at work. Calvin had mastered the intricacies of the

---

[65] For good general treatments, see John H. Langbein, *Prosecuting Crime in the Renaissance: England, Germany, France* (Cambridge, MA: Harvard Univ. Press, 1974); Adhemar Esmein, *A History of Continental Criminal Procedure with Special Reference to France*, repr. ed. (South Hackensack, NJ: Rothman Reprints, 1968).

[66] *Institutes* (1536), dedicatory epistle.

[67] Ibid., chap. 6.35.

[68] Ibid., dedicatory epistle.

Lutheran two kingdoms theory, and converted it to his own use. He had charted a course between the radical antinomianism and radical legalism of his day. He had crafted a theory that balanced freedom and order, liberty and law both within the church and within the state. He had provided a lean and learned apologia for religious liberty that would inspire fellow evangelicals for generations, indeed centuries, to come. This was no small achievement for a man newly converted to the evangelical cause and still in his early twenties.

Calvin's early formulations on religious liberty did betray considerable casuistry, however. Calvin may have reconciled the dialectic of law and liberty, of legalism and antinomianism in his early writings. But to reconcile one dialectic he introduced many others. He drew clear and easy lines between the heavenly and earthly kingdoms, the spiritual and the political life, the coercion and counsel of the law, the essential and indifferent matters of faith, the pious and impious canons of the church, the equitable and inequitable statutes of the state, the governance of the "manifestation" but not of the "manner" of religion, the duty to obey versus the right to petition the magistrate, among many other dualities. To be sure, such line-drawing followed the prevailing humanist methodology used by the leading theologians and jurists of the time.[69] And Calvin was convinced that his "readers, assisted by the very clarity of the arrangement, will better understand" the subject.[70] But such line-drawing did little to produce the authoritative synthesis on religious liberty to which Calvin aspired. Why should Calvin's line-drawing be any more authoritative than a millennium of line-drawing by the Catholic Church? How should the pious believer, cleric, or magistrate, untutored in humanist dialectics, parse and police these fine distinctions in their private and professional lives? Calvin did not say.

Calvin's early formulations on religious liberty were not only casuistic, they were also incomplete. Catholic and Protestant writers of the day viewed religious liberty in both individual and institutional terms. Calvin focussed

---

[69] See generally Neal W. Gilbert, *Renaissance Concepts of Method* (New York: Columbia Univ. Press, 1960). For an important Lutheran antecedent to this method, see *Dialectices Philippi Melanchthonis Libri IIII* (Lugduni, 1534) and id., *Erotemata Dialectices* (1547), reprinted in G.C. Bretschneider, ed., *Philippi Melanchthonis opera quae supersunt omnia* (Halle: C. A. Schwetschke et filium, 1846), 20: 511. For legal antecedents, see discussion in Roderich von Stintzing, *Geschichte der deutschen Rechtswissenschaft* (München/Leipzig: R. Oldenbourg, 1880), 88ff., 241ff. Calvin's contemporary Peter Ramus (1515–1572), whom fellow Calvinists lionized, had developed this line-drawing methodology to such a level of refinement that much of human knowledge was being pressed into an endless series of binary opposites. See generally, Walter J. Ong, *Ramus, Method and the Decay of Dialogue* (Cambridge, MA: Harvard Univ. Press, 1958); W.S. Howell, *Logic and Rhetoric in England* (Princeton: Princeton Univ. Press, 1956); J.J. ver Donk, *Petrus Ramus en de Wiskunde* (Assen: Van Gorcum, 1966).

[70] *Institutes* (1536), chap. 6.38.

principally on the individual and his spiritual liberty vis-à-vis the church and political liberty vis-à-vis the state. He had relatively little to say about the relationships per se of church and state, clergy and magistracy, prelate and prince. Calvin's treatment of church-state relations was derivative of his theory of individual religious liberty in this early period. He seemed content to shorten the legal arm of the church and to lengthen the legal arm of the state. He also seemed content to assign the church to the heavenly kingdom and the state to the earthly kingdom, and to assume that the ontological distinctions between these two kingdoms would provide ample direction and division for ecclesiastical and political officials.

Later Formulations.—Calvin's later formulations on religious liberty had the opposite tendency. As his thinking matured, and he took up his pastoral and advisory duties in Geneva, Calvin began to think in more integrated and more institutional terms. He blurred the lines between the earthly kingdom and heavenly kingdom, between spiritual and political life, law, and liberty. He also focussed more closely and concretely on the institutional responsibilities and relationships of church and state. Whereas the religious liberty of the individual had been a principal concern of Calvin's in the 1530s, religious liberty of the church took priority and precedence thereafter—to the point where the individual's religious freedom would have to yield to the church's in the event of conflict. This new priority was no more clearly demonstrated than in Calvin's actions in the infamous case of Michael Servetus.

It must be emphasized that in his later writings Calvin faithfully repeated his early formulations on religious liberty for the individual. He continued to insist on the cardinal distinction between the "spiritual kingdom" and the "political kingdom."[71] He continued to insist on the spiritual liberty of believers from the coercion of the spiritual law and from superstitious human traditions, and indeed bolstered his earlier arguments with ample new biblical support.[72] He continued to insist on the political liberty of the believer vis-à-vis the political official and civil law. In fact, he peppered his later sermons and commentaries with general endorsements of political liberty for believers

---

[71] *Institutes* (1559), bk. 3, chap. 19.15; bk. 4, chap. 20.1. But note that Calvin now tended to view the two kingdoms theory simply as an expression of the traditional Catholic concept of the inner forum (governed by penitential rules) versus external forum (governed by canon law rules). See above note 24. For Catholic antecedents, see Winfried Trusen, "Forum internum und gelehrtes Recht im Spätmittelalter," *Zeitschrift der Savigny-Stiftung (Kan. Ab.)* 57 (1971): 83.

[72] Ibid., bk. 3, chap. 19.1–8, 14.

and non-believers alike. "There is nothing more desirable than liberty."[73] Liberty is "an inestimable good,"[74] "a singular benefit and treasure that cannot be prized enough,"[75] something that is worth "more than half of life."[76] "How great a benefit liberty is, when God has bestowed it on someone."[77] Calvin emphasized the importance of political suffrage and the franchise in the political community. The "right to vote," he once said, is the "best way to preserve liberty."[78] "Let those whom God has given liberty and the franchise use it."[79] "[T]he reason why tyrannies have come into the world, why people everywhere have lost their liberty . . . is that people who had elections abused the privilege."[80] "I freely admit," Calvin wrote in summary of his position, "that there is no kind of government more salutary than one in which liberty is properly exercised with becoming moderation and properly constituted on a durable basis."[81] Many such passages occur in Calvin's later writings, both formal and informal.[82] Calvin never lost his appetite for the spiritual and political liberty of the individual.

Calvin, however, wove these familiar refrains on individual liberty into robust new orchestrations on law and order. He still insisted that liberty and law, freedom and order belong together. But the law and order side of the equation took prominence in his later writings as he struggled to define the functions and interrelationships of moral, political, and ecclesiastical laws and structures within both the heavenly and the earthly kingdoms. By the time of his 1559 Institutes, Calvin had in effect superimposed on the Lutheran two kingdoms theory his own variant of the Catholic two swords theory. He had assigned the church a legal role in the governance of the earthly kingdom, and the state a moral role in the governance of the heavenly kingdom. At the same time, he had rendered obedience to church officials and law both a spiritual and a civic duty, and obedience to political officials and law both a civic and spiritual duty. Such new sentiments left his familiar views on individual religious liberty both scattered and somewhat indeterminate.

---

[73] Comm. Genesis 39: 1, CO, 23: 502.

[74] Homilies on I Samuel, CO, 29: 544, 30: 185.

[75] Comm. Deut. 18: 14–18, CO, 27: 459.

[76] Comm. Deut. 24.7, CO, 24: 627–628.

[77] Homilies on I Samuel, CO, 29: 555.

[78] Harmony of the Last Four Books of Moses, CO 24: 697.

[79] Sermons on Deut. 18: 14–18, CO 27: 458–460.

[80] Sermons on Deut.5: 18–19, CO, 27, 410–411.

[81] Institutes (1543), chap. 20.7.

[82] See additional such passages in Höpfl, The Christian Polity of John Calvin, 156–60; John T. McNeill, "The Democratic Element in Calvin's Thought," Church History 18 (1949): 153.

The following sections gather up the scattered discussions of religious liberty vis-à-vis (1) the moral law; (2) the positive laws of the state; and (3) the positive laws of the church.

(1) Liberty and Moral Law.—At the foundation of Calvin's later formulations was a newly expanded theory of the moral law, which God in his sovereignty uses to govern both the heavenly and earthly kingdoms.[83] Calvin described the "moral law" much as he had described the "spiritual law" before—as moral commandments, engraved on the conscience, repeated in the Scripture, and summarized in the Decalogue.[84] He used widely varying (and sometimes confusing) terminology to describe this moral law—"the voice of nature," the "engraven law," "the law of nature," "the natural law," the "inner mind," the "rule of equity," the "natural sense," "the sense of divine judgment," "the testimony of the heart," the "inner voice," among other terms.[85] Calvin never developed a systematic taxonomy of these terms or natural law theory akin to that of fellow reformers like Philipp Melanchthon, Johann Oldendorp, or Richard Hooker.[86] Calvin generally used these terms synonymously to describe the norms created and communicated

---

[83] On the importance of the sovereignty of God in Calvin's later writings, see *Institutes* (1559), bk. 1 and discussion in Bohatec, *Budé und Calvin*, 306–345; Beyerhaus, *Studien zur Staatsanschauung Calvins*, 48–107.

[84] *Institutes* (1559), bk. 2, chaps. 7.1, 8.1, bk. 4, chap. 20.15.

[85] Among many other references, see *Institutes* (1559), bk. 2, chaps. 2.22, 7.3–4, 10, 8.1–2; bk. 3, chap. 19.15–16; bk. 4, chap. 20.3, 15, 16; Comm. Rom. 2: 14–15; Sermons on Deuternonomy 19: 14–15, CO, 34: 503ff.; Comm. Harmony of the Four Books of Moses, CO, 24: 209–260; Sermons on the Ten Commandments (Deut. 4: 44–6:4), in CO, 26: 236–432, translated as *John Calvin's Sermons on the Ten Commandments*, trans. and ed. Benjamin W. Farley (Grand Rapids: Baker Book House, 1980). See discussion in Erik Wolf, "Theologie und Sozialordnung bei Calvin," in Erik Wolf, *Rechtstheologische Studien* (Frankfurt am Main: Vittorio Klostermann, 1972), 3, 12–15; I. John Hesselink, *Calvin's Concept of the Law* (Allison Park, PA: Pickwick Publications, 1992), 18–24, 51–85; Höpfl, *The Christian Polity of John Calvin*, 179–180; Jürgen Baur, *Gott, Recht und weltliches Regiment im Werke Calvins* (Bonn, 1965), 26–75; Bohatec, *Calvin und das Recht*, 1–93; John T. McNeill, "Natural Law and the Teaching of the Reformers," *Journal of Religion* 26 (1946): 168.

[86] On Melanchthon's and Oldendorp's formulations, see discussion and literature in Berman and Witte, "The Transformation of Western Legal Philosophy in the Lutheran Reformation," 1611–1635, 1638–1642. On Richard Hooker's formulations, see *Laws of Ecclesiastical Polity* (1586), bk. 1, reprinted in *The Folger Library Edition of the Works of Richard Hooker*, ed. W. Speed Hill (Cambridge: Belknap Press of Harvard Univ. Press, 1977), vol. 1 and discussion in A.P. d'Entrevés, *The Medieval Contribution to Political Thought: Marsilius of Padua and Richard Hooker* (London: Oxford Univ. Press, 1939). For a comparison of Hooker's and Calvin's views, see August Lang, "The Reformation and Natural Law," in *Calvin and the Reformation* (London, 1909), 56–98; P.D.L. Avis, "Richard Hooker and John Calvin," *Journal of Ecclesiastical History* 32 (1981): 19–28.

by God for the governance of humanity, for the right ordering of individual and social lives. He considered the commandments of the Decalogue to be the fullest expression of the moral law,[87] but he grounded many other human customs and habits in this moral law as well.[88]

God makes "three uses of the moral law" in governing humanity, said Calvin, invoking the classic Protestant doctrine of the "uses of the law," which he had mentioned in passing in his earlier writings.[89] First, God uses the moral law theologically—to condemn all persons in their consciences and to compel them to seek his liberating grace. Here Calvin expanded on his earlier discussion of the dialectic between spiritual law and spiritual liberty. By setting forth a model of perfect righteousness, the moral law "warns, informs, convicts, and lastly condemns every man of his own unrighteousness."[90] The moral law thereby punctures his vanity, diminishes his pride, and drives him to despair. Such despair, Calvin believed, is a necessary precondition for the sinner to seek God's help and to have faith in

---

[87] See esp. his commentary on the Decalogue in *Institutes* (1559), bk. 2, chap. 8; Harmony of the Last Four Books of Moses, CO 24: 262–724; and Sermons on the Ten Commandments, CO, 26: 236–432.

[88] These included the headship of the husband to the wife and children (Comm. I Cor. 7: 37; Eph. 5: 31; I Tim. 2), the sanctity of monogamy (Comm. Gen. 26: 10; 38 :24), the duty to take care of the family (Comm. I Tim. 5: 8), breast-feeding (Comm. Gen. 21: 8), primogeniture (Comm. Gen. 27: 11), the obligation to keep promises (Comm. I Cor. 9: 1), the laws of impediments in marriage (Harmony of the Last Four Books of Moses), the need for witnesses in capital murder cases (Ibid.), the need for class distinctions in society (Ibid.), natural law prohibitions against incest (Comm. Gen. 29: 27), murder (Harmony of the Last Four Books of Moses), adultery (Comm. Genesis 26: 10), and slavery (Comm. Genesis 12: 15; Comm. Eph. 6: 1). See discussion and notes in Höpfl, *The Christian Polity of John Calvin*, 180.

[89] For discussion of this doctrine, see John Witte, Jr. and Thomas C. Arthur, "The Three Uses of the Law: A Protestant Source of the Purposes of Criminal Punishment?" *Journal of Law and Religion* 10 (1994): 433 and sources cited therein. For antecedents in Calvin's earlier writings, see *Institutes* (1536), bk. 1.33; *Calvin's Commentaries on Seneca's De Clementia*, bk. 1, chap. 2.2 (Latin text, 24–25, Battles and Hugo trans., 73–77); bk. 1, chap. 22.1 (Latin text, 124–126, Battles and Hugo trans., 301–307). The latter text suggests that Calvin derived his theology of the uses of the moral law not only from his biblical and theological studies but also from his earlier legal and political studies. In this 1532 work, Calvin endorsed classic Greek and Roman doctrines of the purposes, aims, or uses of criminal law and punishment. Both Plato and Seneca had defined these as "retribution," "deterrence," and "rehabilitation." which correspond roughly to Calvin's understanding of the "theological," "civil," and "educational," uses of the moral law. See Plato *Laws*, 9.6 862 E, 11.11 932 C; Plato *Gorgias*, 81, 525B and *Calvin's Commentary on Seneca's De Clementia*, 75, 305. See Seneca, *De Clementia*, bk. 1, chap. 22.1, with *Calvin's Commentary on Seneca's De Clementia*, 301–307. See also the translator's notes in ibid., 137*. For the later elaboration of this analogy between the theological doctrine of the uses of the moral law, and the purposes of the criminal law, see Witte and Arthur, "The Three Uses of the Law."

[90] *Institutes* (1559), bk. bk. 2., chap. 7.6.

God's grace. "[I]t is as if someone's face were all marked up so that everybody who saw him might laugh at him. Yet he himself is completely unaware of his condition. But if they bring him a mirror, he will be ashamed of himself, and will hide and wash himself when he sees how filthy he is."[91] The moral law is that mirror. It drives persons to seek the cleansing "spiritual liberty" that is available to them through faith in God's grace—the liberty of conscience from the condemnation of the moral law.[92]

Second, God uses the moral law civilly—to restrain the sinfulness of non-believers, those who have not accepted his grace. "[T]he law is like a halter," Calvin wrote, "to check the raging and otherwise limitlessly ranging lusts of the flesh. . . . Hindered by fright or shame, sinners dare neither execute what they have conceived in their minds, nor openly breathe forth the rage of their lust."[93] The moral law imposes upon them a "constrained and forced righteousness"[94] or a "civil righteousness."[95] Though their consciences are "untouched by any care for what is just and right," the very threat of divine punishment compels sinners to obey the basic duties of the moral law—to fear God, to rest on the Sabbath, to avoid blasphemy, idolatry, and profanity, to obey authorities, to respect their neighbor's person, property, and relationships, to remain sexually continent, to speak truthfully of themselves and their neighbors.[96]

God coerces sinful consciences to adopt such "civil righteousness" in order to preserve a measure of order and liberty in the sin-ridden earthly kingdom. "Unless there is some restraint, the condition of wild beasts would be better and more desirable than ours," Calvin wrote.[97] Persons need the God-given constraints of conscience in order to survive in "a public community."[98] "Liberty would always bring ruin with it, if it were not bridled by the moderation" born of the moral law.[99] And again: "We can be truly and genuinely happy not only when liberty is granted to us, but also when God

91 Comm. Galatians 3: 19, CO, 5: 535. See also *Institutes*, bk. 2, chap. 7.8. Calvin also liked to use the image of the sinner as debtor, incapable of discharging his debt. See, e.g., Sermon on Deut. 5: 23–27, CO, 26: 396.

92 *Institutes* (1559), bk. 2, chap. 7.8–9; bk. 3, chap. 19.3–6; Harmony of the Last Four Books of Moses, CO, 24: 725; Comm. Gal. 5: 13, CO, 50: 250.

93 *Institutes* (1559), bk. 2, chap. 7.10.

94 Ibid.

95 Ibid., bk. 4. chap. 20.3.

96 Ibid., bk. 2, chap. 8.6–10; Harmony of the Last Four Books of Moses, CO, 24:725ff.; *Sermons on the Ten Commandments*, CO, 26: 236ff.

97 Comm. Jer. 30:9, CO, 38: 617. See also Hesselink, *Calvin's Concept of the Law*, 249–251.

98 *Institutes* (1559), bk. 2, chap. 7.10.

99 Comm. Jer. 30: 9, CO, 38: 617.

prescribes a certain rule and arranges for a certain public order among us so that there may be no confusion."[100]

Third, God uses the moral law educationally—to teach believers, those who have accepted his grace, the means and measures of sanctification, of spiritual development. "We are not our own," says Calvin quoting St. Paul. "[T]he faithful are not given liberty to do whatever seems good to them and that each one follow his own appetite."[101] Even the most devout saints, though free from the condemnation of the moral law, still need to follow the commandments "to learn more thoroughly . . . the Lord's will [and] to be aroused to obedience."[102] The law teaches them not only the "civil righteousness" that is common to all persons, but also the "spiritual righteousness" that is becoming of sanctified Christians. As a teacher, the law not only coerces them against violence and violation, but also cultivates in them charity and love. It not only punishes harmful acts of murder, theft, and fornication, but also prohibits evil thoughts of hatred, covetousness, and lust.[103] Such habits of "spiritual righteousness" are not to be exercised in the heavenly kingdom alone. They are to imbue all aspects of the life of the believer—spiritual and temporal, ecclesiastical and political, private and public. Calvin stressed that Christians must take their faith and conscience directly into the political, public, and external life of the earthly kingdom, "as ambassadors and stewards of the treasure of salvation, of the covenant of God, ... of the secrets of God."[104] By so doing, they not only allow God's glory and image to shine in the earthly kingdom, but they also induce its sinful citizens to seek God's grace.[105]

Calvin's expanded theory of the uses of the moral law of human conscience laid important groundwork for the expansion of political liberty and civil rights. In his earlier writings, Calvin had argued that God imposes various duties on the political office, and that these duties also "constitute" the political liberties of their subjects in the earthly kingdom. When political officials respect the God-given duties of their office, the political liberties of their subjects are amply protected. Now, Calvin argued that God imposes

---

[100] Ibid.

[101] Sermon on Deut. 5:4–7, in CO, 26: 247 and *John Calvin's Sermons on the Ten Commandments*, 63. For the implications of this sentiment for Calvin's doctrine of "free will" of Christians, see the excellent discussion in Bohatec, *Budé und Calvin*, 351–372.

[102] *Institutes* (1559), bk. 2, chap. 7.12.

[103] Ibid., bk. 2, chap. 8.6;

[104] Sermon on Deut. 5: 22, CO, 26: 384 and *John Calvin's Sermons on the Ten Commandments*, 251.

[105] Ibid., bk. 2, chap. 8.51; bk. 3, chaps. 3.9, 6.1, 17.5, 6.1; Comm. I Peter 1: 14, CO, 55: 221

various duties not just on political officials, but on all persons in the earthly kingdom. These include the moral duties, set out in the Decalogue, to respect the person, property, reputation, and relationships of their neighbors. When members of the earthly kingdom respect these God-given duties of communal living, the civil freedoms of their neighbors are amply protected. It was only a short step from this theory of political and civil duties to a theory of subjective civil rights and political freedoms. A person's duty to his neighbor could be easily cast as the neighbor's right to have that duty discharged. A political official's duty to rule citizens justly could be easily cast as the citizen's freedom from unjust rule. Calvin did not take this step into the realm of subjective rights. But his immediate followers, building directly on Calvin's theology, took this step quite easily, calling for a full panoply of civil rights and political liberties at least for Christians.[106]

Calvin's expanded theory of the moral law also laid the groundwork for the expansion of spiritual liberty. Earlier, Calvin had been largely content to view the dialectic of spiritual law and spiritual liberty as a matter of the heavenly kingdom alone. As a consequence, he insisted that liberty of conscience was "a wholly spiritual thing" and could not be construed as a political freedom. Now, with his new emphasis on the omnicompetence of God's sovereignty, Calvin drew the spiritual dialectic of law and liberty into the earthly kingdom as well. God's moral law governs both the heavenly and the earthly kingdoms. Christians are given liberty of conscience to follow this moral law as citizens of both kingdoms. As Calvin put it: "We obtain liberty in order that we may more promptly and more readily obey God in all things," spiritual and temporal.[107] These premises could lead easily to the conclusion that liberty of conscience must be an absolute guarantee in both the heavenly and earthly kingdoms, at least for Christians. Calvin dithered on

---

106 See generally, David Little, "Reformed Faith and Religious Liberty," in Donald R. McKim, *Major Themes in the Reformed Tradition* (Grand Rapids, MI: W. B. Eerdmans, 1992), 196, 200–206; Winthrop S. Hudson, "Democratic Freedom and Religious Faith in the Reformed Tradition," *Church History* 15 (1946): 193; Heinz Schilling, "Calvinismus und Freiheitrechte," *Bijdragen en Mededelingen betreffende de Geschiedenis der Nederlanden* 198 (1987): 403; John Witte, Jr., ed., *Christianity and Democracy in Global Context* (Boulder: Westview Press, 1993), 4–7. For earlier studies, see the compilation in Hermann Vahle, "Calvinismus und Demokratie im Spiegel der Forschung," *Archiv für Reformationsgeschichte* 66 (1975): 183. The doctrine of subjective rights, of course, was not invented by later Calvinists; it was formulated at canon law already in the twelfth and thirteenth centuries, if not before. See Brian Tierney, *Religion, Law, and the Growth of Constitutional Thought, 1150–1650* (Cambridge: Cambridge Univ. Press, 1982), and the dissertation of his student, Charles J. Reid, Jr., "Rights in Thirteenth Century Canon Law: An Historical Investigation" (Ph.D. Diss. Cornell, 1994).

107 Comm. on I Peter 2: 16, CO, 55: 206. See also Institutes (1559), bk. 3, chap. 17.1–2 and discussion in Hesselink, *Calvin's Concept of the Law*, 259–260.

this point—in part constrained by his own strong rhetoric against the antinomianism of the Anabaptists and for the exclusively spiritual character of Christian liberty.[108] His followers, particularly the Dutch pietists and English Puritans, drew this conclusion quite easily.[109]

(2) *Liberty and the Laws of the State.*—In his later writings, Calvin expanded the place and purpose not only of moral law but also of positive law in the two kingdoms. Earlier, Calvin had recognized as positive law only the "political law" of the state, whose authority is rooted in the moral law, and whose jurisdiction is strictly limited to the earthly kingdom. Now, Calvin recognized as positive law both the political law of the state and the ecclesiastical law of the church. Both the state and the church are legal entities, Calvin argued. Each institution has its own forms of organization and order, and its own norms of discipline and rule. Each is called to play a distinct role in the enforcement of Godly government in the community. Each provides "external means or aids through which God invites us into communion with Christ, and keeps us there."[110] Each institution participates in the elaboration of Godly moral law and the enforcement of its inherent "uses." Each helps to define, and to delimit, the province of religious liberty.

God has vested in the state "the temporal power of the sword," said Calvin. As before, Calvin insisted that the magistrate is the vice-regent of God; that he must rule with written positive laws rooted in tradition and morality and guided by equity and justice; that citizens must obey him and his law up to the limits of Christian conscience.[111] But now Calvin offered

---

[108] Compare *Institutes* (1559), bk. 3, chap. 19.14–16 with Ibid., bk. 4, chap. 10.5.

[109] See sources cited supra note 106. See further discussion in O.J. DeJong, "Union and Religion," *The Low Countries History Yearbook* (1981): 29–49.; Karl Schwarz, "Der Begriff Exercitium Religionis Privatum," *Zeitschrift der Savigny-Stiftung* (Kan. Ab.) 105 (1988): 495–518.

[110] *Institutes* (1559), subtitle of bk. 4. ("de externis mediis vel adminiculuis quibus deus in Christi societatem nos invitat et in ea retinet"). It was only in this final edition of the *Institutes* that Calvin clearly defined church and state, together, "as external means" of grace, thereby effectively eclipsing the two kingdoms theory. See also above notes 24 and 71. In the 1536 edition, he had treated in one chapter the topics of "Christian Liberty," "Ecclesiastical Power," and "Political Administration," with strong emphasis on the organic connections among the topics. See *Institutes* (1536), chap. 6. In subsequent editions of his *Institutes*, he had broken up these three topics into separate chapters— taking up "Christian Freedom" in the context of soteriology, "Ecclesiastical Power" in the context of the sacraments, "Political Administration" in the context of the Christian life. See the 1539, 1543, 1545, 1550, 1553, and 1554 editions in CO, 1: 252–1151.

[111] See generally, *Institutes* (1559), bk. 4., chap. 20. In his commentary on the Decalogue, Calvin explained more thoroughly than before the reason that Christians must obey the magistrate up to the limits of conscience:

some refinements both to the structure and to the purpose of political government and law. These refinements, though they did not yield a comprehensive political theory, were pregnant with political implications, which later Protestants helped to deliver.

The *structure* of political governments must be "self-limiting," Calvin said, so that "rulers are checkmated by their own officers" and offices.[112] Such inherent political restraints rarely exist in a monarchy, Calvin believed, for monarchs too often lack self-discipline and self-control, and betray too little appetite for justice, prudence, and Christian virtue.[113] "If one could uncover the hearts of monarchs," Calvin wrote late in his life, "he would hardly find one in a hundred who does not likewise despise everything divine."[114] Thus, "it is safer and more tolerable that government be in the hands of a number of persons who help each other,"[115] such as prevails in an aristocracy, or even better in "a [mixed] system comprised of aristocracy, tempered by democracy."[116] What Calvin had in mind was rule by the "best characters," by the spiritual and moral elite, who were elected to their offices.[117] Mere division of political authority, however, was an insufficient safeguard against political tyranny. Calvin thus encouraged all magistrates to govern through local agencies, to adhere to precedent and written rules, to divide their power among various self-checking branches and officials, to stand periodically for elections, to hold regular popular meetings in order to give account of themselves and to give air to popular concerns.[118] Though Calvin never

---

Now insofar as God has given us in one phrase and in one brief summary the rule to obey all [our] superiors, let us mark that in so doing he does not resign his right. . . . When we are commanded to be obedient to our superiors, the exception remains that nonetheless this must not detract from any of those prerogatives which belong to God, which already been treated in the first table. For we know that the service by which God is worshiped must precede everything else.

Comm. Deut. 5: 16, CO, 26: 309 and *John Calvin's Sermons on the Ten Commandments*, 141–142.

[112] Sermons on II Samuel (1562), in *Supplementa Calvinia*, 1:55.

[113] See, e.g., Sermons on Job 10: 16–17 and Job 19: 26–29, CO, 33: 503, 24: 138; Sermons on Deut. 17: 16–20, CO 27: 479. See the numerous excerpts from other writings collected in Beyerhaus, *Studien zur Staatsanschauung Calvins*, 109–115.

[114] Lectures on Daniel (1561), quoted in McNeill, "The Democratic Element," 159.

[115] Sermon on Deut. 18: 14–18, CO: 28: 459–460.

[116] *Institutes* (1543), chap. 17; *Institutes* (1559), chap. 20.8.

[117] McNeill, "The Democratic Element," 162.

[118] See, e.g., *Institutes* (1559), bk. 4, chap. 20.10–11, 31; Comm. Romans 13: 1–10, CO, 49: 248–251 and discussion in Bohatec, *Calvins Lehre von Staat und Kirche*, 116ff., 619ff.; McNeill, "John Calvin on Civil Government," 24ff.; Höpfl, *The Christian Polity of*

synthesized these various "democratic elements" of political theory,[119] his followers in the Netherlands, England, and New England wove them into a comprehensive theory of political democracy.[120]

The *purpose* of political government and law is, in essence, to help God achieve the civil use of the moral law—to cultivate civil restraint and civil righteousness in all persons, if necessary through the coercive power of the sword. Calvin described this function in various ways. Magistrates are "ordained protectors and vindicators of public innocence, modesty, decency, and tranquility; their sole endeavor should be to provide for the common safety and peace of all."[121] Magistrates have as their "appointed end" "to adjust our life to the society of men, to form our social behavior to civil righteousness, to reconcile us one with another, and to promote general peace and tranquility."[122] Calvin made clear that such magisterial cultivation of the civil use of the law was inherently limited. "It is true that when magistrates create laws, their manner is different from God's. But then their purpose has to do only with the way we govern ourselves with respect to the external civil order to the end that no one might be violated and each might have his rights [protected] and have peace and concord among men. That is their intention when they create laws. And why? [Because] they are mortal men; they cannot reform inner and hidden affections. That belongs to God."[123]

The best means for the magistrate to help cultivate the civil use of the moral law, said Calvin, is through direct enforcement of the provisions and principles of the Decalogue. The magistrate is the "custodian of both tables" of the Decalogue, said Calvin.[124] He is responsible to govern both the

---

John Calvin, 160ff.; M.E. Chenevière, *La pensée politique de Calvin*, repr. ed. (Geneva: Slatkine Reprints, 1970), 181ff.

[119] See McNeill, "The Democratic Element" and Robert M. Kingdon, "Calvinism and Democracy," in John H. Bratt, ed., *The Heritage of John Calvin* (Grand Rapids: Eerdmans, 1973), 177.

[120] See discussion and sources in Harold J. Berman, "Law and Belief in Three Revolutions," *Valparaiso Law Review* 18 (1984): 569, 594–598; Witte, ed., *Christianity and Democracy in Global Context*, 5–7; id., "How to Govern a City on a Hill: The Early Puritan Contribution to American Constitutionalism," *Emory Law Journal* 39 (1990): 41–64; id., "The Plight of Canon Law in the Early Dutch Republic," in R.H. Helmholz, ed., *Canon Law in Protestant Lands* (Berlin: Duncker & Humblot, 1992), 135, 144–147.

[121] *Institutes* (1559), bk. 4. chap. 20.9.

[122] Ibid., bk. 4, chap. 20.2.

[123] Sermon on Deut. 5: 17, CO: 26: 321 and *John Calvin's Sermons on the Ten Commandments*, 159.

[124] *Institutes*, bk. 4, chap. 20.9. See also ibid., bk. 2, chap. 8.11–12; Harmony of the Four Books of Moses, CO, 24: 721–724. For a comparison of Calvin's division of the Commandments between these tables, and that of other Christian and Jewish writers, see Bo Reicke, *Die Zehn Worte in Geschichte und Gegenwart* (Tübingen: Mohr, 1973), 9–42.

relationships between persons and God, based on the first table of the Decalogue, and the multiple relationships among persons, based on the second table. Thus the magistrate is to promulgate laws against Sabbath-breaking, blasphemy, heresy, "idolatry, sacrilege against God's name, against his truth, and other public offenses against religion" that violate the principles of the first table.[125] He is "to defend the worship of God, and to execute vengeance upon those who profanely despise it, and on those who endeavor . . . to adulterate the true doctrine by their errors."[126] The magistrate is also to promulgate laws against homicide, theft, perjury, adultery, inchoate crimes, and other immorality that violate the principles of the second table.[127] By so doing, the magistrate coerces all persons, regardless of their faith, to respect and maintain the "civil righteousness" or "public morality" dictated by God's moral law.

Calvin was convinced that, through this exercise of Godly moral authority, the state magistrate enhances the ambit of religious liberty. By teaching each person the rudiments of Christian morality, even if by force, the magistrate enables those who later accept Christ to be "partially broken in, . . . not utterly untutored and uninitiated in Christian discipline" and discipleship.[128] By upholding minimal standards of Christian morality, the magistrate protects the "public manifestation of religion" and provides a public and peaceful space for Christianity and the church to flourish.[129] By purging the community of overt heretics, idolaters, and blasphemers, the magistrate protects the Godly character of the community and the sanctity of the Church and its members. Individual Christians and the church as a whole thus enjoy greater freedom to exercise the Christian faith.

Calvin did not enhance the magistrate's civil jurisdiction over religious and moral matters without establishing safeguards. First, magistrates were not "to make laws . . . concerning religion and the worship of God."[130] They were only to enforce God's law on religion and worship, especially as it was set forth in the first table of the Decalogue. This principle stood in marked

---

[125] *Institutes* (1559), bk. 4, chap. 20.3

[126] Serm. on Daniel 4: 1–3, CO, 40: 647–651. See discussion in Paul Woolley, "Calvin and Toleration," in John H. Bratt, ed., *The Heritage of John Calvin* (Grand Rapids, MI: Eerdmans, 1973), 137.

[127] Ibid.; see also ibid., bk. 2, chap. 8 and Harmony of the Four Books of Moses, CO, 24: 262–724 for detailed interpretation of the Decalogue as well as the summary in Calvin's *Instruction et confession de foy* (1537), reprinted as John Calvin, *Instruction in Faith*, trans. Paul T. Fuhrmann (Philadelphia: Westminster Press, 1949).

[128] *Institutes* (1559), bk. 2, chap. 8.10.

[129] Ibid., bk. 4, chap. 20.3.

[130] Ibid. (emphasis added).

contrast to both Lutheran and Anglican Protestants, who at the time vested in the magistrate the power to promulgate all manner of establishment and ecclesiastical laws. Second, magistrates were not to enforce God's laws indiscriminately. "We must not always reckon as contentious the man who does not acquiesce in our decisions, or who ventures to contradict us," said Calvin.[131] "We must exercise moderation; so as not instantly to declare every man to be a 'heretic' who does not agree with our opinion. There are some matters on which Christians may differ from each other, without being divided into sects."[132] Third, magistrates were not to enforce God's laws inequitably. Instead, they must seek to adjust their punishments to the capacities of each subject and the dangers of that person's crime. "All teachers have . . . a rule here which they are to follow . . . modestly and kindly to accommodate themselves to the capacities of the ignorant and the unlearned."[133]

> This is what he [Isaiah] means by the metaphor of the bruised reed, that he does not wish to break off and altogether crush these who are half-broken, but, on the contrary, to lift up and support them, so as to maintain and strengthen all that is good in them. We must neither crush the minds of the weak by excessive severity, nor encourage by our smooth language anything that is evil. But those who boldly and obstinately resist . . . must be broken and crushed.[134]

The one person whom Calvin helped the magistrate to "crush" was Michael Servetus—unleashing what has been called "one of the most famous controversies of modern times about religious freedom."[135] The facts are not contested. Servetus, an accomplished Spanish scientist and theologian, was best known in his day for two unrelated acts—the discovery of the circulation of blood in the lungs, and the publication of a 1531 tract, *Concerning the*

---

[131] Serm. I Cor. 11: 6, CO, 49: 722. See also Woolley, "Calvin and Toleration," 144–153.

[132] Comm. Titus 3: 10, CO, 52: 434–435.

[133] Comm. Rom. 1: 14, CO, 49: 18–19.

[134] Comm. Isa. 42: 3, CO, 37: 60–62.

[135] Josef Lecler, *Toleration and the Reformation* (London: Longmans, 1960), 1: 325. Among numerous writings on Servetus and his fate, see Roland H. Bainton, *Hunted Heretic: The Life and Death of Michael Servetus* (Boston: Beacon Press, 1953); Bainton, *The Travail of Religious Liberty*, 72ff.; Richard Nürnberger, "Calvin und Servet: Eine Begegnung zwischen reformatorischem Glauben und modernem Unglauben im 16. Jahrhundert," *Archiv für Reformationsgeschichte* 49 (1958): 196; Jerome Friedman, *Michael Servetus. A Case Study in Total Heresy* (Geneva: Droz, 1978); McNeill, *The History and Character of Calvinism*, 226ff.; Andrew Pettegree, "Michael Servetus and the Limits of Tolerance," *History Today* 40 (1990): 41.

Errors of the Trinity.[136] The latter act was the more controversial, for in his tract Servetus charged the Church with all manner of distortion and confusion in developing its doctrine of God as Father, Son, and Holy Spirit. The book was widely condemned, in Catholic and Protestant circles alike. When Servetus sent a copy to the bishop of Saragossa, the bishop referred him to the Inquisition, which ordered him to appear. Servetus disappeared, surfacing again in 1545, when he sent Calvin a letter posing several queries about the Trinity. Calvin answered his queries, and after several rounds of correspondence sent him a copy of the *Institutes* in an effort to persuade him of his errors. Servetus promptly returned the volume to Calvin, having annotated numerous corrections, and insulting comments in the margins.[137] Calvin broke off the correspondence, confiding ominously to a friend in a letter in 1546, that if Servetus "takes it upon himself to come hither [to Geneva], . . . I shall never permit him to depart alive." In 1553, Servetus published a *Restitutio* of his volume on the Trinity, which, again, was swiftly condemned by Protestants and Catholics. This time Servetus was arrested by Catholic authorities, and brought before the Inquisition. Calvin, among others, furnished the inquisitorial court with documentary evidence of Servetus' heresy and blasphemy, including the copy of his *Institutes* that Servetus had annotated. Servetus managed to escape from his inquisitors. During his flight, Servetus travelled through Geneva—one, but certainly not the only convenient stopping point along the way. On Sunday morning, he attended worship services at a church where Calvin was preaching. He was pointed out to Calvin who had him arrested by the Geneva magistracy. Servetus was indicted before the Geneva council for "horrible, shocking, scandalous, and infectious" heresy, in violation of prevailing local law as well as the law of Justinian. Calvin served as his first accuser and testified among others against him. Servetus, unrepresented by counsel in the case, was convicted. He was ordered to recant and repent. He refused, and was sentenced to death by slow fire at the stake. Calvin supported Servetus's plea for a more merciful means of execution. The magistrate refused, burning Servetus at the stake on October 27, 1553.[138]

Executions for heresy were hardly a novelty in the mid-sixteenth century, let alone in the centuries before. In the same decade of Servetus' death, Queen Mary of England executed some 273 Protestants who resisted her return to

---

[136] For other documents, see Roland H. Bainton, "Documenta Servetiana," *Archiv für Reformationsgeschichte* 44 (1953): 223; ibid., 45: 99.

[137] See collection in CO, 8: 645–720.

[138] For the proceedings, see CO, 8: 721–832 and *Registres de la Compagnie des Pasteurs de Genève au tempes de Calvin* 1553–1564 (Geneva: Droz, 1962), vol. 2, ("Accusation et Procès de Michel Servet").

Catholicism.[139] The following decade, the Duke of Alva, executed nearly 20,000 Dutch Protestants in an attempt to quiet the ferment for reformation in the Netherlands.[140] But executions for heresy were not known in Protestant Geneva, which in Calvin's day had become something of a haven for Protestant non-conformists from throughout Europe.[141] Of the 139 felons known to have been executed in Geneva between 1542 and 1564, Servetus was apparently the only one executed for heresy.[142] It was difficult to justify such executions using the strict biblical logic on which Calvin generally insisted. Banishment of heretics could be grounded easily in Scripture, but execution could not be.[143]

Calvin's critics, most notably Sebastian Castellio,[144] saw Servetus' execution as the inevitable consequence of Calvin's improper enhancement of

---

[139] Lecler, *Toleration and the Reformation,* 2: 351–352.

[140] M. Dierickx, "Die lijst der veroordeelden door de Raad van Beroerten," *Revue Belge de Philologie et d'Histoire* 60 (1962): 415.

[141] See William C. Innes, *Social Concern in Calvin's Geneva* (Allison Park, PA: Pickwick Publications, 1983), 205–219, on religious refugees in Geneva.

[142] Höpfl, *The Christian Polity of John Calvin,* 136. See also E.W. Monter, *Studies in Genevan Government (1536–1605)* (New York, 1967), 152–155; id., "Crime and Punishment in Calvin's Geneva, 1562," *Archiv für Reformationsgeschichte* 64 (1973): 281; Innes, *Social Concern in Calvin's Geneva,* 169n.

[143] See Höpfl, *The Christian Polity of John Calvin,* 172ff., 201ff. Höpfl shows that in his defense of the execution of Servetus, Calvin had to resort exclusively to a "natural law" argument, rather than his usual method of grounding his arguments in Scripture (sometimes supplementing them with natural law arguments). Höpfl writes:

> Perhaps the only contentious issues on which Calvin was prepared to call [exclusively] upon the oracle of natural law and naturalis sensus were the suppression of blasphemy and heresy, and the death-penalty for adultery. Calvin first made use of the former to justify the execution of Servetus; he was plainly on the defensive for adopting a policy which he condemned in papists, indeed for doing the papists' work for them, and had no New Testament support except of the most forced and labored kind. Under these circumstances he was prepared to adduce the *sensus naturae* as dictating that "in every well-ordered polity, religion must have pride of place and is to be preserved intact under the supervision of the laws, as even unbelievers confess.". . . But this was fairly feeble stuff with which to justify death-penalty among Christians.

Ibid., 182.

[144] Among numerous materials on Castellio, see, e.g., Roland H. Bainton, *Studies on the Reformation* (Boston: Beacon Press, 1963), 139–181 (chapter on "Sebastian Casteillo, Champion of Religious Liberty"); U. Plath, "Calvin und Castellio und die Frage der Religionsfreiheit," in Wilhelm H. Neuser, ed., *Calvinus Ecclesiae Genevensis Custos* (Frankfurt am Main: P. Lang, 1982), 191–195; Jean Runzo, "Sebastian Castellio's Scepticism and Religious Toleration," in Fred O. Francis and Raymond P. Wallace, eds., *Tradition as Openness to the Future: Essays in Honor of Willis W. Fisher* (Lanham, M: Univ. Press of America, 1984), 71–88; Werner Kaegi, *Castellio und die Anfänge der Toleranz* (Basel: Helbing & Lichtenhahn, 1953).

the state's power over "the public manifestation of religion." How is the magistrate to distinguish between God's law for religion, which he must enforce, and man's law for religion, which he may not? How is the magistrate to decide whether a doctrinal teaching is blasphemous, idolatrous, or heretical? How is the magistrate to be protected against undue influence by a theologian and pastor as formidable as Calvin? What purpose does civil discipline of such a person serve? "I hate heretics, too," Castellio wrote, as well as blasphemers, idolaters, and other apostates. "But . . . I see two great dangers. And the first is that he be held for a heretic who is not a heretic. This happened in former times, for Christ and his disciples were put to death as heretics, and there is grave reason to fear a recurrence of this in this century. . . . Great care must be exercised to distinguish those who are really seditious from Christians. Outwardly they do the same thing and are adjudged guilty of the same crimes by those who do not understand. Christ was crucified among thieves. The other danger is that he who is really a heretic be punished more severely or in a manner other than that required by Christian discipline."[145] Castellio rebelled particularly against Calvin's endorsement of Servetus' execution for espousing heretical doctrine. "[T]o kill a man is not to defend a doctrine, it is to kill a man. . . . Religious doctrine is not the affair of the magistrate, but of the doctor. What has the sword to do with doctrine?"[146]

Calvin found little convincing in such criticisms, and in his later years he defended his views with ever more bitter vitriol. It is here where Calvin's critics can find his most intemperate statements against religious liberty, and where Calvin casts a dark shadow on his otherwise sophisticated treatment of religious liberty. Calvin's interpretation of a passage about stoning false prophets illustrates his new bombast: "This law at first appears to be too severe. For merely having spoken should one be so punished? But if anybody slanders a mortal man he is punished and shall we permit a blasphemer of the living God to go unscathed? If a prince is injured, death appears to be insufficient for vengeance. And now when God, the sovereign emperor, is reviled by a word, is nothing to be done? God's glory and our salvation are so conjoined that a traitor to God is also an enemy of the human race and worse than a murderer because he brings poor souls to perdition. Some object that since the offense consists only in words, there is no need for such severity. But we muzzle dogs, and shall we leave men free to open their mouths as they

---

[145] Sebastian Castellio, *Concerning Heretics* (1554), ed. Roland H. Bainton (New York: Columbia Univ. Press, 1935), 126, quoting from "Dedication by Martin Bellius to Duke Christoph of Württemberg."

[146] Quoted by Roland H. Bainton, *Sebastian Castellio: Champion of Religious Liberty* (New York, 1951), 75.

please? Those who object are like dogs and swine. They murmur that they will go to America where nobody will bother them. God makes plain that the false prophet is to be stoned without mercy. We are to crush beneath our heel all affections of nature when his honor is involved. The father should not spare the child, nor the brother his sister, nor the brother his brother, nor the husband his own wife or the friend who is dearer to him than life. No human relationship is more than animal unless it be grounded in God."[147] Similar vitriol courses through Calvin's 1554 manifesto *Defense of the Orthodox Christian Faith . . . Against the Manifold Errors of Michael Servetus.*[148] These later utterances catch Calvin in a very dark and defensive mood, and can be used to cast him and his views on religious liberty in a very dark and sinister profile.

(3) *Liberty and the Laws of the Church.*—While God has vested in the state the coercive power of the sword, Calvin argued, He has vested in the church the spiritual power of the Word. God calls the members of the church to be his priests and prophets—to preach the Gospel, to administer the sacraments, to teach the young, to gather the saints, to care for the needy, to communicate God's word and will throughout the world.[149] The church is to be a beacon of light and truth, a bastion of ministry and mission. Just as pious Christians must take their faith into the world to reflect God's image and glory, so the church must take its ministry into the world to project God's message and majesty for all persons to behold.[150]

God has established his church with a distinct and independent polity, Calvin argued. The church's responsibilities must be divided among multiple offices and officers.[151] Ministers are to preach the word and administer the sacraments. Doctors are to catechize the young and to educate the parishioners. Elders are to maintain discipline and order and adjudicate

---

[147] Quoted by Bainton, The Travail of Religious Liberty, 68–69.

[148] CO, 8: 453–644.

[149] Ibid., bk. 4, chap. 1.1–11.

[150] *Institutes* (1559), bk. 4. chap. 1.7–17; Serm. Deut. 5: 22, CO, 26: 384 and *John Calvin's Sermons on the Ten Commandments*, 251–252.

[151] Ibid., bk. 4, chap. 3; "Les ordonnances ecclesiastiques de l'Eglise de Geneve" (1541), reprinted in Amelius L. Richter, *Die evangelischen Kirchenordnungen des sechszehnten Jahrhunderts*, repr. ed. (Nieuwkoop, 1967), 1: 342. See discussion of this ecclesiastical polity in action in Höpfl, *The Christian Polity of John Calvin*, 90–127; Robert M. Kingdon, "Calvin and the Government of Geneva," in Wilhelm H. Neuser (hrsg.), *Calvinus Ecclesiae Genevensis Custos* (Frankfurt am Main: P. Lang, 1984), 49; Elsie A. McKee, *Diakonia in the Classical Reformed Tradition and Today* (Grand Rapids, MI: W. E. Eerdmans Publishing Co., 1989), 15ff., 61ff.; Richard C. Gamble, ed., *Calvin's Ecclesiology: Sacraments and Deacons* (New York: Garland, 1992).

disputes. Deacons are to control the finances of the church and to coordinate the church's care of the poor and needy. Each of these church officials, Calvin believed, is to be elected to his position by church members. Each is subject to the limitation of his own office, and the supervision of his fellow officers. Each is to participate in weekly congregational meetings that allow members to assess their performance and to debate matters of doctrine and discipline. This form of ecclesiastical polity, whose inner workings Calvin discussed in copious detail, was often described by later Calvinists as an "ecclesiastical democracy."

God has vested in this church polity three forms of legal power (*potestas*).[152] First, the church holds doctrinal power, the "authority to lay down articles of faith, and the authority to explain them."[153] Included herein is the authority to set forth its own confessions, creeds, catechisms, and other authoritative distillations of the Christian faith, and to expound them freely from the pulpit and the lectern.[154] Second, the church holds legislative power, the authority to promulgate for itself "a well-ordered constitution" that ensures (1) "proper order and organization," "safety and security" in the church's administration of its affairs; and (2) "proper deceny" and "becoming dignity" in the church's worship, liturgy, and ritual.[155] "When churches are deprived of . . . the laws that conduce to these things," said Calvin, "their very sinews disintegrate, and they are wholly deformed and scattered. Paul's injunction that 'all things must be done decently and in good order' can be met only if order itself and decorum are established through the addition of observances that form a bond of union."[156] Third, and "most importantly," said Calvin, the church has jurisdiction, the authority to maintain discipline and to prevent scandal among its members.[157] The church's jurisdiction, which is rooted in the power of the keys,[158] must remain "wholly spiritual" in character, Calvin insisted.[159] Its disciplinary rules must be "founded upon God's authority, drawn from Scripture, and, therefore, wholly divine."[160] Its

---

[152] For a careful parsing on the meaning of this term, see Höpfl, *The Christian Polity of John Calvin*, 113–114.

[153] *Institutes* (1559), bk. 4, chap. 8.1.

[154] Ibid., bk. 4, chaps. 1.5, 3.4.

[155] Ibid., bk. 4, chap. 10.27–28.

[156] Ibid., bk. 4, chap. 10.27.

[157] Ibid., bk. 4, chap. 11.1. See also Calvin's elaboration in *De Scandalis*, in CO, 8: 1–84, with English translation John Calvin, *Concerning Scandals*, trans. John W. Fraser (Grand Rapids: Eerdmans, 1978).

[158] Ibid., bk. 4, chaps. 11.1–2, 5–6; 12.1.

[159] Ibid., bk. 4. chap 10.5.

[160] Ibid., bk. 4, chap. 10.30.

sanctions must be limited to admonition, instruction, and, in severe cases, the ban and excommunication. Its administration must always be moderate and mild,[161] and left "not to the decision of one man but to a lawful assembly"— ideally a consistory court, with proper procedures and proper deference to the rule of law.[162] In his writings in the 1540s, Calvin conceived this ecclesiastical jurisdiction in modest terms, simply as a way of purging the church of manifest sin and sinners and of policing the purity of the Lord's Supper or Eucharist.[163] By the end of his life, however, these disciplinary codes seemed to have resurrected a good deal of the traditional Catholic canon law and restored to the church consistory courts a good deal of the traditional authority that Calvin and other early Protestants had so hotly spurned. In a 1560 amendment to the ecclesiastical ordinances, which Calvin endorsed, we read:

> The matters and cases which come most commonly before the consistories are cases of idolatry and other kinds of superstition, disrespect towards God, heresy, defiance of father and mother, or of the magistrate, sedition, mutiny, assault, adultery, fornication, larceny, avarice, abduction, rape, fraud, perjury, false witness, tavern-going, gambling, disorderly feasting, gambling, and other scandalous vices: and because the magistrate usually does not favour such gatherings, the consistory will use the ordinary reprimands, namely, brotherly admonition, as sharp and as vehement as the case demands, suspension from the Lord's Supper, deprivation of the Lord's Supper for a stated period of time; and persistent offenders will be publicly named, so that people will know who they are.[164]

Studies of Genevan life during Calvin's tenure show that the consistory courts played a very active role, alongside the city councils, in the protection of spiritual and moral discipline, often cooperating with the magistracy in the enforcement of marriage, poor relief, education, and other laws.[165]

---

[161] Ibid., bk. 4, chaps. 11.3; 12.1–4, 8–11. See also Calvin's *consilia*, in CO, 10: 207– 208, 210–211, urging the consistory "to keep to its own boundaries and limits" and that "excessive strictness should be kept within bounds."

[162] Ibid., bk. 4, chap. 11.5.

[163] See, e.g., *Les ordonnances ecclesiastiques* (1541); CO, 38: 207.

[164] See E. Arnaud, ed., *Documents protestants inédits de XVIe siècle* (Paris, 1872), 72ff., with English translation in Alastair Duke, et al., ed., *Calvinism in Europe 1540–1610: A Collection of Documents* (Manchester: Manchester Univ. Press, 1992), 48.

[165] See, e.g., Walter Köhler, *Zürcher Ehegericht und Genfer Consistorium* (Leipzig: M. Heinsius Nachfolger, 1942), vol. 2; Robert A. Kingdon, "A Fresh Look at Calvin's Attempt to Introduce Discipline into a Reformed Community. The Consistory of Geneva, 1542– 1564," in *Calvin-France-South Africa* (Pretoria: Kital, 1990); W. Fred Graham, *The Constructive Revolutionary: John Calvin and his Socio-Economic Impact* (Atlanta, 1978);

While political law and punishment helps God to achieve the civil use of the moral law, church law and discipline helps God to achieve all three uses of his moral law. By maintaining a pure Godly doctrine and law, the church upholds the theological use of the law to induce sinners to behold their depravity and to seek God's grace. By maintaining structural order and decorum, the church upholds the civil use of the law to deter sinful conduct and to preserve a measure of public righteousness and liberty among its members. By maintaining spiritual discipline, the church upholds the educational use of the law to teach the saints the meaning and measure of sanctification and spiritual righteousness.

Moreover, the church's enforcement of spiritual discipline achieves within ecclesiastical society the same goals of retribution, deterrence, and rehabilitation that the state's criminal law achieves within civil society.[166] Through its spiritual discipline, the church exacts retribution against the sinner, so that God's honor, law, and sacraments can be preserved. It deters both the sinner and others in the church from violations of God's word and will. It corrects and rehabilitates the sinner and brings him back into community with his fellow believers.[167] Calvin saw no difficulty in imposing upon Christian believers both civil and ecclesiastical discipline, and would hear nothing of a double jeopardy defense. Multiple forms and purposes of discipline are inherent in God's moral law, and punishment by the state cannot preclude discipline by the church, or vice-versa.[168]

Calvin's radical expansion of the law and authority of the visible church in his later writings served at once to contract and to expand the province of religious liberty. On the one hand, Calvin contracted the exercise of the individual's spiritual liberty within the church. To be sure, Calvin repeated verbatim his early panegyrics about liberty of conscience from the

---

Herbert D. Foster, "Calvin's Programme for a Puritan State in Geneva, 1536–1541," *Harvard Theological Review* 1 (1908): 391.

[166] See *Institutes* (1559), bk. 4, chap. 11.1:

[T]he whole jurisdiction of the church pertains to the discipline of morals. . . . For as no city or township can function without magistrate and polity, so the church of God . . . needs a spiritual polity. This is, however, quite distinct from the civil polity, yet does not hinder or threaten it but rather greatly helps and furthers it. Therefore, this power of jurisdiction will be nothing, in short, but an order framed for the preservation of the spiritual polity.

[167] Ibid., bk. 4, chaps. 11.3–5; 12.

[168] See, e.g., Ibid., bk. 4, chap. 11.3, illustrating how a drunk or a fornicator would need to be subject to both laws and punishments. See also several good examples respecting questions of marital and sexual life in *Calvin's Ecclesiastical Advice*, trans. Mary Beaty and Benjamin W. Farley (Louisville, KY: Westminster/John Knox Press, 1991) and discussion in Höpfl, *The Christian Polity of John Calvin*, 91ff.

condemnation of the moral law and from superstitious human traditions.[169] He repeated his condemnations of the "innumerable human traditions of the Romanists—so many nets to ensnare miserable souls . . . and to bind the conscience which Christ has set free."[170] But what Calvin gave with one hand, he took with the other. Though Christians might have ample liberty of conscience, they certainly do not have much freedom of exercise as members of the church. They must "freely" bind themselves to obey the church's "well-ordered constitution" and comprehensive code of spiritual discipline. They must "gladly" submit to the mandated forms and habits of worship, ritual, and liturgy so that the church's decorum, discipline, and dignity will not be compromised.[171] They must "voluntarily" restrict their spiritual freedom even in discretionary matters of spiritual living so that weaker members of the church will not be offended and misled. Within the church, individual religious liberty and discretion must give way to corporate religious order and organization. Those who could not submit to the church's strictures were, of course, free to leave the church—a local application of the "right of emigration" provided in the 1555 Religious Peace of Augsburg.[172] But in a community such as Geneva, removal from one of the congregational churches often resulted in banishment from the entire community as well. "What sort of freedom of conscience could there be with such caution and excessive attention to detail?" Calvin once asked himself rhetorically.[173] Not much, thought his critics, despite Calvin's lengthy ratiocinations to the contrary.

While Calvin contracted individual religious liberty, he expanded considerably institutional religious liberty. Indeed, Calvin argued strongly for a measure of ecclesiastical autonomy and a basic separation of the institutions and offices of church and state. "There is a great difference and unlikeness between the ecclesiastical and civil power" of the church and state, said

---

[169] *Institutes* (1559), bk. 3. chap. 19.1–16.

[170] Ibid., bk. 4, chap. 10.1–2.

[171] Ibid., bk. 4, chap. 10.27–31. See, e.g., the strained logic of ibid., bk. 4, chap. 10.31:

> Now it is the duty of Christian people to keep the [church] ordinances that have been established according to this rule with a free conscience, indeed, without superstitition, yet with a pious and ready inclination to obey; not to despise them, not to pass over them in careless negligence. We must be far from openly violating them through pride and obstinancy.

[172] Reprinted in Sidney Z. Ehler and John B. Morrall, eds., *Church and State Through the Centuries: A Collection of Historic Documents with Commentaries* (Newman, MD: Burns & Oates, 1954), 164.

[173] *Institutes* (1559), bk. 4, chap. 10.31.

Calvin.[174] "A distinction should always be observed between these two clearly distinct areas of responsibility, the civil and the ecclesiastical."[175] The church has no authority to punish crime, to remedy civil wrongs, to collect taxes, to make war, or to meddle in the internal affairs of the state. The state, in turn, has no authority to preach the word, to administer the sacraments, to enforce spiritual discipline, to collect tithes, to interfere with church property, to appoint or remove clergy, or to meddle in the internal affairs of the church.[176] When church officials operate as members of civil society, they must submit to the civil and criminal law of the state; they cannot claim civil immunities, tax exemptions, or privileges of forum.[177] When state officials operate as members of the church, they must submit to the constitution and discipline of the church: they cannot insist on royal prerogatives or sovereign immunities.[178] To permit any such interference or immunity between church and state, said Calvin, would "unwisely mingle these two [institutions] which have a completely different nature."[179]

Calvin's principle of separation of church and state bore little resemblance, however, to the modern American understandings of "a high and impregnable wall between church and state."[180] Despite his early flirtations with the two kingdoms theory, Calvin ultimately did not contemplate a "secular society" with a plurality of absolutely separated religious and political officials within them. Nor did he contemplate a neutral state, which showed no preference among competing concepts of the spiritual and moral good. For Calvin, each community is a unitary Christian society, a

---

174 Ibid., bk. 4. chap. 11.3. See also ibid., bk. 4, chap. 20.1–2. Cf. also ibid., bk. 3. chap. 19.15, where Calvin urges that "political kingdom" and "spiritual kingdom" "must always be considered separately; while one is being examined, the other we must call away and turn aside the mind from thinking about the other." In the next paragraph, Calvin seems to equate these two kingdoms with "civil government" and "church laws."

175 Consilium (undated), CO, 10: 223.

176 See Les ordonnances ecclesiastiques (1541); Institutes (1559), bk. 4, chap. 11.3–16, chap. 20.2–4; Consilia, CO, 10: 215–217, 223–224. For a good summary, see McNeill, "John Calvin on Civil Government," 41ff. For a detailed account, see Bohatec, Calvins Lehre von Staat und Kirche, 611ff. Calvin was, in fact, banished from Geneva from 1538–1541 for his objections to magisterial involvement in the appointment and regulation of clergy.

177 Institutes (1559), 4.11.6–16.

178 Ibid., bk. 4. chap. 11.4., chap. 20.1.

179 Ibid.

180 Everson v. Bd. of Education, 330 U.S. 1, 16 (1947). On the derivation of this metaphor, see Mark D. Howe, The Garden and the Wilderness (Cambridge, 1965).

corpus Christianum under God's sovereignty and law.[181] Within this unitary society, the church and the state stand as coordinate powers. Both are ordained by God to help achieve a godly order and discipline in the community, a successful realization of all three uses of the moral law. Such conjoined responsibilities inevitably required church and state, clergy and magistracy to aid and accommodate each other on a variety of levels. These institutions and officials, said Calvin, "are not contraries, like water and fire, but things conjoined."[182] "[T]he spiritual polity, though distinct from the civil polity does not hinder or threaten it but rather greatly helps and furthers it."[183] In turn, "the civil government has as its appointed end . . . to cherish and protect the outward worship of God, to defend sound doctrine of piety and the position of the church . . . and a public manifestation of religion."[184]

Calvin's principles were as much reminiscent of medieval forms of church-state relations as prescient of modern forms. To be sure, Calvin anticipated many of the modern concepts of separation, accommodation, and cooperation of church and state that later would come to dominate Western constitutionalism. But Calvin also appropriated many of the cardinal insights of both the two powers theory of Pope Gelasius and the two swords theory of the Papal Revolution.[185] Like his medieval predecessors, Calvin saw that to maintain its "liberty," the church had to organize itself into its own legal and political entity, and to preserve for itself its own jurisdiction and responsibility. It had to wield its own "sword," its own "power." Calvin differed from his medieval predecessors, however, in insisting on a more democratic form of ecclesiastical and civil polity, a more limited ecclesiastical jurisdiction, and an equality of church and state before God.

Conclusion.—In his haunting book on the *Origins of Totalitarian Democracy*, J.L. Talmon described the eighteenth century French Revolution as the harbinger of modern forms of both liberal democracy and totalitarian fascism.[186] The political ideas of the French Revolution, said Talmon, were sufficiently "protean" and "provocative" to guide both these contemporary political movements along paths that the *philosophes* could never have

---

[181] Herbert Butterfield, "Toleration in Early Modern Times," *Journal of the History of Ideas* 38 (1977): 573, 576.

[182] Homilies on I Sam. 11: 6–10, CO, 29: 659.

[183] *Institutes* (1559), bk. 4, chap. 11.1.

[184] Ibid., bk. 4, chap. 20.2–3.

[185] See generally Berman, *Law and Revolution*; Brian Tierney, *The Crisis of Church and State: 1050–1300* (Englewood Cliffs, N.J.: Prentice-Hall, 1964).

[186] J.L. Talmon, *The Origins of Totalitarian Democracy* (London: Secker & Warburg, 1955).

anticipated. A Lincoln and a Marx, a Roosevelt and a Mussolini could all take inspiration from the core teachings of the French Revolution.

An analogous claim might be made about the sixteenth century Calvinist Revolution—that first broke out in Geneva, and eventually swept over the Netherlands, Scotland, parts of France, England, Switzerland, Germany, Eastern Europe, and America. Calvin's political ideas, too, were sufficiently protean and provocative to inspire a wide range of both totalitarian and democratic tendencies.

It is easy to expose the totalitarian and belligerent tendencies of many leading Calvinists—John Knox, Oliver Cromwell, John Winthrop, John Cotton, Samuel Rutherford, Cotton Mather, to name a few. It is easy to extend beyond Servetus the list of martyrs who were reviled, banished, or executed by Calvinists—Caspar Coolhaas, Jacobus Arminius, Hugo Grotius, Roger Williams, Anne Hutchinson, John Wise, to name a few. It is easy to find Calvinist sermons and pamphlets, on both sides of the Atlantic, earnestly defending all manner of monarchy, slavery, chauvinism, racism, warfare, torture, limited suffrage, religious establishment, apartheid, persecution, and many other forms of pathos. It is easy to weigh the political and legal contributions of the Calvinist tradition against contemporary standards of liberty, and find them wanting. Calvin's writings have provided a seedbed out of which has grown a whole wilderness of tangled political thorns that have strangled the growth of religious and political liberty in many quarters.

Calvin's writings, however, also made profound and lasting contributions to the Western legal and political tradition of religious liberty. The Protestant Reformation inaugurated by Martin Luther in 1517 was, at its core, a fight for religious liberty—liberty of the individual conscience from intrusive canon laws and clerical controls, liberty of political officials from ecclesiastical power and privilege, liberty of the local clergy from central papal rule and oppressive princely controls. Calvin helped to further this cause of liberty, not only in Geneva, but in many other quarters of Western Europe as well. His theory of the Christian conscience provided the cornerstone for the constitutional protections of liberty of conscience and free exercise of religion advocated by later Protestants in France, Holland, England, Scotland, and America. His theory of moral laws and duties inspired a whole range of natural law and natural rights theories, directed, among other things, to the protection of religious liberty. His theory of a congregationalist church polity broke the power of synodical and episcopal centralization, and eventually was used to support concepts of confessional pluralism. His theory of a coequal and cooperative clergy and magistracy provided a strong foundation for later constitutional protections of both separationism and accommodationism. His theory of the moral responsibilities of both church and state to the community lies at the heart of modern theories of social pluralism and civic republicanism.

Calvin's most original and lasting contribution to the Western tradition of religious liberty lay in his restructuring of the liberty and order of the church. Calvin was able to find a way between both the Erastian tendencies of Lutherans and Anglicans that subordinated the church to the state, and the ascetic tendencies of Anabaptists and radicals that withdrew the church from the state and society. He did so by combining ingeniously within his ecclesiology the principles of the rule of law, democracy, and liberty and giving the church a moral responsibility within the entire community.[187]

First, Calvin urged respect for the *rule of law* within the church. He devised laws that defined the church's doctrines and disciplinary standards, the rights and duties of their officers and parishioners, the procedures for legislation and adjudication. The church was thereby protected from the intrusions of state law and the sinful vicissitudes of their members. Church officials were limited in their discretion. Parishioners understood their spiritual duties. When new rules were issued, they were discussed, promulgated, and well known. Issues that were ripe for review were resolved by church tribunals. Parties that had cases to be heard exhausted their remedies at church law. Disgruntled individuals and families that departed from the church left their private pews and personal properties behind them. Dissenting congregations that seceded from the fold left their properties in the hands of the corporate body. To be sure, this principle of the rule of law within the reformed church was an ideal that too often was breached, even in Calvin's day. Yet this principle helped to guarantee order, organization, and orthodoxy within the church.

Second, Calvin urged respect for the *democratic process* within the church. Pastors, elders, teachers, and deacons were to be elected to their offices by the congregation. Congregations periodically held collective meetings to assess the performance of their church officers, to discuss new initiatives within their bodies, to debate controversies that had arisen. Delegates to church councils were to be elected by their peers. Council meetings were to be open to the public and to give standing to parishioners to press their claims. Implicit in this democratic process was a willingness to entertain changes in doctrine, liturgy, and polity, to accommodate new visions and insights, to spurn ideas and institutions whose utility and veracity

---

[187] See further discussion in John Witte, Jr., "The Catholic Origins and Calvinist Orientation of Dutch Reformed Church Law," *Calvin Theological Journal* 28 (1993): 328, 349–351.

were no longer tenable.[188] To be sure, this principle did not always insulate the church from a belligerent dogmatism, even in Calvin's day. Yet this principle helped to guarantee constant reflection, renewal, and reform within the church.

Third, Calvin urged respect for *liberty* within the church. Christian believers were to be free to enter and leave the church, free to partake of its offices and offerings without fear of bodily coercion and persecution, free to assemble, worship, pray, and partake of the sacraments without fear of political reprisal, free to elect their ministers, elders, deacons, and teachers, free to debate and deliberate matters of faith and discipline, free to pursue discretionary matters of faith, the adiaphora, without undue laws and structures. To be sure, this principle, too, was an ideal, that even Calvin compromised, particularly in his actions towards Servetus and in his undue empowerment of the consistory courts in his later years. Yet this principle helped to guarantee constant action, adherence, and agitation for reform by individual members of the church.

It was Calvin's genius to integrate these three cardinal principles of ecclesiology. Democratic processes prevented the rule-of-law principle from promoting an ossified and outmoded orthodoxy. The rule of law prevented the democratic principle from promoting a faith swayed by fleeting fashions and public opinions. Individual liberty kept both corporate rule and democratic principles from tyrannizing ecclesiastical minorities. Together, these principles allowed the church to strike a unique perpetual balance between law and liberty, structure and spirit, order and innovation, dogma and adiaphora. This delicate ecclesiastical machinery did not inoculate Calvinist churches against dissent and schism. Calvinist churches, like all others, have known schism, intolerance, and abuse. But this ecclesiastical machinery did help to render the pluriform Calvinist church remarkably resilient over four centuries and in numerous countries and cultures.

This integrated theory of the church had obvious implications for the theory of the state. Calvin hinted broadly in his writings that a similar combination of rule of law, democratic process, and individual liberty might serve the state equally well. Such a combination, he believed, would provide the best protection for the liberty of the church and its individual members. What Calvin adumbrated, his followers elaborated. In the course of the next two centuries, European and American Calvinists wove Calvin's core insights into the nature of corporate rule into a robust constitutional theory of

---

[188] See, e.g., CO, 10: 220, urging "constant reform and renewal," but warning against "rash changes and constant innovations."

republican government, which rested on the pillars of rule of law, democratic processes, and individual liberty.

John Calvin was certainly not the father of modern religious liberty, as some of his more exuberant champions have claimed. Yet through his writings and example, Calvin provided an indispensable impetus to the realization and integration of individual and corporate religious liberty. No honor roll of religious liberty in the West can properly omit him.

$$\text{---} \ \text{\textcircled{5}} \ \text{---}$$

THOMAS HOBBES:
ON RELIGIOUS LIBERTY AND SOVEREIGNTY
Joshua Mitchell*

It would be fruitful to begin this discussion of religious liberty and tradition in the thought of Hobbes with two of his own characteristically confounding observations. First:

[There is] no other government in this life, neither of *state*, nor *religion*, but *temporal*.[1]

And second:

[I]n the act of our *submission*, consisteth both our *obligation*, and our *liberty*.[2]

---

* Assistant Professor of Government, Georgetown University. Ph.D., University of Chicago (1989). Earlier versions of this article appeared as "Hobbes and the Equality of All Under the One," *Political Theory* 21, no. 1 (1993): 78–100, and "Hobbes: the Dialectic of Renewal and the Politics of Pride," in Mitchell, *Not by Reason Alone* (Chicago: Univ. of Chicago Press, 1993), chap. 2, and are reprinted herin with permission.

[1] Thomas Hobbes, *Leviathan*, Michael Oakeshott ed. (New York: Macmillan Publishing Co., 1962), pt. 3, chap. 39, 340 (emphasis added). See Matt. 12: 25.

[2] Ibid., pt. 2, chap. 21, 163 (emphasis in original). While the terms of the debate are somewhat different in Rousseau, he, too, would agree. See Jean-Jacques Rousseau, *Emile*, Allan Bloom trans. (New York: Basic Books, 1979), bk. 5, 461: "each man who obeys the sovereign obeys only himself, and . . . one is more free under the social pact than in the state of nature."

Both of these statements are bound to perplex the modern mind—accustomed as it is to separating matters of state and religion, and to believing that whatever else liberty might involve, it does not entail the strong form of submission that Hobbes clearly has in mind. What I intend to offer here is a sympathetic overview of Hobbes's theological position by way of an exposition of the two observations cited above. I shall suppose, in other words, that Hobbes was trying to comprehend the meaning of religious liberty within the confines of the categories of thought that he inherited during the turmoil of the Reformation. I will take the view that his position was not a ruse, that he was not an atheist, and that no effort to understand his views of religious liberty and tradition can succeed without placing him within the *biblical* rather than, say, ancient political tradition.

First, then, to the claim that "[there is] no other government in this life, neither of *state*, nor *religion*, but *temporal*."

Against Christian Dualism.—The significance of the Old Testament during the Reformation is not be underestimated. As one commentator has observed:

> [there was an] interest in Hebrew studies which blossomed in England during the late sixteenth and early seventeenth centuries as a consequence of the emphasis that Reformation theologians placed on the reading and understanding of the text which recorded the word of God. The validity of the Old Testament commandments for Christians was an issue of crucial importance during the Reformation.[3]

The reason *why* the Old Testament became important in Reformation theology, briefly, is that the theological and philosophical basis for comprehending the relationship between the orders of reality as it had been thought through within the Catholic Church (under the auspices of Aristotle and Aquinas) had been rejected in favor of an understanding in which the orders of reality (carnal and spiritual) were comprehended historically—and, as I will point out in the essay on Locke, *dialectically*. Here, Catholic *analogical* thinking is supplanted by Protestant *historical* thinking. On such a view, the history of the Jews became crucial to the Protestant project, if you will. Hence the renewed interest in the Old Testament. (One need only peruse the writings of the early Puritans for confirmation.)

In Hobbes's thinking, Moses in particular was important; he was, in fact, the crucial figure in the Old Testament necessary for understanding temporal government. In him was to be found the basis for the stability of government,

---

[3] David S. Katz, *Philo-Semitism and the Readmission of the Jews to England, 1603-1655* (Oxford: Clarendon Press, 1982), 9.

and an answer to the madmen and religious enthusiasts—his conjunction[4]—of his own day. Scientific knowledge could repudiate superstition[5] and is consistent with Scripture.[6] It could not by itself, however, address the deeper issue. It could *clear away* false religions, but not *clarify* the meaning of the true religion. To do this, biblical interpretation was necessary—hence, the *need* for, among other sections of work, Parts III and IV of the *Leviathan*.

As in the theology of Luther, which so shaped subsequent Reformation thinking, Moses' covenant with God is, for Hobbes, a decisive event on the basis of which massive implications (theological and otherwise) follow; Hobbes's interpretation of its meaning, however, is quite different. Where Luther finds in Moses a presage of the utter interiority of faith, which is to be juxtaposed to "the world," Hobbes finds in Moses the foundation of unified sovereignty: political and religious.[7] Where Luther found in Moses the basis of Christian dualism, Hobbes finds a monism of sorts. To put it otherwise, for Hobbes there is only *one* kingdom of God—which neither Moses nor Christ sundered. From this central claim derive the attributes of the Leviathan which are such a stumbling block to the contemporary mind: the right to command obedience and the right of interpretation.

Consistent with the spirit of his scientific enterprise, for Hobbes, the kingdom of God is to be understood in its literal sense. Those who formed a covenant with God—the people of Israel—are of His kingdom.[8] Moreover, only by covenant with God can the right of kingdom be constituted at all.[9] This right of kingdom, when legitimately passed down, is, in effect, the way in which God's presence in the world continues despite His literal absence,[10] despite the fact that His voice can no longer be heard.[11]

---

[4] Hobbes, *Leviathan*, pt. 1, chap. 8, 63–66.

[5] Ibid., pt. 1, chap. 11, 85.

[6] Ibid., pt. 2, chap. 32, 271.

[7] Hobbes does concede that Christ announced *another* world in addition to *this* one; but the other world is not to be found in the deep place within (as it was with Luther), but rather in the *future*, when Christ returns. Until then, there is only *this* world, in which political and religious sovereignty are legitimately united—as it was under Moses.

[8] Hobbes, *Leviathan*, pt. 3, chap. 35, 297.

[9] Thomas Hobbes, *De Cive*, in *Man and Citizen*, Bernard Gert trans. (Gloucester, MA: Humanities Press, 1978), chap. 16, 315.

[10] Hobbes, *Leviathan*, pt. 3, chap. 35, 302.

[11] The importance of God's speech cannot be underestimated in Hobbes. Speech from God, say, to Abraham, *Leviathan*, pt. 3, chap. 35, 297; Genesis 27: 7–8, or to Moses, *Leviathan*, pt. 3, chap. 35, 298; Exodus 19: 5, is the necessary but not sufficient condition for the right of kingdom to be exercised. The additional factor needed is consent and obedience by a particular people, *Leviathan*, pt. 3, chap. 35, 299, by which Hobbes means that the people agree to let one person mediate between them and God. He is perhaps thinking of Exodus 32: 26, where the Sons of Levi consent to obey Moses, God's mediary,

Most significantly, it is through this right, this covenant, that a counterpoint is established to the absence of God in the world.[12] While for the most part absent from present view in the life of humankind, God's *trace* is nevertheless still present. Sovereign authority is the trace of God in history. In Hobbes's words, "Christian sovereigns [are] the only persons whom Christians now hear speak from God."[13]

Hobbes's discussion of the biblical foundation of sovereign authority can actually be broken down into two interrelated components. On the one hand, there is the narrative that surrounds God's original covenant with the people of Israel, its loss, its preparation for renewal through Christ, and finally its realization in a Christian commonwealth. And on the other hand, there is the matter of the sovereign's exclusive right to interpret the law as well as sacred documents. This right, too, derives from God's covenant with Moses. I will consider Hobbes's genealogy of authority first, and then the sovereign's right of interpretation. Both aspects, again, are to be understood to follow from the

---

and do not themselves deign to speak *for* or *of* God. The precedent for this demeanor is drawn from Exodus 20: 19, where the people say to Moses, "*speak now to us, and we will hear thee, but let not God speak to us lest we die,*" ibid., chap. xlii, 378 (emphasis in the original). In *De Cive*, chap. 16, 319, Hobbes cites Exodus 19: 24, 25 for much the same thought. In his words, "[private men] were prohibited with most heavy threats, *to hear God speak*, otherwise than by means of Moses" (emphasis in original). It is not far from this thought to the idea that the individual cannot be judge for himself in matters of good and evil. Ibid., chap.12, 244. A sovereign, an intermediary, is necessary. See, for example, Hobbes's statement that "the will of God is not known except through the state," in *On Man*, in *Man and Citizen*, Bernard Gert trans. (Gloucester, MA: Humanities Press, 1978), chap. 15, 85. The myth of Ixion, invoked by Hobbes at the outset of *De Cive* is also consonant with this idea. For Hobbes, it is by virtue of God's speech that humankind's "own weak reason" receives its corrective. *Leviathan*, pt. 3, chap. 40, 349. While Locke would later make this same argument, his focus was on Christ's clarification of the truth of Adam, not Christ's renewal of the truth of Moses. These are two quite different understandings of biblical history.

[12] See J.G.A. Pocock, "Time, History, and Eschatology in the Thought of Thomas Hobbes," in *Politics, Language, and Time* (New York: Atheneum, 1973), 148–201. Pocock argues, in a manner consistent with the argument presented here, that contrary to the conventional understanding of Hobbes which would have it that history is relatively unimportant in his thought—witness, for example, the non-historical character of the movement from the state of nature to the state of civil association—history, in fact, plays a crucial role. For Hobbes, the Christian God came in the past and promised to come again in the future. Humankind lives between these two infinitely significant moments, yet must be content to live without the presence of God in this moment of history. In important respects this analysis is correct; because of the absence of the divine in the interim of history Hobbes posits an interim solution to the problem of pride: the Leviathan. But this is not the complete story. The other portion is the *ongoing* covenant between God and humankind in history which Hobbes traces back to Moses.

[13] Hobbes, *Leviathan*, pt. 3, chap. 43, 426.

unity of sovereignty—contrary to the frequently made claim (especially during the Reformation!) that Christianity divided sovereignty.

The Geneology of Authority.—The origin of the legitimate authority of the sovereign lies with Abraham: the first to form a covenant with God after the deluge. Ameliorating humankind's "passion-clouded reason," this covenant, though significant, does not, however, make up for the loss of the original pristine relationship between God and Adam.[14] It does, however, represent the first instance in which God's relationship to humankind is mediated through a sovereign, and so amounts to a point of departure that establishes a right pattern which finds its culmination in the Old Testament in Moses.[15] Here the sovereign interprets all law; the people are obedient; the people do not judge in matters of good and evil; and there is a sign that marks them.[16]

After the initial covenant with Abraham,[17] God renewed his covenant with Isaac,[18] Jacob,[19] and Moses.[20] Thereafter it is the priests who rule.[21] Next, because the Israelites were "a people greedy of prophets,"[22] power was transferred to them, though rightly it still remained with the priests. Finally, the people of Israel rejected God and instituted a succession of kings "to

---

[14] Hobbes, *De Cive*, chap. 16,. 310.

[15] The kingdom is *there* with Abraham, but it is not yet *called* a kingdom until Moses. See Hobbes, *Leviathan*, pt. 3, chap. 35, 298.

[16] The sign of circumcision was, in Hobbes's view, a way by which "Abraham and his seed should *retain the memory* of [their] covenant [with God]," *De Cive*, chap. 16, 311 [emphasis added]. Luther, on the other hand, saw it as a challenge to reason—which faith cannot but do. See Brian A. Gerrish, *Grace and Reason, A Study in the Theology of Luther* (Oxford: Clarendon Press, 1962), 19:

> circumcision made the Jews a laughing-stock, so utterly pointless did the practice seem. Luther replies that the point of circumcision is precisely to offend reason, to force it to surrender its vanity. If God had given a token which reason could approve, then man's arrogance would have remained.

Hobbes is concerned with "retaining the memory" of the covenant because, in his view, the crucial problem is that subjects always seem to *forget* their obligation to obey their sovereign. Luther, in turn, thought that the crucial problem was that reason's effort to grasp the message of Christianity—and no doubt he had in mind here the Roman Church—could only corrupt that message.

[17] Gen. 22: 16–18.

[18] Gen. 26: 3–4.

[19] Gen. 28: 13–14.

[20] Exodus 3: 6 and 19: 5–6. See Hobbes, *De Cive*, chap. 16, 314, and *Leviathan*, pt. 3, chap. 40, 343, for his discussion of Abraham, Isaac, Jacob, and Moses.

[21] Hobbes, *De Cive*, chap. 16, 321–22.

[22] Ibid., 323.

judge [them] like all other nations."[23] The kings retained their right to judge in matters both sacred and profane, like Moses and the prophets before them; nevertheless, because the people no longer understood the reason for it, the covenant disintegrated:

> Notwithstanding the government both in policy and religion, were joined, first in the high-priests and afterwards in the kings, so far forth as concerned their right; yet it appeareth by the same holy history, that the people understood it not . . . [and] they took occasion, as oft as their governors displeased them, by blaming sometimes the policy, sometimes the religion, to change the government or revolt from their obedience at their pleasure: and from thence proceeded from time to time the civil troubles, divisions, and calamities of the nation.[24]

This situation was not, however, rectified during or after the exile; for although the covenant was technically renewed, the people of Israel did not promise obedience, which, for Hobbes, is a central feature of a covenant. After this pseudo-renewal, the situation further deteriorated because of the conquest by the Greeks.[25] Christ then prepares the way for a renewal of the covenant with God, for the instauration of sovereign authority anew, for a situation in which the people obey their sovereign in all matters and know the reason for it.[26] Christ, in other words, prepares the way for a time when

---

[23] Hobbes, *Leviathan*, pt. 3, chap. 40, 348. Hobbes's citation, quoted in part, is from 1 Samuel 3: 5. The covenant ends with the election of Saul. See Ibid., chap. 41, 354. The difference between Hobbes and Augustine is nowhere made more clear than on their readings of Saul. See Augustine, *City of God*, Henry Bettenson trans. (New York: Penguin Books, 1972), bk. 17, chap. 7, 731:

> [the Greek (rather than Latin) version of 1 Samuel 15: 23–29 reads]: "The Lord has torn the kingdom *from* Israel, out of your hand." The purpose of this reading is to make it plain that "out of your hand" means the same as "from Israel." Thus the man Saul figuratively personified Israel, the people which was to lose its kingdom when Christ Jesus our Lord should take the kingship under the new covenant, a spiritual instead of physical kingship.

[23] Hobbes insisted that the covenant lost with Saul was renewed through Christ; Augustine insisted that Christ brought about a new, and *spiritual*, kingdom. This Hobbes rejects.

[24] Hobbes, *Leviathan*, pt. 3, chap. 40, 348. Hobbes accuses the subjects of Charles I of, in effect, being Israelites, of no longer knowing why they owed obedience to the king, in *Behemoth*, Ferdinand Tönnies ed. (Chicago: University of Chicago Press, 1990), Dialogue 1, 4. This is the last of seven causes contributing to the English Civil War.

[25] Hobbes, *Leviathan*, pt. 3, chap. 40, 351.

[26] In order for Christians to know the reason why they must obey the sovereign they must be convinced that Jesus did renew the covenant; that is, that He was the Son of God, and that what He said about the necessity of obeying the sovereign had divine authority. The sovereign, again, must have divine authority to rule. In Hobbes's words, "the king, and every other sovereign, executeth his office of supreme pastor by immediate authority from

human beings do not contest with their sovereign as the Israelites did when they no longer knew why they owed him obedience. The story of the Israelites—their *forgetfulness* and lapse into errancy when without the guidance of Moses their intermediary—is the story of all humankind; it is both historically specific and universally applicable. Without "Moses" there is only forgetfulness and errancy. The physical sign of circumcision (that first reminder) required a supplement; this supplement alone has the awful authority to compel attentiveness—and obedience:

> The end of Christ's coming was to renew the covenant of the kingdom of God, and to persuade the elect to embrace it, which was the second part of his office. If then Christ, while he was on earth, had no kingdom in this world, to what end was his first coming? It was to restore unto God, by a new covenant, the kingdom, which being his by the old covenant, had been cut off by the rebellion of the Israelites in the election of Saul.[27]

The lesson is clear: when the Jews instituted a king who would "judge them like all other nations," their passion-clouded reason received no corrective. A "secular" state, one ruled by Saul, offers no antidote for the inevitable errancy of its subjects. The political problem of order can only be solved, it would seem, through the mediation of God's personator in history!

Hobbes continues. The true renewal of the covenant could not have occurred until sovereigns adopted the Christian religion. Prior to that time, and after Christ's death, there is no one authorized interpreter of the Gospels and, consequently, no real Christian commonwealth or church. In Hobbes's words: "a Church and a Christian city is but one thing."[28] Here, then, is a period in which the covenant is uninstituted, even though Christ provided the ground for its renewal. The theoretical difficulty posed is the following: if the Christian commonwealth was not instituted upon Christ's death, how was Christ's truth carried forward in coherent form without a sovereign who had the legitimate authority to interpret that truth for the many? St. Paul, speaking to the church at Thessalonica (Acts 2: 38), points up the difficulty of the situation. In preaching to the Jews that Jesus was the Christ, he lacked authority, and so could only try to persuade. And since the authority of

---

God, that is to say in *God's right* or *jure divino*," ibid., pt. 3, chap. 42, 395 (emphasis in original). Locke would later argue that *after Christ first came* natural reason could know the foundation of morality and duty without the need of a sovereign authority. Hobbes claims that Christ's authority merely convinces human beings of the necessity of obeying the sovereign, of submitting to his authority.

27 Ibid., pt. 3, chap. 41, 355 (emphasis in original).

28 Hobbes, *De Cive*, chap. 17, 368.

interpretation on this matter of Christ was vested in each individual person, every one could agree or not agree for their own reasons.[29]

This situation in which every human being is judge (of the teachings of the apostles who spoke without authority), which for Hobbes is so perilous for collective life, was rectified, however, by what can only be called an inner transformation of those who heard the message of the Gospels: "But in that time, when not the power and authority of the teacher, but *the faith of the hearer*, caused them to [embrace Christ], it was not the apostles that made their own writings canonical, but every convert made them so to himself."[30]

This inner transformation seems to have been aided by that third moment in the Holy Trinity; the Holy Ghost. The Holy Ghost, according to Hobbes, carried forward the work of the One God in the person of the apostles.[31] And this provided a bridge that spanned the dark age between the time of the loss of the covenant and the time of its renewal in the Christian commonwealth.

The era of the Christian commonwealth did not arrive, however, with the conversion of Constantine, when Christianity and sovereign authority finally merged after the work of the Holy Ghost (through the apostles) was completed. According to Hobbes, the very success of the early Church in gaining adherents occasioned the ossification and the consolidation of authority within the church—where it did not belong. This consolidation of authority occurred when the Church began to demand obedience; and the inversion of the Christian message (that human beings owed obedience to the sovereign alone) was "the first knot upon [their] liberty." The second knot was the consolidation of power in the hands of one church; the third was the extension of that power over the whole of the Roman Empire.[32]

Where it could have been the case that the locus for the renewal of Christ's covenant might have been Constantine, the efflorescence of the Roman Church (which appropriated the sovereign's spiritual authority) subverted Christ's message and unwittingly deferred the true instauration of the covenant by placing three knots upon the liberty of humankind.

These three knots were, however, recently cut, and in the reverse order: first Queen Elizabeth broke with the Roman Church; next the Presbyterians undercut the religious monopoly of the Episcopalians; and finally, power was taken away from both.[33] Because of this final act, Christians are at last able to return to the primitive Christianity—the great hope of the Reformation—

---

[29] Hobbes, *Leviathan*, pt. 3, chap. 42, 374-75.

[30] Ibid., 380.

[31] Ibid., 359-61.

[32] Ibid., pt. 4, chap. 47, 498-99.

[33] Ibid., pt. 4, chap. 47, 499.

which inspired the faithful before the Roman Church usurped spiritual authority from the sovereign.

It is finally in England, then, that the kingdom of darkness comes to an end. Not at the time of Constantine, but at the *present* moment is Christ's covenant properly renewed. Here is nothing less than a vision of England's significance in the unfolding of biblical history. God's trace, once lost, is reinstantiated. Now, in matters of faith no Church can intercede; in matters of obedience and interpretation the sovereign has complete authority: this is the meaning of Christ's covenant fulfilled in Hobbes's England. And this at once political and religious arrangement is possible because of a genealogy—and hence a continuity—that can be traced backward in history to the first covenant.

The Sovereign's Right of Interpretation.—Consider now Hobbes's thoughts on authority and interpretation. While he may have been impressed by the case for the unity of sovereignty in the *Republic*, and while his observation, "not till kings were pastors, or pastors kings [could there have been authorized interpretation]"[34] may approximate Plato's observations,[35] the similarity conceals more than it reveals. For Hobbes, it is the absence of God's voice, the opacity of certain portions of Scripture, and the need to have clarity about the meaning of life eternal that causes difficulty. The meaning of Scripture is subject to interpretation; and in order for a city to remain in existence without faction there must be an authorized interpretation. In the final analysis, authorized interpretation makes possible the unity of voice that distinguishes a people from a multitude.[36] The task of the authorized interpreter for the city is to provide an interpretation to which all must accede.

Consider for a moment the problem of dissent. Hobbes is quite clear on this. The city is instituted to protect the people, not *this* or *that* person.[37] Those who dissent from the single voice of the people constitute a city unto themselves; and in this situation the city retains its "primitive right . . . that is, the right of war, as against an enemy."[38] Hobbes would have those for whom natural death is a small concession for the righteous dissent that brings eternal life understand not only that their purported direct covenant with

---

[34] Ibid., pt. 3, chap. 42, 376.

[35] Plato, *Republic*, Richard W. Sterling and William C. Scott trans. (New York: W.W. Norton & Co., 1985), bk. 5, 473d.

[36] Hobbes, *De Cive*, chap. 12, 250.

[37] Ibid., chap. 13, 259.

[38] Ibid., chap. 6, 175. This is also Hobbes's fifth Law of Nature. See Hobbes, *Leviathan*, pt.1, chap. 15, 118.

God is "a lie ... [that is unjust and derives from] a vile and unmanly disposition,"[39] but that it is a misunderstanding of Romans 13: 1,2: "Let every soul be subject unto the higher powers. For there is no power but of God: the powers that be are ordained of God. Whosoever therefore resisteth the power, resisteth the ordinance of God: and they that resist shall receive to themselves damnation."[40] This does not mean there is no place for righteousness, for obeying the word of God. The difficulty, however, is that while human beings must obey God's commands, *the interpretation of their meaning* must be decided by the city.[41] In Hobbes's words, "there is need of an interpreter to make scripture canon."[42]

The interpreter, however, is not merely the translator who understands the language in which the Scriptures were written; above and beyond the translator's task, interpretation falls to one with the authority to interpret.[43] That is, whoever holds the place of Moses in a Christian commonwealth represents God to the people and is thereby authorized to interpret His word.

---

[39] Hobbes, *Leviathan*, pt. 2, chap. 18, 135.

[40] *De Cive*, chap. 11, 240, citing Romans 13: 1–2.

[41] Hobbes, *De Cive*, chap. 17, 343.

[42] Ibid., 349.

[43] Ibid., 349-50. Michael Polanyi has claimed, like Hobbes, that interpretation is dependent on authority; though the authority with which Polanyi is concerned is the scientist's, not the sovereign's. According to Hobbes, the interpretation of scientific truth derives from the proposition itself—which the unaided individual can judge. Religious truth, in turn, derives from the authority of the person propounding it. Ibid., chap.18, 373-75. This, in conjunction with his idea that "the want of science disposes men to rely on the authority of others," *Leviathan*, pt. 1, chap. 12, 93, led Hobbes to the belief that science was wholly beneficent and could not serve sinister ambitions, *Behemoth*, dialogue 2, 96. Polanyi's position is that this tidy distinction breaks down; for as scientific truth becomes ever more sophisticated individuals must undergo an extended period of training in which they must trust in the authority of the person teaching them before they can learn to interpret scientific findings correctly. In Polanyi's view, scientific truth comes increasingly to resemble religious truth, not in terms of its content, but in terms of the relationship between interpretation and authority. See Michael Polanyi and Harry Prosch, *Meaning* (Chicago: University of Chicago Press, 1975), 182-97.

Musing about the future of revolutions, Tocqueville thought they would become increasingly rare precisely because of this relationship between authority and interpretation:

> As men grow more like each other ... it becomes harder for any innovator whosoever to gain and maintain great influence over the mind of a nation. ... For, taking a general view of world history, one finds that it is less the force of the argument than the authority of a name which has brought about great and rapid changes in accepted ideas.

[43] *Democracy in America*, J.P. Mayer ed. [New York: Harper & Row, 1969], vol. 2, pt. 3, chap. 21, 641.

Not only knowledge, but legitimate power is necessary for right interpretation.

Finally, perhaps the best way to understand why Hobbes thought there was a need for one and only one interpreter is to recall the view of biblical history he endorses. In the future Christ will come again (at the end of history), at which point the universal Church will appear.[44] At that time there will be no need for interpreting Scripture written long ago, for the kingdom of God that it portends will be at hand. Interpretation of the revealed Word will give way to the Revelation itself.

In the past, prior to the need for interpretation of the Revelation, the voice of God spoke through particular individuals, the prophets. Prophecy then ceased, and Scripture took its place.[45] Here, the point of mediation between humanity and God shifts from the prophet who reveals to the sovereign who interprets, from the individual to the "public person" of the sovereign.[46] In other words, the individual in this Age of Scripture, if you will, is not the medium of God.[47] For this reason Hobbes claims that it "belongs not to the private man, but to the Church [that is, the sovereign] to interpret Scripture."[48] Because of the position human beings presently occupy in (biblical) history the right of interpretation belongs solely to the sovereign.

Additionally, because God does not presently speak through individual human beings, questions of good and evil are not within their purview. Consequently, Hobbes can say that "[the thing that] disposeth men to sedition, is [the idea] *that the knowledge of good and evil belongs to each single*

---

[44] Hobbes, *Leviathan*, pt. 3, chap. 38, 335-36; see also Ibid., chap. 41, 353.

[45] Ibid., pt. 3, chap. 32, 275. For a different interpretation see David Johnston, *The Rhetoric of the Leviathan* (Princeton: Princeton University Press, 1986). Johnston argues that Hobbes's subordination of prophecy was intended "to transform men and women into the rational and predictable beings they would have to be before [Hobbes's] vision of political society could ever be realized," ibid., 184. Hobbes subordinates prophecy, however, because this is not the age of the prophet. In this age, God "speaks" through the Leviathan.

[46] See Hobbes, *Leviathan*, pt. 1, chap. 16, 127: "the king of any country is the *public* person, or representative of all his subjects" (emphasis in original). And at the same place, "a multitude of men, are made *one* person, when they are by one man, or one person represented . . . for it is the *unity* of the represented, that maketh the person *one*" (emphasis in original).

[47] The full force of this point is shown in Hobbes's treatment of the Scriptural claim that we must obey God above other men. If Christ or His prophets were here, he claims, we could simply listen to them speak; but since we have only Scripture—which does not speak of its own accord—we must listen to it speak through the sovereign. It is God who speaks through such interpretation; hence, in obeying the sovereign we obey God. See Hobbes, *De Cive*, chap. 18, 370.

[48] Hobbes, *Leviathan*, pt. 3, chap. 42, 365.

man."[49] This position is consistent with Hobbes's conclusion about the centrality of human pride; though in this context we see not the reason why the private person cannot sit at Jupiter's table,[50] but why the sovereign can. Biblical history justifies the sovereign's right to do so. Because the sovereign stands between man and God—and this standing-between brings new meaning to the Leviathan's status as a "mortal god"—he is not, qua sovereign, like the private person whose pridefulness receives such acute treatment in Parts I and II of the Leviathan. The sovereign is a public person; the person whose authority and interpretive prerogative are justified by virtue of Christ's renewal of the covenant first fully instantiated in Moses' relationship with God and with His chosen people. Christ did not produce the dualism so many Christians claim that he did. If God the Father unified sovereignty under Moses, there is little reason to doubt that God the Son contravened that first act by which civil peace becomes possible at all.

Of Liberty and Obedience.—"Vain esteem," Hobbes says, is the wellspring of human misery.[51] Hobbes's solution to the problem of vain esteem, of human pride, is, of course, a well known one: "the generation of that great Leviathan, or rather to speak more reverently, of that mortal god to which we owe . . . our peace and defense."[52] While he does leave open the question of what particular form such a mortal God should take (claiming that he does not wish to seem of the opinion "that there is a less proportion of obedience

---

[49] Hobbes, De Cive, chap. 12, 244 (emphasis in original). See also Ibid., chap. 12, 249; and Hobbes, Behemoth, dialogue 3, 144: "common people know nothing of right and wrong by their own meditation; they must therefore be taught the grounds of their duty, and the reasons why calamities ever follow disobedience to their lawful sovereign."

[50] Ixion, the myth goes, was invited by Jupiter to a banquet, at which he fell in love with Juno. Attempting to embrace her he clasped a cloud, from whence the Centaurs, in Hobbes's words, "a fierce, fighting, and unquiet generation," proceeded, De Cive, Preface, 98. In Hobbes's interpretation of the myth, Ixion represents the private man who was invited into the court of politics to consider matters of Justice. He fell in love, not with Justice but with his wife and sister instead; and embracing Justice's shadow thus, gave birth to "those hermaphrodite opinions of moral philosophers, partly right and comely, partly brutal and wild; the causes of all contention and bloodshed." Ibid., 98.

[51] Hobbes, De Cive, chap. 1, 117. See also Albert O. Hirschman, The Passions and the Interests (Princeton: Princeton University Press, 1977), 31, for the view that Hobbes wished "[to found] a state so constituted that the problems created by passionate men are solved once and for all. While this is in some sense correct, Hirschman appropriates this notion for his own purposes: to show that Hobbes was part of that tradition concerned with substituting interest (which was constructive) for passion (which was destructive). The problem with this view is that it fails to give an account of the Leviathan: the figure who is able to mitigate the destructive power of pride. Merely to point out that Hobbes wished to substitute interest for passion does not at all help establish who the Leviathan is or why he is able to mitigate human passions.

[52] Hobbes, Leviathan, pt. 2, chap. 17, 132 (emphasis in original).

due to an aristocracy or democracy than to a monarchy"[53]), he nevertheless provides reasons for believing monarchy to be the best way of averting the massive threat posed by human pride.

Hobbes's consideration of monarchy begins, appropriately enough, with an inquiry into what animates those who rail against it. Are they not really envious of the one whose power elevates him far above the rest? So great is their pride, based as it is on competition with others for honor, that "such men would withdraw themselves from under the dominion of the one God [if they could]."[54]

The envy which animates human beings to despise monarchy is so potent that it leads them, similarly, to reject aristocracy. Aristocracy differs from monarchy only in that it gives *more* humans a voice in the issues of commonwealth than does monarchy. The relative power that distinguishes the few from the many corresponds to the relative power that distinguishes the one from the many. That is, the difference is maintained. Thus, in spite of the fact that more human beings are of elevated status in aristocracy, Hobbes argues that aristocracy differs from monarchy in degree and not in kind. The person animated by envy recognizes this, and therefore calls for the only solution which levels the differences in power and honor between human beings: the institution of democracy.

The institution of democracy, however, has the effect of reconstituting the original condition of equality found in the state of nature, a condition that proved to be so calamitous, and that compelled human beings to enter into a covenant in which they accede to the arbitration of the Leviathan in the first place. While it might be possible to institute a democracy, such a regime is inherently unstable, simply because the many will inevitably abuse the power and honor unavailable to them in an aristocracy or monarchy. The inevitable contestations in a democracy will yield not stability, but faction, which, because "every man esteems [only] according to his own judgment,"[55] leads to civil war and to the death of the commonwealth. Far better is it that matters of judgment be left, "not [to] the persuasion and advice of private men, but [to the] laws of the realm, [and having done this] you will no longer suffer ambitious men through the streams of your blood to wade to their own power."[56]

---

[53] Hobbes, *De Cive*, Author's Preface, 104.

[54] Ibid., chap. 10, 224.

[55] Ibid., chap. 6, 178.

[56] Ibid., Author's Preface, 103. Contrast this to Nietzsche, for whom,

a legal order thought of as sovereign and universal, not as a means in a struggle between power-complexes but as a means of *preventing* all struggle in general . . .

The best state of affairs, then, is monarchy. By submitting to the one who represents the will of the many, the many lose all claims to power and honor and, thus, are equal with respect to each other. As in democracy, the many under monarchy are equal. Yet unlike democracy, power and honor cannot be contested for: "As in the presence of the master, the servants are equal, and without any honor at all; so, too, are the subjects, in the presence of the sovereign."[57]

This reading of Hobbes's defense of monarchy and warning of the perils of pride is a more or less standard one, I recognize. What has *not* been noted is that this seemingly purely *political* arrangement recapitulates aspects of Reformation theological speculation about the (prideful) priesthood *of all* believers under the one sovereign (Christ). What is significant here is not simply that Hobbes endorses monarchy, but that the *form* it takes—the persistent focus upon pride; the demand that pride be attenuated; the assertion that only the sovereign is capable of diminishing it—is so *Christian*. The salvific drama of earthly existence here is a transmuted application of a theological insight for temporal government; *all men* stand equal, prideful, before the one sovereign—the only figure capable of "redeeming" man, and without whom there can be only "death." For the Reformers the sovereign (Christ) is the only *way*; no less could be said of Hobbes's sovereign (Leviathan). In both, *only* the equality of all under the one leads to "salvation."

There is, to be sure, some question whether the many are, in fact, equal under the sovereign, as Hobbes well recognizes. The ability of the weak to kill the strong does, in a manner of speaking, level all differences among human beings.[58] This argument alone, however, is not convincing. What about natural differences among human beings. What are to be made of these?

> Whether therefore men be equal by nature, the equality is to be acknowledged; or whether unequal, because they are like to contest for dominion, it is necessary for the obtaining of peace, *that they be esteemed as equal* . . . [and] *that every man be accounted by nature equal to another*; the contrary to which law is *pride*.[59]

---

would be a principle *hostile to life*, an agent in the dissolution and destruction of man, an attempt to assassinate the future of man, a sign of weariness, a secret path to nothingness.

[56] Friedrich Nietzsche, *The Genealogy of Morals*, trans. Walter Kaufman New York: Random House, 1967, Second Essay, §11, 76 (emphasis in original).

[57] Hobbes, *Leviathan*, pt. 2, chap. 18, 141.

[58] Ibid., pt. 1, chap. 13, 98; *De Cive*, chap. I, 114.

[59] Hobbes, *De Cive*, chap. 3, 143 (emphasis in original).

Human pride is behind the rejection of monarchy and the call for equality and liberty.[60] Those who call for such liberty, aside from not being aware that they, like Augustine's earthly citizens,[61] *really* seek dominion, also do not realize—and here Hobbes is hardly a modern figure—that there is more genuine liberty under a monarch than within a democracy. While it is true that under monarchy only a few have power and honor, it is also the case that only those few will be involved in the contestation for it. Because of this, "the ambitious [few] only will suffer; the rest are protected from the injuries of the more potent."[62]

In a democracy, where all are involved in public matters, where each sees the opportunity to declare his or her eloquence in public life,[63] everyone supposes that they have more liberty than those who have no voice in these matters. Hobbes argues, however, that such liberties are actually grievances under democracy. In what do these consist?

> To see his opinion, whom we scorn, preferred to ours; to have our wisdom undervalued before our own faces; by an uncertain trial of a little vain-glory, to undergo most certain enmities . . . to hate and to be hated, by reason of the disagreement of opinions; to lay open our secret councils and advices to all, to no purpose and without any benefit; to neglect the affairs of our own family: these, I say, are the grievances.[64]

The supposed liberties under democracy reveal themselves to be the means whereby pride is allowed full rein; and this situation can only end disastrously. As we noted earlier: "no society can be great or long lasting, which begins from vainglory."[65] Human society invariably entails certain inconveniences. Those entailed by monarchy deny power and honor to most human beings; yet in return they are provided with the liberty to secure their own preservation as well as *freedom from* the dangerous affliction of pride.

The additional liberty they would receive under democracy, the freedom to enter into public matters, is illusory; for, in the final analysis, it is founded on the fanciful belief that human beings possess the capacities which only

---

[60] Ibid., chap. 10, 228.

[61] See Augustine, *City of God*, bk. 1, Preface, 5: "I cannot refrain from speaking about the city of this world, a city which aims at dominion, which holds nations in enslavement, but is itself dominated by that very lust of domination."

[62] Hobbes, *De Cive*, chap. 10, 227. See also Hobbes, *Behemoth*, dialogue 1, 59: "[human beings enjoy liberty when they enjoy] an exemption from the constraint and insolence of their neighbors."

[63] Hobbes, *De Cive*, chap. 10, 232.

[64] Ibid., 229-30.

[65] Ibid., chap. 1, 113.

that mortal-God, the Leviathan, as well as the immortal God, possess. Such a belief is demonstrable proof of the vanity of humankind, of its pride.

It is possible, of course, to see in this repudiation of the liberty in a democracy a purely political motive: Hobbes simply wished to defend monarchy against democracy. Obedience, he is often inferred to have concluded, was more precious than liberty, notwithstanding his ostensible argument that, again, "in the act of our *submission*, consisteth both our *obligation*, and our *liberty*."[66] This latter claim is not, however, simply a piece of political rhetoric. It may just as easily be viewed as an integral part of his entire argument about how pride may be attenuated. As with many Christian thinkers, human beings are so corrupted by pride that *any* effort on their part to will their own "salvation"—here broadly conceived to include salvation from the death that awaits them in the state of nature—cannot succeed. Prideful creatures acting in freedom always succumb to greater errancy. Only by resisting their pridefulness, by *obeying* the One Sovereign and not believing in the sufficiency of their own efforts, can their undertakings be fruitful. Obedience is the precondition of *genuine* human liberty.

This is a very old thought, not one peculiar to Hobbes's purported defense of absolute government. It is to be found, for example, in the Old Testament in the narrative of Sarah's barren womb.[67] Abraham and Sarah, by themselves, could not bring forth God's chosen people. Their efforts would have only come to naught without the intervention of God. But Abraham *obeys* God's commands, and this obedience is the precondition of the beneficence that follows.

In Augustine, too, obedience is crucial as well. Deference before the Sovereign (God) arrests the pridefulness of human beings who would think their own efforts are the source of their comfort and safety:

> God's instructions demanded obedience, and obedience is in a way the mother and guardian of all the other virtues in a rational creature, seeing that the rational creation has been so made that *it is to man's advantage to be in subjection to God, and it is calamitous for him to act according to his own will.*[68]

As in Hobbes, acting in accordance with one's own will can result only in "death." Obeying the sovereign is the only way for humankind to avoid calamity.

The parallel may be confirmed without hearkening back as far as Augustine, however. Earlier in the Reformation, Luther's insistence that

---

[66] Hobbes, *Leviathan*, pt. 2, chap. 21, 163 (emphasis in original).

[67] Gen. 16: 1.

[68] Augustine, *City of God*, bk. 14, chap. 12, 571 (emphasis added).

obedience to the commandments of God is the precondition for the attainment of true righteousness *and freedom* under Christ[69] comports with Hobbes's position about the need for obedience to the sovereign. No less can be said of Calvin: "For as the surest source of destruction to men is to obey themselves, so the only haven of safety is to have no other will, no other wisdom, than to follow the Lord wherever He leads."[70] It is important to recognize, here, that within Reformation Christianity there are good *religious reasons* for asserting that obedience to the sovereign is the only way to establish true freedom, and that the liberty that withdraws itself from under the sovereign, that claims itself sufficient unto itself, is a species of pridefulness that cannot be countenanced. Without obedience errancy is inevitable; the prideful longing for liberty can lead only to death unless it is linked to obedience.[71]

Hobbes, then, is not simply being rhetorical when he subsumes liberty to obedience; he is voicing an axiom of the Reformation—only here, because Hobbes understands Christianity *not* to have brought about a spiritual kingdom that stands *next to* the City of Man,[72] the insight which other Reformers applied only to the Christian's relationship to God the Son here applies to the citizen's relationship to the sovereign,[73] who, for Hobbes, is the only rightful *personator* of God.[74]

---

[69] See, for example, Martin Luther, "The Freedom of a Christian," in *Luther's Works*, Jaroslav Pelikan ed. (Saint Louis: Concordia Publishing House, 1958), vol. 31, 333-77.

[70] John Calvin, *Institutes of Christian Religion*, Henry Beveridge trans. (Grand Rapids, MI: Eerdmans Press, 1989), bk. 3, chap. 7, 7.

[71] See F.C. Hood, *The Divine Politics of Thomas Hobbes* (Oxford: Clarendon Press, 1964), 174-75: "man's mistaken confidence in his own ability to judge between good and evil is that original sin of pride, in which all men participate. In disobeying his sovereign, the subject repeats the sin of Adam, for he disobeys God." My treatment here of Hobbes is consistent with Hood's; the difference is one of emphasis. Hobbes's politics *is* Divine, but the crucial question is what is his understanding of the relationship between the two Testaments. This question is not made explicit by Hood.

Completely off the mark is Strauss, for whom "the whole scheme suggested by Hobbes [is made possible by] the disenchantment of the world, by the diffusion of scientific knowledge, or by popular enlightenment." Strauss continues, "Hobbes's is the first doctrine that necessarily and unmistakably points to a thoroughly 'enlightened,' i.e., a-religious or atheistic society as the solution of the social or political problem." Leo Strauss, *Natural Right and History* (Chicago: University of Chicago Press, 1953), 198.

[72] Hobbes's claim that "there is therefore no other government in this life, neither of state, nor religion, but temporal," *Leviathan*, pt. 3, chap. 39, 340, must be taken seriously, I suggest. Christ *renews* the Mosaic covenant under which worldly and spiritual government where conjoined.

[73] See Eric Voegelin, *The New Science of Politics* (Chicago: University of Chicago Press, 1952), 152–61. Voegelin sees Hobbes as a gnostic who attempts to "[freeze] history into an everlasting final realm on this earth." Ibid., 161. This gnostic interpretation of Hobbes is only partially correct; while it does recognize that Hobbes "temporalizes" a

Final Thoughts.—With advent of the Reformation, Hegel observed,

> each individual [came to enjoy] the right of deriving instruction for himself from [the Bible], and of directing his conscience in accordance with it. [Because of the Reformation] we see a vast change in the principle by which man's religious life is guided: the whole system of Tradition, the whole fabric of the Church becomes problematical, and its authority is subverted.[75]

Hobbes's thinking is, of course, not easily reconciled with this view—though neither is it wholly opposed to it. He complains in *Behemoth*, for example, that the effect of the controversy between the Pope and the Reformed church was, in effect, to bring the word of God within the reach of the Israelites— which Moses, in receiving the word of God *on the Mount,* had not done. The Pope, in keeping Scripture out of the hands of the people, had acted (rightly!) as Moses had. While the Reformed Church may have been correct in denying authority to the Pope, the effect of the controversy between them undermined the authority of both, for now the word of God was in the hands of the people. "After the Bible was translated into English," Hobbes says, "every man, nay, every boy and wench, that could read English, thought they spoke with God Almighty, and understood what He said."[76]

The reconciliation Hobbes purports to provide to this quandary about authority, interpretation, and liberty, is, first, to bolster the faculty of reason (about which I have spoken little here) and to insist that the light shed by it is a better guide than is tradition. "Read thyself," he says at the outset of *Leviathan*.[77] This clearly derogates the Catholic reliance upon tradition. Yet the liberty—indeed, the responsibility—to use reason's light to cast doubt

---

"transcendent" pattern, what must also be taken into consideration is that for Hobbes, God is absent from history. No author who affirms this can be accused of wishing to freeze this moment of history into an everlasting final realm on earth, for that would violate the insight (which Hobbes and the other Reformers endorse) that between God and Humankind lies a chasm which cannot presently be bridged, and will only be bridged at the end of history. Additionally, Voegelin assumes precisely what Hobbes wishes to deny, viz, that human existence involves both the transcendent and immanent dimension, and that the two must be separated.

[74] See *Leviathan*, pt. 1, chap. 12, 127. Recall that Hobbes does not speak of the Trinity. "Trinity" is a word without a referent. Ibid., chap. 8, 68. Rather, he speaks of the personations of God, of which Moses is one and the rightful sovereign another.

[75] G.W.F. Hegel, *The Philosophy of History*, J. Sibree trans. (New York: Dover Publications, 1956), pt. 3, § 3, chap. 1, 418.

[76] Hobbes, *Behemoth*, dialogue 1, 21. Cf. Hegel, *Philosophy of History*, pt. 3, § 3, chap. 1, 418: "Luther's translation of the Bible has been of incalculable value to the German people. It has supplied them with a People's Book, such as no nation in the Christian world can boast."

[77] Hobbes, *Leviathan*, Author's Introduction, 20.

upon tradition and upon the superstition that constitutes *most* religion does not fully announce the modern era; for conjoined with his call to use reason's light is his call to *defer* to a powerful one who stands over all at that place where reason's light grows dim: where God's Word must be deciphered. Here, he argues, human liberty consists precisely in *not* engaging the interpreting faculty. Here we must accede to one interpretation, and follow Christ who taught us again the lesson that the Jews had forgotten with Saul, viz., that it is our duty to God to obey temporal powers.

In Hobbes, then, reason subverts tradition and liberty presupposes obedience. The first of these insights is one with which we wrestle today, the second has been abandoned by a world more confident about the capacity of reason to enter into domains Hobbes thought only the Sovereign could rightly consider.

JOHN LOCKE:
A THEOLOGY OF RELIGIOUS LIBERTY

*Joshua Mitchell**

Thinking about the dialectic of history does not begin with Marx, Hegel, or even with Kant.[1] Indeed, Hegel's dialectic of history with which we are familiar in *The Phenomenology of Spirit* and in *The Philosophy of Right* emerged only after years of earlier speculation about the meaning of the fulfillment of the Old Testament truth purported to be offered by Christ and the New Testament.[2] We need only turn to Hegel's *The Spirit of Christianity and Its Fate* to see him wrestling with the question of the meaning of Christ's fulfillment of the Old law, a question that lay at the foundation of Reformation theology.[3] Seen in this light, Hegel's mature speculations are not

---

* Professor of Government, Georgetown University. Ph.D., University of Chicago (1989) . This article was originally published as "John Locke and the Theological Foundation of Liberal Toleration: A Christian Dialectic of History," *The Review of Politics* 52, no. 1 (1990): 64. We are grateful for permission to use the article. A version of this article also appeared as "Locke: the Dialectic of Clarification and the Politics of Reason," in Mitchell, *Not by Reason Alone* (Chicago: Univ. of Chicago Press, 1993), chap. 3.

[1] Cf. Scott Warren, *The Emergence of Dialectical Theory* (Chicago: University of Chicago Press, 1984), for the claim that Kant marks the beginning of this kind of speculation.

[2] See, for example, *The Positivity of the Christian Religion* and *The Spirit of Christianity and Its Fate* in G.W.F. Hegel, *Early Theological Writings*, trans. T.M. Knox (Philadelphia: University of Pennsylvania Press, 1948).

[3] The biblical passage which expresses this notion most succinctly is the proclamation by Christ in Matthew 5: 17: "Think not that I have come to destroy the law,

entirely new. They are a philosophical transmutation of his earlier speculations; speculations which were themselves linked to a long established theological tradition concerned with what could be called the meaning of the dialectic of biblical history. Hegel, then, really comes rather late onto the scene of this kind of thinking.[4]

All this is common knowledge within departments of Religion. In Political Science, however, we still labor under the illusion that to speak of the dialectic of history is, in the same breath, to invoke Hegel—or perhaps Marx. This need not be so, as a consideration of the Christian thought out of which Hegel's philosophical dialectic of history arose clearly demonstrates. And this is my concern here. What I will argue is that Locke's doctrine of toleration rests on a rather sophisticated reading to the meaning of Christ's fulfillment of the Old Testament, and therefore that it is first and foremost a theological argument about the dialectic of biblical history.[5]

---

or the prophets: I am come not to destroy, but to fulfill." Charles Taylor describes Hegel's dialectic in precisely these terms. See Charles Taylor, *Hegel and Modern Society* (Cambridge: Cambridge University Press, 1979), 49: "*Aufhebung* [is Hegel's term] for the dialectical transition in which the lower stage is both annulled and preserved in a higher one."

See Steven B. Smith's "Hegel's Discovery of History," *Review of Politics* 45 No. 2 (1983): 163–87, for an excellent discussion of the relationship of Hegel's early theological works to his later philosophy of history.

[4] See Henning Graf Reventlow, *The Authority of the Bible and the Rise of the Modern World* (Philadelphia: Fortress Press, 1985), for the claim that biblical criticism (of the sort with which Hegel was concerned early on) originates not in Germany but rather in England, notably in the thought of Wycliffe (1320–1384). Importantly for my purposes here, Reventlow claims that Locke is but one of a long line of thinkers in England whose biblical interpretation and political thought is intertwined.

See also Eldon Eisenach's *Two Worlds of Liberalism* (Chicago: University of Chicago Press, 1981). Eisenach casts light on that moment of liberal thought which has received too little attention: the political import of the God who reveals Himself through and throughout history. Liberal thought, in Eisenach's view, is concerned with freedom *and* Providence. In this essay I focus on Locke's understanding of God's revelation in history, and suggest that the best way to understand its political significance is to ask a seemingly simple question of the authors we study who wrote extensively about theology: how do they conceive the meaning of Christ's fulfillment of the Old Testament law?

[5] Strauss notes that had Locke really believed that the two Testaments provided the foundation of political order, he would have written a "Politique tirée des propres paroles de l'Écriture Sainte" rather than his *Two Treatises of Government*. See Leo Strauss, *Natural Right and History* (Chicago: University of Chicago Press, 1974), 205. While a treatment of the *Two Treatises* is beyond the scope of this essay, the opposition Strauss suggests is a false one. Dunn is quite helpful on this point. In his words, "the *Two Treatises* [are] saturated with Christian assumptions—and those of a Christianity in which the New Testament counted very much more than the Old." See John Dunn, *The Political Thought of John Locke* (Cambridge: Cambridge University Press, 1969), 99. While Locke's theory of government does not "consist of properly arranged quotations from scripture," Strauss, *Natural Right*, 205, it is not the secular theory Strauss would make it out to be. Likewise,

Bearing this larger framework in mind, I will first make some preliminary comments about Locke's argument for separating the spiritual and political realms, and about his view of why and when they were first separated, then turn to the rather important question of why heterodoxy remains in the world illuminated by Christ's light. I will then more thoroughly consider Locke's view of the fulfillment offered by Christ. The meaning of Christ's fulfillment is crucial for understanding Locke's position. Contemporary attempts to resurrect Locke's doctrine of toleration which all the while disregard the significance of Christ are, I think, quite misguided.[6] A discussion of the meaning of Christ's fulfillment will help clarify the overall dialectic of the history Locke has in mind; and on the basis of this dialectic, the reason why toleration is necessary will fully emerge. Finally, I will conclude with some remarks about both Locke and Hobbes.

The Two Realms and Their Origin.—

> The care of souls cannot belong to the civil magistrate because his power consists only in outward force; but true and saving religion consists in the inward persuasion of the mind, without which nothing can be acceptable to God.[7]

The distinction between the interior realm of faith and the exterior realm of power is the cornerstone of Locke's call for toleration. For Locke, of course, power belongs to the realm of "outward things," not the interior realm in which reasoned conviction is the judge. Power, therefore, cannot change conviction; the two operate in different dimensions. While under compulsion, reason can neither comprehend nor disclose for itself the requirements for salvation. Even if it were true that power and compulsion could bring about a change, the resultant conviction,

---

Locke's doctrine of toleration is not a secular doctrine. It is more akin to a "politique tirée des propres paroles de l'Écriture Sainte" than has been imagined.

6 See, for example, Jeremy Waldron's recent "Locke: Toleration and the Rationality of Persecution," in Susan Mendus, ed., *Justifying Toleration* (Cambridge: Cambridge University Press, 1988), 61–86. While Waldron's intention to extract for us today what is viable in Locke's doctrine of toleration is commendable, his philosophical rendering of it misses the mark. Waldron concludes that Locke's argument "appeals to and is concerned with the interests of the persecutors and with the danger that, in undertaking intolerant action, they may exhibit a less than perfect rationality," ibid., 85. In the following theological analysis of Locke's position I show that Locke's understanding of rationality was broader than Waldron wishes to allow. Rationality cannot be equated with interest in Locke.

7 John Locke, *A Letter Concerning Toleration* (Indianapolis: Bobs-Merrill, 1955), 18.

[which puts human beings] under the necessity to quit the light of their reason, and oppose the dictates of their consciences, and blindly to resign themselves up to the will of their governors and to the religion which either ignorance, ambition, or superstition had chanced to establish [could never assure salvation].[8]

Reasoning human beings, in a word, must be allowed to come to their own convictions without outside interference. Magistrates, therefore, should not exercise their power in matters of religious conviction. The use of power would blot out the light of reason which alone can illuminate the path to salvation. All this, as I have said, is well known.

While Locke's claim that the imposition of exterior power blocks the path to salvation is well known, however, not enough attention has been given to what Locke says about the relevance of Christ's first coming for his doctrine of toleration. Locke argues, for example, that prior to the coming of Christ the use of power for religious purposes *was* condoned in the Old Testament, as a way of extirpating idolatry—for here reason was unenlightened and worshiped a false God. Locke, in fact, provides two complementary explanations of why present-day Christians need not follow the Old Testament in this respect. First, he claims, the Old Testament injunction to root out idolatry pertains only to a *particular* people isolated in a small corner of the world, not to all peoples now under the sway of Christ's *universal* message. In Locke's words, "'Hear, O Israel,' sufficiently restrains the obligations of the law of Moses only to that people."[9]

Second, while the Jewish commonwealth was a theocracy, necessitated by the tendency of inadequately enlightened reason to go astray,[10] the New Dispensation revealed to reason the true foundation of duty, whereafter the use of power—that is, political power—subverted rather than aided its disclosure. Because of the New Dispensation, political power and religious duty could and, indeed, had to be separated. Only after Christ's first coming,

---

8 Ibid., 19.

9 Ibid., 42.

10 This, in effect, is the position Hobbes also adopts, though Hobbes claims that this was the case *after* Christ's first coming as well! The Leviathan, like Moses before him, is granted the right to interpret because reason remains unilluminated by God; it tends to go astray, to get caught up in itself. See, for example, Thomas Hobbes, *Leviathan*, ed. Michael Oakeshott (New York: Macmillan, 1962), 87-97, where, because reason cannot know first principles (God), it falls into superstition. See also Hobbes' reference to the myth of Ixion in *De Cive*, trans. Bernard Gert (Gloucester, Mass.: Humanities Press, 1978), 97–98. Here Ixion is not allowed to sit at Jupiter's table because the result is always "contention and bloodshed." From the first passage we learn that humankind *cannot* know God; from the second, that it *should not* be tempted to try. The political solution to the pride of those who do try is the Leviathan: the king of the children of pride.

in other words, *were there two realms*. It is because of this radically new situation that Locke concludes that religious affairs ought not to be impinged upon by political power. His argument *for* toleration, for separating religion from politics is—to put it bluntly—a *theological* argument:

> For the commonwealth of the Jews, different in that from all others, was an absolute theocracy; nor was there, or could there be any difference between that commonwealth and the Church. . . . But there is no such thing under the Gospel as a Christian commonwealth. . . . [Christ], indeed taught men how, by faith and good works, they can obtain eternal life; but He instituted no commonwealth.[11]

After the New Dispensation, then, political power was anathema to the discovery of duty. The earlier (and necessary) relationship between power and religious truth was sundered by Christ's illumination of the foundation of duty. Thereafter, attempts to channel conviction, to destroy heterodoxy, by the use of power must be seen in their true light: "These things, and all others of this nature, are much rather marks of men striving for power and empire over one another than of the Church of Christ."[12]

Of Heterodoxy.—The use of power, then, should never be used to convert one person to the orthodoxy of another. The light of reason can only shine from within each individual soul which (enlightened by the reason it possesses) is always orthodox unto itself. When the light of reason is subverted, the universal message brought by Christ—in contradistinction to the particular message brought by God to the people of Israel[13]—*never gains hold*. The universal message brought by Christ can only be received when the reason is not impinged upon by exterior force. To persecute the heterodoxy of others does not eliminate "otherness," but rather maintains and ossifies it. The universality of the Christian message *can* overcome heterodoxy, but only provided that reason is given the latitude to discover it.

Christian truth, the light that was revealed, then, demands that Christians accept heterodoxy, that they be tolerant. This paradox: that universality and heterodoxy are not inconsistent, derives from what Locke considers to be the truth of the New Dispensation: by the light of reason mankind can accede to the universal morality brought by revelation provided that political power not overstep its rightful jurisdiction—and only by the light of reason.

---

[11] Locke, *Letter*, 43.

[12] Ibid., 13.

[13] See John Locke, *The Reasonableness of Christianity*, ed. George W. Ewing (Washington: Regnery Gateway, 1965), §240, 168: "yet that revelation [the Old Testament] was shut up in a little corner of the world. . . . But our Savior, when he came, *threw down this wall of partition*" (emphasis added).

Why Heterodoxy Remains.—Locke's tolerance of heterodoxy, of "difference," I have so far attributed to his conviction that the universal message of the New Dispensation requires it. By virtue of a revealed truth that provides the foundation for a universal morality and duty discoverable by the light of reason, and that applies to humankind as a whole, particular differences must be tolerated.

The underlying conviction of his call for toleration is, as I have said, that by not intervening with the use of political power, these differences will *diminish* because the revealed truth of Christ *now* provides humankind with a foundation which, prior to His first coming, had not been fully clarified. This conviction we will have occasion to consider in greater detail when we turn to a discussion of the significance of Christ.[14] In the interim, however, we must consider why, if the New Dispensation provides the foundation for a universal concept of morality and duty, heterodoxy remains in the world. In Locke's answer to this question we discover why the religious factionalism which, for example, so troubled Hobbes is, for him, an overrated problem: it is an artifact of a misunderstanding about *who* Christ is, and about what was made possible in virtue of his first coming.

"The Yoke That Galls Their Necks".—The misunderstanding that contributes to the continuation of heterodoxy stems from a confusion about the right relationship between the two worlds. Misconceiving their purview, the magistrates have used political power to quell religious heterodoxy.[15]

> The stirs that are made proceed not from any peculiar temper of this or that
> church or religious society, but from the common disposition of all mankind,

---

[14] Note that the *Reasonableness* was written six years *after* the *Letter* (in 1695), and that while this conviction is there in the *Reasonableness*, it is merely consistent with the sentiment expressed in the *Letter*. In the *Letter*, however, the justification for tolerance is not expressed in terms of the unconcealment of reason. Perhaps Locke was working toward that notion in the *Letter* and fully articulated it later, in the *Reasonableness*. Cf. J.W. Gough, *John Locke's Political Philosophy* (Oxford: Clarendon Press, 1950), 175, for the claim that Locke's thoughts on toleration had already coalesced in 1659. Regarding Gough's more general claim that "the essential question [of Locke's toleration] is a political one," ibid., 176, I argue, to the contrary, that Locke's doctrine of toleration is essentially theological.

[15] Hobbes, of course, argues that the task of the sovereign is precisely that: to exercise political—or rather "temporal"—power in matters of doctrinal interpretation (though not, he claims, in matters of faith.) See Hobbes, *De Cive*, 344–45: "[Christ did not come] into the world to teach *logic*. It remains therefore that the judges . . . of controversies, be the same with those whom God by nature had instituted before, namely, those who in each city are constituted by the sovereign" (emphasis in original).

who when they groan under any heavy burden endeavor naturally to shake off the yoke that galls their necks.[16]

It is not religious difference in itself that is the cause of civil contention. Rather, external power instills enmity in the hearts of those who are threatened by it, who through their natural resistance become threats to civil order. Political power impinging upon the religious domain occasions civil resistance. The supposed causal connection between religion and civil disorder is, therefore, spurious. It is because of differential treatment, because of partiality in respect to political power, that heterodoxy persists in a form which is threatening to civil order:

> It is not the diversity of opinions (which cannot be avoided), but the refusal of toleration to those that are of different opinions (which might have been granted), that has produced all the bustles and wars that have been in the Christian world upon the account of religion.[17]

Leaders of this world who have attempted to eradicate heterodoxy, to create within a civil community an orthodox religious community as well, have created a situation in which the partiality they employ has turned a not intransigent theological difference into a difference which is menacing to society. The "other" who is (merely) theologically different becomes the "other" who is socially *evil*. By confusing the two worlds, religious difference, which should not have a detrimental effect on civil life, becomes socially demonic.[18] Separate the two worlds, render each its due, and the evil that

---

[16] Locke, *Letter*, 54.

[17] Ibid., 57.

[18] Luther expressed a similar sentiment with his claim that when the two worlds, spiritual and carnal, are confused "the door is opened for all manner of rascality, for the world as a whole cannot receive or comprehend [spirit]." Martin Luther, "Temporal Authority," in Helmut T. Lehmann, ed., *Luther's Works* (Philadelphia: Fortress Press, 1967) 45: 92. It should be made explicit here that for both Luther and Locke the argument for separating the political and religious realm *is itself a theological argument*. The implications of this have not been understood fully by those who see in Protestantism the agency which evacuates religion from the political sphere, and applaud it (Troeltsch, Weber, Wolin, and Pocock), or by those who see the same and decry the disenchantment it occasions (MacIntyre, Neuhaus). Neuhaus claims, for example, that

> [the] vacuum with respect to political and spiritual truth is the naked public square. If [the West] is overthrown, the root cause of the defeat would lie in the impossible effort to sustain that vacuum. [John Courtney] Murray is right: not communism, but the effort to establish and maintain the naked public square would be the source of the collapse.

Richard John Neuhaus, *The Naked Public Square* (Grand Rapids, MI: Eerdman's Publishing Co., 1984), 85.

accompanies religious difference in a world where the civil and the religious are conflated will disappear. Eliminate partiality and what manifests itself as evil once again becomes mere religious difference. The turbulence associated with religious faction then dissipates. To put the matter simply: the attempt to bring God into the world *through politics* results not in good, but rather in evil; and conversely, in order to diminish evil in the world, mankind must not conflate the two realms:

> [If the commonwealth and church would each] contain itself within its own bounds—the one attending to the worldly welfare of the commonwealth, the other to the salvation of souls—it is impossible that any discord should ever have happened between them.[19]

Religious difference, then, need not become demonic. Provided that political forces external to the religious heterodoxy are not brought to bear, it will not be a difference *that makes a difference*.[20] It will not be a threat to civil peace.

Of Heresy and Schism.—But while this explanation may satisfactorily account for a certain amount of difference, of heterodoxy (which, with time, will be ameliorated because of the universal message brought by Christ!), it does not provide an explanation for those heterodoxies that are self-generated, that is, of those generated from *within* a particular religious community and not attributable to the imposition of power from without. To explain these, Locke writes a postscript to the *Letter* on the matter of heresy and schism.

Thus far we have seen Locke decouple the linkage between religious heterodoxy and politics by recurring to the truth of the New Dispensation: separate the two worlds, he claims, and each can act properly within its own purview; and as a corollary, Christianity contributes to, rather that detracts from, civil peace.[21] Not Christianity, but rather Christianity misconceived,

---

[19] Locke, *Letter*, 59.

[20] Locke is really concerned with two kinds of differences that make a difference: (1) heterodoxy and (2) differences among different religions. Regarding this second type, Locke argues that persons of different religious orientation cannot be heterodox to each other. Heterodoxy only occurs within a religious community where "the rule of faith and worship are of the same religion," *Letter*, 59. This latter type of difference is so foreign so as not to be a threat to civil peace at all. Difference of this sort, Locke seems to suggest, does not occur within one state and therefore is not troubling, though it can be a source of contention between states.

[21] As I have already pointed out, toleration, for Locke, is necessary because of the truth of Christianity. It should not be surprising, therefore, for him to say: "those are not to be tolerated who deny the being of God. Promises, covenants, and oaths, which are the bonds of human society, can have no hold on the atheist. The taking away of God, though but even in thought, dissolves all," *Letter*, 52.

has led to religious factionalism and political warfare. And like all misconceptions, this one, too, can be corrected. Heterodoxy due to the incursion of political power into the religious domain is not the source of irreconcilable differences that matter politically.

The more difficult case of which to give such a benign account, however, is precisely the case which so troubled Hobbes, *viz.*, where the interpretation of the meaning of the two Testaments yields different conclusions about the right relationship between the political and religious realms, and where such politically disastrous interpretations cannot be attributed to external power, to "the yoke that galls their necks." Yet Locke clearly believes, as we shall see shortly, that the revelation of the foundation of duty by Christ does provide enough light now—at this moment of history *after* his first coming—to produce something of a consensus about the meaning of Christian duty among reasonable men and women.[22]

Because of this conviction (one scarcely noted by political theorists), the most significant problem for Locke is the imposition of political power upon religious freedom, rather than heresy and schism. The foundation of duty having been revealed, differences of interpretation not attributable to external power can be obviated provided "what is manifestly contained in the sacred text"[23] serves as a guide. This certainty about the perspicuity of Scripture can be found in Luther's formulations,[24] though, significantly, not in those of Hobbes—whose political vision also rests on an interpretation of Scripture. And the reason for this difference in conviction between Locke and Hobbes

---

[22] See John Locke, *An Essay Concerning Human Understanding* (Oxford: Clarendon Press, 1975), bk. 1, chap. 1, § 5, 45: "[human beings] have light enough to lead them to the knowledge of their Maker, and the sight of their duties"; and Ibid., bk. 1, chap. 19, § 21, 698: "*Revelation* is natural *Reason* enlarged by a new set of Discoveries communicated by GOD immediately" (emphasis in original).

[23] Locke, *Letter*, 62. In Locke's definition, a heretic or schismatic is a person who separates from or adds on to that content. In Revelation 22: 18–19, John enjoins everyone "that heareth the words of the prophecy of this book" neither to add on to or subtract from it.

[24] For Luther, the content of the scripture is revealed in the abyss of powerlessness where the Gospel is grasped "with other eyes [than] carnal reason doth [have]," Martin Luther, "Lectures on Galatians," in Lehmann, *Works*, 27: 86. In the abyss of powerlessness, when the Christians realize that the will cannot will what God wills them to will, the light of the Gospel is revealed, to borrow Locke's language. For Locke, because Christ supplemented the natural light of reason, Christians can with their reason discover the content "manifestly contained" in the Gospel. The abyss of powerlessness (and the will necessary to encounter it) do not occasion the light that illuminates. It is simply there to be seen. There is an understandable content, and though some may "separate from" or "add on to" it, the content remains there to be seen by all who possess the faculty of reason. Luther, in other words, finds the *will* the key to the meaning of the Gospel, while Locke finds the key in the faculty of *reason*.

can be understood quite simply in terms of what they account Christ to have brought into the world.[25] Because of the clarity that Christ brought into the world, heresy and schism are not politically significant problems for Locke. They can be allayed by adhering to what is there, in Scripture.

Difference Is Not Problematic.—At the theoretical level, then, the two kinds of difference—heterodoxy, on the one hand; and heresy and schism, on the other—are not intransigent problems. In the final analysis, both can be overcome by a right reading of the Gospel. Far from being the source of political turmoil and religious faction, the New Dispensation provides the ground for civil peace. The New Dispensation does not undermine political life, it supports it. Rather than exacerbate difference, it diminishes it— because toleration is made necessary by the New Dispensation itself. Although this seems to contradict the claim that there is but one true God, toleration is, in fact, consistent with it; for only through the use of unimpeded reason can the one God's truth be known and salvation assured:

> [In the event that I am not persuaded of the truth of a religion] in my own mind, there will be no safety for me in following it. No way whatsoever that I shall walk in against the dictates of my own conscience will ever bring me to the mansions of the blessed.[26]

Although I will not dwell on it here, the implication that this rudimentary fact has for worship and community is, for Locke, quite clear. While a common form of worship within a community gives the *appearance* that the one true God is being worshiped, unless inner belief is present among the worshipers, outward appearance will be deceptive. It is inner belief that gives substance to outward worship.[27] Without the former, a common form of worship is vacuous. Unity of worship under compulsion does not necessarily indicate a worship of the one true God. God's truth makes its way into the mind of the person whose reason is unconstrained. Proper worship can only follow from this. Insist on a common form of worship and God's light is lost; accept the paradoxical notion that all may worship as the light of their reason

---

[25] Where, for Locke, Christ brought into the world the light and foundation of Christian duty, for Hobbes, Christ renewed the covenant with God, which renewal grants the sovereign the authority to interpret the Gospel. In Locke's case, the light of revelation shines brightly enough (now) for all to interpret (along the same lines because Christ revealed the necessary foundation). In Hobbes's case, Christ was not the revealer, but the renewer; reason remains in the dark, as it were, after Christ as well as before His first coming.

[26] Locke, *Letter*, 34.

[27] Ibid., 35.

informs them, and God's light once again enters the world.[28] The one true God is revealed to and in a heterodox world.

The Meaning of Christ's Fulfillment.—In several places along the way I have discussed the central significance Locke attaches to the first coming of Christ. It is now time for a more systematic treatment of that subject. To put the issue in its proper theological context the question is the following: "What is the religious truth of the Old Testament that is subsequently fulfilled by Christ?" A fully adequate account of Locke's answer would have to include a consideration of his argument about how faith in Christ makes up for the inability to act righteously without fail; about how the law of the Old Testament still rules—only now, in conjunction with faith, righteousness is again possible. In this formulation the interiority of faith does not *supersede* the exteriority of the law (Luther's formulation), but is a supplement to it that corrects for the loss of obedience and righteousness in Adam. Christ supplements, he does not reconstitute the foundation of righteousness. The law, for Locke, still stands: "The law [cannot] be taken away or dispensed with, without changing the nature of things, or overturning the measures of right and wrong; and thereby introducing and authorizing irregularity, confusion and disorder in the world."[29]

I will not, however, focus on Locke's understanding of the relationship between the Old law and faith. Instead, I will turn to an important theme in Locke's understanding of the meaning of Christ's fulfillment: the gradual *unconcealment* of His truth to those who expected in Christ not a final redemption but a renewal of the earthly kingdom.

The Unconcealment.—Anticipating a literal kingdom, the hearers of Christ were unprepared, Locke claims, for his message of the heavenly kingdom to come, and the unconcealment of this truth to them is the story of Christ's first coming.[30]

---

[28] It is for this reason that church affiliation must be completely voluntary. See Ibid., 20–26. All must be free to choose the church in which they worship, according to their own conviction. Much has been made of Locke's voluntarism. Indeed, it seems consistent with the supposed atomism of the liberal soul. Locke's voluntarism, however, must be seen in terms of his conclusions about the dialectic of biblical history and not in terms of the analytical distinction between atomistic and socially constituted human beings, a distinction which plagues contemporary readings of Locke, and of Hobbes as well.

[29] Locke, *Reasonableness*, §180, 136.

[30] Mircea Eliade, *A History of Religious Ideas* (Chicago: University of Chicago Press, 1984), vol. 2, § 224, 359–61, for an excellent synopsis of the three theological explanations possible for the delay of the parousia: either a more fervent apocalyptic hope;

Recall for a moment that, for Locke, Adam was granted natural reason by God, a natural reason which, as part of the Old Dispensation, is still regnant.[31] Against this backdrop, Locke argues, Christ's message was gradually revealed. Put another way, although reason is present from the beginning, it was not sufficiently enlightened prior to Christ:

> Though the works of nature, in every part of them, sufficiently evidence a deity; yet the world made so little use of their reason, that they saw him not where even by the impressions of himself he was easy to be found. Sense and lust blinded their minds in some, and a careless inadvertency in others; and fearful apprehension in most . . . gave them up into the hands of their priests; to fill their heads with false notions of the Deity.[32]

In this unenlightened mode, Locke claims, societies ruled by priests were concerned with the accouterments of religion but not with virtue and moral duty, the real cement of a society. Barely retaining their integrity, societies continued with just enough of this cement to "tie [them] together in subjection."[33] Lacking a foundation in Christian virtue, they were held together—but not in freedom:

> The illuminative truth of reason *did* rule the minds of a few human beings prior to Christ, notably the philosophers, [but it was] too hard a task for unassisted reason, to establish morality, in all its parts, upon its true foundation; with a clear and convincing light.[34]

Moreover, philosophers, assisted by a natural reason which "makes but a slow progress and little advance in the world,"[35] had no way to make the laws of reason authoritative. The great majority of human beings do not have the leisure to enlarge their knowledge; hence, they cannot know, but must

---

a deferment of the kingdom until some future date; or a new life possible now because of Christ. Locke takes the second and third alternative.

[31] Locke, of course, makes much of this grant of reason when discussing government in *An Essay Concerning the True Original, Extent, and End of Civil Government* in Peter Laslett, ed., *Two Treatises of Government* (Cambridge: Cambridge University Press, 1988) (hereinafter "*Second Treatise*"). The other grant given by God to Adam in the beginning— the right of dominion—is the foundation for Locke's doctrine of property.

[32] Locke, *Reasonableness*, §238, 165.

[33] Ibid., §241, 170.

[34] Locke, *Reasonableness*, §241, 170. Augustine, much earlier, expressed the same thought in his *City of God*. The heading of bk. 2, chap. 7 reads: "The conclusions of the philosophers are ineffective as they lack divine authority. Man is easily corrupted and the God's examples influence him more than the argument of man." Augustine, *City of God*, trans. Henry Bettenson (New York: Penguin Books, 1984), 54.

[35] Locke, *Reasonableness*, §241, 171.

believe.[36] And because belief is predicated on authority,[37] the law of reason discovered by the philosophers could not be disseminated.

A fortunate attribute of the faculty of reason, however, is that while it discovers for itself only slowly, "nothing seems hard to our understanding, that is once known."[38] And because of Christ's revelation, the true foundation of virtue and moral duty has been disclosed. By its authority, revelation was able to accomplish what the philosophers could not: extend the rule of reason to those who previously could not have attained it; cure the defects of local versions of morality and supplant it with a universal morality;[39] and, finally, level differences in knowledge between those who once had the leisure to know and those who did not. Now both groups stand before the revealed truth and are informed by it.[40]

Christ's Three-Part Revelation.—Christ, then, gradually revealed the truth to those who had believed what the priests had told them: that the Messiah would renew the earthly kingdom. This gradual revelation by Christ was actually tripartite: first, miracles He performed; second, intimations that He was the Messiah; and third; open declarations to that effect.[41]

The performance of miracles was designed to convince without speech that Christ was the Messiah.[42] Although chronologically farthest removed from the revelation of who Christ was, miracles are, in an important sense, the foundation upon which the second and third parts of Christ's revelation rests. Without miracles there could be no proof that a divine *interruption* in the regularities of nature had occurred. In Locke's words, "for miracles [are]

---

[36] Locke, *Reasonableness*, §243, 179. MacPherson's argument on this point is quite unsatisfactory. He claims that Locke's intention is to show that "the laboring class, beyond all others, is incapable of living a rational life," C.B. MacPherson, *The Theory of Possessive Individualism* (Oxford: Oxford University Press, 1962), 226, and that this served as a justification for the political disenfranchisement of all wage earners. Locke, however, is not concerned with wage earners in the passage cited; he is concerned to show that Christ's revelation is the Divine supplement to the natural reason of the philosophers.

[37] This statement accords with Hobbes's formulation, though where Hobbes roots authority in the lawful sovereign, the personator of God, Locke roots it in Christ, the second moment of God!

[38] Locke, *Reasonableness*, §243, 177.

[39] Ibid., 176.

[40] Luther's notion of the equality of all human beings before Christ resonates in this Lockean formulation. For both thinkers, Christ levels all heretofore-considered-significant differences. See Luther, "Temporal Authority," in *Works*, 45: 117: "there is no superior among Christians, but Christ Himself and Christ alone."

[41] Locke, *Reasonableness*, §§57–61, 35–39.

[42] Ibid., §29, 18.

that foundation on which believers of any divine revelation must ultimately bottom their faith."[43]

Intimations in speech, parables come closer to open declaration but are not yet that. By intimations Christ still conceals himself in order that He may fulfill His mission.[44] Had Christ declared openly who He was, He would have been set up as an earthly king;[45] for the children of Abraham had no other thoughts of the Messiah, "but of a mighty temporal prince."[46] This was not Christ's mission. His hearers, therefore, had to be prepared for the truth "in degrees,"[47] through intimations, through parables.[48]

Finally, prior to His death, and after He had fulfilled His mission on earth, Christ openly declares His kingdom. But significantly, it is only after

---

[43] John Locke, *A Discourse of Miracles*, in I.T. Ramsey, ed., *John Locke*, (Stanford: Stanford University Press, 1958), 86. It was Locke's position that "the holy Men of Old . . . had outward Signs to convince them of the Author of [the] Revelations [they received]," Locke, *Essay*, bk. 4, chap. 19, § 15, 705, and that these signs have now ceased. What, then, is to be made of the claims by enthusiasts that they had received revelations from God? Locke argues that reason must be the judge of such claims. That enthusiasts *believe without reasons* disqualifies their claims. Reason is the standard by which claims of the receipt of revelation must be judged. "Reason," however, is not here to be opposed to revelation, as much contemporary scholarship is apt to do. See James Tully, "Governing Conduct," in Edmund Leites, ed., *Conscience and Casuistry in Early Modern Europe* (Cambridge: Cambridge University Press, 1988), 59: "[In Locke's view] God spreads Christianity by the same mode of governance as other opinions are spread." Christianity is the true religion, ascertainable by the light of reason, to be sure; yet the light of reason acquires its brightness by being guided by the *practices* in a Christian commonwealth:

> Christian philosophers have come closer to demonstrating ethics than the pre-Christians, but this is not because, as they assume, they have an independent rule of reason to test moral principles. It is rather because their first principles are derived from Revelation. We grow up with the Gospel from the cradle. It seems 'natural' to us and we take it for 'unquestionable truths.' Rationalists think they have discovered the foundations of morality, but they only 'confirm' Revelation. We would be lost without it. Revelation is the foundation of reason, of what we take to be 'self-evident.

Ibid. Locke's liberalism presupposes that Christianity is the foundation upon which politics of a certain sort may be built.

[44] Locke, *Reasonableness*, §§62–74, 39–49. Strauss saw in Locke's exposition of Christ's gradual unconcealment an explication more of Locke's view of the necessity of caution when speaking or writing for the public than of the truth of Christ. See Strauss, *Natural Right and History*, 207.

[45] Locke, *Reasonableness*, §74, 48.

[46] Ibid,. §140, 98.

[47] Ibid., §139, 98. See also Ibid., §156, 115, where, in a reference to John 16: 12, Christ spoke obscurely because his hearers *could not bear it.* The burden of Locke's Christology rests upon John 1: 5 ("And the light shineth in darkness; and the darkness comprehended it not").

[48] Locke, *Reasonableness*, §124, 85.

Christ's death that His truth (now openly declared) is fully understood,[49] though not immediately. Even after Christ died, his disciples could not bear the truth of the kingdom He professed, though they more than anyone else had been prepared for it, and had received open declarations of it. Because they could not bear it, there was the need for the Holy Ghost, which gave the apostles "a full and clear sight and persuasion."[50]

With the advent of the Holy Ghost the meaning of Christ's kingdom is fully revealed: He came to "give a full and clear sense" to the Law and of the kingdom (and to what was necessary to enter into it), "free from the corrupt glosses of the scribes and the pharisees."[51] This clarification reaffirmed the need to do good works; only now such works had to be conjoined with the need for faith. The full effect of this conjunction was to bring the world out of the "Egyptian darkness" and into the light of God initially possessed by the people of Israel alone; only now it is not one people who may claim it, but the whole of humanity.[52]

At that point the movement from concealment to unconcealment reaches its conclusion. The authority of God, once given only to the people of Israel, and the foundation of virtue and moral duty in reason, once possessed only by the philosophers, are now united in the full revelation and enlightenment

---

[49] This dialectic of death and revelation is found, in philosophical form, in Hegel's thought as well. There, in its starkest formulation, *Geist* reveals itself to itself on the "slaughter bench" of history. G.W.F. Hegel, *Reason in History* (Indianapolis: Bobbs-Merrill, 1953), 27.

[50] Locke, *Reasonableness*, §156, 115. See also Ibid., §156, 116: "my death and resurrection, and the coming of the Holy Ghost, will speedily enlighten you; and *then* I shall make you know the will of the father" (emphasis in original). On this reading, the Enlightenment is the Age of the Holy Ghost! In Hegel's view, similarly, the Holy Ghost was also necessary for the apostles to be imbued with the divine. Speaking of the time when Christ openly declares His kingdom, Hegel says, "now for the first time Jesus ventures to speak to his disciples of his impending fate; but Peter's consciousness of the divinity of his teacher at once assumes the character of faith only; the faith which senses the divine but which is not yet a filling of his whole being with the divine, not yet a reception of the Holy Ghost." *The Spirit of Christianity*, 267.

We should recall that for Hobbes, too, the Holy Ghost was the agent of the acceptance of the truth of Christianity. For Hobbes, however, the Holy Ghost acted only when there was no authority present to interpret Scripture. See Hobbes, *Leviathan*, 380. When an authority emerges the unauthorized hearer of the Gospel no longer has the right of interpretation. In Hobbes's view, in other words, Christ does not provide the light by which the reason possessed by every human being may know the truth of Scripture once it has been unconcealed—as Locke would have it.

[51] Locke, *Reasonableness*, §188, 140.

[52] Ibid., §§238–41, 165–173. A piece of evidence Locke cites for the universalization of what once was a particular claim is the fact that the apostles went out "amongst the nations." Ibid., §240, 168.

accomplished by the Holy Ghost.[53] Now the light of reason, first granted to Adam, shines *with authority* in virtue of Christ.

Locke's Dialectic of Biblical History: An Overview.—Reason, according to Locke, was granted to Adam in the beginning. This was, of course, natural reason, the natural reason which was granted *by* God, but which had not yet received assistance *from* God. At its best, this was the reason of the philosophers, which was not yet authoritative for all human beings.

Thus, while reason *was there from the beginning*, it is not yet *conscious of its authority* until the death of Christ.[54] With the death of Christ enough light is cast for the reasoning human being to come to know the truth of Christianity: the Universal Religion. By being tolerant Christians reconcile themselves to the truth of their faith, and the very ethical structure of the cosmos. By being tolerant the Christian accepts who Christ was: the clarifier of the truth of the Old Testament. By being tolerant Christians reconcile themselves to the dialectic of biblical history, a dialectic which reveals that the ontological reality of human life was transformed with the first coming of Christ. It was Christ who made it possible for Christians to reside in two realms which complement but which must nonetheless be separated, one from the other. Toleration is rooted in theology, not politics.

Final Thoughts.—Locke's doctrine of toleration, and hence of religious freedom, was the theoretically necessary outcome of his understanding of the dialectic of biblical history. In the course of this essay I have argued that the reasonableness of toleration, for Locke, can be understood fully only in the context of his Christianity; it cannot be reduced to a calculus of interest, nor to purely political considerations. It arises, more precisely, within the

---

[53] See Leo Strauss, "Athens or Jerusalem," in *Studies in Platonic Political Philosophy* (Chicago: University of Chicago Press, 1983) for a discussion of the alternatives of reason and divine dispensation. Locke claims that these alternatives have been united by the New Dispensation. See, for example, Locke, *Reasonableness*, §245, 185:

> The view of heaven and hell [given to us through Revelation] will cast a slight upon the short pleasures and pains of this present state, and give attractions and encouragements to virtue, which reason and interest and the care of ourselves cannot but allow and prefer. Upon this foundation, and upon this only, morality stands firm and will defy all competition.

The natural reason employed by the philosophers to discover the human good, is guided toward that good by the revelation that supplements natural reason.

[54] Hegel comes to mind here. Writing about faith in *The Spirit of Christianity*, he notes that, "faith in the divine is only possible if in the believer himself there is a divine element which rediscovers itself, its own nature, in that on which it believes, even if it be unconscious that what it has found *is* its own nature. Hegel, *Spirit of Christianity*, 266.

Reformation debates about the meaning—political or otherwise—of Christ's fulfillment of the Old Law, and cannot be disentangled from Reformation categories without rendering it incoherent.

In the contemporary debate about toleration, the reflexive recurrence to Locke surely evinces this incoherence. In these times, when the line of demarcation between politics and religion is growing increasingly obscure, Locke's claim that these two domains must remain distinct offers a certain comfort. Yet there is an irony about this claim that is almost always overlooked: the argument for separating religion and politics—for *disenchanting* the political world, as it were—*is itself a theological argument*. At the outset of the Reformation, it should be remembered, Luther made a variant of this same argument.[55]

In these times we must ask whether the *coherence* of the claim for the need to separate religion and politics must itself rest on a religious conviction of a certain sort. Locke thought that it must; we increasingly labor to maintain that separation without it. Liberal thought, concerned as it has been right from the beginning with freedom, is today turning a blind eye to religion, seeing it as a hostile force to be contended with rather than as a resource through which human freedom—in all its aspects—can be fully comprehended. Tocqueville (who also believed in the separation of religion and politics) saw this development already in the nineteenth century:

> Alongside these religious men [who wish to return to aristocracy] I find others whose eyes are turned more to the earth than to heaven; partisans of freedom . . . I think [they] should hasten to call religion to their aid, for they must know that one cannot establish the reign of liberty without that of mores, and mores cannot be firmly founded without beliefs. But they have seen religion in the ranks of their adversaries, and that is enough for them; some of them openly attack it, and others do not dare to defend it.[56]

It was Locke's conviction (and Tocqueville's as well) that religious liberty and political liberty were allies rather than adversaries. At century's end, it seems, religious liberty is a threat to liberal thought—at least as it is understood and defended in many prominent universities.

Political thought, however, achieves its coherence against the backdrop of the adequacy of a larger set of theological formulations and provisional answers. In abandoning that backdrop, contemporary liberal thinkers have given up the high ground to those whose theological vision *is* different and,

---

55 Again, see Luther, "Temporal Authority," in *Works*, 45: 92.

56 Alexis de Tocqueville, *Democracy in America*, ed. J. P. Mayer (New York: Harper & Row, 1968), Author's Introduction, 17.

consequently, antagonistic toward liberal thought. Rather than answering back, as Locke did, with a theological vision that seeks to do justice to human freedom and liberty, that seeks to comprehend the extant political situation in the light of larger theological issues, liberal thinkers have either ignored or attacked religion.

Having renounced the attempt to find a moderate theology, however, condemns to oblivion their attempt to find a moderate politics. When the theological center is abandoned religion doesn't go away; it shows itself in immoderate forms. Locke is salutary today because he recognized that religion, though *separable* from politics, undergirds politics. Contemporary liberals have, unfortunately, disregarded his understanding even while they have endorsed the conclusions that follow from it.

— ❧ 7 ❧ —

ROUSSEAU'S CIVIL RELIGION
AND THE IDEAL OF WHOLENESS

W. Cole Durham, Jr.[*]

T
he idea of civil religion has taken on new life ever since Robert Bellah brought it back into circulation with his seminal *Works on Civil Religion in America.*[1] It has taken hold as a sophisticated way to characterize the recognition accorded to religion in a wide variety of ceremonial contexts in American public life, ranging from references to deity in the inaugural addresses of United States presidents to the use of the phrase "In God We Trust" on currency. The notion extends not only to explicit references to deity, but to public veneration for the founding documents of the republic.[2] Among other things, the notion has been invoked by legal scholars as a devise for thinking about the borderline between permissible and impermissible manifestations of religion in public life,[3] and more

---

[*] Professor of Law, J. Reuben Clark Law School at Brigham Young University. B.A., Harvard (1972); J.D., Harvard Law School (1975).

[1] Robert N. Bellah, *Works on Civil Religion in America,* Daedelus (Winter, 1967); Robert N. Bellah, *Beyond Belief: Essays on Religion in a Post-Traditional World* (Berkeley: Univ. of California Press, 1970); Robert N. Bellah & Phillip E. Hammond, *Varieties of Civil Religion* (San Francisco: Harper & Row, 1980).

[2] Sanford Levinson, "The Constitution in American Civil Religion," *Supreme Court Review* (1979): 123.

[3] Sanford Levinson, "The Confrontation of Religious Faith and Civil Religion: Catholics Becoming Justices," *DePaul Law Review* (1987): 1047; Michael M. Madigan, "The

generally, it has provided a fruitful vehicle for thinking about society's religious dimensions.

Bellah, of course, derived the notion of civil religion from Rousseau's chapter on this subject at the end of *The Social Contract.* Drawing on Rousseau's conception, Bellah identified features of American life that appear to constitute the expressions and rites of this civil religion. Further, he sketched out some of the key doctrines on this trans-sectarian religion: "the existence of God, the life to come, the reward of virtue and the punishment of vice, and the exclusion of religious intolerance."[4] While both the phenomena and doctrines identified in Bellah's depiction in American civil religion parallel those suggested by Rousseau, the resulting conception of civil religion seems much more superficial than Rousseau's original idea. In my view, Rousseau's analysis of civil religion is grappling with something much deeper than a thin veneer of religiosity used as a non-controversial way of appealing to diverse religious beliefs on ceremonial and patriotic occasions. If my argument is correct, it plays the same role in Rousseau's analysis of the religious dimension of society that the concept of the general will plays in his analysis of society's political dimension. Even more profoundly, it constitutes Rousseau's effort to wrestle with the religious dimensions of the problem of community. But this wrestling is in some ways inconclusive: It captures Rousseau's prescient sense for the ambiguities and tensions inflicted on society by the onslaught of modernity. My aim in this essay is to contribute to a deeper understanding of Rousseau's theory of civil religion, thereby enriching our understanding of Rousseau's conception of the religion and politics in community.

Civil Religion and the Ambiguities of Community.—Rousseau's civil religion is puzzling—deeply puzzling. The depth of the bewilderment is evidenced by claims that the penultimate chapter of *The Social Contract* has "aroused more criticism than all the rest of the book, and in particular has often been held contradictory to everything its author elsewhere utters of religion."[5] The difficulty stems not only from Rousseau's proverbial surface ambiguity and contradictoriness, though both are present in abundant measure, but also from the more fundamental tensions between toleration and social

---

Establishment Clause, Civil Religion, and the Public Church," *California Law Review* 81 (1993): 293; Yehudah Mirsky, Note, "Civil Religion and the Establishment Clause," *Yale Law Journal* 95 (1986): 1237.

[4] Robert N. Bellah, "Civil Religion in America," *Daedelus* (Winter, 1967).

[5] E. Wright, *The Meaning of Rousseau* 86 (New York: Russell & Russell, 1963). See also A. Cobban, *Rousseau and the Modern State* 84 (London: G. Allen & Unwin, Ltd., 1934).

solidarity—between particularity and wholeness—which pervade his thinking about religion and politics. What Cassirer has called "the problem of Jean-Jacques Rousseau"[6] appears in all its recalcitrant vitality in the domain of the civil religion, and analysis of the problem's religious dimensions cannot help but illuminate its integrally related political aspects. In fact, if a principal thesis of this essay is correct, Rosseau's political thought may be conceived as the articulation of the political implications of a fundamentally (if uniquely Rosseauian) religious perception of the nature of man.

(1) *Abstract Theory or Historical Account.*—The ambiguity and complexity of Rousseau's conception of religion and politics becomes apparent as soon as one turns to a close textual analysis of the chapter on civil religion in the *Social Contract.* In the opening lines of that chapter, Rousseau asserts, "[a]t first, men had no kings save the gods, and no government save theocracy."[7] But what does he mean here by "at first?" Is he alluding to the imaginary time described in the *Discourse on the Origin of Inequality* before social life had generated any artificial faculties? Or is the reference to that still pre-civil condition that has been characterized as "a state of *de facto* society which is a 'fallen' state of nature"?[8] At another level, does the subsequent phrase, "if the study of history were developed from this point of view [*i.e.*, in consonance with the sketch of religious history he provides],"[9] imply that the "at first" he speaks of was actually within historical time? If so, the implication would seem to be that his analysis of the relationship of natural and civil religion is intended not merely as a matter of abstract theory, about the place of religion in society, resting on "mere conditional and hypothetical reasonings,"[10] but as historical analysis. This would contrast with his study of the relationship of natural and civil man, which is more clearly hypothetical and imaginary.

Further, just as it is unclear whether "at first" is a reference to abstraction or to history, so it is not obvious whether the stress in the remainder of the sentence is on the first clause or the second. Is Rousseau saying something

---

6 E. Cassirer, *Das Problem Jean-Jacques Rousseau,* 41 *Archiv für Geschichte der Philosophie* 177, 177 (1932). This essay has appeared in translation. E. Cassirer, *The Question of Jean Jacques Rousseau,* P. Gay trans., (Bloomington: Indiana Univ. Press, 1963).

7 J. -J. Rousseau, *The Social Contract* IV, viii, in *The Social Contract and Discourses* 1, 129, G.D.H. Cole trans., (New York: E.P. Dutton, 1950) (hereinafter *Social Contract*).

8 Hoffman, "Rosseau on War and Peace," *American Political Science Review* 57 (1963): 317, 318.

9 *Social Contract* IV, viii, at 133.

10 J.-J. Rousseau, *A Disclosure on a Subject Proposed by the Academy of Dijon: What is the Origin of Inequality among Men, and Is It Authorized by Natural Law?,* in *Social Contract and Discourses* 175, 198, G.D.H. Cole trans., (New York: E.P. Dutton, 1950) (hereinafter *Inequality*).

about whether religion is a feature of the state of nature, so that man in that isolated condition could truly be said to have no king but the God of natural religion? Or is the sentence more ironical in tone, making a historical assertion that primitive regimes were in effect theocracies? The second is probably the more obvious reading, but the ambiguity about whether Rousseau's account of the evolution of religion is abstract or historical should not be overlooked. It may be linked to a deeper uncertainty about whether religion is natural or inherently social.

The ambiguity continues in the subsequent sentences, but shifts to an exploration of the role religion plays in rulership. At first, man "reasoned like Caligula, and, at that period, reasoned aright."[11] Since Rousseau had associated such reasoning—which conceived of rulers and subjects as beings of different orders[12]—with the thought of Hobbes and Grotius, and criticized it as a doctrine conducive to tyranny,[13] it would seem that he had in mind a period or condition (the ambiguity of historicity remains) substantially "later" than the pure state of nature. By asserting that these first men "reasoned aright," Rousseau may have intended to imply that especially before the onset of social corruption, man was correct in perceiving that he need not acknowledge any sovereign other than divinity as revealed in nature (including himself). Assuming that "society with the divine" does not constitute a type of social existence which is already beyond nature, this interpretation does not preclude the possibility that Rousseau is talking here about the pure state of nature. What is correct about the Caligula-type reasoning on this view is its recognition that beings of the same order have no right to dominate each other, and perhaps, that there is a grain of truth in Caligula's perverted belief in his own divinity. On the other hand, Rousseau may merely have been implying that in those early days when men had not yet developed the capacity (i.e., the weakness) to accept "equals as masters,"[14] and when the psychic tension created by the fact of government accordingly led men to ascribe divinity to their rulers, men "reasoned aright" in recognizing that the resultant social scheme was one in which religion and politics were totally fused. They had correctly perceived the tenor of their times, even if they had succumbed too easily to the wiles of Caligula. Under

---

[11] *Social Contract* IV, viii, at 129.

[12] Presumably, the reasoning of Caligyla referred to is the same as that referred to earlier, according to which Caligula reasoned from the natural superiority of shepherd to sheep to the conclusion "either that kings were gods, or that men were beasts." *Social Contract* I, ii, at 5.

[13] Ibid.

[14] Ibid. IV, viii, at 129.

this interpretation, Rousseau appears at the very least to be speaking of civil society, and his meaning may be historical as well.

(2) *Polytheism and Pluralism.*—Turning from the ambiguities about Rousseau's starting point in the chapter on civil religion, one is next puzzled by his explanation of the emergence of polytheism, which turns out on analysis to suggest Rousseau's reflections on pluralism in modern society. Superficially, the account seems plausible enough: as two groups come into conflict with one another, it soon becomes apparent that one god cannot serve two peoples, and so national divisions lead to polytheism, which in turn leads to intolerance. National religion, as opposed to natural religion, is thus dependent on consciousness of other national entities in a way that is subtly reminiscent of the vain and corrupting comparison that lies at the core of Rousseau's notion of *amour-propre*.[15]

At this level, pluralization appears as both cause and consequence of disintegration of a once unified golden age. But how does Rousseau's account explain the phenomenon of cults with multiple deities in a single state? A retreat from strict historicity is the easy response, but the difficulty goes deeper. According to Rousseau's statement of the argument, "[f]rom the mere fact that God was set over every political society, it followed that there were as many gods as peoples."[16] The picture is one in which a society whose political and religious life is totally integrated inevitably creates and worships a deity shaped in the image of its own interests. But if deities are merely the projection of the interests of social entities, how are multiple deities in a society to be explained except as a manifestation of multiple conflicting sub-groups in the larger social entity? And if this is the explanation of polytheistic national cults, how did the larger social entities ever coalesce if each deity was the reflection of conflicting social interests in a pluralistic world? Going a step further, how were the dangers of split sovereignty and loosened bonds of social solidarity that Rousseau associates with Christianity avoided in the polytheistic cults of Sparta and Rome?[17]

Rousseau might have answered that political unification is made possible (or is followed) by the emergence of a polytheistic theology which integrates in a single religion the divergent interests represented by the various deities. But if that is Rousseau's meaning, will not shifts in the balance of power among competing subsocieties necessitate the emergence of a sophisticated "priestly class" (intellectual idealogues) who can make the necessary

---

[15] Cf. *Inequality* at 241-42.

[16] *Social Contract* IV, viii, at 129.

[17] See text accompanying notes 42–47, below.

adjustments in social theology but who can also subtly dominate society in the process?

Stated differently, Rousseau's analysis of polytheistic religion accurately suggests that if religion provides a means for integrating and harmonizing the conflicting interest groupings within a civil society, one can expect power struggles aimed at getting the definitive oracles of a society (e.g., courts, legislatures) to take sides in endorsing the symbolic hegemony or ranking of the society's competing "gods." In any event, why does Rousseau say that polytheism leads to intolerance and not tolerance?[18] Leaving aside the fact that his account ultimately describes the emergence of a paganism which was everywhere "one and the same religion,"[19] he may be saying that internal cohesion is purchased at the price of intensified religio-political rivalry at the international level—an insight that suggests considerable cause for concern at a time of rising ethnic and nationalist rivalries. In light of Rousseau's preference for small republics, in which internal cohesion is probably easier to maintain, this may reflect a considered judgment that the price is worth paying. This judgment would, of course, have been more defensible in a pre-nuclear age. But the full cost must be counted: not only would the multiplication of national entities in the form of small republics lead to increased "theological and civil intolerance"[20] (at the international level), which would seem to be an evil in itself in Rousseau's scheme,[21] but in addition, since unavoidable national rivalries would inevitably focus attention on divergent doctrines in "national theologies," communities would be distracted from shared values which are much more likely to be in harmony with the truths of natural religion. National homogeneity is purchased at the price of heightened risk of international conflict and reduced likelihood of finding shared values conducive to a peaceful international order.

In a sense, Rousseau responds to the problem of international intolerance, but his reply is not particularly comforting. The argument is that "in pagan times, . . . there were no wars of religion . . . precisely because each State, having its own cult as well as its own government, made no distinction between its gods and its laws."[22] That is, there were no religious wars not because there were no wars, but because the wars were primarily political. Wars were religious only in the very limited sense that because of the high degree of religious and political integration maintained in those early

---

[18] See *Social Contract* IV, viii, at 129.

[19] Ibid. at 131.

[20] Ibid.

[21] See ibid. at 129.

[22] Ibid.

societies, "[p]olitical war was also [incidentally] theological."[23] But if the primary international problems are warfare itself and the loss of perspective resulting from religious and ideological polarization, it is not helpful to be told that the harms remain, but that politics and not religion is the culprit.[24] The difference in mode does not appear to be a difference in substance, particularly given the starting assumption that political and religious modes of social life are highly integrated.

To recognize that the allegation of "no wars of religion" is exaggerated or misleading, however, is not to come to terms with the phrase's meaning in Rousseau's deeper analysis of religion in society. For some reason, it seems very important to Rousseau to stress the fundamentally political nature of pagan theology and pagan wars. There is nothing so absurd, in his mind at least, as "the erudition which in our days identifies and confuses the gods of different nations . . . As if there could still be anything in common to imaginary beings with different names."[25] But when the Greeks engaged in an analogous practice, it was meaningful, because at that time there was political substance to the religious comparisons. "[R]ediscovering their gods among the barbarians . . . [was a] way they had of regarding themselves as the natural sovereigns of such peoples."[26] The loss of political substance, Rousseau may be saying, together with the correlative marginalization of religion from political life, has transformed a once meaningful exercise in religious thought into a hopelessly ridiculous example of theological pedantry. What is unclear is the extent to which the scorn for comparative religion was intended as a subtle critique of the meaningfulness of all theological wrangling, or deeper still, as a disguised claim that religion has never held the ultimate key to social life.

Further on, in a footnote to his comments on the historical oddity of the Jews' refusal to recognize their conquerors' gods, Rousseau makes a somewhat paradoxical remark that sheds further light on his views about the relation of religion and politics: "It is quite clear," he states, "that the Phocian war, which was called 'the Sacred War,' was not a war of religion. Its object was the punishment of acts of sacrilege, and not the conquest of unbelievers."[27] One would think that punishment of acts of sacrilege was a religious enterprise, and that conquest of unbelievers (nothing is said of

---

[23] Ibid.

[24] Contentions that recent warfare in Bosnia was not really religious, but was in fact the result of political manipulation of religious groupings, is similarly non-consoling: changing the labels does not reduce the devastation.

[25] Ibid.

[26] Ibid.

[27] Ibid. at 130 n.2.

conversion) was an essentially political concern. Accordingly, Rousseau's cryptic footnote appears to be somehow reversed: contrary to what he says, it would seem that "the Sacred War" was religious and not political.

His meaning emerges, however, when one proceeds to the next paragraph. "[T]here was no way of converting a people except by enslaving it, and there could be no missionaries save conquerors."[28] While that sentence could appear in a book attempting to justify religious warfare (or suppression of religion by a political society confident of its ideological legitimacy), the meaning seems to be that the integration of religion and politics in pagan society was so complete that people simply could not conceive of any reason for changing religion except for political conquest. "The obligation to change cults being the law to which the vanquished yielded, it was necessary to be victorious before suggesting such a change.[29] Pagan wars were not religious wars, because their aim was extension of sovereignty and not oppression for the sake of something imaginary. Apparently then, Rousseau's footnote was implying that the sacrilege at issue in the so-called "Sacred War" was political and not religious; what was at stake in the war was something religious in form but political in substance. The concern was not so much with mere personal beliefs as with political recalcitrance.

(3) *The Public Dimension of Religion.*—If this is Rousseau's meaning, then his statement about "[e]very religion . . . being attached solely to the laws of the State which prescribed it"[30] may be more radical than it appears at first glance. He may be implying that by its very nature, religion is a matter of state, and not of personal conscience, or at least that religion necessarily has a public dimension that cannot be confined to the private sphere, as classical liberal theory has argued.[31] The possible response that Rousseau is merely describing contingent historical events at this juncture and is not attempting to say anything about the fundamentally public or private character of

---

[28] Ibid. at 130-31.

[29] Ibid. at 131.

[30] Ibid. at 130.

[31] In effect, Rousseau seems to be recognizing that what Josè Casanova has described as "public religion" is a necessary feature of life in human communities. See José Casanova, *Public Religions in the Modern World,* (Chicago: The Univ. of Chicago Press, 1994), 40-66. Given Rousseau's affinities for republican communities, and the fact that republican theory at the time did not require the state to be neutral on matters of public good (whether religious or secular), see John Witte, "The Essential Rights and Liberties of Religion in the American Constitutional Experiment," *Notre Dame Law Review* 71 (1996): 371, 385–88, Rousseau's position in this regard appears to be a manifestation of his republicanism. As Professor Witte has noted, "civil republicans sought to imbue the public square with a common religious ethic and ethos—albeit one less denominationally specific and rigorous than that countenanced by the Puritans." Ibid. at 386.

religion is not completely satisfying. For in many ways, the call for a civil religion is a call for a new paganism, and much of the controversy concerning the civil religion has centered precisely on the issue whether reintegration of religion and politics will eventuate in obliteration of respect for private conscience.

Such concerns are exacerbated when one realizes the possible implications of Rousseau's relative equanimity in depicting conquerors as missionaries and conversion as enslavement.[32] Earlier in *The Social Contract*, Rousseau had rejected Grotius' contention that conquest could legitimate slavery.[33] Grotius had argued that since the victor has the right to kill the vanquished, the latter "can buy back his life at the price of his liberty,"[34] and hence that enslavement after conquest is permissible. In response, Rousseau claimed that war was a "relation, not between man and man, but between State and State. . . ."[35] If it were possible "to kill the State without killing a single one of its members,"[36] (and Rousseau pointed out that it was feasible to avoid the killing of additional "members" as soon as these surrendered), then there was no right of execution and hence, no right of enslavement.[37] But if this is Rousseau's position, condoning *religious* "enslavement" after conquest would seem to imply a view of religion as part of the state—as an aspect of defeated sovereignty which could justifiably be extirpated.

The extent to which Rousseau would in fact tolerate such intolerance is unclear. His historical or quasi-historical account is ambiguous in this regard. It speaks of the republican Romans as believing that the gods of a vanquished people were "subject to their own [gods] and compelled to do them homage"[38] and contrasts the imperial Romans who granted both their own gods and the gods of the vanquished "the rights of the city."[39] The ambiguity lies in the fact that Rousseau seems to view favorably the gradual development of tolerance for the vanquished, but in light of his deeper conviction that the evolution from republic to empire constituted a pattern of

---

[32] See above, p. 5 & n.22. Of course, in his later assessment of the evils of paganism, he states, [i]t is bad . . . when it becomes tyrannous and exclusive, and makes people bloodthirsty and intolerant." *Social Contract* IV, viii, at 135. But this is not necessarily inconsistent with acceptance of political imposition of a new state religion by conquerors who are concerned to prevent "political sacrilege" and secure obedience (enslavement) to new laws—not, that is, if political order is the crucial priority.

[33] Ibid. I, iv, at 9.

[34] Ibid.

[35] Ibid. at 10.

[36] Ibid. at 11.

[37] Ibid.

[38] Ibid. IV, viii, at 131.

[39] Ibid.

decay, it is not clear whether he regards the toleration of later paganism as a sign of progress or disintegration. In either case, the implication seems clear that pagan religion was intimately connected with and ultimately subordinate to politics. "So far from men fighting for the gods, the gods, as in Homer, fought for men."[40] The republican Romans "left the vanquished their gods as they left them their laws,"[41] and the imperial Romans, having dissipated their inheritance, gave virtue and vice equal sway in the city. In describing the early societies in which religion and politics had remained integrated, then, Rousseau was describing a mode of life in which politics reigned supreme.

(4) *The Perils of Transcendence.*—And then came Jesus. Although there had been some inkling of the separation of religion and politics among his Jewish forebears,[42] it was Jesus' separation of theological and political systems that led to what Rousseau regarded as a terrible oxymoron—a spiritual kingdom on earth—which "made the State no longer one."[43] The pagans, unable to believe that religion could ultimately be separated from politics,

> looked on the Christians as really rebels, who, while feigning to submit, were only waiting for the chance to make themselves independent from their [the pagans'] masters, and to usurp by guile the authority they pretended in their weakness to respect. This was the cause of their persecutions.[44]

The question of persecution, then, was perceived not as a matter of respect or disregard for private dignity, but as a matter of politics and sovereignty. In a world in which religion could not be conceived as something meaningful apart from politics, there could be no such thing as a kingdom "not of this world," or loyal allegiance to two sovereigns. Pagans, Rousseau was saying, were not bigots; they were deeply conscious of the dangers of allowing religion and not politics to dominate public order. The "fancy the Greeks had for rediscovering their gods among the barbarians" was not absurd erudition. Ultimately, the question being raised was whether religion should have an immanent or a transcendent role with respect to the public order, and the pagans feared the domination of transcendence.

In light of the subsequent history, Rousseau maintains that the fears of the pagans were justified. Once given political power, "the humble Christians changed their language, and soon this so-called kingdom of the other world

---

40 Ibid.

41 Ibid.

42 Ibid. at 130.

43 Ibid. at 131.

44 Ibid.

turned, under a visible leader, into the most violent of earthly despotisms."[45] The cult of transcendence resulted in a

> double power and conflict of jurisdiction . . . [which] made all good polity impossible in Christian States; and men have never succeeded in finding out whether they were bound to obey the master or the priest.[46]

This critique is full of venom for Catholicism and clericalism, but it is not clear how far Rousseau thought its logic should be pushed. It was not only Jesus who taught of a higher kingdom. Pagan philosophical conceptions of natural law were just as likely to inspire humble Socratic "gadflies" or hierophants of an ideal kingdom not yet come, just as capable of creating a jurisdictional rift in human allegiance that had revolutionary dimensions, and just as corruptible in the sense of germinating rationales for domination, oppression and tyranny once a semblance of the ideal acquired power to govern. Is the "history lesson" merely an attack on Roman Christianity and more generally on the type of bureaucratized idealism which creates institutional rifts in the state and therefore "leads to a sort of mixed and anti-social code which has no name"?[47] Or is it a deeper lesson in the perils of transcendence?

At the beginning of *The Social Contract*, Rousseau had stated that "the social order is a sacred right which is the basis of all rights. Nevertheless, this right does not come from nature, and must therefore be founded on conventions."[48] The question is what guides the conventions? In light of the doctrine of the general will, Rousseau's answer seems to be that the ideal polity will result from a distillation of values immanent in society. Viewed from this perspective, the lesson of religious history seems to be part of a frontal attack on any human attempt to seek ultimate social norms from the higher realms postulated by religion. But as soon as this interpretation is advanced, it is confronted with the problem of explaining Rousseau's deep respect for Gospel Christianity, his natural religion, and, as it were, "everything its author elsewhere utters of religion."[49] What emerges is a seemingly impossible dilemma. If transcendence is dangerous, as Rousseau's pagans and his history seem to suggest, it can only be eliminated if one is willing to sacrifice what many regard as the core of human existence. The practical difficulty of making this sacrifice is magnified when one reflects that

---

[45] Ibid. at 131-32.

[46] Ibid. at 132.

[47] Ibid. at 134.

[48] Ibid. I, I, at 4.

[49] See above, p. 1 & n.1.

while, as Rousseau notes, the Kings of England and the Czars of Russia may be able to root out the clergy,[50] it would be virtually impossible for them to stamp out the lure of utopia and the sense of a higher justice. On the other hand, as soon as the concern for transcendent values finds acceptance, the danger of split sovereignty arises (except, perhaps, in perfect societies) and unless the votaries of these higher norms are incorruptible, there is always the fear that "the priestly interest [will become] . . . stronger than that of the state."[51] As the response to Bayle and Warburton suggests, Rousseau may be attempting to strike a middle course. Unlike Bayle, who maintained that "religion can be of no use to the body politic,"[52] Rousseau was conscious that "no State has ever been founded without a religious basis."[53] And unlike Warburton, who thought Christianity to be the strongest support for the state, he perceived Christianity as having an enervating effect on the crucial social bonds of the political constitution.[54]

(5) *The Relationship of Religion and Politics.*—What is unclear in the articulation of this "middle course" is whether religion has more than merely instrumental value. Rousseau concludes his chapter on the Legislator with the remark, "[w]e should not, with Warburton, conclude that politics and religion have among us a common object, but that, in the first periods of nations, the one is used as an instrument for the other."[55] Rousseau is thus deeply conscious of the Legislator's need to "have recourse to an authority of a different order, capable of constraining without violence and persuading without convincing."[56] To the extent that the Legislator "credit[s] the gods with [his] own wisdom, . . . in order to constrain by divine authority those whom human prudence could not move,"[57] his use of religion is purely instrumental.

But even in the account of the Legislator, it can be argued that there is a religious element which goes beyond mere instrumentalism. The qualifications of the Legislator constitute a kind of secular saintliness. Blessed with prophetic insight, he must live in the world without being of the world, "beholding all the passions of men without experiencing any of them . . ."[58]

---

[50] Cf. *Social Contract* IV, viii, at 132-33.

[51] Ibid. at 133.

[52] Ibid.

[53] Ibid.

[54] Ibid.

[55] Ibid. II, vii, at 41-42.

[56] Ibid. at 40.

[57] Ibid. at 40-41.

[58] Ibid. at 37.

He must not only manipulate awe for the divine in others, but must himself be infused with "sublime reason far above the range of the common herd."[59] In short, he must approach divinity in his own being. "It would take gods to give men laws."[60] Transformed by some miracle so that he stands outside politics, he must discern the inner workings of religious life among the people for whom he is to legislate. Even to manipulate their awe, if his "manipulation" is to endure,[61] he must understand deeply the sources of reverence within their society. Just as in the political realm, he must perceive and articulate the general will, so in the religious sphere he must recognize the harmonics of social spirit, in order that he may legitimately mold the social institutions which will yield a society at one with itself. Seeing the end from the beginning, he must

> feel himself capable, so to speak, of changing human nature, of transforming each individual, who is by himself a complete and solitary whole, into part of a greater whole from which he in a manner receives his life and being; of altering man's constitution for the purpose of strengthening it; and of substituting a partial and moral existence for the physical and independent existence nature has conferred on us all.[62]

While it remains true, then, that the Legislator relies on religion in laying the foundations of a polity, he does not employ it as an opiate, *i.e.*, as a mask and palliative for illegitimate domination. Within himself, there is a religious dimension to the wisdom required for his task and to the process by which his desires are purged and his perspective distanced from the particularity of the society for which he will legislate. And within society, it is his perception of an immanent religiosity that enables him to integrate religious and political factors in social life so that they can operate synergistically for the creation of a more perfect polity than would otherwise have been possible. In both respects, the role of religion is not *merely* instrumental, not shallowly manipulative.

At the same time, the precise nature of the religiosity of the Legislator and "his" society remains unclear: it is a strangely secular blend of charisma and the numinous. Lycurgus, in many ways the least religious of Rousseau's legislative paradigms,[63] is the only great legislator explicitly mentioned in text

---

[59] Ibid.

[60] Ibid. at 38.

[61] Cf. ibid. at 41: "Idle tricks form a passing tie; only wisdom can make it lasting."

[62] Ibid. at 38.

[63] Greek tradition portrays Lycurgus as receiving certain edicts from the oracle at Delphi which were supposed to be either his laws themselves or the divine sanction for his laws. After completing his legislation, he is supposed to have starved himself to death at

in the chapter on the Legislator, although Calvin is mentioned in footnote[64] and there are allusions to the accomplishments of Moses, Numa and Mohammed.[65] In *The Government of Poland*, Rousseau seems to suggest that it is Moses—the most religious of legislators—who has achieved the deepest success. Not only has he transformed a "herd of servile emigrants into a political society, a free people;"[66] in addition, his legislation has been so "proof against time, fortune, and conquest . . . [that even] today, when that nation no longer exists as a body, its legislation endures and is as strong as ever."[67]

Lycurgus was able to transform the Spartans into "beings more than merely human"[68] and Numa was able to change "robbers into citizens,"[69] but nothing has been as lasting as Israel. None of this is mentioned in *The Social Contract*, and accordingly, it is not clear where on the spectrum of religiosity between Moses and Lycurgus Rousseau's ideal Legislator will be found. But in any case, whatever the nature of the religiosity Rousseau perceives at the founding (and foundation) of ideal society, it seems apparent that his alternative to Warburton and Bayle goes beyond cynical instrumentalism in its view of the relation of religion and politics. At the deepest level, Rousseau's alternative may be not so much an attack on traditional religion as a philosophical critique of religion as transcendence; it may be a plea for philosophers to turn from a Platonic heaven in order to discover the light immanent in the cave of social life.

(6) *The Religions of Man and Citizen.*—Having described the "history" of religion, Rousseau turns to his analysis of the two primary and "non-

---

Delphi after pledging the Spartans not to change the laws until his return. See W. Durrant, *The Story of Civilization: Part II: The Life of Greece* 78 (N.Y.: Simon & Schuster, 1939). But Rousseau appears to make no reference to the religious dimension of Lycurgus' accomplishment.

[64] *Social Contract* II, vii, at 39 n.1, 41 n.1.

[65] See ibid. at 41.

[66] J.-J. Rousseau, *The Government of Poland* 6 (W. Kendall trans., Library of Liberal Arts, Indianapolis: Bobs-Merrill, 1972) (hereinafter *Poland*).

[67] Ibid.

[68] Ibid. at 7.

[69] Ibid.

worthless"[70] modes of religious life in society: "the religion of man, and that of the citizen."[71]

> The first, which has neither temples, nor altars, nor rites, and is confined to the purely internal cult of the supreme God and the eternal obligations of morality, is the religion of the Gospel pure and simple, the true theism, what may be called natural divine right or law (*droit divin naturel*). The other, which is codified in a single country, gives it its gods, its own tutelary patrons; it has its dogmas, its rites, and its external cult prescribed by law; outside the single nation that follows it, all the world is its sight infidel, foreign, and barbarous; the duties and rights of man extend for it only as far as its own altars. Of this kind were all the religions of early peoples, which we may define as civil or positive divine right or law (*droit divin civil ou positif*).[72]

The names he gives the two types of religion suggest a parallel between natural and civil modes of life in religion and politics. But if the parallel is intended, its meaning is far from clear. There is a deep sense in which religion, like political life, is good or bad for Rousseau depending on whether it remains true to nature or becomes unnatural.[73] But as much as Rousseau yearns for the state of nature, he is convinced that civilized man cannot return to that happy condition.[74] Is "the true theism" of natural religion by analogy something which is forever lost to man? It would seem not, because the principal tenets of the natural religion, which are intimated in the passage above and developed by the Savoyard Vicar in the *Emile*,[75] are to be incorporated in the civil religion, which has only the following simple dogmas:

> [t]he existence of a mighty, intelligent, and beneficent Divinity, possessed of foresight and providence, the life to come, the happiness of the just, the

---

[70] The third mode, identified with religions "of the Lamas and of the Japanese, and . . . Roman Christianity" is dismissed as so obviously defective that it doesn't warrant discussion. "All that destroys social unity is worthless; all institutions that set men in contradiction to himself are worthless." *Social Contract* IV, viii, at 134. The two major modes are presumably not worthless in either of these senses.

[71] Ibid.

[72] Ibid.

[73] See Wright, *The Meaning of Rousseau*, at 113.

[74] See J. Shklar, *Men and Citizens: A Study of Rousseau's Social Theory* 10 (London: Cambridge Univ. Press, 1969); Cassirer, *Das Problem*, at 54; C. Vaughan, *The Political Writings of Jean Jacques Rousseau* 1: 13 & n.2 (1915, reprinted New York: Wiley, 1962) (with citations to numerous passages in Rousseau's minor works and letter where the possibility of returning to nature is dismissed as absurd).

[75] See generally *Creed of a Savoyard Priest*, in J.-J. Rousseau, *Emile* 228-278 (B. Foxley trans., (New York: E.P. Dutton, 1972) (hereinafter *Emile*).

punishment of the wicked, the sanctity of the social contract and the laws . . . [and a proscription of] intolerance.[76]

On the other side of the parallel, given the depth of Rousseau's sensitivity to the dangers of social corruption, it seems almost surprising that the civil religion should be so thoroughly infused with (if not identical to) the religion of the citizen. Describing the latter's vices, Rousseau notes that it is "founded on lies and error, it deceives men, makes them credulous and superstitious, and drowns the true cult of the Divinity in empty ceremonial."[77] Moreover, it breeds intolerance and violence,[78] which are simply religious manifestations of *amour propre* (the corrupting form of love).

Despite these flaws, the civil religion ultimately proposed bears such a pronounced resemblance to the religion of the citizen that there is a tendency to identify the two, even though it is not clear whether Rousseau conceived of the civil religion as a synthesis of the religions of man and citizen, or as the most attractive of two mutually exclusive alternatives chosen after weighing the costs and benefits of each. In either case, it is clear that the attraction of the citizen religion lies in its ability to promote social solidarity. Its capacity to strengthen the state by stimulating love for the laws and a willingness to put country before self is contrasted with the tendency of pure Christianity to divert attention from the affairs of this world, to destroy the love for worldly glory and heroism, and in general, to undermine those passions which are

---

[76] *Social Contract* IV, viii, at 135. With regard to the relationship of the Savoyard Vicar and the civil religion of the *Social Contract*, Ernest Wright has made the following remarks:

> The *Social Contract* and *Emile*, with the Vicar's Profession in it, were written at the same time; they were not only published together, but are so interpenetrated that the first is reproduced all but entire within the second. . . . The Vicar believes in his religion because it does not seem individual to him, but, in reason, universal; yet he would tolerate all other religions which are tolerant in turn, condemning only those which hold that we are damned if we do not believe them. Having no power to prohibit such intolerance, he can only do his best to discourage it. Meanwhile, as a member of the state, he devoutly follows its religious ordinances. The Contract offers a religion to support the state. Its dogmas are about identical with those of the Vicar; but any further dogmas will be tolerated in the individual unless they are themselves intolerant—unless they say we shall be damned for not believing them. If they do, the state may do more than discourage them, it may prohibit them, and whoso holds them may therefore be excluded from the state as unfit for membership.

Wright, *The Meaning of Rousseau*, at 89 n.1. See also Cobban, *Rousseau and the Modern State*, at 79 (chapter on civil religion represents only one aspect of Rousseau's conception of the place of religion in the life of society).

[77] *Social Contract* IV, viii, at 135.

[78] Ibid.

necessary to preserve the state in a pagan world. Rousseau seems to acknowledge that the *truly* Christian society would be beyond reproach in all the crucial respects:

> Everyone would do his duty; the people would be law-abiding, the rulers just and temperate; the magistrates upright and incorruptible; the soldiers would scorn death; there would be neither vanity nor luxury.[79]

But "a society of true Christians would not be a society of men."[80] The real evil of Christianity in the actual world is its tendency to relinquish government to the corrupt and to be timid in responding to the emergence of corruption. "[A] single self-seeker or hypocrite . . . would certainly get the better of his pious compatriots."[81] The true Christian is unwilling to compromise his personal goodness for the sake of the state; he is unwilling to learn (in the Machiavellian sense) to do the necessary "bad things." Even though incorruptible in itself, Christianity—the religion of man alone—is incapable of safeguarding the virtue of the state.

(7) *The Ambiguities of Intolerance.*—Within the complex web of tensions and ambiguities that constitutes Rousseau's proposal of a civil religion, the most perplexing issue is how the seeming apostle of tolerance could recommend a scheme so ominous and severe in its intolerance. Repeatedly, critics have characterized the chapter on civil religion as "unfortunate."[82] There is good evidence that the chapter was hastily written,[83] and some have thought that much of the difficulty with the civil religion in general and the problem of intolerance in particular could be ascribed to this fact. But Rousseau had suggested the possibility of a civil religion as early as 1756 in a letter to Voltaire:

> I would therefore like the adoption in each state of a moral code, or of a kind of profession of civic faith, which included on the positive side the social maxims which everybody would be bound to admit and on the negative side the fanatic maxims which one would be bound to reject, not as impious but as seditious. Thus every religion which could be reconciled with the code would be admitted,

---

[79] Ibid. at 136.

[80] Ibid.

[81] Ibid.

[82] See, e.g., H. Höffding, *Jean Jacques Rousseau and His Philosophy* 131 (W. Richards & L. Saidla trans., New Haven: Yale Univ. Press, 1930); Cobban, *Rousseau and the Modern State*, 88.

[83] See Vaughn, *The Political Writings of Jean Jacques Rousseau*, 1: 87; E. Wright, *The Meaning of Rousseau*, 86; C. Hendel, *Jean-Jacques Rousseau Moralist* 2: 231 (Indianapolis: Bobbs-Merrill, 1934).

every religion which could not be reconciled would be proscribed, and everybody would be free to have no other religion than the code itself.[84]

However hastily the chapter that appeared in *The Social Contract* in 1762 was written, its basic thesis had obviously had considerable time to mature.

The Social Contract's intolerant tolerance is accordingly all the more puzzling. Despite the tolerant tone of both the letter to Voltaire and the dogma proscribing intolerance in the tenets of the civil religion, there is something deeply disturbing about the severity of the sanctions to be imposed on citizens unwilling to make the civic profession of faith.

> While [this faith] . . . can compel no one to believe . . . [its dogmas], it can banish from the State whoever does not believe them—it can banish him, not for impiety, but as an anti-social being, incapable of truly loving the laws and justice, and of sacrificing, at need, his life to his duty. If any one, after publicly recognizing these dogmas, behaves as if he does not believe them, let him be punished by death: he has committed the worst of all crimes, that of lying before the law.[85]

The severity of these provisions is underscored when one reflects that if the civil religion is essential to every state, one who cannot subscribe to its tenets has nowhere to flee.[86] Fears of oppressive intrusion into matters of private conscience are not allayed by the assurance that "subjects . . . owe the Sovereign an account of their opinions only to such an extent as they matter to the community,"[87] because Rousseau has earlier stressed that "the Sovereign is sole judge of what is important . . . for the community to control."[88] Like Locke and Milton before him, Rousseau appears to have few qualms about banning atheism and Catholicism from his otherwise tolerant world,[89] and his enthusiasm in *The Government of Poland* for exploiting education, patriotism, public festivals and (by implication) all the institutions of the civil religion for the inculcation of political virtue makes it difficult to say how broad a swath he would allow the state to cut in narrowing the domain of private conscience. The willingness to exclude atheists is particularly puzzling in light of the fact that one of the fundamental teachings

---

[84] *Lettre à Voltaire*, Aug. 18, 1756, C.G. II, 303-24, quoted in M. Einaudi, *The Early Rousseau* 206-07 (Ithaca, N.Y.: Cornell Univ. Press, 1967). For the actual text read by Voltaire, see Leigh, "Rousseau's Letter to Voltaire on Optimism," *Studies on Voltaire* 30 (1964): 247.

[85] *Social Contract* IV, viii, at 139.

[86] See A. Cobban, *Rousseau and the Modern State*, 83.

[87] *Social Contract* IV, viii, at 138.

[88] Ibid. II, iv, at 28.

[89] See ibid. IV, viii, at 139-40.

of *Julie ou La Nouvelle Heloise* was the possibility of the creation of an ideal society (Clarens) founded on the mutual toleration and respect of an atheist (Wolmar), who participated only in the outer form of religious worship (church attendance for the sake of appearance), and a devout believer (Julie).[90] Beyond fears of oppression, there are residual questions about how Rousseau, who attached such great value to sincerity, could advocate a system of church-state relations which was bound to induce hypocrisy—the shell of outer compliance—in a considerable portion of the citizenry.[91]

(8) *Ambiguities in the Conception of Community.*—The depth of the ambiguity on the issue of toleration is reflected in the breadth of the spectrum of interpretations it has spawned. The oppressive aspects of the civil religion have provided strong support for those who have urged a totalitarian or communitarian view of Rousseau. Arguing at the beginning of the twentieth century that "the 'individualism' of Rousseau . . . [is] nothing better than a myth,"[92] C.E. Vaughan lamented,

> It is grievous to think that a man like Rousseau should have done his utmost to fight against the light, to drive the world back into the darkness from which it was at last struggling to escape.[93]

Despite his recognition that Rousseau's aim was to "unite the truth and nobility of Christianity with the civic fervour," the ardent patriotism, of the purer forms of Paganism,"[94] Vaughan was convinced that Rousseau's overriding concern was to buttress the state's interest in making certain that the public duties of its citizens were "discharged not only with strictness, but with zeal."[95] The inevitable consequence, he thought, would be the glaring moral evil of persecution.[96]

The communitarian interpretation advanced by Vaughan has been a recurrent theme in Rousseau criticism.[97] Two variations on the general theme

---

[90] See C. Hendel, *Jean-Jacques Rousseau Moralist*, 2: 232; A. Cobban, *Rousseau and the Modern State*, 81.

[91] See, e.g., C. Vaughan, *The Political Writings of Jean Jacques Rousseau*, 1: 90-93.

[92] Ibid., 1.

[93] Ibid., 90.

[94] Ibid., 88.

[95] Ibid., 89.

[96] Ibid.

[97] See, e.g., E. Barker, *Introduction to The Social Contract* xxxviii (1947, paperback, N.Y.: Oxford Univ. Press, 1960); H. Maine, *Popular Government* 157, 160 (N.Y.: H. Holt, 1886); K. Popper, The Open Society and Its Enemies 2: 50 (London: G. Routledge & Sons, Ltd., 1945); Taine, *Les origines de la France contemporaine*, Vol. I, *L'Ancien Régime* 319 (Paris: Hachette, 1876).

are worth noting. Alfred Cobban, while recognizing the collectivist impulses in the civil religion, noted by way of caveat that the "Civil Religion by itself must be held to represent only one aspect of [Rousseau's] conception of the place of religion in the life of society."[98] Relying primarily on the strong spirit of toleration manifested elsewhere in Rousseau's works, he contended that the seeming tendency to place matters of state above matters of conscience may have been not so much a reflection of collectivist convictions as a consequence of an effort to assess religion from a strictly political perspective in the political writings.[99]

Such a view is not without foundation in the text of *The Social Contract*. Rousseau initiates his discussion of the relative merits of the religions of man and citizen with the phrase, "In their political aspect. . . ."[100] Even when, at the conclusion of his critique of Christianity and just prior to his description of the civil religion, he says, "But, setting aside political considerations, let us come back to what is right (*droit*) . . .,"[101] the ambiguity of the word "*droit*" obscures whether he is attempting to step back from the political frame of reference in order to determine what is "right" from the perspective of both religion and politics, or whether he is merely saying, polemics aside, let us determine what right or law (*droit*) ought to be from the perspective of the ideal, but still political, sovereign. To the extent the second of these alternatives corresponds to Rousseau's meaning, the Cobban argument imposes significant constraints on attempts to use the civil religion in efforts to portray Rousseau as a totalitarian.

The second variation on the communitarian theme also recognizes the collectivist elements in Rousseau's thought, but sees them not as an evil but as part of a brilliant early attempt to grapple with the emerging problem of the disintegrating social solidarity and community life that the industrial revolution brought in its train. In the words of Sheldon S. Wolin,

> Few men have been more deeply at odds with society than Rousseau; fewer still have spoken as powerfully of the need for community. Yet this was not one more paradox in the most paradoxical of thinkers. Because Rousseau felt his own alienation so deeply, he was prepared to sacrifice more for society, as well as to demand more from it . . . . Rousseau's solution for the ills of society was not to beckon men to the woods, nor to advocate the destruction of all social interdependencies. He proposed, instead, a paradox: let us create a society which causes men to grow closer to one another, to become so strongly solidary that

---

[98] Cobban, *Rousseau and the Modern State*, 79.

[99] See ibid., 86-87.

[100] *Social Contract* IV, viii, at 134.

[101] Ibid., 138.

each member will be made dependent on the whole society and, by that very fact, be released from *personal* dependencies.[102]

The civil religion in this perspective is not an instrument of oppression but a healing tonic for the anguish of alienation and separation in society. It is one of the channels through which the individual finds meaning and fulfillment in his own life through identification with the larger community. It contributes to the process by which a "love of the fatherland, which is to say love of the laws and of liberty . . . [comes to make up the citizen's] entire existence"[103] and by which citizens come to regard

their own existence merely as a part of that of the State [community], [so that] they . . . at length come to identify themselves in some degree with this greater whole, to feel themselves members of their country, and to love it with that exquisite feeling which no isolated person has save for himself . . . .[104]

It was from the vantage point of this communitarian perception of Rousseau that Durkheim analyzed the civil religion: politics alone cannot insure social cohesion, since social cohesion requires a "spontaneous agreement of wills" which in turn depends at least in part on an "intellectual communion" of an essentially religions nature; the civil religion is comprised of that minimal measure of religiosity necessary to assure inward and outward performance of civil responsibilities (to provide the citizen with "a religious reason for doing his duty); it is thus not only a means to but also a mode of social solidarity and cohesion.[105] In general, the principal characteristic of the second variation is to explain the potentially intolerant strains in Rousseau's thought as part of a deeper perception that the individual is not merely the solitary man wishing to be left alone with his conscience, but also the social man deeply in need of community with his fellows.[106] In this context, the concern for toleration tends to be overshadowed by the concern for wholeness.

The other side of Rousseau's ambiguity with regard to toleration is reflected in the views of those who continue to maintain that Rousseau's primary aim with the civil religion was to promote toleration. It is too easy to

---

[102] S. Wolin, *Politics and Vision: Continuity and Innovation in Western Political Thought* 368–69, 371 (Boston: Little Brown, 1960).

[103] Rousseau, *Poland, 19.*

[104] J.-J. Rousseau, "A Discourse on Political Economy," in *The Social Contract and Discourses* 283, 307–08, G.D.H. Cole trans., New York: E.P. Dutton, 1950) (hereinafter *Political Economy*).

[105] See E. Durkheim, *Montesquieu and Rousseau: Forerunners of Sociology* 132-34 (Ann Arbor, Mich.: Univ. of Michigan Press, 1965), 132-134.

[106] Cf. M. Einaudi, *The Early Rousseau*, 13, 17.

forget that Rousseau lived at a time when established churches remained the order of the day. The model of Calvinistic Geneva may have been influential in molding his suggestion that the civil religion be "established" in the ideal society.[107] Without entering into the complex questions about the sources of the civil religion, what is significant is the contrast between the religious establishments of his day and the comparatively slight "establishment" of religion Rousseau was prepared to accept.[108] The dogmas of the civil religion were to be "few, simple, and exactly worded, without explanation or commentary."[109] The critique of Christianity makes it apparent that Rousseau would not permit state support for the civil religion to include aid to a priestly establishment.[110] Beyond issues of public morality and duty, each man may have

---

[107] In the *Letters from the Mountain*, Rousseau acknowledged that the Genevan constitution was the model for his political institutions. *Lettres écrites de la montague*, 3 O.C. at 809, summarized in Einaudi, *The Early Rousseau*, 264–66, esp. 266 n.81 (referring to conflicting views of Candaux and Derathé, Einaudi supports the view that even if the philosophical sources of the *Social Contract* have little relation to Geneva, the inspiration of the book—at least several of its chapters—is Genevan in its very essence). The relationship of Rousseau to Geneva is not without ambiguity, see Einaudi, *The Early Rousseau*, 30 n.10 (for references to the literature), and the conditions which prompted him to leave Geneva again after his return in 1754 should have made him more sensitive to the dangers of any type of state-endorsed creed. On the other hand, Rousseau may have thought that such dangers could be eliminated simply by making it clear that the established creed of the civil religion was not to be sustained and interpreted by an established clergy. Cf. *Social Contract* IV, viii, at 139. Given that hypothesis, together with Rousseau's life-long love for his native city (despite difficulties after 1754), see Einaudi, *The Early Rousseau*, 30–33, many of the intolerant aspects of the civil religion—its anti-Catholicism, anti-atheism, and willingness to impose a state creed—may reflect at least in part veneration for Geneva.

For an analysis of Calvinistic influence on the civil religion, see L. Cordier, *Jean Jacques Rousseau und der Calvinismus: Eine Untersuchung über das Verhältnis Rousseaus zur Religion und Religiösen Kultur seiner Vaterstadt* 133–87 (Langensalza: Beyer, 1915).

[108] Cf. John Witte, *The Essential Rights and Liberties, in the American Establishment*, 388-89 (discussing "slender" or "soft" types of religious establishment even in the post-revolutionary United States).

[109] *Social Contract* IV, viii, at 139.

[110] *See* ibid. at 132-33. Cf. Rousseau, *Poland*, 20 & 49 (foreigners and priests should be stripped of their pedagogical positions; appointment of bishops should be left for the most part with the king; *i.e.,* some establishment remains, but gradually undermined through state control of education). In the Letter to d'Alembert, Rousseau describes the clergy of Geneva as "a body of philosophic and pacific theologians, or rather a body of officers of morality and ministers of virtue." J.-J. Rousseau, *Politics and the Arts: Letter to M. d'Alembert on the Theatre* 14 (A. Bloom, trans. 1960, Cornell Paperbacks, Ithaca, N.Y.: Cornell Univ. Press, 1968). "Philosophic and pacific" appears to imply tolerance, and while there is always the danger that "ministers of virtue" can exercise their authority in totalitarian ways, Rousseau seems to be praising them precisely because they have not acted in that way. The teaching seems to be that even where there is an established clergy,

what opinions he pleases, without its being the Sovereign's business to take cognizance of them; for, as the Sovereign has no authority in the other world, whatever the lot of its subjects may be in the life to come, that is not its business, provided they are good citizens in this life.[111]

The civil religion thus allows broad latitude with regard to personal beliefs, in the absence of what the United States Supreme Court might call "compelling state interests" to the contrary.[112] Viewed from this perspective, much that sounds collectivist in Rousseau's church-state theory is no more than the recognition that there are some limits to the state's obligation to respect the individual beliefs of its citizens. In the words of C.W. Hendel,

> This doctrine of civil religion was intended to do away with all persecutors. It was not meant to sanction a dogmatic theology and inquisition . . . . The practical intention of the chapter on *Civil Religion* was thus to exclude intolerance and to establish religious liberty . . . Rousseau's statement of his meaning was complicated by the fact that he himself was profoundly convinced of the necessity of religion to morals and the social order which depends ultimately upon the moral will of men.[113]

According to this interpretation, the supposed collectivist implications of the civil religion may reflect nothing more than the extreme difficulty of maintaining state neutrality toward matters of personal religious belief without accelerating the secularization of society.[114] Current literature concerning church-state relations in America and in Europe is replete with evidence that this continues to be one of the thorniest problems of constitutional law[115]—a problem that even (especially?) Rousseau would have trouble resolving cleanly.

---

it ought to limit the exercise of its authority so that it is no more coercive than the civil religion.

[111] *Social Contract* IV, viii, at 139.

[112] *See, e.g.,* Sherbert v. Verner 374 U.S. 400, 403 (1963). Of course, as the critics of Rousseau's communitarian would be quick to point out, Rousseau's idea of what is "compelling" is much too broad for modern liberal taste.

[113] C. Hendel, *Jean-Jacques Rousseau Moralist*, 2: 231–42.

[114] Cf. Vaughan, *The Political Writings of Jean Jacques Rousseau*, 94 (Rousseau was concerned with stemming tide of secularism on the one hand while stripping Christianity of superstition on the other).

[115] James Davison Hunter, *Culture Wars: The Struggle to Define America* (New York: Basic Books, 1991); José Casanova, *Public Religions in the Modern World* (Chicago: The Univ. of Chicago Press, 1994); David Martin, *A General Theory of Secularization* (New York: Harper Colophon Books, 1978); See School Dist. Of Abington v. Schempp, 374 U.S. 203, 225 (1963); Choper, *The Establishment Clause and Aid to Parochial Schools, 56 California Law Review* 56 (1968): 260; R. Drinan, "The Constitutionality of Public Aid to Parochial Schools," in *The Wall Between Church and State* 55, 66–68 (D. Oaks, ed.,

Some scholars have viewed the tensions in the civil religion as evidence that Rousseau's attitude toward religion was essentially pragmatic. Schinz, for example, claims that for Rousseau, the meaning of religion lies solely in its efficacy in ensuring human happiness, and that its truth is dependent upon the fulfillment of that task.[116] To the extent that the civil religion is conducive to social peace and to the development of a sense of identification with the community which deepens the individual's sense of meaning and worth, it is conducive to human happiness, and by pragmatic criteria is sufficiently "true" to be imposed on the citizenry. A pragmatic conception of religion obviously makes it easier to adopt an instrumental view of the role of religion in the state, and if Rousseau was a pragmatist in this respect, his seeming casualness in balancing the advantages of the religion of the citizen against those of "the true theism" would be more easily understood. It is only by adopting this type of pragmatic conception of Rousseau that Grimsley is able to explain the paradox of Rousseau's emphasis on religious sincerity on the one hand and his apparent demand for a public avowal of the civil religion—whether or not it is believed—on the other.[117] Rousseau, he claims,

> favours the religion which commands the greatest number of adherents, for this seems likely to make for political and civil stability. . . . [C]onsiderations of public order far outweigh any question of the truth or falsity of particular religious dogmas. The effectiveness of a national religion is to be determined by its ability to strengthen the unity and stability of the State rather than by its

---

Chicago: Univ. of Chicago Press, 1963); Katz, "Freedom of Religion and State Neutrality," *Univ. of Chicago Law Review* 20 (1953): 426; P. Kauper, *Religion and the Constitution* (Baton Rouge, La.: Louisiana State Univ. Press: 1964); Maier, "Kirche—Staat—Gesellshchaft: Historisch-politische Bemerkungen zu Ihrem Verhaltnis," *Essener Gesprache zum Thema Staat und Kirche* 1: 12 (Munster Aschendorff, 1969); Scheuner, "Erorterungen und Tendenzen im gegenwartigen Staatskirchenrecht der Bundesrepublik," *Essener Gesprache zum Thema Staat und Kirche* 1: 108, 112 (Munster: Aschendorff, 1969); Obermayer, "Religious Schools and Religious Freedom: Proposals for Reform of the German Public School System," American Journal of Comparative Law 16 (1968): 552; H. Quaritsch, "Kirchen und Staat: Verfassungsund staatstheoretische Probleme der staatkirchenrechtlichen Lehre der Gegenwart," *Der Staat* 1: 175 & 278, reprinted in H. Quaritsch & H. Weber, *Staat und Kirchen un der Bundesrepublik: Staatskirchenrechtliche Aufsatze 1950-1967* at 265 (Berlin: Bad Homburg, v.d.H., 1967); von Zezschwitz, "Staatliche Neutralitatspflicht und Schulgebet," *Juristenzeitung* 1966: 337.

[116] A. Schinz, *La Pensee de Jean-Jacques Rousseau* 466, 506 (1962), summarized in Cassirer, *Das Problem*, 115. See also A. Schinz, *La Pensee religieuse de J.-J. Rousseau et ses recents interpretes* (Paris: F. Alcan, 1927).

[117] R. Grimsley, *Rousseau and the Religious Quest* (Oxford: Clarendon Press, 1968), 81–84. See also ibid., 43.

spiritual value; it is the social, not the religious function of the national cult which contributes to its real effectiveness.[118]

The problem with the pragmatic interpretation is that it fails to take Rousseau's religiosity seriously enough. It is far too ready to concede that religion is subordinate to politics in Rousseau's thought. This tendency is particularly distressing in Grimsley, who except for his discussion of the civil religion, renders a vivid account of the depth and meaning of Rousseau's unique but deeply sincere religiosity. Whether or not one agrees with Cassirer that the essential mistake of the pragmatic interpretation is its failure to recognize that the core of Rousseau's conception of religion "is to be found not in the problem of happiness but in the problem of freedom,"[119] there is something fundamentally unsatisfying about an account which portrays Rousseau as forgetting all concern for "true theism" and individual sincerity as soon as political expedience so requires. Either that, or there is something profoundly perverse about Rousseau himself.

Tensions of Transcendence and Immanence in Rousseau's Civil Religion.—Up to this point, my effort has been to depict as thoroughly as I could the ambiguities I perceive in Rousseau's chapter on the civil religion. The pervasiveness of ambiguity that I sense should be apparent, and should be understood as a caveat to the interpretation which follows. In a very deep sense, Max Imboden may be correct when he says "the contradictions in Rousseau are not coincidental; they are an image and an expression of contradictions which reside in ourselves and which are implicit in our world."[120] The problem of Rousseau may be that he sensed the contradictions and tensions of the modern world too clearly, and allowed them to seep into almost every line he wrote. And yet, Rousseau himself always insisted that "one great principle" was evident in all his books.[121] I certainly make no pretensions to having discovered some "one great principle." But I am interested in arguing that whatever that principle may be (if it exists at all), it has a more deeply religious cast than is commonly supposed. If I am correct, the consequence is that while many of the ominous aspects of the civil

---

[118] Ibid., 82.

[119] Cassirer, *Das Problem*, 115.

[120] M. Imboden, *Rousseau und die Demokratie* (Tubingen: Mohr, 1963), quoted in Ecstein, *Rousseau's Theory of Liberty* (Review of Otto Vossler's *Rousseau's Freiheitslehre*), *Journal of Historical Ideas* 1965: 291, 293.

[121] J.-J. Rousseau, *Rousseau juge de Jean-Jacques, Troisieme dialogue*, in *Oeuvres completes* 9: 287 (Paris: Hatchette., 1871-77). See also P. Gay, *Introduction* to Cassirer, *Das Problem*.

religion remain, they take on a fundamentally different meaning—a meaning which suggests that Rousseau was conscious of the threatening aspects of the civil religion but conceived them not as a danger of collective coercion but as a burden of collective guilt.

(1) *Rousseau's Religiosity.*—The starting point of the argument is essentially biographical; it takes as authentic the large number of declarations of faith scattered throughout Rousseau's works and his life.[122] Of course, Rousseau was not religious in any conventional sense. Although he was twice close to an ecclesiastical vocation, albeit in two different faiths,[123] this is little more indicative of his own inner religiosity than his soupline conversion to Catholicism and his subsequent reconversion to the Geneva church, which was more a reflection of patriotic zeal than a commitment to particular religious practices.[124] The outer trappings of faith mattered little to Rousseau. But there were simple things that mattered deeply. Nature was always a source of spiritual rejuvenation and became increasingly a kind of refuge from loneliness in his later years.[125] Regarding immortality, Rousseau wrote to Voltaire,

> All the subtleties of metaphysics can well sharpen my pains, they will never shake my faith in the immortality of the soul. I feel it, I believe it, I want it, I hope it, I will defend it until my last breath.[126]

He held with religious fervor to the Pelagian heresy with its denial of the doctrine of original sin and affirmation of moral freedom and moral accountability; his critique of society was fundamentally a defense of the primordial innocence of man. A yearning for innocence and simplicity was an integral part of his image of paradise.[127] Rousseau thought the ultimate happiness would include complete interpersonal openness. Just as men in the Christian paradise would be transparent to God's gaze, so men would become

---

[122] See generally notes 119–132, above, and accompanying text. But cf. J. Shklar, *Men and Citizens*, 108 (religion did not play any direct part in Rousseau's own emotional life and did not move him deeply).

[123] R. Grimsley, *Rousseau and the Religious Quest*, 12.

[124] See generally ibid., 2–34. Regarding the second conversion, see J.-J. Rousseau, *Confessions* VIII, 365 (J. Cohen, trans. 1954) (hereinafter *Confessions*).

[125] See R. Grimsley, *Rousseau and the Religious Quest*, 29.

[126] *Lettre à Voltaire*, Aug. 18, 1756, Leigh version at 294, quoted in M. Einaudi, *The Early Rousseau*, 206–07.

[127] See R. Grimsley, *Rousseau and the Religious Quest*, 92.

transparent to each other.[128] As Grimsley notes, the innocence of such individuals

> in the sight God enables them to enjoy . . . [a] spontaneous interpenetration of consciousness. The mutual confidence of Clarens has . . . [this] quality of pure innocence and transparence, but it has a higher spiritual value than the unreflecting innocence of primitive man, since it is based on a clear awareness of purity and openness of heart.[129]

The "illumination" on the road to Vincennes was almost Pauline in nature: "I beheld another universe and became another man."[130] In the new vision that emerged, compassion was recognized as a vital natural sentiment which had the capacity to insulate man from the corrupting influences of society if properly nurtured.[131] Finally, a deep reverence for conscience—for what Kant in a parallel vein referred to as "the moral law within"—is manifested throughout Rousseau's works. The profundity of this reverence is apparent in the words of the Savoyard Vicar:

> Conscience! Conscience! Divine instinct, immortal voice from heaven; sure guide for a creature ignorant and finite indeed, yet intelligent and free; infallible judge of good and evil, making man like to God! In thee consists the excellence of man's nature and the morality of his actions; apart from thee, I find nothing in myself to raise me above the beasts—nothing but the sad privilege of wandering from one error to another, but the help of an unbridled understanding and a reason which knows no principle.[132]

Rousseau never unambiguously adopted the creed of the Savoyard Vicar. Half way through the Vicar's confession, there is an interlude in which

---

128 Ibid., 118.

129 Ibid. The notation of transparence in Rousseau was developed by Jean Starbinski, in his *Jean-Jacques Rousseau, la transparence et l'obstacle* (1958). In his Foreword, Starbinski states, "Rousseau longs for the communication and the transparence of hearts; but he is frustrated in his expectation, and, choosing the contrary path, he accepts and provokes the obstacle, which allows him to withdraw into passive resignation and the certitude of his innocence." Quoted in M. Einaudi, *The Early Rousseau*, 12 n.22.

130 *Confessions* VIII, 327. I take Grimsley's statement that the illumination was not a "strictly religious experience, in spite of the apocalyptic language with which Rousseau was later to describe it," R. Grimsley, *Rousseau and the Religious Quest*, 14, to imply merely that it was not religious in the conventional sense. It was archetypally religious within the style of Rousseau's religiosity.

131 See *Inequality*, 226-27; *Emile* IV, 215. For an analysis of the differences in the relation of the beneficent sentiments to amour de soi and amour-propre in the two weeks, see J. Charvet, *The Social Problem in the Philosophy of Rousseau's Religiosity* (Cambridge: Cambridge Univ Press, 1974).

132 *Emile* IV, 254.

Rousseau[133] acknowledges, "I saw any number of objections which might be raised; yet I raised none, for I perceived that they were more perplexing than serious, and that my inclination took his part."[134] That carefully qualified statement of Rousseau's intellectual reaction to the Vicar's views was never rescinded. At the emotional level, however, the impact of the Vicar's creed was overpowering. "It seemed to me as if I were listening to the divine Orpheus when he sang the earliest hymns and taught men the worship of the gods."[135] In part, the ambiguity of Rousseau's intellectual response may have reflected a deep sense of unworthiness to serve as a prophet of natural religion. "By your own showing," he said to the Vicar, "the inner voice must be my guide, and . . . when it has long been silenced it cannot be recalled in a moment."[136] Whatever the case, one cannot escape the feeling that Rousseau had lived his life in the shadow of the Savoyard priest; his life-long dialogue with that saintly image is expressive of the core of his religiosity.

(2) *The Call of Conscience: Religiosity in Education and Legislation.*—In light of that consideration and also because the *Emile* and *The Social Contract* were written almost simultaneously, it is vital to understand the relationship of the religiosity of Rousseau the Educator to that of Rousseau the Legislator. Until this relationship is understood, the civil religion will continue to appear as an anomalously superficial chapter in an otherwise profoundly religious outlook. It will continue to be conceived as something having no more religious depth than the "civil religion" which has been perceived by Robert Bellah and others[137] in such ritualistic commonplaces as the habitual invocation of divinity in inaugural addresses, in Congress, and in courts; in the reference to deity on currency; and in the public celebrations associated with Independence Day, Memorial Day, and Veteran's Day. There is no question that Rousseau paid considerable attention to the details of public pomp when making his recommendations in *The Government of Poland*, and this may have reflected his attempt to suggest ways of institutionalizing the civil religion. But surely civil religion is more than the mere external ritual of patriotism. It is impossible to read the Vicar's confession of faith without realizing that Rousseau was sensitive to something more deeply personal in

---

[133] See ibid., 226 ("I myself was this unhappy fugitive" who was cared for by the Savoyard priest).

[134] Ibid., 258.

[135] Ibid.

[136] Ibid.

[137] See, e.g., A. Greeley, *The Denominational Society: A Sociological Approach to Religion in America,* (Glenview, Ill.: Scott, Foresman, 1972), 156 ff.; W. Herberg, *Protestant, Catholic, Jew,* (Garden City, N.Y.: Doubleday, 1955), 77–88, 263–65.

religion than patriotic ceremony or the inner fire of patriotism itself. To fail to recognize this fact is to forget that

> [t]he incomparable power which Rousseau the thinker and writer exercised over his time . . . [is derived from] his own completely personal dynamics of thought, feeling, and passion . . . [which enabled him to repudiate and destroy other] molds in which ethics and politics, religion as well as literature and philosophy were cast.[138]

At the conclusion of the Vicar's confession, Rousseau writes,

> I have transcribed this document not as a rule for the sentiments we should adopt in matters of religion, but as an example of the way in which we may reason with our pupil without forsaking the method I have tried to establish. So long as we yield nothing to human authority, nor to the prejudices of our native land, the light of reason alone, in a state of nature, can lead us no further than to natural religion; and this is as far as I should go with Emile. If he must have any other religion, I have no right to be his guide; he must choose for himself.[139]

These words express Rousseau's ultimate attitude toward the place of religion in an ideal education. With only minor modifications, however, they also express Rousseau's conception of the proper place of religion in the ideal polity. The simple tenets of the civil religion are not an expression of the sentiments a Legislator should impose on his people, but an example of the institutions he will create in "reasoning" with his people in the attempt to awaken in them a love of virtue. In both education and politics, Rousseau appears to be recommending the most tolerant of approaches. Neither the Educator nor the Legislator imposes his own dogmas by means of human authority or national prejudice;[140] both simply establish those tenets which the light of reason alone, in the state of nature, could lead men to embrace. Both recognize that there are some things that the ignorant pupil cannot be allowed to do because of the extreme danger to personal (or social) well-being, and hence, ways are found to protect the pupil and the people from themselves, without direct coercion or apparent human domination.[141] For the Legislator, religion in these contexts serves as a means of "constraining

---

138 See Cassirer, *Das Problem*, 35–38.

139 *Emile* IV, 278.

140 Cf. ibid., 239 (Vicar stresses he is not preaching his own opinion but merely explaining it).

141 For a summary description of this non-direct guidance in the Emile and an argument that more than mere duplicity and masked domination is being recommended by Rousseau, see J. Charvet, *The Social Problem*, 45–63.

without violence."[142] But even then, dogmas are mandatory which are both agreeable to all in the light of reason and which constitute "social sentiments without which a man cannot be a good citizen or a faithful subject."[143] The essential justification for the civil religion, like the justification for Emile's religious training, is its inherent reasonableness; the limits on dogma derive from the fact that reason can lead us no further than to natural religion. If the citizen is to subscribe to any additional beliefs, the Legislator, like the Educator, has no right to be his guide; the citizen must (and can) choose for himself. In short, Rousseau seems to be saying that the Legislator should follow the example of the Savoyard Vicar in treating the Protestants and Catholics in his community alike. Like the Vicar, he should strive "to get them [members of all faiths] to love one another, to consider themselves brethren, to respect all religions, and each to live peaceably [i.e., tolerantly] in his own religion."[144]

The Vicar's neo-Cartesian arguments for the existence of God and the external world[145] and his Kant-like argument for the immortality of the soul[146] are not as important for an understanding of Rousseau's religiosity as his perception of the nature of ultimate human satisfaction. "Supreme happiness," the Vicar says, "consists in self-content; [in order] that we may gain this self-content we are placed upon this earth and endowed with freedom, we are tempted by our passions and restrained by conscience."[147] Ultimate happiness is thus obtainable only through exercise of moral agency, and is attained by achieving harmony with conscience. When freed from the corruption of the material passions,

> we behold with joy the supreme Being and the eternal truths which flow from him; when all the powers of our soul are alive to the beauty of order and we are wholly occupied in comparing what we have done with what we ought to have done, then it is that the voice of conscience will regain its strength and sway; then it is that the pure delight which springs from self-content, and the sharp regret for our own degradation of that self, will decide by means of overpowering feeling what shall be the fate which each has prepared for himself.[148]

---

[142] *Social Contract*, II, vii, at 40.

[143] Ibid. at IV, viii, at 139.

[144] *Emile* IV, 274.

[145] Ibid., 229-39.

[146] Ibid., 244-46.

[147] Ibid., 244.

[148] Ibid., 246.

The path to joy is thus the path to reunion with conscience. It is because of conscience that "[t]here is nothing sweeter than virtue."[149]

But while conscience is the deepest, surest, and ultimately the only adequate guide to full expression of being,

> [C]onscience is timid, she loves peace and retirement . . . . She is discouraged by ill-treatment; she no longer speaks to us, no longer answers to our call; when she has been scorned so long, it is as hard to call her as it was to banish her.[150]

Not only do the evils of individual and social life deaden the voice of conscience, but there is a sense in which conscience is not self-activating: "To know good is not to love it; this knowledge is not innate in man; but as soon as his reason leads him to perceive it, his conscience impels him to love it . . . ."[151] Religion performs an important function in helping to overcome problems that derive from both of these features of conscience. With regard to the first, religion provides social reinforcement which helps to inhibit "ill-treatment;" with regard to the second, it can perform an important function in helping to awaken conscience so that the love for good is stirred to life. When Rousseau talks of the importance of religion in teaching the citizen to "love his duty,"[152] then, it seems reasonable to think that his primary concerns are with shielding and awakening conscience, for it is only conscience that can teach man to love his duties in the deepest sense. But only a religion of reason can walk the fine line between teaching the individual of the goods which the innate voice of conscience will then recognize and love, and dominating the individual in such a way that conscience is deadened. No sham religion which attempts to manipulate human beings through religious chicanery can tap the well-springs of the inner forum. Accordingly, when Rousseau suggests that the ideal Legislator must resort to religion in order that the people "might obey freely, and bear with docility the yoke of the public happiness,"[153] he is not calling for mystification of the masses but explaining that only conscience can generate a love for nobility and virtue before the fruits of either have been experienced.[154] It is in light of this perception that he warns, "The great soul

---

[149] Ibid., 255.
[150] Ibid., 254.
[151] Ibid., 253.
[152] *Social Contract* IV, viii, at 138.
[153] Ibid. II, vii, at 41.
[154] Cf. *Emile* IV, 250.

of the legislator is the only miracle that can prove his mission. . . . Idle tricks form a passing tie; only wisdom can make it lasting."[155]

The absorption with conscience also helps to explain why Rousseau was so little concerned about the outer form of religion and the theological controversies of denominationalism. Describing his return to Protestantism in Geneva, Rousseau wrote,

> The Gospel being, in my opinion, the same for all Christians, and fundamentals of dogma only differing over points that men attempted to explain but were unable to understand, it seemed to me to rest with the Sovereign alone in each country to settle the form of worship and the unintelligible dogma as well. It was therefore, I thought, the citizens' duty to accept the dogma and follow the cult of their country, both as prescribed by law. . . . In a word, philosophy, whilst attaching me to what was essential in religion, had freed me from the host of petty forms with which men have obscured it. Considering that for a reasonable man there were no two ways of being a Christian, I considered also that everything to do with form and discipline in each country belonged to the province of the law.[156]

So long as dogma and cult were prevented from obscuring the central appeal to conscience, issues of cult and dogma were of little significance. In fact, Rousseau was so concerned with emphasizing what he regarded as the inner essence of religion, "the purely internal cult of the supreme God,"[157] that he failed to appreciate that depriving particular organized religions the right to believe in their own exclusive validity and to act accordingly could itself strike at the heart of something essential to sincere religious life. Secular persecution of the religious was not a phenomenon with which he was familiar, although he detested intolerant atheism.[158] In any event, the conviction that natural religion embodies the fundamental truths that were available to reason for the awakening of conscience, together with the lack of concern for matters of form—so long as outer religion was not authoritarian and hence inimical to the natural unfolding of conscience—enabled Rousseau to argue for a civil religion which could integrate the religions of man and citizen.

(3) *Civil Religion a Synthesis of Religions of Man and Citizen.*—I suggested earlier that one of the fundamental ambiguities of the chapter on civil religion relates to whether Rousseau conceived of civil religion as a synthesis of the

---

[155] *Social Contract* II, vii, at 41.

[156] *Emile* IV, 365-66.

[157] *Social Contract* II, viii, at 134.

[158] See, e.g., Grimsley, *The Religious Quest*, 14.

religions of man and citizen, or as an imperfect option reflecting the need to choose between two mutually exclusive alternatives.[159] If one conceives of the civil religion as the cultivation of conscience in society, however, one is led to the conclusion that Rousseau's meaning lies closer to synthesis. The Savoyard Vicar is the paradigmatic representation of the integration of the religions of man and citizen at the level of the individual. A saint of the natural religion, he nonetheless performs the rites of outer religion with deep reverence.[160] He regards

> all individual religions as so many wholesome institutions which prescribe a uniform method by which each country may do honour to God in public worship; institutions which may each have its [sic] reason in the country, the government, the genius of the people, or in other local causes which make one preferable to another in a given time or place. I think them all good alike, when God is served in a fitting manner. True worship is of the heart. God rejects no homage, however offered, provided it is sincere.[161]

The Vicar teaches all the dogmas of the civil religion, and he teaches them in a way that awakens conscience without smothering it. He does not rely on institutional authority or superstition. Rather, he simply attempts to keep his own life in harmony with conscience and to strengthen the wholesome and legitimate bonds that bind men to each other, whatever outer form those bonds may take. He is content to allow the harmony of his own life to beckon to the conscience of others, awakening the yearning for wholeness in them not by coercion, but by tolerant example.

The difficulty for Rousseau is to determine how the integration apparent in the life of the Vicar can be realized at the level of the state. The problem is twofold. There is the threshold question about what it means for the state to keep its life in harmony with the "collective conscience,"[162] and the more difficult question about whether the state can arouse the individual conscience in the same manner as does the Savoyard Vicar—by example and without coercion. Needless to say, Rousseau's central attempt to grapple with these problems occurs in the context of his discussion of the general will. It will not be possible in this paper to enter into a detailed analysis of that doctrine, but it is important to recognize the parallels between the quest for conscience in politics and religion. For in a very deep sense, Rousseau's ideal

---

[159] See p. 20, above.

[160] See *Emile* IV, 273.

[161] Ibid., 272.

[162] I find Durkheim's phrase particularly apt in this context.

was the union of these two dimensions of social life.[163] The civil religion, in its attempted synthesis of the religions of man and citizen, reflected a yearning for integration of political and religious life in a social setting reconciled with individual and collective conscience.

A few illustrative examples will have to suffice in suggesting the significance of the connections between Rousseau's notion of the general will and his religious thought regarding the quest for conscience. In the course of analyzing tensions between private wills and the general will in the *Discourse on Political Economy*, Rousseau wrote,

> [U]nhappily personal interest is always found in inverse ratio to duty, and increases in proportion as the association grows narrower, and the engagement less sacred; which irrefragably proves that the most general will is always the must [sic] just also, and that the voice of the people is in fact the voice of God.[164]

The general will, like the religious conscience, speaks with a "celestial voice."[165] Both are infallible, except when misled by the voices of passion and faction:

> [T]he general will is always right and tends to the public advantage; but it does not follow that the deliberations of the people are always equally correct. Our will is always for our own good, but we do not always see what that is; the people is never corrupted, but it is often deceived . . . .[166]

Similarly,

> [C]onscience never deceives us; she is the true guide of man; it is to the soul what instinct is to the body; he who obeys his conscience is following nature and he need not fear that he will go astray . . . . Conscience is the voice of the soul, the passions are the voice of the body . . . . [Is it] strange that these voices often contradict each other? . . . [C]onscience is the best casuist; and it is only when we haggle with conscience that we have recourse to the subtleties of argument.[167]

Just as private virtue and ultimate private satisfaction consist in harmony with conscience, so public virtue and ideal political existence are the reflection of social life in accord with the dictates of the general will. In *The*

---

[163] See Powers, "The Earthly Ciy of Jean-Jacques Rousseau," *Southwestern Social Science Quartery* 40 (1959): 125, 137.

[164] Rousseau, *Political Economy*, 291.

[165] Cf. p. 33 & n.124, above.

[166] *Social Contract* II, iii, at 26.

[167] *Emile* IV, 249-50.

Social Contract, Rousseau stated, "The first and most important deduction from the principles we have . . . laid down is that the general will alone can direct the State according to the object for which it was instituted, i.e. the common good."[168] And in the *Discourse on Political Economy*, he claimed that

> [i]f you would have the general will accomplished, bring all the particular wills into conformity with it; in other words, as virtue is nothing more than this conformity of the particular wills with the general will, establish the reign of virtue.[169]

It is ultimately this "reign of virtue" with which Rousseau is most fundamentally concerned. Whether in religion or politics, it is life in accordance with that which is universal in all men—conscience—that is the necessary condition of life in ideal society. This is not merely a reflection of the fact that ideal society cannot function without virtue. It is a recognition that in the final analysis, only conscience can identify the ideal, and that no form of social life short of a reign of virtue can still the innate restlessness and discontent which is the inevitable reaction to and condemnation of the non-ideal. For Rousseau, then, nothing short of total harmony with conscience can constitute the ideal. One of the corollaries of that conviction is that ultimate individual and social satisfaction can only be found through self sacrifice and self discipline. Just as one can only "find" oneself in society by "losing" one's entire self in the social compact, so one can only find wholeness at all levels of life by losing oneself in the path of virtue. The civil religion, by demanding obedience to the tenets of the natural religion and to the dictates of the social contract[170]—hopes to promote a "finding" of harmony with conscience in both religious and political life. It seeks to integrate the yearning for wholeness in religion (the religion of man) and in politics (the religion of the citizen) into a unitary harmony with universal conscience.[171]

In order to see more clearly how Rousseau imagined that the ideal of wholeness—as manifested in his vision of the state and his belief in the need for inculcation of virtue in the citizenry—could be reconciled with the ideals of non-coercion and tolerance, it will be useful to return to the account of the

---

[168] *Social Contract* II, i, at 23.

[169] Rousseau, *Political Economy*, 298.

[170] See *Social Contract* IV, viii, at 139.

[171] For more detailed analysis of the significance of Rousseau's religious convictions for his political thought, see F. Glum, *Jean Jacques Rousseau: Religion und Staat* (Stuttgart: W. Kohlhammer, 1956); Willhoite, "Rousseau's Political Religion," *Review of Politics* 27 (1965): 501. Both of these authors maintain that an understanding of Rousseau's religious theory is crucial to an understanding of his political thought. See Glum, 29; Willhoite, 501.

Savoyard Vicar. Rousseau's initial reaction to the Vicar's Spartan way of life (or more accurately, perhaps, Rousseau's initial reaction to the ideal of the austere existence as it first emerged in his inner intellectual history) was to exclaim, "What gloomy ideas! . . . . If we must deny ourselves everything, we might as well never have been born; and if we must despise even happiness itself who can be happy."[172] He could not understand the paradox of losing in order to find.[173] One of the reasons the Vicar's profession of faith had such deep meaning to him was that it was offered in response to a plea to explain the paradox.[174] "I will open my whole heart to yours," the Vicar had told him,

> You will see me, if not as I am, at least as I seem to myself. When you have heard my whole confession of faith, when you really know the condition of my heart, you will know why I think myself happy, and if you think as I do, you will know how to be happy too.[175]

Not surprisingly, the answer to the paradox that the Vicar provides centers on conscience. Supreme happiness and self-content derives from life in accordance with conscience, and austerity is vital if conscience and not passion is to emerge as the central pillar of the soul.

(4) *Rousseau's Republican Monasticism.*—The crucial question from the perspective of the ideals of non-coercion and tolerance is how the vital regimen of austerity is to be imposed or elicited by the state. Taine described Rousseau's state as a "layman's monastery," claiming that "in this democratic monastery which Rousseau establishes on the model of Sparta and Rome, the individual is nothing and the state everything."[176] While the metaphor is apt, the characterization of the "monastery" as lacking all concern for the individual is misleading, since the "monastery" Rousseau envisions would be operated in the spirit of the Savoyard Vicar, or of Dostoevsky's Father Zossima. I mention Father Zossima not only because there are strong similarities between him and Rousseau's Vicar, but also because in a number of ways, his argument for "monasticism"—for the ideal of austere virtue—sheds light on the parallel argument in Rousseau. "The world has proclaimed the reign of freedom,"[177] Father Zossima observes, "but what do we see in

---

[172] Rousseau, *Emile*, 227.

[173] See ibid.

[174] See ibid., 228.

[175] Ibid.

[176] Taine, *Les Origines*, 323, 321, quoted in Gay, *Introduction* to Cassirer, *Das Problem.*

[177] F. Dostoevsky, *The Brothers Karamazov*, Book VI: *The Russian Monk* 289 (C. Garnett, trans., New York: Modern Library, 1960). The parallels between the Vicar and

this freedom? Nothing but slavery and self-destruction!" One is reminded immediately of the famous phrase at the beginning of *The Social Contract*: "[m]an is born free; and everywhere he is in chains." In Father Zossima's view, the essence of the "world's" doctrine of freedom is the multiplication of desires, leading to spiritual suicide among the rich and envy and murder among the poor. In both cases, the effect is what Rousseau might have called the death of conscience and the possibility of true freedom constituted by conformity with conscience. "Interpreting freedom as the multiplication and rapid satisfaction of desires," Father Zossima continues, "men distort their own nature, for many senseless and foolish desires and habits and ridiculous beliefs are thus fostered. They live only for mutual envy, for luxury and ostentation." Rousseau described the same phenomenon in terms of *amour-propre* and the decadence of society. Father Zossima then describes a "champion of freedom" who, when deprived of tobacco while in prison almost betrayed his cause in order to obtain tobacco to satisfy his craving. "How can such a one fight?" Father Zossima asks,

> [W]hat is he fit for? He is capable perhaps of some action quickly over, but he cannot hold out long. And it's no wonder that instead of gaining freedom men have sunk into slavery. Instead of serving the cause of brotherly love and the union of humanity, man have fallen, on the contrary, into dissension and isolation . . . . And therefore the idea of the service of humanity, of brotherly love and the solidarity of mankind, is more and more dying out it the world. Indeed this idea is sometimes treated with derision. For how can a man shake off his habits, what can become of him if he is in such bondage to the habit of satisfying the innumerable desires he has created for himself? He is isolated, and what concern has he for the rest of humanity? Men have succeeded in accumulating a greater mass of objects, but the joy in the world has grown less.

"The monastic way is very different," Father Zossima contends. "I subdue my proud and wanton will and chastise it with obedience, and with God's help I attain freedom of spirit and with it spiritual joy." It is noteworthy that Father Zossima does not say, "The leader of the monastery subdues my proud and wanton will and demands obedience." Both he and Rousseau were conscious that the life in accordance with conscience cannot be coerced; it is necessarily individual, though it is probably easier to achieve such a life within a community striving toward that end than in a corrupt society in which one

---

Father Zossima could be worked out in considerable detail. For purposes of this paper, however, I will refer almost exclusively to the passage contained in Book VI, 2 (e), pp. 288–90 in the Signet Classics edition. Unless otherwise indicated, quotation from Father Zossima may be found on those pages.

must make the effort alone.[178] In a sense, the real problem with the monastic way was that it was likely to be too individualistic, not that the individual would be crushed. Father Zossima was sensitive to those critics who charged: "You have secluded yourself within the walls of the monastery for your own salvation, and have forgotten the brotherly service of humanity." Implicit in this criticism is a deeper perception of the danger that the pursuit of personal wholeness leads away from society and into isolation—a danger of which Rousseau was acutely aware, as manifested by his criticism of the other-worldliness of Christianity. "But we shall see," Zossima responds, "which will be most zealous in the cause of brotherly love. For it is not we, but they [the critics of monasticism] who are in isolation, though they don't see that." In this view, it is the monks who are in tune with the hearts of the people, and the "salvation of Russia comes from the people."

Rousseau would be less inclined to speak in terms of salvation, and he would undoubtedly be uncomfortable with the notion of a monastic class that would contribute in a mysterious way to the coming of some distant millennium. But his thought parallels that of Father Zossima insofar as it suggests that the pursuit of wholeness in the individual may be in deeper harmony with the pursuit of wholeness at the level of society than superficial analysis would suggest. Rousseau too had sensed that "the people is never corrupted."[179] He believed that the simple men seeking unity with conscience, like the Russian monks, were more in tune with the "hearts of the people" (the general will) than the sophisticated rationalists of his day. He was convinced that ideal society is ultimately unobtainable without the austere "monastic" discipline of virtue, but it is not clear how optimistic he was about the possibility of actualizing the ideal.[180] The uncertainty and possible pessimism in this regard underscores the fact that he did not believe

---

[178] In this regard, it is worth recalling that Father Zossima had said to Alyosha—who in many respects stood in the same relationship to Father Zossima as Rousseau did to the Vicar—"you will go forth from these walls, but will live like a monk in the world. . . . Life will bring you many misfortunes, but you will find your happness in them, and will bless life and will make others bless it—which is what matters most." Ibid., 261. Father Zossima's prophecy implies a faith that the saintly life can exist in the secular world if the individual chooses to accept its discipline. More importantly, it suggests that the deep fulfillment that flows from the discipline of virtue can be found in the "outer world." The tragic difficulty for figures like the Vicar and Alyosha is the virtual impossibility of remaining "unspotted"—a difficulty which increases the attractiveness of the community aspiring to virtue. But whatever the problems of coexistence of virtue and vice, it is important to note that like Rousseau, Alyosha experienced teaching by example without domination; he was in no sense imprisoned or otherwise dominated in the monastery; and he remained very much an individual.

[179] See Social Contract II, iii, at 26.

[180] See Shklar, Men and Citizens, 8.

men could be forced into social heaven. In the letter to Voltaire regarding the Lisbon earthquake, Rousseau had asked,

> Do kings of this world have some right of inspection in the other world and are they empowered to torment their subject [sic] on earth to force them to go to paradise? Clearly all human government must be limited by its nature to civil duties and in spite of anything that the sophist Hobbes may have said, when a man is a good servant of the state he must not render account to anybody of the way in which he serves God.[181]

This passage could be interpreted as implying that while the state may not attempt to force men into religious paradise, it may "force men to be free"[182] in the sense of forcing them to enter the ideal civil state by (coercively) imposing a regimen of virtue. But such an interpretation would be inconsistent with Rousseau's conception of the ideal. The "reign of virtue" of which Rousseau dreams cannot be imposed by force, because conscience—the key to the ideal condition—would be smothered in the process. A more reasonable interpretation would view Rousseau as holding that while men may be forced to enter civil society, which constitutes a crucial threshold position that must be attained before the ultimate pursuit of social wholeness can begin, they can no more be forced into ideal society than into religious paradise. Entry into the civil condition

> produces a very remarkable change in man, by substituting justice for instinct in his conduct, and giving his actions the morality they had formerly lacked. Then only, when the voice of duty takes the place of physical impulses and right of appetite, does man, who so far had considered only himself, find that he is forced to act on different principles, and to consult his reason before listening to his inclinations.[183]

The essence of this "very remarkable change" is that conscience has been awakened. The morality that was impossible as long as man was totally dominated by instinct has become possible with the emergence of the potential freedom which Rousseau perceives to be the only alternative to enslavement to the passions. Like the Savoyard Vicar teaching Rousseau, or Rousseau teaching Emile, the state can play a supportive role in the cultivation of life in accordance with conscience. It can protect the individual from the actions of others which might damage the unfolding of conscience, even if that means restraining others in some cases. But it is the individual

---

181 Quoted in M. Einaudi, *The Early Rousseau*, 206.

182 See *Social Contract* I, vii, at 18.

183 Ibid. I, viii, at 18.

himself who must recognize that the regimen of virtue is necessary to the attainment of wholeness, and he must impose that law upon himself. Ultimately, Rousseau seems to believe, the individual pursuing wholeness is forced to recognize that oneness with self is impossible apart from oneness with others; the individual is accordingly "forced to act on different principles; his conscience leads him to love his duty, and to seek to actualize the dictates of the general will; he becomes "zealous in the cause of brotherly love"—of social harmony and tolerance and oneness; and possibly, if a people becomes genuinely united in imposing the regimen of virtue on itself, the ideal of *The Social Contract* will become real.

There can be no doubt that Rousseau was conscious of the dangers of the ideal of austerity; he was deeply conscious of that which was ominous in the yearning for wholeness which was manifested in his civil religion and in his political theory in general. But far from conceiving of the foreboding austerity of his ideal as a justification of collective coercion, he recognized that forced imposition of virtue would result not in life in accordance with conscience, but in life under the slavery of fear. His civil religion must accordingly be conceived not as a program of coercion, but as a depiction of the interplay of the religions of man and citizen in supporting growth toward and maintenance of the ideal civil polity. The severity of the sanctions imposed on those who do not adhere to the civil religion is not part of an attempt to impose the civil religion by force, but a reflection of the need to restrain some individuals from inhibiting the growth of conscience in others. In Rousseau's mind, the regimen of virtue which was the ultimate aim of the civil religion could only be perceived as oppressive by those who had not remained open to the inner voice of conscience and its overpowering yearning for wholeness. The transparence of wholeness, he seemed to think, can only seem oppressive to the guilty, who have something to hide, and who prefer the privacy of isolation to the purging path of virtue.

If my interpretation of Rousseau's civil religion is correct—if civil religion represents an attempt to synthesize the religions of man and citizen in order to promote and maintain but not coerce religious and political life in harmony with individual and social conscience—it may shed light on an apparent inconsistency in Rousseau's images of utopia. Professor Shklar has argued that Rousseau had two models of utopia—a Spartan city and a tranquil household—and that the two stand in polar opposition to each other.[184] In her view,

---

[184] Shklar, *Men and Citizens*, 3–4.

The Spartan city excludes all private affections and associations, not only the family. It precludes contemplative and universal religiosity, as all inclinations are bent before xenophobia, communal isolation and pride, and a virtue that is sustained by the pressure of public opinion rather than by benevolence or love. Village life would seem infinitely more attractive by comparison. Self-love here leads effortlessly to a love of humanity. A Christianity designed to comfort and console can flourish here. . . .Nevertheless, this is not a faultless state either. It is stultifying in its dullness. The peasant or man of the Golden Age is brutish and stupid. He is quite capable of irrational violence when he confronts anyone other than his family. . . .Only the artificially created village, the cultivated family withdrawing to the land really seemed idyllic. This, too, has its flaws; the impact of civilization cannot be shaken off by mere physical escape. Its psychological imprint is indelible and warps or destroys these efforts to retreat into rustic life. . . .The wish to play a public role, to develop one's civic capacities, to belong to a purposeful order, to take part in an organized drama, is as much a part of a morally adult life as the desire to be a self-sufficient whole, united only with those whom one loves and independent of all that interferes with one's real needs. Choose, however, one must, or rather ought, even though one never does. To recognize the choice, at the very least, is to escape from the unthinking misery of actuality.[185]

The two utopias, as I understand them, are articulations of the religions of man (the tranquil household) and citizen (Sparta). If the civil religion was intended by Rousseau as a synthesis of these two religions, as I contend it was, then the argument that Rousseau intended the two utopias to stand in irreconcilable opposition to each other is incorrect. In the actual world of history and society, it may well be that there is no practical means of integrating the two poles of the civil religion. But that does not imply that Rousseau's vision of utopia was intentionally fragmentary and dualized. On the contrary, Rousseau's statement of the ideal, with all its ambiguity and contradictoriness, was an attempt to depict a mode of life in which all the divergent strands of the ideal could be fused together in a unified harmony with conscience. That which is deeply puzzling about the civil religion is a reflection of the complexity of the quest for wholeness.

---

[185] Ibid., 31–32.

—∽ 8 ∾—

EDMUND BURKE'S
TOLERANT ESTABLISHMENT
*Michael W. McConnell**

T he events of 1776 through 1791 are well known to students of church-state relations, as are the views of the key participants, including Jefferson and Madison, Washington and Henry, Backus and Leland. It is less well known that during the same period in Britain, the issues of church and state were debated no less extensively than in America, but with a quite different conclusion. In those debates, without a doubt, the leading figure was Edmund Burke.

The issues of establishment and toleration occupied Burke's attention throughout his 40 years as a statesman and man of letters. His first published work, *A Vindication of Natural Society*,[1] was a satirical defense of revealed religion against the attacks of Lord Bolingbroke, and his last, the *Letters on a*

* William B. Graham Professor of Law, University of Chicago Law School. B.A., Michigan State University (1976); J.D., University of Chicago (1979). The author is grateful to the Morton C. Seeley Endowment Fund and the Arnold and Frieda Shure Research Fund for financial support during preparation of this article, and to David Currie, Ralph Lerner, Dan Kahan, Albert Asschuler, Elenn Kagan, Daniel Ritchie, Martin Marty, Joseph Cropsey, David Smlin, Gerard Bradley, Stephen Gillis, Philip Hamburger, Thomas Berg, Stephen Schulhofer, and Gareth Jones for helpful comments on earlier drafts, and to Jeff Seitzer for valuable research assistance. A longer version of this article was published in 1995 Supreme Court Review 393-462, and is reprinted in part herein with permission of the publisher.

[1] *The Works of the Right Honorable Edmund Burke* (1756, rev. ed. Boston: Little, Brown, 1865), 1: 1–66 (hereinafter cited as "*Works*").

Regicide Peace,[2] related the enormities of the French Revolution to the aggressive atheism of the *philosophes*. Above all, in his life-long struggle to protect the civil rights of Roman Catholics (especially in Ireland), Burke advocated, organized, and sacrificed for a particular vision of the relation of church and state under the English constitution. Burke's vision is all the more significant because of its apparently stark opposition to the central conception of these issues adopted in America. Here, almost every stripe of opinion on matters of religion and government adheres to one version or another of church-state "separation."[3] Burke, by contrast, maintained that "in a Christian commonwealth the Church and the State are one and the same thing, being different integral parts of the same whole."[4]

For Burke, the religious establishment was not antithetical to, but a integral part of, England's system of civil and political liberty. For him the establishment was an instrument of moderation, restraint, and even toleration. He insisted that "[i]f ever there was anything to which, from reason, nature, habit, and principle, I am totally averse, it is persecution for conscientious difference in opinion."[5] Burke thus presents a profound alternative to the American resolution of the church-state problem—but one equally grounded in liberal constitutionalism. At a time when the American constitutional principles of nonestablishment and free exercise are mired in a tension and contradiction that the Supreme Court seems unable to resolve, it may be instructive to see how Burke sought to reconcile the principles of establishment and toleration, and how he understood both to fit into the wider framework of his "constitution of freedom."[6]

Burke's Personal Religious Commitment.—Before turning to Burke's positions on establishment and toleration, it is well to begin with a brief summary of his religious commitment. There is little doubt that Burke was a committed and devout Christian. His editor J. G. A. Pocock calls him "the

---

[2] *Works*, 5: 233-508; 6: 1-113.

[3] See Carl H. Esbeck, "Five Views of Church-State Relations in Contemporary American Thought," *Brigham Young University Law Review* 1986: 371; Steven D. Smith, "Separation and the 'Secular': Reconstructing the Disestablishment Decision," *Texas Law Review* 67 (1989): 955.

[4] Speech on the Petition of the Unitarians (May 11, 1792), *Works* 7: 43.

[5] Speech on the Acts of Uniformity (Feb. 6, 1772), *Works* 7: 10.

[6] The term "constitution of freedom" comes from Burke's great speech to his constituents at Bristol, in which he defended his support for the Catholic Relief Act in the aftermath of the Gordon riots. Speech at Bristol, Previous to the Election (Sept. 6, 1780), *Works* 2: 416.

pious Burke,"[7] and his most recent biographer, Conor Cruise O'Brien, says he was a "devout Christian."[8] Burke lived his adult life as an Englishman and a faithful member of the Church of England, but he was born in Ireland of Catholic stock at a time when the Penal Laws kept the Catholic majority in humiliating submission to the Protestant minority, called the "Ascendancy." Burke's mother was a practicing Catholic her entire life, as was his wife, while nominally a convert to the established church. His father, a lawyer, converted to Anglicanism as a young man, apparently for the purpose of being able to practice his profession. Conor Cruise O'Brien hypothesizes that much of Burke's posture toward the Catholics of Ireland is driven by a sense of guilt about his father's opportunistic apostasy.[9] Burke was baptized and (for the most part) raised in the (Anglican) Church of Ireland. He attended a rural Catholic school as a boy, a Quaker school in his youth, and institutions of the established church (Trinity College, Dublin, followed by the Inns of Court) for higher education. Although suspected of secret Catholicism for most of his life (political cartoons generally depicted Burke in the robes of a Jesuit, and at critical junctures in his political career Burke's enemies accused him of being a Jesuit and a Jacobite[10]), the actual evidence suggests that he was deeply committed to the adopted faith of his father.[11]

One might expect that a person of this background would feel cynical and resentful toward both (perhaps all) religions—toward the hegemonic religion to which he had become attached by a combination of coercion and opportunism and toward the subjected religion, which he had forsworn, as well. This was not Burke's reaction. Instead, Burke warmly defended his adopted religion from its philosophical and political detractors, and at the same time worked tirelessly and at great political cost to free the Catholic faith of his ancestors from the oppression of the Protestant Ascendancy. In

---

[7] J. G. A. Pocock, Editor's Introduction, in Edmund Burke, *Reflections on the Revolution in France* (1790, Indianapolis: Hackett Pub. Co., 1987), xvii (hereinafter cited as "*Reflections*").

[8] Conor Cruise O'Brien, *The Great Melody: A Thematic Biography of Edmund Burke* (Chicago: Univ. of Chicago Press, 1992), 588 (hereinafter cited as "*Great Melody*"). Similarly, Burke's 19th Century biographer, Thomas MacKnight, described him as "sincerely attached to the principles of the Christian religion." Thomas MacKnight, *History of the Life and Times of Edmund Burke* (London: Chapman & Hall, 1858), 3: 164 (hereinafter cited as "*Life and Times*"). Some scholars, however, suggest that Burke was a hidden skeptic. See, e.g., Harvey Mansfield, Jr., "Burke and Christianity," *Studies of Burke and His Time*, 9 (1968): 864-65.

[9] Great Melody, 13–14.

[10] Ibid., 50; *Life and Times*, 202–03, 422–23 .

[11] There have been persistent rumors that Burke sought last rites as a Catholic on his deathbed, see *Great Melody*, 590, but this is based entirely on conjecture.

part, Burke defended "religion" (usually identified in the generic) on social grounds—as the "basis of civil society and the source of all good and of all comfort."[12] But it went deeper than that. Burke believed that "atheism is against, not only our reason, but our instincts,"[13] and his letters and writings are filled with references to the divine order and judgment. Burke wrote to a friend that "I am attached to Christianity at large; much from conviction; more from affection."[14]

Burke responded to the traumatic conversion of his father by minimizing the differences between the abandoned and the adopted faith.[15] "The Catholics of Ireland," he claimed, "have the whole of our *positive* religion: our difference is only a negation of certain tenets of theirs."[16] Indeed, in the *Reflections*, Burke made the remarkable claim: "So tenacious are we [the English] of the old ecclesiastical modes and fashions of institution that very little alteration has been made in them since the fourteenth or fifteenth century."[17] Considering the doctrinal and ecclesiological tergiversations that the English church had undergone during that period, Burke's observation evinces an uncommonly powerful desire to obliterate the differences between the Catholic and Anglican communions. He might claim that "[w]e are Protestants, not from indifference, but from zeal";[18] but the Protestantism to which he referred was one that had made peace with Roman Catholicism,[19]

---

[12] Reflections, 79.

[13] Ibid., 80.

[14] Thomas W. Copeland, ed., *The Correspondence of Edmund Burke* (Cambridge & Chicago: Cambridge Univ. Press, 1970), 6: 215 (hereinafter cited as "*Correspondence*").

[15] Burke took a similar approach to the relation between his adopted Englishness and his natal Irishness. In a letter to the head of the Catholic Committee of Ireland, Burke wrote:

You do me Justice in saying in your Letter of July, that I am a "true Irishman." Considering as I do England as my Country, of long habit, of long obligation and of establishment, and that my primary duties are here, I cannot conceive how a Man can be a genuine Englishman without being at the same time a true Irishman, tho' fortune should have made his birth on this side of the Water. I think the same Sentiments ought to be reciprocal on the part of Ireland, and if possible with much stronger reason.

Letter to John Keogh (Nov. 17, 1796), *Correspondence*, 9: 113.

[16] Letter on the Affairs of Ireland (1797), *Works*, 6: 425.

[17] *Reflections*, 87.

[18] Ibid., 79-80.

[19] Ibid., 79: "Violently condemning neither the Greek nor the Armenian, nor, since heats are subsided, the Roman system of religion, we prefer the Protestant."

allowed persons of various doctrinal persuasion to "live quietly under the same roof,"[20] and had embraced toleration as "a part of Christianity."[21]

Finally, while it is surely dangerous to deduce a statesman's theology from public statements and writings on political themes, these sources convey an impression that Burke understood religion almost exclusively as a source of a moral code, of hope and consolation on earth, and of rewards and punishments in the life to come. In his private notebook, Burke wrote that "The Principle of Religion is that God attends to our Actions to reward and punish them."[22] Notably lacking in Burke's extensive speeches and writings about religion is any reference to the central tenet of mainstream Christianity: the vicarious atonement of Jesus Christ and redemption through faith in Him.[23] Indeed, to the best of my knowledge, Burke never mentions Christ (though he frequently mentions God), and he rarely quotes the Bible.[24] So far was Burke from the evangelical position on the Bible that he called it a "vast collection of different treatises" and a "most venerable, but most multifarious collection of the records of the divine economy."[25] His assertions about religion in his private notebook are bereft of Biblical reference or support. On the other hand, Burke did not move in the direction of rational religion, so attractive to many of his contemporaries. That would be the religious equivalent of the metaphysics and abstraction that he so deplored in politics. "I know the Clergy, shamed and frightened at the Imputation of Enthusiasm, endeavour to cover Religion under the Shield of Reason, which will have some force with their Adversaries. But God has been pleased to give mankind an Enthusiasm to supply the want of Reason; and truely, Enthusiasm comes nearer the great and comprehensive Reason in its effects, though not in the

---

[20] Speech on a Bill for the Relief of Protestant Dissenters (Mar. 17, 1773), *Works*, 7: 29.

[21] Ibid., 25.

[22] Edmund Burke, *Religion of No Efficacy, Considered as a State Engine*, in H. H. F. Somerset, ed., *A Notebook of Edmund Burke* (Cambridge: Cambridge Univ. Press, 1957), 67 (hereinafter cited as "*Notebook*"). The *Notebook* was apparently written between 1750 and 1756, but not published. Compare *Reflections*, 140: "The body of all true religion consists, to be sure, in obedience to the will of the Sovereign of the world, in a confidence in his declarations, and in imitation of his perfections. The rest is our own."

[23] In his *Notebook*, Burke articulates a theology of works righteousness that is decidedly unorthodox from a Protestant point of view. "[O]ur Performance of our Duty here," he writes, "must make our fate afterwards." *Notebook*, 72.

[24] A rare exception is his quotation of *Matthew* 18: 22–23, in a rebuke to certain Protestant Dissenting clergy who opposed the extension of toleration to a wider category of Dissenters, in his Speech on a Bill for the Relief of Protestant Dissenters (Mar. 17, 1773), *Works*, 7: 30.

[25] Speech on the Acts of Uniformity (Feb. 6, 1772), *Works*, 7: 18-19.

Manner of Opeation, than the Common Reason does."[26] Since "enthusiasm," at this time, was a term of opprobrium (meaning something like fanaticism), this was a remarkable choice of words.

By his own admission, Burke found the great controversies over religious doctrine—he gives predestination as an example—"obscure," and did not see why "we should not leave things as the Divine Wisdom has left them."[27] His own personal approach to theological doctrine is summarized in his Speech on a Bill for the Relief of Protestant Dissenters: "I have as high an opinion of the doctrines of the Church as you. I receive them implicitly, or I put my own explanation on them, or take that which seems to me to come best recommended by authority."[28] His reluctance to embrace the full doctrinal position of the Church of England may be attributable to a hidden adherence to at least some aspects of Catholicism, but his independent attitude toward ecclesiastical authority is distinctly Protestant—and in his latitudinarianism he revealed himself, ironically, as a true son of the Church of England, the church most strenuously committed, over its history, to the broad accommodation of doctrinal and liturgical differences.

It is fair to say, then, that Burke was a religious man, but not a sectarian. "All the principal religions in Europe stand upon one common bottom," he wrote in 1795. "The support that the whole or the favored parts may have in the secret dispensations of Providence it is impossible to tell."[29] He was attached to the fundamentals of what today might be called "mere Christianity," but did not dwell upon the doctrinal differences that separated his Catholic ancestors from his Protestant co-communicants. Burke's great commitment was to arrest the advance of militant atheism, as it appeared in the revolutionaries of France and, he thought, in the some of their extreme Protestant sympathizers in England.

---

[26] *Notebook*, 67.

[27] Ibid., 29. On one occasion, Burke claimed to have read all of the theological publications on all sides that were written during the 17th and 18th centuries. He reached the conclusion that such studies tended merely to confuse, and so he had elected to cling fast to the Church of England. *Parliamentary History*, 21 (1780-81): 710, paraphrased in Thomas H. D. Mahoney, *Edmund Burke and Ireland* (Cambridge: Harvard Univ. Press, 1960), 98 (hereinafter cited as "Mahoney").

[28] Speech on a Bill for the Relief of Protestant Dissenters (Mar. 17, 1773), *Works*, 7: 28.

[29] Letter to William Smith, Esq., on the Subject of Catholic Emancipation (Jan. 29, 1795), *Works*, 6: 368. See also Letter to Richard Burke, Jr., on Protestant Ascendency in Ireland (1793), in *Works*, 6: 400: "I do not pretend to take pride in an extravagant attachment to any sect." Significantly, Burke participated in Presbyterian worship services at the time of his investiture as Lord Rector of Glasgow University—evincing an ecumenism rare for his day. *Life and Times*, 3: 76.

Burke's Defense of the Established Church.—Burke was an unapologetic champion of the established church as part of the time-honored constitutional structure of England. "We are resolved," he declared, "to keep an established church, an established monarchy, an established aristocracy, and an established democracy, each in the degree it exists, and no greater."[30] But as we shall see, Burke's establishment is different, both in purpose and in character, from the prototypical established church. Ordinarily, established churches are either theocracies, in which a powerful church exercises some or all of the power of secular government, for advancement of the truths of a particular religion, or state-run churches, in which a powerful government controls the church and uses it for advancement of the purposes of the state. Through history, we have seen both; but the latter is more common, and was so in Burke's day. In the English tradition, the latter position has been termed "Erastianiam."[31] Under an Erastian system, the church is used by the sovereign as a supplementary means of social control, so that to the power of the laws is added the suasion of the priest and the fear of eternal punishment. The roots of the position in English political theory go back to Richard Hooker, and in more extreme form, Thomas Hobbes.

(1) The role of the establishment in Burke's constitution.—Burke defended the established Church of England, but he did so on neither theocratic nor Erastian grounds. His defense in no way rested on any claim that the Church of England is the true faith. Theological correctness was not the point. "It is not morally true," he said, "that we are bound to establish in every country that form of religion which in *our* minds is most agreeable to truth, and conduces most to the eternal happiness of mankind."[32] The Anglican Church held its position in England by prescription; it was the embodiment of the religious experience of the English people over a long period of time (as the Presbyterian Church was of the Scottish and the Roman Catholic of the Irish). Burke was no theocrat. But by the same token, Burke criticized the view that the claim of religion to public support is based on its social utility. "If you attempt to make the end of Religion to be its Utility to human society," he wrote in an unpublished notebook, "to make it only a sort of supplement to the Law, and insist principally upon this Topic, as is very common to do, you then change its principle of Operation, which consists of

---

30 *Reflections*, 80.

31 See generally Weldon S. Crowley, "Erastianism in England to 1640," *Journal of Church & State* 32 (1990): 549.

32 Speech on the Petition of the Unitarians (May 11, 1792), *Works*, 7: 42 (emphasis in original).

Views beyond this Life, to a consideration of another kind, and an inferior kind; and thus, by forcing it against its Nature to become a Political Engine, you make it an Engine of no efficacy at all."[33] Thus he broke with the two dominant traditions of alliance between church and state.

Burke's principal defense of the establishment is found in a section of his greatest work, *Reflections on the Revolution in France*, which was inspired by the confiscation of the property of the Church in France by the revolutionaries and its subordination to political control. In the *Reflections*, he set out to outline "the true principles of our constitution in church and state."[34] There he observes that the established church is "the first of our prejudices," but quickly adds that it is "not a prejudice destitute of reason, but involving in it profound and extensive wisdom."[35]

The purpose of the establishment, Burke explains, is the "consecration of the state." By this he does not mean that the state is holy or exempt from criticism. On the contrary, it means that those who hold power in the state are "infused" with the "sublime principle" that "they should not look to the paltry pelf of the moment nor to the temporary and transient praise of the vulgar, but to a solid, permanent existence in the permanent part of their nature."[36] Government must be viewed as a "holy function"—not in the sense that it is above criticism, but in the sense that it must conform, in "virtue and wisdom," to principles higher than itself.[37] The established church thus stands as a reminder that those in power "act in trust, and that they are to account for their conduct in that trust to the one great Master, Author, and Founder of Society."[38] It is a moral check on the abuse of power.

It is the democratic element in the English constitution that most needs this kind of check. Oppression of the minority by the majority "will extend to far greater numbers and will be carried on with much greater fury than can almost ever be apprehended from the dominion of a single scepter," Burke wrote.[39] Princes are inherently more constrained because they must act

---

[33] *Notebook*, 67. Burke was not, however, above making an argument based on social utility when it suited his purposes. See, e.g., *Reflections*, 69:

Nothing is more certain than that our manners, our civilization, and all the good things which are connected with manners and with civilization have . . . depended for ages upon two principles and were, indeed, the result of both combined: I mean the spirit of a gentleman and the spirit of religion.

[34] Letter to Phillip Francis (Feb. 20, 1790), *Correspondence*, 6: 92.

[35] *Reflections*, 80.

[36] Ibid., 81.

[37] Ibid., 83.

[38] Ibid., 81.

[39] Ibid., 110.

through others. By contrast, "where popular authority is absolute and unrestrained, the people have an infinitely greater, because a far better founded, confidence in their own power." It is of "infinite importance," therefore, that the people "should not be suffered to imagine that their will, any more than that of kings, is the standard of right and wrong."[40] "When they are habitually convinced that no evil can be acceptable . . . to him whose essence is good, [the people] will be better able to extirpate out of the minds of all magistrates, civil, ecclesiastical, or military, anything that bears the least resemblance to a proud and lawless domination."[41]

In particular, the function of the establishment is to ensure continuity with the established traditions of the society. Religion makes us aware that the civil order is but a part of the timeless moral order ordained by the universal sovereign, and not the mere choice of passing majorities.[42] Associate the state with the church, and the people will not be so ready as they otherwise might be to "chang[e] the state as often, and as much, and in as many ways as there are floating fancies or fashions."[43] To avoid

> the evils of inconstancy and versatility, ten thousand times worse than those of obstinacy and the blindest prejudice, we have consecrated the state, that no man should approach to look into its defects or corruptions but with due caution, that he should never dream of beginning its reformation by its subversion, that he should approach to the faults of the state as to the wounds of a father, with pious awe and trembling solicitude.[44]

The established church is a bulwark against hasty and incautious change.

Burke's view of establishment illuminates his disagreement with social contract theory, and thus with the more radical idea that the people have the right, at any time, to alter or abolish their form of government and to institute one more to their liking.[45] God—not the people—is the ultimate "institutor and author and protector of civil society." God willed the state, and His will is "the law of laws and the sovereign of sovereigns."[46] In a famous passage of the *Reflections* seemingly addressed to Locke, Burke conceded that "Society is

---

[40] Ibid., 82.

[41] Ibid., 83.

[42] Ibid., 85. Burke returns to this theme in his "Appeal from the New to the Old Whigs" (August, 1791), Edmund Burke, *Further Reflections on the Revolution in France*, ed. Daniel E. Ritchie (Indianapolis: Liberty Fund, 1992), 160–66 (hereinafter cited as "*An Appeal*").

[43] *Reflections*, 82.

[44] Ibid., 84.

[45] See *An Appeal*, 123, 157–58, 175.

[46] *Reflections*, 86.

indeed a contract"—but that it "ought not to be considered as nothing better than a partnership agreement in a trade of pepper and coffee, calico, or tobacco, or some other such low concern, to be taken up for a little temporary interest, and to be dissolved by the fancy of the parties." It must be "looked on with reverence." It is "a partnership not only between those who are living, but between those who are living, those who are dead, and those who are to be born." Thus, the authority of the sovereign—even the people—is constrained by the immutable order ordained by God. "Each contract of each particular state is but a clause in the great primeval contract of eternal society, . . . according to a fixed compact sanctioned by the inviolable oath which holds all physical and all moral natures, each in their appointed place." This divine law, he wrote, is not subject to the "will" of the people, who "are bound to submit their will to that law." Thus, it is in a case of "the first and supreme necessity only, a necessity that is not chosen but chooses," that a people have the right to dissolve the bands of society.[47] The established church, in Burke's view, is nothing more than "our recognition of a seigniory paramount"[48]—a recognition, like that in the American Pledge of Allegiance, that the nation is "under God" and therefore limited and constrained in its use of power.

Thus, far from augmenting the authority of the sovereign, as in the typical Erastian establishment, the established church in Burke's vision is a means of limiting power.

It is noteworthy that Burke's assessment of the effect of the establishment in England was shared by his philosophical *bête noire*, Jean-Jacques Rousseau—though Rousseau deplored what Burke celebrated. According to Rousseau, "the Kings of England have established themselves as heads of the church, . . . [b]ut with this title they have made themselves not so much masters as ministers, and have acquired not so much the right to change the church as the power to preserve it."[49] Thus he concludes, to his disgust, that "there are two powers, two sovereigns, in England."[50] To Rousseau, unlike Burke, this division of authority between church and state is "manifestly bad," because "all institutions that set man at odds with himself are worthless."[51] The point of a civil religion, to Rousseau, is to "join[] divine worship to a love of the law" and to "mak[e] the homeland the object of the

---

[47] Ibid., 84–85.

[48] Ibid., 86.

[49] Jean-Jacques Rousseau, *The Social Contract*, trans. M. Cranston (Harmondsworth: Penguin, 1968) (hereinafter cited as "*Social Contract*").

[50] Ibid., 180.

[51] Ibid., 181.

citizens' adoration."[52] To Burke it is to remind both the rulers and the people of the limitations of the law and the obligations of the nation to a higher and more permanent order.

Burke does not maintain that enforcement of an established church throughout the dominion, regardless of the circumstances and predispositions of the people, would produce these salutary effects. Burke himself notes that when an attempt is made to impose an established church contrary to the "genius and desires" of the nation (giving Scotland at the time of Charles I as an example, but surely thinking of Ireland in his own time), such a "usurpation" will "excite[] a most mutinous spirit in that country."[53] In the United States, the early establishments produced more "mutiny" than they did "virtue and wisdom." But that does not mean the United States can do without "consecration." In an odd way, the Constitution of the United States performs much the same role that the established church performed in Burke's vision. The remedy against hasty and incautious change is the written constitution. As Madison stated in *Federalist* No. 44:

> The sober people of America are weary of the fluctuating policy which has directed the public councils. They have seen with regret and indignation that sudden changes and legislative interferences, in cases affecting personal rights, become jobs in the hands of enterprising and influential speculators, and snares to the more industrious and less informed part of the community. . . . They rightly infer, therefore, that some thorough reform is wanting, which will . . . give a regular course to the business of society.[54]

The Constitution is our bulwark against change—our guarantee that passing majorities, inflamed by "floating fancies or fashions," will not "destroy the entire fabric." And the Constitution itself is protected by a quasi-religious status in the popular mind.

Moreover, rather than an established church, it is our First Amendment that most plainly serves as a reminder that legitimate government is limited by the immutable principles of a higher Authority. I have observed in another place that our Free Exercise Clause stands as a recognition that even the democratic will of the people is subordinate, in principle, to the commands of God as perceived in the individual conscience, and that in such a nation, with such a commitment, totalitarian tyranny is a philosophical impossibility.[55] Religion—the recognition of an authority higher than the State—is thus

---

52 Ibid.

53 Speech on the Acts of Uniformity (Feb. 6, 1772), *Works*, 7: 8.

54 J. Madison, *The Federalist no. 44*, ed. C. Rossiter (New York: Penguin, 1961), 282.

55 Michael W. McConnell, "The Origins and Historical Understanding of Free Exercise of Religion," *Harvard Law Review* 103 (1990): 1516.

central to the constraint of governmental power in both Burke's England and Madison's America, though Burke accomplishes this by incorporating the spiritual authority into the constitution of the State while Madison does so by placing the conscience of the individual above the civil authority. The two systems may appear to be opposites, but the true opposite of both is the totalitarian system first introduced in France, where the State, embodying the "general will," is the highest authority and both established church and individual conscience are subjugated to it.

   (2) *The character of the established church in Burke's constitution.*—As has been noted, establishments typically serve the function of social control, by which the sovereign employs the church to reinforce the dictates of the law or—in the theocratic alternative—uses the coercive power of the state to enforce the doctrines and practices of the religion. Burke's establishment does neither. It is largely, though not entirely, independent of state control and also largely, but not entirely, indifferent about matters of doctrine and practice.

   The people of England, Burke explains, have "made their church, like their king and their nobility, independent."[56] This independence is essential if the establishment is to perform its constitutional function, for "[r]eligion, to have any force on men's understandings, indeed to exist at all, must be supposed paramount to laws, and independent for its substance upon any human institution."[57] Independence is attained in the English system by endowing the church with sufficient private property that it is dependent neither upon "the unsteady and precarious contribution of individuals" nor upon the vagaries of Parliamentary appropriation. "They certainly never have suffered, and never will suffer, the fixed estate of the church to be converted into a pension, to depend on the treasury and to be delayed, withheld, or perhaps to be extinguished by fiscal difficulties."[58] As one dependent on the largesse of others would know, such fiscal difficulties "may sometimes be presented for political purposes."[59] If the clergy depended upon

---

[56] *Reflections*, 88.

[57] *Tract on the Popery Laws* (c. 1761), *Works*, 6: 338.

[58] *Reflections*, 88.

[59] Ibid. One might speculate that Burke's sensitivities on this score were heightened by his own experience. Early in his career, he resigned an official pension of £ 300 per year because it would have made him, in effect, a perpetual retainer to his then-employer William Gerard Hamilton. Later in the same year, Burke unexpectedly inherited an estate of approximately the same value—an inheritance that secured his independence to the same extent that the earlier pension would have imperiled it. *Life and Times*, 177-83. Though no commentator has noted the connection, Burke's depiction of the situation of the Church in the *Reflections* has a certain autobiographical flavor.

appropriations from the Parliament, rather than the security of earnings from the glebe lands of the church, they would be subordinate to the civil authorities, and subject to their whim and control. Thus, "[t]he people of England think that they have constitutional motives, as well as religious, against any project of turning their independent clergy into ecclesiastical pensioners of state. They tremble for their liberty, from the influence of a clergy dependent on the crown; they tremble for the public tranquillity from the disorders of a factious clergy, if it were made to depend upon any other than the crown."[60]

This "independence" was not, of course, absolute. Burke agreed that government has a "general superintending control" over the "publicly propagated doctrines of men." Such control is essential to "provide adequately for all the wants of society."[61] But Burke did not expect, or intend, this "control" to include the power to determine the doctrines and practices of the Church of England. "As an independent church, professing fallibility, she has claimed a right of acting without the consent of any other; as a church, she claims, and has always exercised, a right of reforming whatever appeared amiss in her doctrine, her discipline, or her rites."[62] In support of this independence, Burke invoked the ancient medieval principle, developed during the papacy of Gregory VII, of the "liberty of the Church."[63] It was this aspect of the establishment—the independence of the Church through its base of private property—that was the first major casualty of the revolution in France.

There may be some tension between Burke's emphasis on the independence of the church as an essential part of the constitution and his statement that "[r]eligion is so far, in my opinion, from being out of the province or the duty of a Christian magistrate, that it is, and it ought to be, not only in his care, but the principal thing in his care; because it is one of the great bonds of human society, and its object the supreme good, the ultimate end and object of man himself."[64] But Burke goes on to describe the magistrate's "right and duty" as "to watch over [the church] with unceasing vigilance, to protect, to promote, to forward it by every rational, just, and prudent means."[65] The "care of the magistrate" thus seems to involve

---

[60] *Reflections*, 88.

[61] Speech on the Petition of the Unitarians (May 11, 1792), *Works*, 7: 42.

[62] Speech on the Acts of Uniformity (Feb. 6, 1772), *Works*, 7: 7.

[63] Ibid. On the "freedom of the church," see Harold Berman, *Law and Revolution* (Cambridge: Harvard Univ. Press, 1983), 88–99, 105.

[64] Speech on the Petition of the Unitarians (May 11, 1792), *Works*, 7: 43.

[65] Ibid.

ministering to the church, as Rousseau had pointed out, rather than being its master.

Burke rejected outright the option of leaving the church solely to the voluntary support of its members. "They who think religion of no importance to the state have abandoned it to the conscience or caprice of the individual; they make no provision for it whatsoever, but leave every club to make, or not, a voluntary contribution towards its support, according to their fancies."[66] Obviously he thought withdrawal of support would weaken the church, but he did not explain his reasoning. Perhaps he considered it self-evident, but if so, this is peculiar. Burke was a sophisticated student of economics, whose thinking paralleled and in some respects anticipated the work of Adam Smith.[67] Smith made the plausible economic argument that ministers of the gospel "who depend altogether for their subsistence upon the voluntary contributions of their hearers" were likely to be superior in "[t]heir exertion, their zeal and industry," to those who derive their support from a "fund to which the law of their country may entitle them," whether it be a landed estate, a tithe, or an established salary or stipend.[68] Burke presumably would respond that a voluntary system renders the clergyman dependent on the popularity and regard of his parishioners and that this is no better than dependence on the political authorities. But while a church forced to be more attentive to its adherents may lose "independence," it is questionable that it would become "weaker." In this, Burke may be reflecting his episcopal ecclesiology, which would carry less weight with Presbyterian Smith.

There is reason to believe that Burke's (and Rousseau's) portrayal of the independence of the Church of England during this period was greatly exaggerated. Appointment of church officers and control over church benefices could hardly fail to give the government effective control. One historian has commented that "at no other time [than the eighteenth century] was the influence of state over church so great. . . . The privileged clergy were an integral part of the extravagant patronage network which dictated how England was governed, and high office in the church was determined by political considerations."[69] Burke's failure to acknowledge this situation is particularly striking in light of his criticism of the use of favors and offices by

---

[66] First Letter to Sir Hercules Langrishe (Jan. 3, 1792), *Works*, 4: 257.

[67] See Donal Barrington, "Edmund Burke as an Economist," *Economica* 21 (1954): 252.

[68] Adam Smith, *An Inquiry into the Nature and Causes of the Wealth of Nations*, vol. 2, bk. 5, chap. 1, pt. 3, art. 3, 309 (1776; Chicago: Univ. of Chicago Press, 1976).

[69] Eric J. Evans, *The Contentious Tithe* (London & Boston: Routledge & K. Paul, 1976), 2

the King to dominate the Parliament.[70] The *Reflections* must be understood as Burke's portrayal of the ideal type of the English constitution, often in romantic and exaggerated terms—not as a hardheaded analysis of the realities.

One of the popular criticisms of the Church, with which Burke had no sympathy, was the contrast between the wealth enjoyed by higher members of the clergy and the poverty and simplicity of the apostles and the early church. In Burke's understanding of the function of the Church in the constitutional order, it was necessary that high church officials be able to present themselves with sufficient pomp that they would command respect among the secular nobility and political powers. The very point of the established church is to remind government officials (and the people) of the higher authority of God. Yet the "people of England know how little influence the teachers of religion are likely to have with the wealthy and powerful of long standing . . . if they appear in a manner no way assorted to those with whom they must associate, and over whom they must even exercise, in some cases, something like an authority." What must the secular powers think of the clergy, Burke asks, "if they see it in no part above the establishment of their domestic servants?"[71] Accordingly, Burke would have the Church "exalt her mitred front in courts and parliaments" and "show to the haughty potentates of the world . . . that a free, a generous, and informed nation honors the high magistrates of its church; that it will not suffer the insolence of wealth and titles, or any other species of proud pretension, to look down with scorn upon what they looked up to with reverence."[72]

As would be expected of Burke, a properly ordered state church should take its doctrinal bearings not from theological theory, but from "the established opinions and prejudices of mankind."[73] As in his politics, Burke anchors his theology in prescription—in the settled customs and opinions of

---

[70] See, e.g., Speech on Economical Reform (Feb. 11, 1780), *Works*, 2: 265–364.

[71] Ibid., 90. Burke acknowledged that

If the poverty were voluntary, there might be some difference. Strong instances of self-denial operate powerfully on our minds, and a man who has no wants has obtained great freedom and firmness and even dignity. But as the mass of any description of men are but men, and their poverty cannot be voluntary, that disrespect which attends upon all lay poverty will not depart from the ecclesiastical.

Ibid.

[72] Ibid. In this passage, Burke evinces the same respect mixed with disdain for aristocratic pomp and privilege that he later reveals in his brilliant *Letter to a Noble Lord*, *Works*, 5: 171–229.

[73] Speech on the Petition of the Unitarians (May 11, 1792), *Works*, 7: 43.

the great mass of the people over long periods of time.[74] This grounding in prescription protects the church from rapid and improvident alteration and at the same time insulates it from the will of the sovereign—and more particularly, inhibits its use as an instrument of revolutionary tyranny. It is better to tolerate "imperfection"—which will exist in all human institutions—than to experience frequent religious "alterations," which lead to "religious tumults and religious wars."[75]

A final characteristic of the established church, in Burke's vision, is that it is tolerant. "I am persuaded that toleration, so far from being an attack upon Christianity, becomes the best and surest support that possibly can be given to it," Burke declared.[76] "Zealous as I am for the principle of an establishment, so just an abhorrence do I conceive against whatever may shake it. I know nothing but the supposed necessity of persecution that can make an establishment disgusting. I would have toleration a part of establishment, as a principle favorable to Christianity, and as a part of Christianity."[77] The rationale and the limits of this toleration will be explored in greater detail below. But for present purposes it is important to note that Burke distinguished—as few among his party did—between the rights of dissenters from the established church to preach, teach, and worship,[78] and the movement for liberalization *within* the Church of England.

The line he drew between questions of toleration and establishment can perhaps best be seen in two debates in the early 1770s (long before the French Revolution raised the stakes in the English debates over church and state). In 1772, more than 200 Anglican clergy petitioned Parliament to be excused from adherence to several of the Thirty-nine Articles of Faith of the Church of England, and were warmly supported by most of Burke's friends and allies in the Whig Party. To their surprise, Burke delivered an oration against the petition, in which he maintained that the petition did not present a question of toleration, but of the right of the people of England to maintain a Church in accordance with their own theological principles.[79] The

---

[74] See Letter to William Smith, Esq., on the Subject of Catholic Emancipation (Jan. 29, 1795), *Works*, 6: 368; for Burke's famous defense of the principle of prescription in political affairs, see Speech on Reform of Representation (May 7, 1782), *Works*, 7: 94–97.

[75] Speech on the Acts of Uniformity (Feb. 6, 1772), *Works*, 7: 10–11.

[76] Speech on a Bill for the Relief of Protestant Dissenters (Mar. 17, 1773), *Works*, 7: 25.

[77] Ibid.

[78] Speech on a Bill for the Relief of Protestant Dissenters (Mar. 17, 1773), *Works*, 7: 21, 21-28.

[79] Speech on the Acts of Uniformity (Feb. 6, 1772), *Works*, 7: 5–19. The bill was defeated, and subsequently a significant body of Anglican clergy resigned their livings and joined the ranks of the Rational Dissenters.

complaint, he said derisively, "is not toleration of diversity in opinion, but that diversity in opinion is not rewarded by bishoprics, rectories, and collegiate stalls."[80] The following year, however, a group of dissenting clergy sought repeal of the requirement that they adhere to certain of the Thirty-nine Articles.[81] This time, Burke switched camps and supported the Dissenters, making what might seem to be the obvious distinction between the right to preach and the right to preach as a clergyman of the Church of England. At the time, most observers regarded this as a reversal of position, because for most the battle lines were drawn between supporters of the establishment and advocates of theological change, but for Burke the two positions were entirely consistent.

Burke rejected coercion as a means of maintaining the establishment. Compulsion in matters of religion, he believed, is not only wrong but ineffective, for the conscience cannot be changed on account of force or convenience.[82] This meant that government power over religion was limited; it could give support and encouragement to beliefs that already were widely held, but could not impose beliefs on an unwilling populace. "Religion," he said, "is not believed because the laws have established it, but it is established because the leading part of the community have previously believed it to be true."[83] He nonetheless recognized that "men must believe their religion upon some principle or other, whether of education, habit, theory, or authority."[84] One important means of supporting religion is through education. He noted that "[o]ur education is in a manner wholly in the hands of ecclesiastics, and in all stages from infancy to manhood." By this means, "we attach our gentlemen to the church."[85]

These, then, are the characteristics of Burke's establishment: independence, stability, and toleration. Burke was less inclined to defend other aspects of the establishment, which were not so easy to reconcile with his vision. The right of the Church to compel payment of tithes, for example, was the most irksome and unpopular aspect of the establishment during this

---

[80] Speech on the Acts of Uniformity (Feb. 6, 1772), *Works*, 7: 15.

[81] This requirement was not generally enforced, but Burke argued that "connivance"—the discretionary nonenforcement of the law—is "an engine of private malice or private favor, not of good government." Speech on a Bill for the Relief of Protestant Dissenters (Mar. 17, 1773), *Works*, 7: 33. If penal laws "may be roused from their sleep, whenever a minister thinks proper, as instruments of oppression, then they put vast bodies of men into a state of slavery and court dependence." Ibid., 7: 26.

[82] *Tract on the Popery Laws* (c. 1761), *Works*, 6: 335.

[83] Ibid., 338.

[84] Letter to Richard Burke, Jr. on Protestant Ascendency in Ireland (1793), *Works*, 6: 395.

[85] *Reflections*, 87.

period, and did more to bring the Church into conflict and disrepute with the ordinary people of England than any other.[86] The tithe was in effect a tax, typically a tenth, on agricultural production and sometimes on the fruits of commerce or labor, with numerous and chaotic exceptions resting on custom, precedent, statute, and caselaw. Far from uniting the people and fostering respect for the divine representatives on earth, the tithing system led to widespread public disaffection and an appearance (if not the reality) of clerical oppressiveness.[87] It could not have escaped Burke's attention that this system was inimical to his vision of the role of the Church. His only direct comments on the tithe, in a letter to his son, evinced great sympathy for Irish farmers who resisted the exaction.[88] Burke presumably found it difficult to attack the tithing system outright, however, for in legal form the tithes were an appurtenance of real property, of ancient provenance, not much different in their legal standing from any other nonpossessory property interest.[89] Thus, in his defense of the establishment we may perceive a discreet silence about the tithe. Instead, he argued optimistically that a greater security of the real property of the Church might render the collection of tithes less vital: "I heartily wish to see the Church secure in such possessions as will not only enable her ministers to preach the Gospel with ease, but of such a kind as will enable them to preach it with its full effect, so that the pastor shall not have the inauspicious appearance of a tax-gatherer."[90]

Another aspect of the establishment that Burke found distasteful was the exclusion of religious dissenters from political franchise and office, through the Corporation and Test Acts. Although in the early 1760s he was willing to countenance the exclusion of Catholics from public office (but not the vote) in Ireland,[91] he later favored removal of all political disabilities in both

---

[86] See generally Evans, *The Contentious Tithe*.

[87] It was also an inefficient and counterproductive tax, as it discouraged both the improvements of the landlord and the cultivation of the farmer, as Adam Smith pointed out. Smith, *An Inquiry into the Nature and Causes of The Wealth of Nations*, vol. 2, bk. 5, chap. 2, pt. 2, art. 1, 363. Given Burke's attention to the issues of public economics, and general agreement with Smith on such matters, it is likely that he was aware of this critique.

[88] Letter to Richard Burke, Jr. on Protestant Ascendency in Ireland (1793), *Works*, 6: 399–400.

[89] *The Contentious Tithe*, 8–9, 17. About one-third of the rights to tithes were owned by private persons, most of them derived from the sale of monastic properties at the time of Henry VIII. Ibid., 12, 17.

[90] Speech on Dormant Claims of the Church (Feb. 17, 1772), *Works*, 7: 142. Burke's optimism had some basis in fact: during the last half of the eighteenth century, there was a "decisive shift in the source of income of many of the better endowed clergy" from tithes to direct ownership of land. *The Contentious Tithe*, 8.

[91] Tract on the Popery Laws (c. 1761), *Works*, 6: 311.

England and Ireland on account of religion.[92] In the aftermath of the confiscation of Church properties by the revolutionary government in France and the praise of the Revolution by Rational Dissenters (such as Richard Price) in England, however, Burke spoke against wholesale repeal of the Test Act as applied to those who favored elimination of the established church.[93] His generally admiring 19th Century biographer, Thomas MacKnight, maintained that "there is perhaps no act of his life so difficult to defend" as this speech,[94] and two years later, Burke appeared to back away from the position, excusing the English Test Act on the ground that it had become a "dead letter."[95] Certainly, in his affirmative defense of the establishment in the *Reflections* and elsewhere, Burke never advocated or defended the imposition of any civil or political disabilities on religious dissenters.

Toleration.—As has already been seen, Burke supported both strong establishment and capacious toleration. In this, he stood virtually alone among the statesmen and advocates of his day. At risk of oversimplification, these may be divided into three camps.[96] First were the evangelical separationists, led by the Baptists, a faction more numerous and influential in America than in Britain. Evangelical separationists opposed the establishment both because they deemed it erroneous on theological grounds and because they thought government support rendered the clergy subservient to the state, and they supported the widest possible toleration or free exercise in matters of religion because they considered religion to be the central and most important activity of life. Second were the secularists, led by so-called "Rational Dissenters" like Richard Price and Joseph Priestly. While superficially aligned with the evangelical separationists—both opposed the establishment—the secularists sought to reduce the role of religion in public life and generally believed that scientific ideas should supplant the superstition and revealed religion of the past. While the evangelical separationists stressed that religion is too sacred to be subject to human interference, the secularists maintained that religion is—or should be— irrelevant to the state. Third were the establishmentarians, such as Lord North and the great William Blackstone. By Burke's day, it was *de rigueur* to recognize a degree of toleration as part of the establishment; but this

---

[92] See Letter to the Hon. Edmund S. Pery (July 18, 1778), *Works*, 6: 202.

[93] Speech on the Petition of the Unitarians (May 11, 1792), *Works*, 7: 41–58.

[94] *Life and Times*, 3: 310.

[95] First Letter to Sir Hercules Langrishe (Jan. 3, 1792), *Works*, 4: 252–53.

[96] These positions are set forth in greater detail and nuance in Ursula Henriques, *Religious Toleration in England, 1787–1833* (Toronto: Univ. of Toronto Press, 1961).

toleration was typically grudging, and held to a narrow compass. Blackstone, for example, wrote that "undoubtedly all persecution and oppression of weak consciences, on the score of religious persuasions, are highly unjustifiable upon every principle of natural reason, civil liberty, or sound religion. But care must be taken not to carry this indulgence to such extremes, as may endanger the national church."[97] In actual disputes over the extension of toleration, the establishmentarians were almost invariably opposed.[98]

It should be noted that the enthusiasm of all three of these positions for toleration of Roman Catholics (the most burning religious issue of the era) was decidedly lacking. To the evangelicals, Catholicism represented the gravest of theological error; to the secularists and rational dissenters Catholicism was superstitious and unenlightened; to the establishmentarians the constitutional status of the Protestant religion was a central tenet of the Glorious Revolution. It was widely held that the Glorious Revolution of 1688—the political heritage of Burke's Whig party—was a victory over Papism, and thus that the suppression of Catholicism was part of the fundamental constitutional fabric of the realm, at least as long as Catholics maintained their potentially subversive loyalty to a foreign power, the Pope in Rome.[99] Antipathy toward Papists was widespread, and was one of the few attitudes that evangelical separationists, secularists, and establishmentarians had in common.

Burke's advocacy of toleration was tied most particularly to his outrage over the oppression of the Catholics of Ireland, but extended to other

---

[97] William Blackstone, *Commentaries on the Laws of England*, vol. 4, bk. 4, chap. 4, 51 (1769; Chicago: Univ. of Chicago Press, 1979) (hereinafter cited as "*Blackstone's Commentaries*"). In a similar vein, Lord North, the head of government, told Burke in 1778 that "his ideas of toleration were large, but that, large as they were, they did not comprehend a promiscuous establishment"—meaning that he opposed any relaxation of the sacramental test. Letter to the Hon. Edmund S. Pery (July 18, 1778), *Works*, 6: 201.

[98] Opposition to the extension of toleration proceeded along two dimensions. First, establishmentarians were disposed to support toleration only to those whose ideas were reasonably close to the national consensus. Thus, Dissenting clergy who affirmed 36 of the 39 Articles were freely permitted to preach, while those who dissented more fundamentally were (at least in theory) not. This was the issue involved in Burke's speech on a Bill for the Relief of Protestant Dissenters (Mar. 17, 1773), *Works*, 7: 25. Second, tolerant establishmentarians generally supported extension of the protection of natural rights to dissenters, but resisted extension of the equal benefits of government action. See Philip A. Hamburger, "Equality and Diversity: The Eighteenth-Century Debate About Equal Protection and Equal Civil Rights," *Supreme Court Review* 1992: 318–22.

[99] See ibid., 57; Ursula Henriques, *Religious Toleration in England, 1787–1833* (Toronto: Univ. of Toronto Press, 1961), 77–79, describing the Tory theory that the Corporation and Test Acts were "fundamental laws" of the Union. Burke summarizes this arguement in his First Letter to Sir Hercules Langrishe (Jan. 3, 1792), *Works*, 4: 245, and refutes it, ibid., 257–70.

Dissenters from the established church as well—up to the point where they became political factions hostile to the constitutional structure of the land. As the French Revolution unfolded, Burke became alarmed at the connection between what he called "fanatical atheism"[100] and the spread of Jacobinism, which he considered the greatest of all threats to the constitution, to liberty, order, and religion, and all the more convinced that revealed religion is a vital protection against totalitarianism. He could not, therefore, view religion as a purely private matter, bereft of political significance, as many religious reformers were wont to do. Rather, he developed a theory in which toleration was part of a general strategy, together with establishment, to maintain the social and cultural preconditions for limited government.

   (1) Burke's efforts on behalf of Catholic emancipation.—Surpassing even his commitment to the Anglican establishment was Burke's lifelong struggle for toleration of Roman Catholics, especially in Ireland. In a letter to his son, Richard, who was serving as agent to the Catholic Committee of Ireland, Burke stated: "There are few things I wish more . . . than that the established churches would be continued on a firm foundation in both kingdoms. When I say few I mean to be exact; for some things, assuredly, I have nearer my heart, namely, the emancipation of that great body of my original countrymen."[101] There was no more consistent strand in Burke's political life. Burke first articulated his argument against the Irish Penal Laws in his Tract Relative to the Laws Against Popery in Ireland,[102] which he began in 1761, but never published. He restated and developed the arguments in numerous speeches and letters throughout his career, including his brilliant Speech at Bristol, Previous to An Election on September 6, 1780,[103] in which he defended his position to constituents unhappy with his outspoken advocacy of Catholic emancipation. Writing in 1795, Burke recalled that he had begun to work against the Penal Laws in Ireland "four or five and thirty years ago" and that he had been "ever since, of the same opinion on the justice and policy of the whole and of every part of the penal system."[104]

   The Irish Penal Laws in Burke's day were harsh and unyielding. Burke claimed that they were worse than "any scheme of religious persecution now existing in any other country in Europe, or which has prevailed in any time

---

   [100] Letters on a Regicide Peace, Works, 5: 363.

   [101] Letter to Richard Burke, Jr. (Mar. 23, 1792), Correspondence, 7: 118 (emphasis in original).

   [102] Published in Works, 6: 299–360. Unfortunately, all that survives is a substantial fragment, some of which is taken from a rough draft.

   [103] Published in Works, 2: 367-24.

   [104] Second Letter to Sir Hercules Langrishe (May 26, 1795), Works, 6: 51.

or nation with which history has made us acquainted."[105] All monks, friars, and priests not then actually in parishes were banished from the kingdom under Queen Anne, on penalty of death if they should return, with rewards for apprehending them and penalties for harboring them. "As all the priests then in being and registered are long since dead," Burke commented, "and as these laws are made perpetual, every Popish priest is liable to the law."[106] In addition, the Catholic people of Ireland were subjected to severe civil disabilities, among them being: denial of the vote, exclusion from public office, military service, higher education, and the practice of law (even as a clerk), denial of the right to bear arms even in self-defense, susceptibility to search without warrant, denial of the right to buy or lease real property for any period exceeding 31 years, denial of the right to devise property by will or by primogeniture, insecurity of property (if children of Catholic property owners converted, they could seize their parents' property and leave only the life estate), destruction of parental rights in the event a Catholic's spouse converted, and prohibition of teaching. Any child who was educated in a Catholic school in another country was stripped for life of any right to legal capacity or property ownership, and so were the persons who sent or maintained them, unless the child abjured the Catholic faith within six months of return. Enforcement of these restrictions was by trial before Protestant magistrates and juries, often with the burden of proof shifted to the Catholic defendant.[107]

Some of these laws applied to Protestant Dissenters in Ireland, and similar laws to Catholic and Protestant Dissenters in England and Scotland as well.[108] Protestant Dissenters who swore oaths of allegiance and supremacy and subscribed to a declaration against popery were exempted from the penalties of the Penal Laws. In theory, Dissenting clergymen could not be licensed to preach unless they subscribed to the Thirty-nine Articles (except those pertaining to church governance and infant baptism), though this was virtually a "dead letter" in England.[109] The Corporation and Test Acts precluded Catholics and Protestant Dissenters from holding public office in England—unless they attended mass according to the rites of the Church of England and subscribed to certain articles of faith, including a denial of transubstantiation. And many of the civil disabilities described in the

---

[105] *Tract on the Popery Laws* (c. 1761), *Works*, 6: 318.

[106] Ibid., 317.

[107] Ibid., 302–17.

[108] For a description of the English Penal Laws, see *Blackstone's Commentaries*, vol. 4, bk. 4, chap. 4, 53–58. The Irish Penal Laws and various Catholic Relief Acts of the period are reproduced in appendices to Mahoney, 325–42.

[109] First Letter to Sir Hercules Langrishe (Jan. 3, 1792), *Works*, 4: 252–53.

preceding paragraph (including prohibitions on the Catholic mass, on Catholic education, and with respect to property) applied to Catholics in England and Scotland as well as in Ireland—though, as Blackstone pointed out, "these laws are seldom exerted to their utmost rigor."[110] But by far the harshest Penal Laws were those applicable to the Catholics in Ireland. These were not anachronisms: with only a few exceptions, these laws were actually enforced by the Protestant minority, who controlled all political and judicial power and who profited by their monopoly on public privileges. The Irish Parliament, far from representing the interests of the Catholic majority, was actively hostile to them.[111]

The perennial argument against admission of Catholics to the rights of citizens was that they were disloyal to the British government—that either because of their lingering loyalties to the Stuart line or their allegiance to the Pope in Rome, they might be expected to side with the Catholic powers of Europe in conflict with the King. As Blackstone argued:

> If once they [papists] could be brought to renounce the supremacy of the pope, they might quietly enjoy their seven sacraments, their purgatory, and auricular confession, their worship of reliques and images; nay even their transubstantiation. But while they acknowledge a foreign power, superior to the sovereignty of the kingdom, they cannot complain if the laws of that kingdom will not treat them upon the footing of good subjects.[112]

These suspicions were all the stronger with regard to the Catholics of Ireland, who might, in addition to any disloyalty arising from their Catholicism, be expected to chafe against their subordination to the English and to the Protestant ruling class.

Burke strenuously sought to refute these claims. As to the generalized danger that Catholics would be loyal to the Pope as a foreign power, Burke labeled the claim a "commodious bugbear,"[113] and pointed to recent events in England and Canada to prove that the Catholic citizens had "cast off all foreign views and connections" and had resolved to "stand or fall with their country."[114] He could not, of course, deny that the Catholics of Ireland were

---

[110] *Blackstone's Commentaries*, vol. 4, bk. 4, chap. 4, 56-57.

[111] First Letter to Sir Hercules Langrishe (Jan. 3, 1792), *Works*, 4: 253.

[112] *Blackstone's Commentaries*, vol. 4, bk. 4, chap. 4, 54.

[113] First Letter to Sir Hercules Langrishe (Jan. 3, 1792), *Works*, 4: 280.

[114] Speech at Bristol, Previous to the Election (Sept. 6, 1780), *Works*, 2: 400, describing the outpouring of Catholic support for the Crown during the American Revolution; First Letter to Sir Hercules Langrishe (Jan. 3, 1792), *Works*, 4: 304, describing the loyalty of Canadian Catholic citizens.

restive under the current regime, but the "real cause" of the disorders in Ireland was not their Catholicism; it was their persecution. The Popery laws

> divided the nation into two distinct bodies, without common interest, sympathy, or connection. One of these bodies was to possess *all* the franchises, *all* the property, *all* the education: the other was to be composed of drawers of water and cutters of turf for them. Are we to be astonished, when, by the efforts of so much violence in conquest, and so much policy in regulation, continued without intermission for near an hundred years, we had reduced them to a mob?[115]

There was no reason to think the Catholics "adverse to our Constitution," when in fact "our statutes are hostile and destructive to them."[116] To treat the Catholics as disloyal is the best way to make them disloyal.

Progress toward reform was slow. In his first attempt, as private secretary to the Chief Secretary in Ireland from 1761 to 1764 (Burke's first public position), he won support from the Privy Council for a modest proposal: to allow six regiments of Catholic Irish to be formed to defend England's ally, Portugal, at Portuguese expense. It was thought that this would help to dispel the persistent suspicion that the Catholic majority were disloyal to Britain, and serve as a bridge toward enlargement of civil capacities. But even this small step was defeated in the Irish Parliament, because of fears that arming the Catholics could prove dangerous.[117]

The next opportunity came in 1778, when Burke was Member of Parliament for Bristol. Burke induced Sir George Savile, a Protestant of aristocratic family with large land holdings in Ireland, to introduce legislation lifting some of the more egregious penalties on the practice of Catholicism in England, and Lord Richard Cavendish introduced a second bill authorizing the Irish Parliament to pass similar relief for the Catholics of that land. Although Burke was undoubtedly the prime mover of these measures behind the scenes, he neither made the motions nor spoke in favor of the bills on the floor of the House, largely because of widespread insinuations that he was too close to the Catholic cause. The bills were enacted, and the Irish Parliament followed suit with a somewhat more limited bill of relief, which Burke later described as a "first faint sketch of toleration, which did little more than disclose a principle and mark out a disposition."[118] Burke was widely given the credit in Ireland for passage of these measures, and it is reported that the King was influenced to sign by an "Address and Petition to the Throne"

---

[115] First Letter to Sir Hercules Langrishe (Jan. 3, 1792), *Works*, 4: 247.

[116] Speech at Bristol, Previous to the Election (Sept. 6, 1780), *Works*, 2: 416.

[117] For an account of this episode, see Mahoney, 14-15.

[118] Speech at Bristol, Previous to the Election (Sept. 6, 1780), *Works*, 2: 403-04.

Burke had drafted some 14 years before, which was preserved and presented to the monarch.[119] Burke himself attributed the change in opinion that enabled passage of the bills to the crisis precipitated by the American Revolution, which made it imperative that all the subjects of Britain be conciliated and united.[120]

The next step was introduction of a similar measure in Scotland. This, however, was blocked by the fierce opposition of an organization called the Protestant Association, led by the fanatical Lord George Gordon, which stirred up angry mobs in Edinburgh and Glasgow. So furious was the anti-Catholic sentiment in Scotland that James Boswell, a Scot, advised Burke that if he pressed ahead for a Catholic Relief Act for that country "there would be as desperate a Rebellion against Government as in the day of Charles the Second."[121] While the bill was pending, in 1780, Gordon presented a petition from the Protestant Association demanding repeal of the English Relief Act. He led a mob of some 60,000 people to Parliament to present the petition. The mob, which one historian has called "unparalleled in the history of parliament," forced entering members of the Lords and Commons to wear blue cockades and shout "No Popery!", violently attacking those who resisted (including such luminaries as the Archbishop of York, the Bishop of Lincoln, the Duke of Northumberland, and the Chief Justice Mansfield).[122] Burke later described the scene to his Bristol constituents, stating: "I do not wish to go over the horrid scene that was afterwards acted. Would to God it could be expunged forever from the annals of this country! But since it must subsist for our shame, let it subsist for our instruction."[123]

There ensued a week of riots during which Catholic churches were looted and burned, homes and other property destroyed, many members of Parliament roughed up, and Burke's home, family, and person threatened. It is reported that Burke repeatedly ventured among the mob, announcing his identity and his support for the Relief Act.[124] Burke matched his physical courage outside with unstinting opposition to repeal of the Act inside. As he described it:

In this audacious tumult, . . . I, who had exerted myself very little on the quiet passing of the bill, thought it necessary then to come forward. I was not alone; but . . . I may and will value myself so far, that, yielding in abilities to many, I

---

[119] See Mahoney, 69–74; 2 *Life and Times*, 236–46.

[120] Speech at Bristol, Previous to the Election (Sept. 6, 1780), *Works*, 2: 400-04.

[121] Quoted in Mahoney, 92.

[122] Ibid., 93–94.

[123] Speech at Bristol, Previous to the Election (Sept. 6, 1780), *Works*, 2: 410.

[124] Mahoney, 95; *Life and Times*, 366.

yielded in zeal to none. With warmth and with vigor, and animated with a just
and natural indignation, I called forth every faculty that I possessed, and I
directed it in every way in which I could possibly employ it. I labored night and
day. I labored in Parliament; I labored out of Parliament. If, therefore, the
resolution of the House of Commons, refusing to commit this act of unmatched
turpitude, be a crime, I am guilty among the foremost.[125]

Burke prevailed and the Act survived, but the King and the government
privately made clear that they would not support any further reform of the
Penal laws, for fear of future violence.[126] Indeed, the House of Commons
passed (though the Lords rejected) a bill offered by Sir George Savile as a sop
to the Protestant Association, which would restrain the "Papists, or persons
professing the Popish religion, from teaching, or taking upon themselves the
education or government of the children of Protestants." Burke took a
spirited part in debate against the bill, defending Catholic education and the
rights of parents to direct the education of their offspring.[127]

Later, he found himself under attack in his Bristol constituency for his
activities in support of the Relief Act, and he delivered a major address
defending his role, and the propriety of religious toleration. "I could do
nothing but what I have done on this subject," he told them, "without
confounding the whole train of my ideas and disturbing the whole order of
my life."[128] This was an issue on which Burke would follow his conscience
rather than the wishes of his constituents. "No man carries further than I do
the policy of making government pleasing to the people," he said. "But the
widest range of this politic complaisance is confined within the limits of
justice. . . . I never will act the tyrant for their amusement."[129]

Burke paid a price. He failed of reelection—in large part because of
opposition to his efforts on behalf of toleration—and thenceforth served in
Parliament as a member for a pocket borough.

After this time, the principal arena for reform of the Irish Penal Laws
shifted to the Irish Parliament (from which Catholics were excluded as both
electors and members). Burke remained active in the cause, corresponding
with members of the Irish Parliament as well as leaders in the movement for
reform. Many of these letters were also published and served as public
advocacy. Among these, Burke's *Letter to a Peer of Ireland* (Lord Kenmare,
then head of the Catholic Association) in 1782,[130] and *Letter to Sir Hercules*

---

[125] Ibid., 412-13.

[126] Mahoney, 96.

[127] See Speech at Bristol, Previous to the Election (Sept. 6, 1780), *Works*, 2: 98–99.

[128] Ibid., 388.

[129] Ibid., 421.

[130] Published in *Works*, 4: 217–39.

Langrishe (a member of the Irish Parliament and moderate advocate of reform) in 1792,[131] are classics, and contributed significantly to the passage of reform legislation in those years. The 1782 Act removed restrictions on purchasing, inheriting, and bequeathing land and legitimated most of the priestly functions of parish priests. The 1792 Act opened the practice of law to Catholics, removed the ban on religious intermarriage, permitted Catholic schools, and removed the ban on foreign education of Catholic children. Burke considered the latter Act so timorous as to be "no relief" and opposed it in favor of stronger measures.[132]

In 1790, in recognition of Burke's guiding role, the Catholic Committee of Ireland hired Burke's son, Richard, as its agent for the campaign for enfranchisement and other reform. As the chairman of the Committee observed, "The many obligations we are under to the Zeal and brilliant Abilities of the Father inspire us with the strongest reliance on the Son for his most strenuous exertions and able assistance in our behalf."[133] Burke wrote a series of letters to his son in that capacity, discussing the circumstances in Ireland and the reasons for further reform, with great sophistication and detail. The most serious problem, as perceived by Burke, was that the intransigence of the Protestant authorities were driving the Catholics to violence, as well as to an association with the revolutionary principles emanating from France. Anticipating Gandhi, Burke urged on the Catholic Irish a strategy of "still, discontented, passive obedience" in lieu of a "giddy unsupported resistance."[134]

Largely as a result of the efforts of father and son,[135] the British government pressured the Irish Parliament to enact a third Catholic Relief Act in 1793, extending to qualified Catholic citizens the rights to vote, to serve on juries, to hold military commissions, and to obtain university degrees, provided they took an oath that, among other things, denied the infallibility of the pope and abjured any intention to disturb the established church. Catholics remained excluded from parliament and other high offices of government, and the hostility between the Protestant government and the Catholic majority continued to fester.

---

[131] Published in *Works*, 4: 241-306.

[132] See Letter to Viscount Kenmare (Feb. 21, 1782), *Correspondence*, 4: 405–18. This letter is a commentary on an earlier version of the bill, in which aspects of the Penal Laws that were not being repealed were explicitly reenacted, thus giving the impression that it was "neither more nor less than a renewd act of universal, unmitigated, indispensable, exceptionless, disqualification," ibid., 407.

[133] Quoted in Mahoney, 162.

[134] Quoted in ibid., 202.

[135] Ibid., 211.

In the summer of 1794, Burke retired from Parliament, but his political allies, the Portland Whigs, returned to power in coalition with Pitt—a coalition that is deemed the beginning of the modern Conservative Party. Hopes were raised for a complete Catholic emancipation in Ireland when Burke's friend and political patron, Earl Fitzwilliam, was named Lord Lieutenant of Ireland, and immediately set about a thorough program of reform. Burke consulted actively with Fitzwilliam. Comprehensive reform legislation was introduced in the Irish Parliament, and a half million signatures were reportedly gathered in support. Within a few months of Fitzwilliam's arrival, however, the King announced his strong opposition to the emancipation plans, and the government instructed Fitzwilliam to use his "Zeal and Influence" to prevent any further proceeding on the emancipation bill.[136] Within a few weeks, Fitzwilliam had been dismissed. According to Burke's Irish sources, the country was "now on the brink of civil war."[137] Burke himself wrote to Fitzwilliam that "My heart is almost broken."[138] No more was accomplished in Burke's lifetime, and Ireland descended into an era of violence and rebellion.

(2) *Burke's position on toleration for other religious persuasions.*—Burke extended his advocacy of toleration to all of what he called "serious religion." He explained that "[e]ven the man who does not hold revelation, yet who wishes that it were proved to him, who observes a pious silence with regard to it, such a man, though not a Christian, is governed by religious principles. Let him be tolerated in this country. Let it be but a serious religion, natural or revealed, take what you can get. Cherish, blow up the slightest spark: one day it may be a pure and holy flame."[139] Thus, he supported the right of all to hold and teach their opinions. This included not just Catholics and Protestant dissenters, but Jews and other non-Christians as well. To be sure, Burke undertook no specific Parliamentary action to repeal the laws against Judaism in England. But in a speech condemning Admiral Rodney's plunder of the Jewish merchants of the Dutch Island of St. Eustatius during the war against the Netherlands, Burke asserted that the Jews are a people whom it was the special object of humanity to protect rather than abuse.[140] And in a private letter to a Catholic friend, Burke commended the Austrian Emperor's

---

[136] Quoted in ibid., 250.

[137] Letter from Rev. Thomas Hussey (Feb. 26, 1787), *Correspondence*, 8: 162.

[138] Quoted in Mahoney, 256.

[139] Speech on a Bill for the Relief of Protestant Dissenters (Mar. 17, 1773), *Works*, 7: 37.

[140] *Parliamentary History*, 22 (1781–82): 223–26, paraphrased in Thomas H. D. Mahoney, *Edmund Burke and Ireland* (Harvard: Harvard Univ. Press, 1960), 111.

extension of toleration to the Jews and indicated his support for such a measure in England—while opining that the nation was not yet ready for it, and that it could not pass without ministerial support.[141]

Burke is, of course, well known for his campaign against oppression in India. In addition to his attacks on the civil oppression and economic exploitation of the Indian people, Burke inveighed against the East India Company's "indignities to the Indian Priesthood."[142] He studied Halhed's Code of Hindu law intently in preparation for his case against Warren Hastings and—according to Charles Fox—"spoke of the piety of the Hindoos with admiration, and of their sacred functions with an awe bordering on devotion."[143] Burke described the Indian people to a Protestant Dissenter skeptical of his efforts as "twenty millions of Dissenters from the Church of England, in Asia," who had "real grievances which God forbid any of the Dissenters in Europe should have more feeling of, in their Persons, than any of them appear to have in any sympathy with the Sufferers."[144]

Burke was, however, ambivalent about new religions. "The only faint shadow of difficulty" with regard to religious toleration, he wrote in his first work on the subject, the *Tract on the Popery Laws*, "is concerning the introduction of new opinions." While new opinions may have been "favorable to the cause of truth," according to Burke, "[e]xperience has shown" that they are not "always conducive to the peace of society." Not only are new religious sects typically prone to "tumultuous and disorderly zeal," but they also are "the cause of the bitterest dissensions in the commonwealth" on account of their resistance to the present establishment. While Burke did not ultimately find this to be a sufficient basis for persecution, he could understand why it might persuade "a man of sense and of integrity."[145] Some 30 years later, Burke's suspicion and distaste for new religions—this time the Unitarian Society—had only increased: "Old religious factions are volcanoes burnt out; on the lava and ashes and squalid scoriæ of old eruptions grow the peaceful olive, the cheering vine, and the sustaining corn. . . . But when a new fire bursts out, a face of desolations comes on, not to be rectified in ages." Therefore, he said, "when men come before us, and rise up like an exhalation from the ground, they come in a questionable shape," and we must "try

---

[141] See Mahoney, 113.

[142] Henry Richard, Lord Holland, *Memoirs of the Whig Party* (London: Longman, Brown, Green, & Longman, 1852), 1: 5-6.

[143] Ibid., 6.

[144] Letter to Richard Bright (May 8 & 9, 1789), *Correspondence*, 5: 470.

[145] *Tract on the Popery Laws* (c. 1761), *Works*, 6: 336–37.

whether their intents be wicked or charitable, whether they bring airs from heaven or blasts from hell."[146]

Like John Locke before him,[147] Burke openly disavowed toleration of atheists, though it is unclear what this would mean in practice. To Burke, this appeared no contradiction, for atheism, to him, was the *absence* of religious conscience, not a variety of it. Thus, he could say that "I would respect all conscience" in the same speech in which he said that atheists "are never to be supported, never to be tolerated."[148] Atheism, he maintained, was "the most horrid and cruel blow that can be offered to civil society."[149]

With the coming of the French Revolution and the support it received in Ireland from the United Defenders and in England from many of the Rational Dissenters (including Reverend Richard Price, whose sermon in support of the Revolution inspired Burke to write the *Reflections*), Burke became less accommodating toward those dissenting Protestants who, he believed, were the vanguard of Jacobinism (hence atheism) in the British Isles. He had learned from the French experience that persons of this description were capable of acts of anti-religious fanaticism, and thus that they posed a serious danger to traditional religion. Burke attacked those Protestants who welcomed the assault on the Catholic Church in France; they are "miserable bigots" who "hate sects and parties different from their own more than they love the substance of religion."[150] He detected a revolutionary—even an atheistic—tendency in some strains of Protestant dissent. He disliked the very term "Protestant," because it emphasized what it was not (that is, not Catholic) rather than any affirmative doctrine.[151] In this, "Protestantism"— that is, opposition to Catholicism—was similar to atheism, which undermined the traditional basis of morality, hope, and order without substituting anything in its place. In one dark letter, he referred to "certain Protestant Conspirators and Traitors, who were acting in direct connexion with the Enemies of all Government and all Religion."[152]

---

[146] Speech on the Petition of the Unitarians (May 11, 1792), *Works*, 7: 46.

[147] See John Locke, *A Letter Concerning Toleration*, in J. Locke, *The Works of John Locke* (London 1823 and 1963 photo. reprint), 6: 46-47.

[148] Speech on a Bill for the Relief of Protestant Dissenters (Mar. 17, 1773), *Works*, 7: 36: "At the same time that I would cut up the very root of atheism, I would respect all conscience,—all conscience that is really such, and which perhaps its very tenderness proves to be sincere."

[149] Ibid.

[150] *Reflections*, 131.

[151] Letter to Richard Burke, Jr. on Protestant Ascendency in Ireland (1793), *Works*, 6: 393–94; see also First Letter to Sir Hercules Langrishe (Jan. 3, 1792), *Works*, 4: 257, 263, criticizing Protestantism as "mere negation."

[152] Letter to John Keogh (Nov. 17, 1796), *Correspondence* , 9: 115.

When the Unitarian Society petitioned in 1790 for repeal of the Test and Corporation Acts—a measure Burke had been willing to entertain in former years[153]—he shifted to a position of opposition. He explained in a letter to Richard Bright, a prominent dissenter and a neighbor of Burke's at Beaconsfield, that he was "less desirous than formerly I had been, of become active in the service of the Dissenters." He had previously been willing to overlook "many things which appeared to me, perhaps not so commendable in the conduct of those who seem'd to lead them" because he had thought them "animated with, a serious, humane hatred of Tyranny, oppression and corruption in all persons in Power." But he had "found by experience" that they were "of a direct contrary character"—that they were attempting to draw England into an imitation of the French Revolution, which would be "highly dangerous to the Constitution and the prosperity of this Country."[154] He proposed that the House of Commons form a committee to "examine into the conduct of the dissenters, the doctrines respecting the established church which they had recently avowed, and all that part of their conduct, to which he had adverted," and pledged that he would "hold himself bound to vote for the repeal of the test and corporation acts" if his fears proved unfounded.[155]

It is interesting that the ground of Burke's objection to the non-Trinitarian Protestants is similar in form to the stereotypical objection to Roman Catholics: that they would subvert the English Constitution and lead to the establishment of tyranny. The difference was not one of principle, but of empirical circumstance: "The whole question of the danger depends on the facts."[156] The Catholics, Burke knew, were loyal citizens made disloyal only by the force of oppression. By contrast, "we know that [the Unitarians] not only entertain these opinions [in support of the French Revolution], but entertain them with a zeal for propagating them by force." He predicted that the radical dissenters would "employ[] the power of law and place to destroy establishments, if ever they should come to power sufficient to effect their purpose: that is, in other words, they declare they would persecute the heads of our Church." Thus, for Burke, "the question is, whether you should keep

---

[153] See T. C. Hansard, *Parliamentary History of England* 28 (1790, 1816): 441 (hereinafter cited as "*Parliamentary History*"): "had the question been brought forward ten years ago, Mr. Burke said, he should have voted for the appeal. At present, in his opinion, a variety of circumstances made it appear imprudent to meddle with it." See also Letter to the Hon. Edmund S. Pery (July 18, 1778), *Works*, 6: 202.

[154] Letter to Richard Bright (Feb. 18, 1790), *Correspondence*, 6: 83.

[155] *Parliamentary History*, 28: 442. He also proposed that the sacramental test, which "he was convinced" was "an abuse of that sacramental rite," should be replaced with an oath not to subvert the constitution of the Church of England. Ibid., 441.

[156] Speech on the Petition of the Unitarians (May 11, 1792), *Works*, 7: 52.

them within the bounds of toleration, or subject yourself to their persecution."[157] It is easy to say, in retrospect, that Burke's comments on this subject seem overwrought, but this was the world's first confrontation with revolutionary internationalism and the rest of Europe was being swept into its vortex. Even so, Burke did not propose to add any new limitations or penalties on those he deemed so dangerous: he urged only that the occasion was not ripe for the lifting of incapacities that already existed.

The limits of toleration, according to Burke, arise solely because of the possibility that an ostensibly religious sect will turn out to be a political faction, and not on account of differences of a theological nature. "If religion only related to the individual, and was a question between God and the conscience," Burke explained, "it would not be wise, nor in my opinion equitable, for human authority to step in."[158] A tolerant government should permit the espousal of "not only very ill-grounded doctrines, but even many things that are positively vices," where they are not incompatible with the good of the commonwealth.[159] The only legitimate basis for restraint upon religious freedom is that "the person dissenting does not dissent from the scruples of ill-informed conscience, but from a party ground of dissension, in order to raise a faction in the state."[160] On the floor of Parliament, Burke read from the "political catechism" of the Unitarians to show that it "contained no precept of religion whatsoever," but was "one continued invective against kings and bishops."[161] He claimed that the religious assemblies of the Unitarians had been "turned into places of exercise and discipline of politicks; and for the nourishment of a Party which seems to have Contention and power, much more than Piety for its Object," and which "is proceeding systematically, to the destruction of this Constitution in some of its essential parts."[162]

Burke had no respect for what he called "political theologians and theological politicians."[163] "[P]olitics and the pulpit are terms that have little agreement," he said. "No sound ought to be heard in the church but the healing voice of Christian charity. The cause of civil liberty and civil government gains as little as that of religion by this confusion of duties. . . . Surely the church is a place where one day's truce ought to be allowed to the

---

[157] Ibid., 48.

[158] Ibid.

[159] First Letter to Sir Hercules Langrishe (Jan. 3, 1792), Works, 4: 258.

[160] Speech on a Bill for the Relief of Protestant Dissenters (Mar. 17, 1773), Works, 7: 30.

[161] Parliamentary History, 28: 436.

[162] Letter to Richard Bright (Feb. 18, 1790), Correspondence, 6: 84, 83.

[163] Reflections, 10.

dissensions and animosities of mankind."[164] On the other hand, he observed that religion is not the "only cause of enthusiastic zeal and sectarian propagation." There is "no doctrine whatever on which men can warm, that is not capable of the very same effect."[165] Indeed, while recognizing that "[r]eligion is among the most powerful causes of enthusiasm,"[166] Burke more often treated religion as a source of restraint, stability, and order, and found the anti-religious zealotry of the revolutionaries far more frightening.

(3) *Burke's arguments for toleration.*—To some extent, Burke's arguments for toleration resembled those commonly offered in enlightened circles. Persecution was cruel, ineffective, hypocritical, and bad for business.[167] Burke expressed these points with his usual panache, but the substance of the arguments is not much different from that in Locke, Bayle, or Spinoza. Certainly, experience showed that the persecution of Catholics in Ireland was ineffectual: "Ireland, after almost a century of persecution, is at this hour full of penalties and full of Papists."[168] The effect of the Penal Laws was not to persuade, convert, or uplift, but merely to injure. "We found the people heretics and idolaters; we have, by way of improving their condition, rendered them slaves and beggars: they remain in all the misfortune of their old errors, and all the superadded misery of their recent punishment."[169] Over the course of 30 years Burke denounced this oppression, appealing to ideals of humanity, Christianity, and Englishness:

> I can never persuade myself that anything in our Thirty-nine articles, which differs from their articles, is worth making three millions of people slaves, to secure its teaching at the public expense; and I think he must be a strange man, or strange Christian, and a strange Englishman, who would not rather see Ireland a free, flourishing, happy *Catholic* country, though not *one* Protestant existed in it, than an enslaved, beggared, insulted, degraded Catholic country, as

---

[164] Ibid., 10-11. See also *Parliamentary History*, 28: 439:

he agreed with his right hon. friend that the church and the pulpit ought to be kept pure and undefiled, and that politics should not be adverted to in either. With equal propriety might theological discussions, he said, be taken up in that House, and questions solely religious be debated there.

[165] *Letters on a Regicide Peace, Works*, 5: 361.

[166] Ibid.

[167] On the latter point, see Speech at Bristol, Previous to the Election (Sept. 6, 1780), *Works*, 2: 406, arguing that Catholics were among the "best manufacturers" in England and might be forced to emigrate to Holland if the Penal Laws were not reformed.

[168] *Tract on the Popery Laws* (c. 1761), *Works*, 6: 334.

[169] Ibid., 341.

it is, with some Protestants here and there scattered through it, for the purpose, not of instructing the people, but of making them miserable.[170]

In typical Enlightenment fashion, Burke argued that "[i]t is not permitted to us to sacrifice the temporal good of any body of men to our own ideas of the truth and falsehood of any religious opinions."[171] Like many advocates of toleration, Burke attacked the hypocrisy of those who condemned the persecution of Protestants in Catholic France but excused the persecution of Catholics in Ireland. How could they "persuade themselves that what was bad policy in France can be good in Ireland, or that what was intolerable injustice in an arbitrary monarch becomes . . . an equitable procedure in a country professing to be governed by law"?[172] To Burke it was absurd to maintain "that the names of Protestant and Papist can make any change in the nature of essential justice."[173] "Toleration is good for all, or it is good for none."[174]

In two important respects, however, Burke's arguments diverged from the typical Enlightenment arguments for toleration. First, he declined to ground religious rights on any abstract theory of natural rights—whether derived from Locke's social contract, evangelical principles of soul liberty, or philosophical notions of the rights of man. "Toleration," to Burke, was "a part of moral and political prudence."[175] Contrary to both evangelical separationists and secularists, Burke maintained that the English people have "never laid it down as an universal proposition . . . that nothing relative to religion was [a Parliamentary] concern but the direct contrary."[176] "It is the interest, and it is the duty, and because it is the interest and the duty, it is the right of government to attend much to opinions; because, as opinions soon combine with passions, even when they do not produce them, they have much influence on actions."[177] Far from leading him to conclude that government should therefore seek to *control* opinion, however, this meant to Burke that the government should pursue a broad policy of toleration, reserving to itself the authority to intervene in cases of genuine danger to the "peace, order, liberty, and . . . Security" of society.[178] He thus insisted on judging claims for toleration on their individual merits, in light of "the

---

[170] Letter to Richard Burke, Jr. (Mar. 23, 1792), *Correspondence* 7: 118.

[171] Ibid., 394.

[172] *Tract on the Popery Laws, Works*, 329–330.

[173] Ibid., 329.

[174] Speech on a Bill for the Relief of Protestant Dissenters (Mar. 17, 1773), *Works*, 7: 29.

[175] First Letter to Sir Hercules Langrishe (Jan. 3, 1792), *Works*, 4: 258.

[176] Speech on the Petition of the Unitarians (May 11, 1792), *Works*, 7: 46.

[177] Ibid., 44.

[178] Ibid.

peculiar and characteristic situation of a people," and his "knowledge of their opinions, prejudices, habits, and all the circumstances that diversify and color life."[179] He adhered to this approach not only with regard to the Unitarians, whom he distrusted, but with regard to the Irish Catholics, whom he did not. Thus, in arguing for representation of Catholics in the Irish Parliament, he insisted that "I do not put the thing on a question of right," that "the whole question comes before Parliament as a matter for its prudence," and that the issue was one of "discretion."[180] This was in marked contrast not only to most advocates of toleration in Britain, whether sectarian or secularist, but also to opinion in the American states of that time, where there were wide disagreements on questions of establishment but seemingly universal agreement that liberty of conscience or the free exercise of religion were natural and inalienable rights.[181]

Burke's reluctance to embrace natural rights was not peculiar to the subject of religious toleration, but was consistent with his wider view that the institutions upon which liberty depends are grounded in ancient usage (that is, in "prescription") and that an abstract doctrine of human rights, on the French model, is subversive of those institutions and incapable of substituting any other practical system of liberty-protecting institutions in its place. His view is not inconsistent with the principle of natural rights, but with the ability of human beings to discern the nature of natural rights through speculative and abstract reason.[182]

Second, Burke's arguments differed from some advocates of toleration, for whom toleration was part of an effort to reduce the power of "superstition"

---

[179] Ibid., 45.

[180] First Letter to Sir Hercules Langrishe (Jan. 3, 1792), *Works*, 4: 292. Similarly, in an essay "On the State of Ireland," written for Secretary of State Henry Dundas, Burke wrote, speaking for the Catholic Committee:

[T]he Roman Catholics ask a share in the privilege of election; not as a matter of speculative right, not upon general principles of liberty, or as a conclusion from any given premises, either of natural or even of constitutional right. They ask it as a protection, and a requisite security which they now have not, for the exercise of legal right. They ask it from a practical sense of the evils they feel by being excluded from it. It is necessary for the free enjoyment of their industry and property, to secure a fair dispensation of justice, both criminal and civil and to secure them that just estimation and importance, without which, in human tribunals, they cannot obtain it.

Correspondence of the Right Honorable Edmund Burke, eds. Fitzwilliam & Bourke (London: F. & J. Rivington, 1844), 4: 65, 67.

[181] See Michael W. McConnell, "The Origins and Historical Understanding of Free Exercise of Religion," 1455–56.

[182] See Peter J. Stanlis, *Edmund Burke and the Natural Law* (Ann Arbor: Univ. of Michigan Press, 1958).

and to confine religion to the merely private. In this, Burke had something in common with the Baptist and other evangelical advocates of religious freedom who were so influential in the movements for disestablishment and free exercise in the American states. Burke was well aware that some persons advocated toleration out of "a cold apathy, or indeed rather a savage hatred, to all Religion, and an avowed contempt of all those points on which we [Christians] differ, and on those about which we agree."[183] Burke's advocacy of toleration, by contrast, was never based on the view that religion is unimportant or injurious. He maintained that "the glorious and distinguishing prerogative of humanity [is] that of being a religious creature,"[184] and was contemptuous of those who tolerated because of indifference: "[t]hat those persons should tolerate all opinions, who think none to be of estimation, is a matter of small merit. Equal neglect is not impartial kindness."[185]

True toleration, Burke said, is the toleration of those who "think the dogmas of religion, though in different degrees, are all of moment, and that amongst them there is, as amongst all things of value, a just ground of preference. They favor, and therefore they tolerate."[186] Burke is not like Jefferson, who based his toleration on the proposition that "it does me no injury for my neighbour to say there are twenty gods, or no god. It neither picks my pocket nor breaks my leg."[187] Toleration, according to Burke, is based on an appreciation of the importance of religion and on the conviction that the "serious religion[s], natural or revealed,"[188] all contain a significant common element, in contrast to their "common enemy," secular or atheistic philosophy. "I shall never call any religious opinions, which appear important to serious and pious minds, things of no consideration. Nothing is so fatal to religion as indifference, which is, at least, half infidelity. As long as men hold charity and justice to be essential integral parts of religion, there can be little danger from a strong attachment to particular tenets in faith."[189] The English,

---

[183] Letter to Thomas Hussey, *Correspondence*, 8: 245–46.

[184] Speech on a Bill for the Relief of Protestant Dissenters (Mar. 17, 1773), *Works*, 7: 35.

[185] *Reflections*, 132.

[186] Ibid.

[187] Thomas Jefferson, *Notes on the State of Virginia* (1787), ed. W. Peden (Chapel Hill: Univ. of North Carolina Press, 1955), 159.

[188] Speech on a Bill for the Relief of Protestant Dissenters (Mar. 17, 1773), *Works*, 7: 37.

[189] Letter to William Smith, Esq., on the Subject of Catholic Emancipation (Jan. 29, 1795), *Works*, 6: 365. ,See also Letter to a Peer of Ireland (1782), *Works*, 4: 229: "until we come to respect what stands in a respectable light with others, we are very deficient in the temper which qualifies us to make any laws and regulations about them."

Burke said, "would reverently and affectionately protect all religions because they love and venerate the great principle upon which they all agree, and the great object to which they are all directed."[190]

This theme became increasingly prominent in Burke's arguments as the totalitarian doctrines of the French Revolution spread through Europe. Burke came to view the spread of Jacobinism as the great evil and the "centre" of his "whole politics."[191] For Burke, the French Revolution was intimately connected to the question of religion. He maintained that "fanatical atheism" was "the principal feature in the French Revolution." "Without reading the speeches of Vergniaud, François of Nantes, Isnard, and some others of that sort," he said, "it would not be easy to conceive the passion, rancor, and malice of their tongues and hearts. They worked themselves up to a perfect frenzy against religion and all its professors." The philosophers who inspired the Revolution "had one predominant object, which they pursued with a fanatical fury—that is, the utter extirpation of religion."[192] This had an effect on his advocacy of toleration. In addition to the standard arguments for toleration, Burke concluded that it was imperative for the traditional religions of Europe to put aside their doctrinal divisions and unite against this "common enemy."[193]

Burke maintained that persecution could undermine—but could not effectually support—religion. In the *Tract on the Popery Laws*, he denied "that it is in a man's moral power to change his religion whenever his convenience requires it. If he be beforehand satisfied that your opinion is better than his, he will voluntarily come over to you, and without compulsion, and then your law would be unnecessary; but if he is not so convinced, he must know it is his duty in this point to sacrifice his interest here to his opinion of his eternal happiness, else he could have in reality no religion at all.[194] As Conor Cruise O'Brien has pointed out, this passage has a "poignant ring," in light of the probable fact that Burke's father was one of those who betrayed his "duty" by sacrificing his "opinion of his eternal happiness" to the necessitudes ("convenience") of legal practice—and that Burke himself could pursue his political career only on account of that betrayal.[195] Perhaps that is why, in a letter to his son written 30 years after the *Tract*, Burke stated:

---

[190] *Reflections*, 132.

[191] Letter to William Smith, Esq., on the Subject of Catholic Emancipation (Jan. 29, 1795), *Works*, 6: 367.

[192] *Letters on a Regicide Peace*, *Works*, 5: 361.

[193] Letter to William Smith, Esq., on the Subject of Catholic Emancipation (Jan. 29, 1795), *Works*, 6: 368.

[194] *Tract on the Popery Laws* (c. 1761), *Works*, 6: 335.

[195] *The Great Melody*, 42.

Strange it is, but so it is, that men, driven by force from their habits in one mode of religion, have, by contrary habits, under the same force, often quietly settled in another. They suborn their reason to declare in favor of their necessity. Man and his conscience cannot always be at war. If the first races have not been able to make a pacification between the conscience and the convenience, their descendants come generally to submit to the violence of the laws, without violence to their minds.[196]

This, too, has an autobiographical ring, perhaps more authentic than the first. But this insight made Burke all the more opposed to the persecution in Ireland, for the Penal Laws were not devised to encourage conversion to Anglicanism, but solely to encourage apostasy from Catholicism. "What do the Irish statutes?" he asked. "They do not make a conformity to the *established* religion, and to its doctrines and practices, the condition of getting out of servitude. No such thing. Let three millions of people but abandon all that they and their ancestors have been taught to believe sacred, and to forswear it publicly in terms the most degrading, scurrilous, and indecent for men of integrity and virtues, and to abuse the whole of their former lives, and to slander the education they have received, and nothing more is required of them."[197] The "deeper evil," Burke perceived, was not persecution, but that the persecution was purely destructive.[198] The Protestant Ascendancy in Ireland had this in common with the atheist philosophers of France and the Radical dissenters of England: in each case, the object is not to convert the people to a better and truer religion, but to destroy traditional religious faith and leave in its place only a "dreadful void."[199] He deemed it "madness and folly" to drive men "from any *positive* religion whatever into the irreligion of the times, and its sure concomitant principles of anarchy."[200]

The spread of Jacobinism—along with a rising spirit of rebellion—in Ireland gave Burke's advocacy against the Protestant Ascendancy a new urgency. Catholicism ought to be a force for stability and order, but persecution was turning Catholics into allies of Jacobinism and revolution. He wrote to an Irish parliamentarian that "in Ireland particularly the Roman Catholic religion . . . ought to be cherished as a good, (though not as the most preferable good, if a choice was now to be made,) and not tolerated as an inevitable evil." As matters stand, "the serious and earnest belief and practice of [Catholicism] by its professors forms . . . the most effectual barrier, if not

---

[196] Letter to Richard Burke, Jr. on Protestant Ascendency in Ireland (1793), *Works*, 6: 395.

[197] Ibid., 396.

[198] Ibid., 393

[199] Ibid., 395.

[200] Letter on the Affairs of Ireland (1797), *Works*, 6: 426.

the sole barrier, against Jacobinism."[201] But instead, as he wrote to another member of the (Protestant) Irish Parliament, the suppression of Catholicism is "partly leading, partly driving into Jacobinism that description of your people whose religious principles, church polity, and habitual discipline might make them an invincible dike against that inundation."[202] He elaborated:

> You make a sad story of the Pope. *O seri studiorum!* It will not be difficult to get many called Catholics to laugh at this fundamental part of their religion. Never doubt it. You have succeeded in part, and you may succeed completely. But in the present state of men's minds and affairs, do not flatter yourselves that they will piously look to the head of our Church in the place of that Pope whom you make them forswear, and out of all reverence to whom you bully and rail and buffoon them. Perhaps you may succeed in the same manner with all the other tenets of doctrine and usages of discipline amongst the Catholics; but what security have you, that, in the temper and on the principles on which they have made this change, they will stop at the exact sticking-places you have marked in *your* articles? You have no security for anything, but that they will become what are called *Franco-Jacobins*, and reject the whole together.[203]

This was Burke's nightmare: the Protestant Ascendancy and the principles of the French Revolution, tyranny and anarchy, advancing in combination in Ireland, and nothing he could do seemed to make any difference.

Conclusion: The Connection Between Toleration and Establishment.—The central preoccupation of Burke's political thought is with the restraint of power. As Conor Cruise O'Brien has emphasized in his recent biography, the animating theme—what he calls, after Yeats, the "Great Melody"—of Burke's career is his opposition to the abuse of power: in the American colonies, Ireland, France, and India.[204] In each of these situations, men in authority over others, but not restrained by the authority of the law, exercised essentially unlimited power, to the detriment of those in whose names they were supposed to govern. To others, even to Burke's usual political allies, these presented different questions altogether, but to Burke, the "malignancy" was the same: "I think I can hardly overrate the malignity of the principles of Protestant ascendancy, as they affect these countries, and as they affect Asia,—or of Jacobinism, as they affect all Europe and the state of human society itself. The last is the greatest evil. But it readily combines with the

---

[201] Ibid.

[202] Second Letter to Sir Hercules Langrishe (May 26, 1795), *Works*, 6: 380-81.

[203] Ibid., 381.

[204] *Great Melody*, xxiii

others, and flows from them. Whatever breeds discontent at this time will produce that great master-mischief most infallibly."[205]

Arbitrary power is the precise opposite of the constitution of freedom; legitimate government is more than the mere will of the sovereign. In a speech directed against the claim by Warren Hastings, head of the East India Company, of "arbitrary power" over the people of India, Burke declaimed:

> Arbitrary power is a thing which no man can give. My lords, no man can govern himself by his own will; much less can he be governed by the will of others. We are all born—high as well as low—governors as well as governed—in subjection to one great, immutable, pre-existing law, a law prior to all our devices and all our conspiracies, paramount to our feelings, by which we are connected in the eternal frame of the universe, and out of which we cannot stir.[206]

In his *Appeal from the New to the Old Whigs*, Burke wrote: "Neither the few nor the many have a right to act merely by their will, in any matter connected with duty, trust, engagement, or obligation."[207] Thus, to Burke, "the important, but at the same time the difficult problem to the true statesman," is to use "moral instruction" and "civil constitutions" to impose restraint on the immoderate exercise of power.[208]

Religion—the consciousness of that "great, immutable, preexisting law" to which Burke appealed in his speech against Hastings—is essential to the restraint of power. Without religion, "it is utterly impossible," according to Burke, that those in power (whether monarchs, aristocrats, or the people) should "empt[y] themselves of all the lust of selfish will." Knowledge that God's will is superior to man's is the strongest security against the possibility that the people might imagine that their will "is the standard of right and wrong." Thus, "[a]ll persons possessing any portion of power ought to be strongly and awfully impressed with an idea that they act in trust, and that they are to account for their conduct in that trust to the one great Master, Author, and Founder of society."[209]

For most people within a society, the established church is the best guarantor of this sensibility of restraint. The Church of England reflects and represents the long-standing beliefs of the major part of the nation, and thus speaks with the authority of prescription. Such a religion, Burke maintained, is "well fitted to the frame and pattern of your [the English] civil constitution"; it is a "barrier against fanaticism, infidelity, and atheism"; it "furnishes

---

[205] Second Letter to Sir Hercules Langrishe (May 26, 1795), *Works*, 6: 379.

[206] *Speeches*, 4: 357–58, or *Works*, 7: 99.

[207] *An Appeal*, 157.

[208] Ibid., 158.

[209] *Reflections*, 83, 82, 81.

support to the human mind in the afflictions and distresses of the world, consolation in sickness, pain, poverty, and death"; and it "dignifies our nature with the hope of immortality, leaves inquiry free, whilst it preserves an authority to teach, where authority only can teach."[210] "[T]his national Church Establishment is a great national benefit," he said, "a great public blessing."[211] Indeed, Burke maintained, the English people "do not consider their church establishment as convenient, but as essential to their state." It is "the foundation of their whole consitution."[212]

But there are some in England and many more in Ireland who, for reasons of conscience and conviction, adhere to a religious faith other than that established by law. They, too, deserve the support and encouragement of the law. Their articles of faith may contain error (as indeed, the established church may contain error) and may not be the best, but all religions impart some measure of the truth of the sovereignty of God and therefore the restraint of man. "Do not promote diversity," Burke thus advised, but "when you have it, bear it; have as many sorts of religion as you find in your country; there is a reasonable worth in them all."[213] Burke declared that he would "never call any religious opinions, which appear important to serious and pious minds, things of no consideration. . . . As long as men hold charity and justice to be essential integral parts of religion, there can be little danger from a strong attachment to particular tenets in faith."[214]

Moreover, any attempt to root out dissenting faiths and replace them with the established church is likely to prove not just unsuccessful, but counterproductive. It is easier to destroy faith than to replace it with another. This is what Burke saw to be the consequence of the persecution of Catholics in Ireland, where the Penal Laws were "partly leading, partly driving into Jacobinism that description of [the Irish] people whose religious principles, church polity, and habitual discipline might make them an invincible dike against that inundation."[215] This persecution, to Burke is "madness and folly." There is no conceivable justification for "driving men . . . from any *positive* religion whatever into the irreligion of the times, and its sure concomitant principles of anarchy."[216]

---

[210] Speech on the Petition of the Unitarians (May 11, 1792), *Works*, 7: 57.

[211] Ibid., 56.

[212] *Reflections*, 87.

[213] Speech on a Bill for the Relief of Protestant Dissenters (Mar. 17, 1773), *Works*, 7: 36-37.

[214] Letter to William Smith, Esq., on the Subject of Catholic Emancipation (Jan. 29, 1795), *Works*, 6: 365.

[215] Second Letter to Sir Hercules Langrishe (May 26, 1795), *Works*, 6: 380-81.

[216] Letter on the Affairs of Ireland (1797), *Works*, 6: 426.

In these circumstances, Burke maintained that differences among religions must take second seat to the more important conflict between religion and its detractors. "If ever the Church and the Constitution of England should fall in these islands," he wrote, "it is not Presbyterian discipline nor Popish hierarchy that will rise upon their ruins. . . . It is the new fanatical religion, now in the heat of its first ferment, of the Rights of Man, which rejects all establishments, all discipline, all ecclesiastical, and in truth all civil order, which will triumph."[217] It was therefore just as important to tolerate and protect conscientious members of other faiths as it was to support the established church. He responded to a member of Parliament who opposed extension of toleration to those whom Burke called "conscientious Dissenters":[218]

> The honorable gentleman would have us fight this confederacy of the powers of darkness with the single arm of the Church of England,—would have us not only fight against infidelity, but fight at the same time with all the faiths in the world except our own.[219]

Toleration and establishment are therefore not inconsistent principles, but alternative strategies for attaining the same objective: to nurture and strengthen the religious sensibilities that are the best and most reliable source of moral restraint. Burke strove his entire life to uphold constitutional principles of balanced government and incremental change that would protect against the dangers of arbitrary power. But in the end, he said, quoting Vergil's *Aeneid*, "[w]e have but this one appeal against irresistible power—

> If you have no respect for the human race and mortal arms,
> Yet beware the gods who remember right and wrong.[220]

---

[217] Letter to Richard Burke, Jr. on Protestant Ascendency in Ireland (1793), *Works*, 6:398.
[218] Speech on a Bill for the Relief of Protestant Dissenters (Mar. 17, 1773), *Works*, 7: 35.
[219] Ibid., 37.
[220] *An Appeal*, 160. Burke quoted, of course, in Latin.

9

RELIGIOUS LIBERTY AND RELIGION
IN THE AMERICAN FOUNDING REVISITED

Ellis Sandoz*

R ecent writers on the subject of religious liberty in America today paint a picture that would have both astonished and appalled even the most enlightened members of the founding generation of this country. For this was quite plainly a Christian country from the perspective of the founding generation generally, and even those of its luminaries who for whatever reasons disdained denominational affiliation or public worship held biblical religion in high esteem as fundamental to the civilization and to the public virtue of the rising new republic.[1] The fact verges on self-evidence, to

---

* Professor of Political Science, Louisiana State University. B. A., L.S.U. (1951); M.A., L.S.U. (1953); *Dr. Oec. Publ.*, University of Munich (1965).

[1] For example, beginning with Thomas Jefferson's presidency and lasting until well after the end of the Civil War, church services were conducted regularly in the chamber of the U. S. House of Representatives, often with the president and members of the cabinet in attendance. President Jefferson secured the newly formed U. S. Marine Corps Band to play for divine worship on occasion. When the band's playing proved not to be the best, the president connived with the director and commandant to recruit some eighteen Italian musicians into the Corps to improve its quality. Cf. Anson P. Stokes, *Church and State in the United States* (New York: Harper, 1950), 1: 499–507; Helen Cripe, *Thomas Jefferson and Music* (Charlottesville, Univ. Press of Virginia 1974), 24–26. Jefferson's biographer writes that President Jefferson "was going to great pains to attend divine services in the House of Congress. One Federalist observer . . . believed that it went far to prove that 'the idea of bearing down and overturning' the religious institutions of the country, which in his opinion had been 'a favorite object,' had been given up. Jefferson did not need to give up that object since he had never had it." Dumas Malone, *Jefferson the President: First Term,*

quote one authority: "Who can deny that for them the very core of existence was their relation to God?"[2]

1801–1805, vol. 4 of *Jefferson and His Time* (Boston: Little, Brown, 1970), 199. On Jefferson's religion more fully the decisive sources are in Dickinson W. Adams, ed., *Jefferson's Extracts from the Gospels: "The Philosophy of Jesus" and "The Life and Morals of Jesus"* (Princeton: Princeton Univ. Press 1983), esp. 14–25. The present paper generally extends, amplifies, and refines aspects of the argument central to Ellis Sandoz, *A Government of Laws: Political Theory, Religion and the American Founding* (Baton Rouge: Louisiana State Univ. Press, 1990), esp. 125–217; also Ellis Sandoz, "Foundations of American Liberty and Rule of Law" and Ellis Sandoz, "Philosophical Foundations of Our Democratic Heritage: A Recollection," *Presidential Studies Quarterly* 24 (1994): 605–617 and 669–673; Ellis Sandoz, "Philosophical and Religious Dimensions of the American Founding," *Intercollegiate Review* 30 (Spring 1995): 27–42. On Jefferson's and other founders' religious views see Sandoz, *A Government of Laws*, 141–62. For a sermon preached in the Capitol by a minister invited for the purpose at Jefferson's suggestion, see John Hargrove, *A Sermon on the Second Coming of Christ, and on the Last Judgment. Delivered the 25th December, 1804, Before both houses of Congress at the Capitol in the City of Washington* reprinted in Ellis Sandoz, ed., *Political Sermons of the American Founding Era, 1730–1805* (Indianapolis: Liberty Press, 1991), 1573–96. On President Jefferson's presence for a sermon delivered by his fiery Baptist supporter the Elder John Leland in 1802 see Malone, *Jefferson the President: First Term*, 106–109.

[2] Carl Bridenbaugh, *Spirit of '76: The Growth of American Patriotism Before Independence, 1607–1776* (New York: Oxford Univ. Press, 1975), 118. Church membership in America in 1780 is estimated at 59 percent of the population with a surge of increase after the onset of the Second Great Awakening in 1790; see Patricia U. Bonomi and Peter R. Eisenstadt, "Church Adherence in the Eighteenth-Century British American Colonies," *William and Mary Quarterly*, 3rd ser., 39 (1982): 274.

> American Christianity became a mass enterprise. The eighteen hundred Christian ministers serving in 1775 swelled to nearly forty thousand in 1845. The number of preachers per capita more than tripled; the colonial legacy of one minister per fifteen hundred inhabitants became one per five hundred. . . . The Congregationalists, which had twice the clergy of any other American church in 1775, could not muster one-tenth the preaching force of the Methodists in 1845.

Nathan O. Hatch, *The Democratization of American Christianity* (New Haven: Yale Univ. Press, 1989), 4.

In terms of demographics, at the end of the colonial period America had fewer than three million people of whom about one-sixth were slaves. There were some 3,005 religious congregations or churches of which all but 50 were Protestant, with the largest number being Congregationalist (658), Presbyterian (543), Baptist (498), Anglican/-Episcopalian (including the Methodists): (480), Quakers (298), German and Dutch Reformed (251), followed by Lutheran (151), miscellaneous minor groups (76), and the 50 Roman Catholic congregations, located mainly in large Eastern towns and in Maryland. There were fewer than 2,000 Jews, concentrated in New York, Philadelphia, Newport, Charleston, and Savannah. Nine of the thirteen colonies had established churches at the beginning of the Revolution. When the Federal Convention met in Philadelphia in 1787, all of the New England states but Rhode Island retained their virtually established Congregational churches; Maryland and South Carolina retained the Anglican/-Episcopalian establishment, a connection given up by Virginia, North Carolina, and Georgia; New York and New Jersey retained only vestiges of their earlier connections with

Tendencies Toward Radical Privatization of Religion and Its Effects.—In considering the perspectives of those who laid the foundations of liberty in America, including freedom of conscience, it seems useful to pause at the outset to notice the quagmire into which American society has plunged on the subject of religious freedom—if legal literature is any indication, at least. Jurisprudence in this area has been called "a maze," "in significant disarray," "a conceptual disaster area," "inconsistent and unprincipled," and not unlike the adventures of "Alice in Wonderland."[3] The flavor is given in 1993 by another legal writer who begins his analysis from that oracle of post-modern nihilistic deconstructionism, the nineteenth-century German thinker Friedrich Nietzsche whose Zarathustra exclaimed: "God is dead! God remains dead! And we have killed him!"[4] The writer concludes his essay as follows:

> The effect of selective post-modernism is to allow secular ideologies to use political muscle to advance their causes, including using the public schools to inculcate their ideals, without even the psychological constraint of liberal neutrality, but at the same time to preserve liberal formalism in court to ensure that religion is not included in the public dialogue. Thus, in New York City the children are read *Heather Has Two Mommies* in the first grade and given information on anal intercourse in the sixth; but, as the Tenth Circuit recently held, *The Bible in Pictures* must be removed from the shelf of the fifth grade classroom library. [If you dispute the fact that God is dead, the author continues,] you have the inalienable right to sing, weep, laugh, and mumble, so long as you do it in private. That is the freedom of religion in the post-modern age.[5]

Perhaps this is merely hyperbole—or a sign of salutary social progress, depending on how one looks at it. But the alarm has been sounded by distinguished scholars. Thus, from their perspective, radical privatization of

---

the Episcopal and Dutch Reformed churches; Rhode Island, Pennsylvania, and Delaware never had established churches. Establishment continued in America long after ratification of the Constitution and the Bill of Rights, lasting until 1833 in Massachusetts, despite all the earlier efforts of Isaac Backus and the Baptists. Anson P. Stokes, *Church and State In the United States*, 1: 273–74.

3 Quoted from Steven G. Gey, "Why is Religion Special? Reconsidering the Accommodation of Religion Under the Religion Clauses of the First Amendment," *University of Pittsburgh Law Review* 52 (1990): 75, citations omitted. It is not my purpose here to summarize case law bearing on freedom of religion except as this may be related to my theme. For a concise summary of that subject, however, see Henry J. Abraham, *Freedom and the Court: Civil Rights and Liberties in the United States*, 5th ed. (New York and Oxford: Oxford Univ. Press, 1988), 277–392.

4 Friedrich Nietzsche, *Thus Spake Zarathustra* (New York, Modern Library ed., 1970), 5; quoted from Michael W. McConnell, "'God is Dead and We have Killed Him!' Freedom of Religion in the Post-modern Age," *Brigham Young University Law Review* 1993: 163.

5 Ibid., 188. Citations omitted.

religion is a tendency to be reckoned with in contemporary America. It has as one of its most objectionable effects, as Michael McConnell indicates, leaving the avowedly religiously neutral atheism of the politically-correct secular state by default as the officially sanctioned ideology inculcated in public schools. Harold J. Berman concurs. As he wrote as long ago as 1979, the result closely approximates in George Washington's America the pattern of institutions and state-imposed ideology fostered through the unquestionable orthodoxy of Marxism-Leninism in the former Soviet Union:

> The Soviet Constitution provides for the separation of church and state and for freedom of religion. . . . Thus atheism, by claiming to be not a religion, but a science or a philosophy, is in fact "established," and traditional religions such as Christianity, Judaism, and Islam are withdrawn from public discourse. It seems to me that this example shows quite well that it is not, in and of itself, the constitutional guarantee of freedom of religion from governmental control or support that is our final protection against religious oppression.[6]

It should also be noticed that the quest for a sufficiently innocuous and comprehensive definition of the *religion* that Americans may, after all, be free to exercise under terms of the First Amendment leads one commentator to the reductionist extreme of identifying it in terms of primitive totemistic belief systems[7] that our founders are likely to have considered a caricature. Religious *substance* is and has been a principal care of Americans because it lies at the core of our culture. Whatever the broad applications, the precious heritage of America is biblical faith and religious liberty on the biblical pattern. Totemism, proceduralism, and broad classification working hand-in-hand with deconstructionism are unsatisfactory in this sphere. Such

---

[6] Harold J. Berman, *Faith and Order: The Reconciliation of Law and Religion* (Atlanta: Scholars Press, 1993), 219.

[7] Gey, "Why Is Religion Special?", 167, following Stanley Ingber, "Religion or Ideology: A Needed Clarification of the Religion Clauses," *Stanford Law Review* 41 (1989): 233, 285; Ingber, in turn, bases on Emile Durkheim's long-outdated pioneering study in the sociology of religion *The Elementary Forms of Religious Life*, trans. J. W. Swain (1915; rpr. New York: Macmillan, 1965), 62:

> Thus we arrive at the following definition. A religion is a unified system of beliefs and practices relative to sacred things, that is to say, things set apart and forbidden—beliefs and practices which united into one single moral community called a Church, all those who adhere to them.

The English book is a translation of *Les Formes élémentaires de la vie religieuse* (Paris: F. Allen, 1912), a study of magic written in the French positivist mode that now is suggested for American constitutional law. Cf. the discussion in Abraham, *Freedom and the Court*, 283–95.

exceptionalism may pose significant problems in an age of generics, but it lies inconveniently close to the heart of the matter.[8]

Similarly, the United States has prized personal liberty generally on the pattern of, and in continuity with, the English Whig and common law traditions distantly represented by Sir Edward Coke, Magna Carta, and the ancient constitution of England as that tradition was reaffirmed in the seventeenth century and revivified during the founding as a central element. Thus, American liberty is not Jacobin liberty, it is argued.[9] Religion and

---

[8] For a general discussion of the fact and problem see Jack P. Greene, *The Intellectual Construction of America: Exceptionalism and Identity from 1492 to 1800* (Chapel Hill: Univ. of North Carolina Press, 1993), esp. 141–42, 148–49, 170–72, 182–83, and 196:

> Some evangelical clergy [in the 1780s, 1790s and later] even evoked the millennial expectations of the early puritan settlers and once again touted their country as "God's American Israel" for whom "the honor" of giving "the true religion" to the world had been "reserved." . . . [Many were able] "to look forward, with pleasing hope, to a day when America will be the praise of the whole earth; and shall participate, largely, in the fulfillment of those sacred prophecies which have foretold the glory of Messiah's kingdom."

Internal quotations from Ezra Stiles' election sermon *The United States Elevated to Glory and Honour* (New Haven: Thomas & Samuel Green, 1783) and Richard Furman's *America's Deliverance and Duty* (Charleston: W. P. Young, 1802), also citing Ruth H. Bloch, *Visionary Republic: Millennial Themes in American Thought, 1756–1800* (Cambridge: Cambridge Univ. Press, 1985). America's exceptionalism, including religious uniqueness, is a theme of David Ramsay's *The History of the American Revolution,* (Philadelphia: R. Atkin & Son, 1789; rpr. ed. Lester H. Cohen, Indianapolis: Liberty Classics, 1990), whose final sentence reads: "May the Almighty Ruler of the Universe, who has raised you to Independence, and given you a place among the nations of the earth, make the American Revolution an Era in the history of the world, remarkable for the progressive increase of human happiness," ibid., 2: 667.

[9] For example, in what may have been his last letter to James Madison, Thomas Jefferson wrote:

> In the selection of our Law Professor [for the University of Virginia], we must be rigorously attentive to his political principles. You will recollect that before the revolution, Coke Littleton was the universal elementary book of law students, and a sounder whig never wrote, nor of profounder learning in what were called English liberties. You remember also that our lawyers were then all whigs. But when his black-letter text, and uncouth but cunning learning got out of fashion, and the honied Mansfieldism of Blackstone became the student's hornbook, from that moment, that profession (the nursery of our Congress) began to slide into toryism, and nearly all the young brood of lawyers now are of that hue. They suppose themselves, indeed, to be whigs, because they no longer know what whigism or republicanism means. It is in our seminary the vestal flame is to be kept alive; it is thence it is to spread anew over our own and the sister States. . . . Take care of me when dead, and be assured that I shall leave with you my last affections.

liberty were understood by the founders to be linked in important ways. In reflecting on the spirit of '76 late in life, John Adams pointedly summarized matters in a letter to Thomas Jefferson:

> The *general principles*, on which the Fathers Achieved Independence, were the only Principles in which that beautiful Assembly of young Gentlemen [representing the numerous religious denominations of the country at the time of the Revolution] could Unite. . . . And what were these *general Principles*? I answer, the general Principles of Christianity, in which all those Sects were United: And the *general Principles* of English and American Liberty, in which all those young Men United, and which had United all Parties in America, in Majorities sufficient to assert and maintain her Independence. Now I will avow, that I then believed, and now believe, that those general Principles of Christianity, are as eternal and immutable, as the Existence and Attributes of God; and those Principles of Liberty, are as unalterable as human Nature and our terrestrial, mundane System.[10]

Thomas Jefferson to James Madison, February 17, 1826, in Merrill D. Peterson, ed., *Thomas Jefferson: Writings*, Library of America ed. (New York: Literary Classics of the U.S., Inc., 1984), 1512–15. (Jefferson died less than five months later, on July 4, 1826, the same day as did John Adams; James Madison died on June 28, 1836, the last of the founders.) For the particularities of this tradition of liberty and rule of law see John Phillip Reid, "The Jurisprudence of Liberty: The Ancient Constitution in the Legal Historiography of the Seventeenth and Eighteenth Centuries" in Ellis Sandoz, ed., *The Roots of Liberty: Magna Carta, Ancient Constitution, and the Anglo-American Tradition of Rule of Law* (Columbia and London: Univ. of Missouri Press, 1993), 147–231, 292–320; also, James R. Stoner, Jr., *Common Law and Liberal Theory: Coke, Hobbes, and the Origins of American Constitutionalism* (Lawrence, Kan.: Univ. of Kansas Press, 1992), esp. 13–68. Regarding Whig versus Jacobin liberty, the point is made by J. G. A. Pocock in "The Machiavellian Moment Revisited: A Study in History and Ideology, *Journal of Modern History* 53 (1981): 72: "English and American history [must] be studied in its own terms, which are Whig and not Jacobin." An important recent study is Harold J. Berman, "The Origins of Historical Jurisprudence: Coke, Selden, Hale,"*Yale Law Journal* 103 (1994): 1651.

[10] John Adams to Thomas Jefferson, June 28, 1813, in Lester J. Cappon, ed., *The Adams-Jefferson Letters: The Complete Correspondence Between Thomas Jefferson and Abigail and John Adams*, (New York: Simon and Schuster, 1959; rpr., 1971), 2: 339–40. In two preceding paragraphs (summarized by the inserted bracketed passage) Adams had written as follows:

> Who composed that Army of fine young Fellows that was then before my Eyes? There were among them, Roman Catholicks, English Episcopalians, Scotch and American Presbyterians, Methodists, Moravians, Anababtists, German Lutherans, German Calvinists, Universalists, Arians, Priestleyans, Socinians, Independents, Congregationalists, Horse Protestants, House Protestants, Deists and Atheists; and "Protestans qui ne croyent rien ['Protestants who believe nothing']." Very few however of several of these Species. Never the less all Educated in the *general Principles* of Christianity: and the general Principles of English and American Liberty.

The treasury of Anglo-American civilization's religious and constitutional attainment as manifested in the founding is a triumph of faith and reason of millennial significance, as the founders themselves tended to believe. If one looks to the founding for any guidance, it ill-accords with the fact for its substance to be equated in contemporary jurisprudence of the Constitution with irrational primitivism in religion and fundamentalistic positivism, a philosophy averse to all "transcendental moonshine." [11] Their common root

---

> Could my Answer be understood, by any candid Reader or Hearer, to recommend, to all the others, the general Principles, Institutions or Systems of Education of the Roman Catholicks? Or those of the Quakers? Or those of the Presbyterians? Or those of the Menonists? Or those of the Methodists? or those of the Moravians? Or those of the Universalists? or those of the Philosophers? No.

Ibid., 2: 339; spelling, capitalization and punctuation as in the original.

[11] Thus Professor Gey argues that

> since Immanuel Kant's publication of the *Critique of Pure Reason*, theistic forms of religion have been unable to rely upon the traditional logical proofs of God's existence. This transformation in the nature of theistic religion rendered God unknowable and placed theistic religion on the same foundation with nontheistic religion—a manifestation of human faith alone.

A. J. Ayer, Bertrand Russell, and (of course) Sigmund Freud are cited in support. Gey, "Accommodation of Religion," 168–69, 186–87. Is this seriously asserted, or is the author putting us on? Whatever the case (and I hope it is the latter), let it be noticed that the critique of neo-Kantian positivism as a satisfactory instrument for philosophizing generally and for exploring human reality theoretically specifically has been tellingly conducted from a number of perspectives which serve radically to discount the sweeping assertions made by Gey. Cf. Eric Voegelin, *The New Science of Politics* (Chicago: Univ. of Chicago Press, 1952), 1–26; and Lezek Kolakowski, *The Alienation of Reason: A History of Positivist Thought*, trans. N. Guterman (Garden City, N. Y.: Anchor Books, 1968). Generally, it may be remarked that the so-called philosophical proofs of the existence of God are intended to be epideictic, not apodictic. They are never the central justification of the truth of faith which rests upon apperceptive *experience*. For this class of experience see, for example, Saint Augustine, *Confessions*, Bk. X; trans. H. Chadwick (Oxford: Oxford Univ. Press, 1991), 179–220. As Stephen F. Brown explains matters in the context of Christian mysticism (a pertinent context) quoting Bonaventure:

> *Behold, if you can, this most pure Being.* From all that has been said about the theory of illumination . . . and the indubitability of the existence of God . . . , it is obvious that the "reasons" or proofs which Saint Bonaventure offers for the existence of God, insofar as they imply the existence of God, are not considered by him as proofs or reasons which first make known the existence of God, since the existence of God is evident in itself and is immediately known in the proposition "God exists." Hence, the reasons taken from the exterior world, although not denied by Saint Bonaventure, are not of primary importance; they are rather stimuli inducing us to think and to become aware of the immediacy of our cognition of God. The being perceived in any created being cannot be perceived in its ultimate meaning without the knowledge of the Being which is God. Neither can any absolute and final and evident truth be known with

Perry Miller three decades ago identified as "obtuse secularism,"[12] a persuasion now often heard in the trendy babel of neo-Marxian dialects. Such a decoding of their intent or meaning, it seems safe to say, definitely was not

---

certitude without the divine light shining through the objects and ideas. This light is always there; we have but to pay full attention to it. When we bring to full awareness the content of our first idea, it is impossible for us to think that God does not exist. . . . [T]he existence of God is included in the notion of God. We may deny His existence, but the denial is not evident and cannot be evident. We may believe that we do not know God, because we are ignorant of the meaning of the term "God," but if we go to the bottom of our knowledge and conceive God as "being itself," there is no possibility of giving our assent to the denial of His existence. See Étienne Gilson, *The Philosophy of Saint Bonaventure* [trans. Illtyd Trethowan (London: Sheed & Ward, 1938)], chap. 3: "The Evidence for God's Existence," 107–26.

Bonaventure, *The Journey of the Mind to God*, trans. Philotheus Boehner, ed. with intro. and notes by Stephen F. Brown (Indianapolis: Hackett Publishing, 1993), 67–68n151.

As Étienne Gilson elsewhere remarks, seriously to consider Kant's view of religious philosophy we must break "the habit of identifying him with the *Critique of Pure Reason* and of forgetting the existence of the *Critique of Practical Reason* altogether." É. Gilson, *The Spirit of Medieval Philosophy*, trans. A. H. C. Downes (New York: Charles Scribner's Sons, 1936), 16–17. The phrase "transcendental moonshine" is used by A. E. Taylor, *Aristotle* (1919; rev. ed., New York: Dover Publications, Inc., 1955), 30. For an informed discussion of the nature of faith and related matters, see Wilfred C. Smith, *Faith and Belief* (Princeton: Princeton Univ. Press, 1979).

The rational desert Professor Gey imagines for religion is not so desolate after all, as we see, and as can further be seen from Eric Voegelin's late writings, such as the essays on "Immortality," "The Gospel and Culture," "Reason," and "Quod Deus Dicitur," all included in Eric Voegelin, *Published Essays, 1966–1985*, ed. E. Sandoz, vol. 12, *The Collected Works of Eric Voegelin* (Baton Rouge: Louisiana State Univ. Press, 1990-), 12: 52–94, 172–212, 265–91, 376–94. The entertaining page on the "God Is Dead" movement is to the point of the discussion herein:

But the movement has also its comic touch: The God who is declared dead is alive enough to have kept his undertakers nervously busy by now for three centuries. Yet the life he is leading, before and after his death, is troubled and complicated. When interrogated by eminent thinkers, he does not seem to be sure whether he is a substance or a subject (Spinoza/Hegel), or perhaps both, or whether he perhaps does not exist at all, whether he is personal or impersonal, whether conscious or unconscious, whether rational or irrational, whether spirit only or matter too (Spinoza), whether he is perhaps only a regulative idea (Kant), whether he is identical with himself or not, or whether he is something entirely different (Heidegger). What is absolute in this ambiguous debate about the Absolute is its deadly seriousness. The only one permitted to laugh in the situation appears to be God.

Eric Voegelin, *In Search of Order*, vol. 5, *Order and History* (Baton Rouge: Louisiana State Univ. Press, 1956–1987), 5: 67.

[12] Perry Miller, "From Covenant to Revival" in John M. Mulder and John F. Wilson, eds., *Religion in American History: Interpretive Essays* (Englewood Cliffs, N. J.: Prentice-Hall, 1978), 160.

what any of the founders had in mind. And it seems not to be what the general run of the American public today has in mind, either.[13] If such critics as Professors McConnell and Berman are right, those in public policy positions and charged with husbanding the American system of ordered liberty may have occasion to reflect on the ancient adage of good government: *salus populi suprema lex esto*—the wellbeing and security of the people is the supreme law.[14]

---

[13] It is doubtless a sign of the widespread dismay and resentment of the American people in matters religious that both houses of Congress overwhelmingly voted for and President William J. Clinton promptly signed into law in November, 1993, P. L. 103–141, entitled the *Religious Freedom Restoration Act of 1993*, characterized in the press "as one of the most important measures affecting religious liberty since the Bill of Rights was ratified in 1791," *Baton Rouge Advocate*, Nov. 6, 1993, 2E.

The text of the statute includes, in pertinent part, the following provisions:

> Sec. 2. Congressional Findings and Declaration of Purposes. (a) Findings. The Congress finds that—(1) the framers of the Constitution, recognizing free exercise of religion as an unalienable right, secured its protection in the First Amendment to the Constitution; (2) laws "neutral" toward religion may burden religious exercise as surely as laws intended to interfere with religious exercise; (3) government should not substantially burden religious exercise without compelling justification; (4) in Employment Division v. Smith, 494 U. S. 872 (1990) the Supreme Court virtually eliminated the requirement that the government justify burdens on religious exercise imposed by laws neutral toward religion; and (5) the compelling interest test as set forth in prior Federal court rulings is a workable test for striking sensible balances between religious liberty and competing prior governmental interests. (b) Purposes.—The purposes of this Act are—(1) to restore the compelling interest test as set forth in Sherbert v. Verner, 374 U. S. 398 (1963) and Wisconsin v. Yoder, 406 U. S,. 205 (1972) and to guarantee its application in all cases where free exercise of religion is substantially burdened; and (2) to provide a claim or defense to persons whose religious exercise is substantially burdened by government.
>
> Sec. 3. Free Exercise of Religion Protected. (a) In General.—Government shall not substantially burden a person's exercise of religion even if the burden results from a rule of general applicability, except as provided in subsection (b). (b) Exception.—Government may substantially burden a person's exercise of religion only if it demonstrates that application of the burden to the person— (1) is in furtherance of a compelling governmental interest; and (2) is the least restrictive means of furthering that compelling governmental interest. (c) Judicial Relief.—A person whose religious exercise has been burdened in violation of this section may assert that violation as a claim or defense in a judicial proceeding and obtain appropriate relief against a government.

Quoted from United States Code Service, Advance Legislative Service (c) 1993 Lawyers Cooperative Publishing. Public Law 103–141, 103rd Congress, 1st Session, 103 P. L. 141; 1993 H.R. 1308; 107 Stat. 1488.

[14] A theme of Sir Edward Coke and John Selden in the debate over the *Petition of Right*; see John Selden's words in retort to Coke's quotation of the maxim (in which he added "*et libertas popula summa salus populi*"—[and the people's liberty is their supreme

In this vein, there is the elementary premise that, under *free government* in the liberal tradition that has shaped our politics since the seventeenth century, there exists the indispensable requirement of nurturing a *community's* cohesion and well-being—a point suggested by the drift of the Preamble's "promote the general Welfare, . . . secure the Blessings of Liberty to ourselves and our Posterity." Otherwise there can be no possibility of free government at all, but only the alternatives of anarchy or coercive apolitical oppression. As James Madison and "Publius" remarked on more than one occasion, representative majority rule (government of, by, and for the people) is the republican principle that must inevitably be served, even as we seek the means to avoid majoritarian evils leading to tyranny and, thereby, to preserve individual liberties. We are unaccustomed to thinking of Madison from the perspective of his championing of the community's well being and popular government as first priorities. As Marvin Myers remarks, "Madison's lifelong concern with the dangers of majority rule has sometimes obscured the source of that concern: his prior commitment to popular government."[15] That a

---

wellbeing]) in Robert C. Johnson et al, eds., *Proceedings in Parliament, 1628*, (New Haven: Yale Univ. Press, 1977–1983), 2: 183; cf. 173–74.

[15] Marvin Myers, ed., *The Mind of the Founder: Sources of the Political Thought of James Madison* (Indianapolis: Bobbs-Merrill, 1973), 408. Myers is quoted and the implications analyzed in a manner pertinent to our general argument here in Drew R. McCoy, *The Last of the Fathers: James Madison and the Republican Legacy* (Cambridge, England: Cambridge Univ. Press, 1989), 137–40. James Madison, writing in April 1787, defines the *republican principle* as follows: "[T]he fundamental principle of republican Government [is] that the majority who rule in such Governments, are the safest Guardians both of public Good and of private rights." James Madison, *Vices of the Political System of the United States*," in William T. Hutchinson, et al., eds., *The Papers of James Madison* (Chicago: Univ. Of Chicago Press, 1975–), 9: 354. As is well-known, the Constitution as theorized by John Jay, James Madison and Alexander Hamilton under the pseudonym *Publius*, is calculated to remedy the worst evils of majoritarian rule without destroying liberty and republicanism in the process, the goal of Justice under rule of law being their objective. Thus, *in Federalist No. 22* Publius writes: "that fundamental maxim of republican government, which requires that the sense of the majority should prevail." In *Federalist No. 58*: "In all cases where justice or the general good might require new laws to be passed . . . the fundamental principle of free government would be reversed. It would no longer be the majority that would rule." In *Federalist No. 78*: "that fundamental principle of republican government, which admits the right of the people to alter or abolish the established constitution whenever they find it inconsistent with their happiness." Quoted from Jacob E. Cooke, ed., *The Federalist* (Middletown, Ct.: Wesleyan Univ. Press, 1961), 139, 397, 527. To this may be added the following from *Federalist No. 51*:

> In a free government, the security for civil rights must be the same as for religious rights. It consists in the one case in the multiplicity of interests, and in the other, in the multiplicity of sects. . . . *Justice is the end of government. It is the end of civil society. It ever has been, and ever will be pursued, until it be obtained, or until liberty be lost in the pursuit.* . . . In the extended republic of the United States, and among the great variety of interests, parties and sects which it

community unified by fundamental convictions beyond the calculation of merely material interests actually existed, and that it was considered vital for the success of America's republican experiment, was attested by John Jay writing as Publius near the beginning of *The Federalist Papers*:

> It has until lately been a received and uncontradicted opinion, that the prosperity of the people of America depended on their continuing firmly united, and the wishes, prayers, and efforts of our best and wisest Citizens have been constantly directed to that object. . . . I have . . . often taken notice, that Providence has been pleased to give this one connected country, to one united people, a people descended from the same ancestors, speaking the same language, professing the same religion, attached to the same principles of government, very similar in their manners and customs, and who, by their joint counsels, arms and efforts, fighting side by side through a long and bloody war, have nobly established their general Liberty and Independence. . . . A strong sense of the value and blessings of Union induced the people, at a very early period, to institute a Federal Government to preserve and perpetuate it.[16]

A century before Publius wrote, John Locke justified majoritarian rule on the principle that the community is vital to free government, and a community must move in one direction: this can only be that of the greater number and force, as the *sine qua non* of free government—that is, government based on the consent of the people.[17] This theory of politics as

---

> embraces, a coalition of a majority of the whole society could seldom take place on any other principles than those of justice and the general good; and there being thus less danger to a minor from the will of the major party, there must be less pretext also, to provide for the security of the former, by introducing into government a will not dependent on the latter; or in other words, a will independent of the society itself.

Ibid., 351–53 (emphasis added).

[16] *Federalist No. 2*, ibid., 8, 9, 10.

[17] John Locke, the father of modern constitutionalism, stoutly maintained that all governments begun in peace "had their beginning laid on that foundation, and *were made by the Consent of the People.*" Locke, *The Second Treatise of Government*, § 104, in Peter Laslett, ed., John Locke, *Two Treatises of Government; A Critical Edition with an Introduction and Apparatus Criticus* (Cambridge, England: Cambridge Univ. Press, 1963), 354. Moreover, § 106: "That the *beginning of Politick Society* depends upon the consent of the Individuals, to joyn into and make one Society; who, when they are thus incorporated, might set up what form of Government they thought fit," ibid., 355. The majoritarian principle is seen in this light, as had been said in §§ 95 and 96:

> When any number of Men have *so consented to make one Community* or Government, they are thereby presently incorporated, and make *one Body Politick*, wherein the *Majority* have a Right to act and conclude the rest.
>   96. For when any number of Men have, by the consent of every individual, made a *Community*, they have thereby made that *Community* one

grounded in consent and consecrated to liberty and justice is given authoritative statement in the opening lines of the Declaration of Independence. From it arises the indispensable fiction that every man's consent to law is given in an act of parliament or of the legislative body more generally. As Sir Thomas Smith who was Secretary of State to Queen Elizabeth stated the principle in 1589:

> all that ever the people of Rome might do either in *centuriatis comitiis* or *tributis*, the same may be done by the parliament of England which representeth and hath the power of the whole realm, both the head and the body. For every Englishman is intended to be there present, either in person or by procuration and attorneys, of what preeminence, state, dignity or quality soever he be, from the prince, be he king or queen, to the lowest person of England. And the consent of the parliament is taken to be every man's consent.[18]

Body, with a Power to Act as one Body, which is only by the will and determination of the *majority*. For that which acts any Community [sic], being only the consent of the individuals of it, and it being necessary to that which is one body to move one way; it is necessary the Body should move that way whither the greater force carries it, which is the *consent of the majority*: or else it is impossible it should act or continue one Body, *one Community*, which the consent of every individual that united into it, agreed that it should; and so every one is bound by that consent to be concluded by the *majority*. And therefore we see that in Assemblies impowered to act by positive Laws, where no number is set by that positive Law which impowers them, the *act of the Majority* passes for the act of the whole, and of course determines, as having by the Law of Nature and Reason, the power of the whole.

Ibid., 349–50 (emphasis as in original). Locke's vogue in pre-Revolutionary America was great, especially in the 1760s and 1770s when the nature of government was being debated: 11% of all citations in publications by Americans in the former decade were to Locke (often to the *Essay Concerning Human Understanding*), who was the most frequently cited individual author; 7% of all citations were to him in the following decade, a tie for most frequent with Montesquieu. The single most frequently cited *book* in the period 1760–1805, it should be noted was the Bible, with 34% of all citations in publications by Americans over a forty-five year period. See Donald S. Lutz, "The Relative Influence of European Writers on Late Eighteenth-Century American Political Thought," *American Political Science Review* 78 (1984): 192–93. In his famous 1744 pamphlet Elisha Williams ("Philalethes"), remarks on having "given a short sketch of what the celebrated Mr. Lock [sic] in his *Treatise of Government* has largely demonstrated; and in which it is justly to be presumed all are agreed who understand the natural rights of mankind." Elisha Williams, *The Essential Rights of Protestants* (Boston: S. Kneeland & T. Green, 1744) in Sandoz, ed., *Political Sermons of the American Founding Era*, 59.

[18] Cited from Smith's *De Republica Anglorum*, ed. L. Alston with a preface by F. W. Maitland (Cambridge, England: the Univ. Press, 1906), bk. 2, chap. 1, in F. W. Maitland, *The Constitutional History of England: A Course of Lectures* (Cambridge, England: Cambridge Univ. Press, 1926), 255. Also Sir Francis Bacon: "in an Act of Parliament every man's consent is included." F. Bacon, *New Abridgement of the Law*, 1: 79, in James H. Kettner, *The Development of American Citizenship, 1608–1870* (Williamsburg, Va., and

Those of our citizens today who evidently find the American political tradition so odious as to seem intent on dismantling or transforming it have grasped the essentially political nature of our constitutional system, even as they reach for levers of power. Perhaps citizens who prudently regard democracy as the worst form of government except for all the others, who wish to preserve and continue to adapt rule of law and ordered liberty as these have historically evolved since 1776, need to nurture consensus in the politically effective community before it is fractured beyond all repair. Ingenuity moderated by the kind of common sense reflected in Justice Robert H. Jackson's "celebrated warning"[19] in the 1949 *Terminiello* case may be to the point: "There is a danger that, if the Court does not temper its doctrinaire logic with a little practical wisdom, it will convert the constitutional Bill of Rights into a suicide pact."[20] And that, too, was not the founders' intention.

Theoretical and Historical Basis of Religious Liberty.—My principal concern here is to clarify something of the historical and theoretical ground of American religious liberty as it emerged in the founding generation with particular attention to the role of James Madison. In addition, the attempt is made to suggest the cogency of this perspective as an enduring legacy of American freedom considered, not merely as a time-bound and parochial achievement, but as a philosophically acute and politically astute insight into the institutionalization of just order in society. To these ends I shall briefly reflect on the basis of concern with religion and religious liberty as matters of compelling importance to human beings; discuss several reasons justifying toleration and leading to the principle of liberty of conscience; and pay attention to the role especially of James Madison in institutionalizing religious liberty in Virginia. That activity, it turned out, became the immediate background for the drafting and ratification of the federal Constitution and Bill of Rights.

To begin with, there are certain philosophical considerations. Thus, the key problem underlying the matter of religious liberty is the theoretical question of the right relationship between the temporal and spiritual realms of reality, and secondary to that, the practical question of how the

---

Chapel Hill, N. C.: Univ. of North Carolina Press, 1978), 32. "The Constitution had institutionalized methods of expressing and redressing grievances; Congress was no local parliament, representing only part of an empire, but was the legitimate embodiment of the whole people." Ibid., 340. See, also, the concluding portion of the quotation from Locke in the previous note.

[19] Abraham, *Freedom and the Court*, 238 n.170.

[20] Terminiello v. City of Chicago, 337 U. S. 1, 37 (1949), Jackson, J., dissenting; cf. Chief Justice Warren Burger's majority opinion in Haig v. Agee, 453 U. S. 280 (1981).

relationship can optimally be institutionalized in ordering society. To use the New Testament terms favored by James Madison, for instance, this requires that the community "Render . . . unto Caesar the things which are Caesar's; and unto God the things that are God's." It also means taking to heart the Gospel's principle: "My kingdom is not of this world."[21]

Human experience intimates that reality is not exhausted by the temporal and spatial sphere but that the world or civilized existence is surmounted or comprehended by the divine, eternal, and transcendental reality apperceived as the spiritual realm called God. Such a layered or stratified structure of reality, articulated in levels from the material to divine reality and participated in by men through a human nature that is the epitome of being, is—despite the inroads of radical French Enlightenment—still the common coin of Western civilization for Americans into the period of the eighteenth-century founding. It supplies the background for any discussion of our subject that wishes to avoid hopeless anachronism or the obtuse secularism that often vitiates inquiry. We can rightly be reminded of the injunction to understand the founders as they understood themselves as a worthwhile standard, provided only that we be allowed to draw the implications of their thinking from a theoretical perspective. From the specific perspective of our subject, the following observation has recently been made:

> It is important to remember that the framers and ratifiers of the first amendment found it conceivable that a God—that is, a universal and transcendental authority beyond human judgment—might exist. If God might exist, then it is not arbitrary to hold that His will is superior to the judgment of individuals or of

---

[21] Matthew 22: 21; John 18: 36 (King James Version). Thus, Madison commended

> a system which, by a due distinction, to which the genius and courage of *Luther* led the way, between what is due to Caesar and what is due God, best promotes the discharge of *both* obligations. . . . A mutual independence is found most friendly to practical religion, to social harmony, and to political prosperity.

Madison to Rev. F. L. Schaeffer, December 3, 1821, Henry A. Washington, ed., *The Writings of Thomas Jefferson*, Congress ed. (Washington, D. C.: Taylor & Maury, 1853–54), 3: 242. In writing of the debate in the Virginia General Assembly in 1786 over enactment of Thomas Jefferson's Statute for Religious Liberty, Madison remarks that the members recoiled at inserting the words "Jesus Christ" into the preamble when it was successfully argued

> that the better proof of reverence for that holy name wd be not to profane it by making it a topic of legisl. discussion, & particularly by making his religion the means of abridging the natural and equal rights of all men, in defiance of his own declaration that his *Kingdom was not of this world.*

Elizabeth Fleet, ed., "Madison's 'Detached Memoranda,' " *William & Mary Quarterly*, 3rd ser., 3 (1946): 556 (emphasis added). This document is undated; the editor believes it probably was written soon after Madison's retirement from the presidency in 1817.

civil society. Much of the criticism of a special deference to sincere religious convictions arises from the assumption that such convictions are *necessarily* mere subcategories of personal moral judgments. This amounts to a denial of the possibility of a God (or at least of a God whose will is made manifest to humans).[22]

As has been suggested, Americans at the time of the founding were virtually unanimous in embracing such views—not merely as (here) hypotheses in Enlightenment fashion, but as articles of their living faith.

In the eighteenth-century horizon of our inquiry, *liberty* (including religious liberty) is distinguished from *license*. The understanding endures that the genuinely free man is one who lives in accordance with truth and justice, so that liberty, law, reason, and revelation are interrelated symbols of order that cannot be separated from one another. Sir Edward Coke's *Institutes*, along with his *Reports* the hornbook of John Adams and Thomas Jefferson, and the basis of legal education into the mid-1770s and later, expounds this understanding of the relationship between liberty and law. Coke writes that the primary meaning of *libertates* in Magna Carta is "the Laws of the Realm, in which respect this Charter is called, *Charta libertatum*. 2. It Signifieth the freedomes, that the Subjects of England have. . . ."[23] This is in harmony with the philosophers' insight that a free man is precisely one who lives in accordance with reason and highest truth. Reason (*nous*) is related to the individual in the same manner that law (*nomos*) is related to society, so that rule of law is the governance of God and reason. Conversely, the slave is any human being (regardless of social status) who so deforms or perverts his nature that life is dominated by ungoverned passions. These reign in a brutish dominion wherein instrumental reason secures the ways to gratification, whether of private desire or of political *libido dominandi*, as in the tyrannical man of Plato—or, perhaps, the putative normal man of Hobbes.[24] From the

---

[22] Michael W. McConnell, "The Origins and Historical Understanding of Free Exercise of Religion," *Harvard Law Review* 103 (1990): 1409, 1497 (emphasis as in original). Hereinafter cited as "Origins . . . of Free Exercise of Religion."

[23] Sir Edward Coke, *Second Part of the Institutes of the Laws of England* . . . ([1641]; London: M. Flesher & R. Young, 1642), 47.

[24] Plato, *Republic* 435ff; 571b–578e; *Laws* 689a–e; Aristotle, *Politics* 1254b5–1255a2; 1287a18–35; Hobbes, *Leviathan*, chaps. 5, 6, 11, 15. It is important to observe that the philosophical anthropology of Plato and Aristotle finds its *equivalent* in the hierarchical conception of human nature adopted by James Madison, where it is perhaps derivative mainly from Scottish Enlightenment writings, especially those of Francis Hutcheson and the common sense school as mediated by John Witherspoon in college. Thus, Madison deals with the springs of human action in terms of a psychological model of man that places virtue at the top, in preference to rational self-interest, which is to be preferred to the passions. As in classical philosophy, the order of worth is inversely proportional to the order of innate power. Hence, the triumph of virtue in the individual—justice and the

horizon of evangelical Protestant Christianity (the controlling horizon of our founders and of the communities they represented), the free man is the man of faith who stands in divine grace, in the law of liberty of Christ's embrace symbolized as "the way, the truth and the life," out of a free response of the contrite heart to the divine appeal expressive in *amor Dei* and, within mortal limitations, a blameless life: "whoso looketh into the perfect law of liberty, and continueth *therein*, he being not a forgetful hearer, but a doer of the work, this man shall be blessed in his deed."[25]

These convergent lines of insight into order pose the problem of the founders as much as they convey something of the background of their convictions. For it is manifestly possible, and appears from all I know to be likely, that the representatives of the American communities of the time that we collectively designate as our founders were both men of conviction and men of sufficient divergence in their specific convictions as to embrace liberty of conscience as not merely the prudential device of statesmen but, as reflective men of faith and varying degrees of zeal, out of humble recognition

---

public good in society—or even of rational self-interest, requires auxiliary assistance from institutions and from historically ingrained habit ("prejudices") in a carefully constructed social system. The pattern will be familiar from such places as *The Federalist Papers*, nos. 10, 49 and 51. See the discussion in McCoy, *The Last of the Fathers: James Madison and the Republican Legacy*, esp. 39–83 and passim. McCoy stresses the importance of David Hume for Madison's thought. Ibid., 42–44. There are hints of the equivalent of Socrates' anthropological principle from the *Republic* (368d–e) as McCoy reflects in successive chapters on "the character of the good statesman" and "the character of the good republic," ibid., 9, 39. "The struggles to maintain the supremacy of reason over passion and of public virtue over narrow self-interest run through this work like recurring themes in a symphony," writes Daniel Walker Howe in reviewing McCoy's book in *William & Mary Quarterly*, 3rd ser., 47 (1990): 142. Cf. Sandoz, *A Government of Laws*, 80–104, 170–85. See also, Susan Ford Wiltshire, *Greece, Rome and the Bill of Rights* (Norman and London: Univ. of Oklahoma Press, 1992); Carl J. Richard, *The Founders and the Classics: Greece, Rome, and the American Enlightenment* (Cambridge, Mass.: Harvard Univ. Press, 1994).

    [25] John 14: 6; James 1: 25. Cf. James 2: 12; 1 John 2: 7–8, 15–17; Galatians 6: 2; 2 John 5. A counterpoint to the argument here that the American founders were Christian can be seen in John M. Murrin, "Religion and Politics in America from the First Settlements to the Civil War," in Mark A. Noll, ed., *Religion and American Politics: From the Colonial Period to the 1980s* (New York and Oxford: Oxford Univ. Press, 1990), 19–43. But even Murrin must acknowledge that "Jefferson and Madison along with George Washington, John Adams, Benjamin Franklin, and nearly all of the Founding Fathers claimed to be Christians" all the while insisting that "hardly any of them was," ibid., 29; "the Founding Fathers all claimed to be 'Christians,' " ibid., 35. The problem is tricky and obviously controverted, to say the least. And this is very curious argumentation. The founders are famous for their veracity and sense of honor; they *said* (thus, presumably *thought*) they were "Christians" in some defensible sense of the term. My view is that there is ample evidence to take the founders at their word: why not? Indeed, how exceedingly odd that we don't! Cf. the discussion in J. C. D. Clark, *The Language of Liberty, 1660–1832* (Cambridge, England: Cambridge Univ. Press, 1994), 335–81.

of the limits of human knowledge. In other words, there is an unavoidable need to separate the question of exactly what the founders believed and what they saw as requisite to the establishment of a compound republic that would not founder on the rock of religious division, the bane of modern Western history. "Torrents of blood have been spilt in the old world, by vain attempts of the secular arm, to extinguish Religious discord, by proscribing all difference in Religious opinion," Madison wrote in 1785.[26] Moreover, the zeal with which they and their several communities sought to serve and propagate the truth of ultimate reality was effectively curbed by taking to heart the judicious Richard Hooker's timeless maxim of moderation: *"Think ye are men, deem it not impossible for you to err."*[27] This admonition plants the seed of toleration and propagates the saving doubt essential to any free government that is ineluctably grounded in the consent of heterogeneous communities. It fosters civility and squarely places reliance upon *persuasion* as the basis of liberty of conscience for individual persons and of peace for society.

American Tradition and Liberty of Conscience for Religious Reasons.—Some such set of considerations would seem to underlie the American political decisions of prohibiting a religious establishment and of ensuring freedom of conscience. These are compromises without which the country probably could not have been constituted and almost certainly could not have endured. Behind these compromises loom, however, the whole array of problems arising from concerns about the moral and philosophical rectitude of a political establishment not formally anchored in the community's nurture and acceptance of a coherent account of the good that attends to all levels of reality, including divine Being. How is the bridge between the philosophical and theological anthropology of classical philosophy and general Christianity—the core structuring elements of the American community at the time of the founding—to be erected and sustained so as to ground the political life of the country morally and ontologically without formal institutional support? What seems to be lacking in the American experiment with free government is coercive means to make men free, to maintain the consensus along lines of the philosophical and biblical teachings universally embraced at the time. Put otherwise, where and how would the sustaining

---

[26] James Madison, "Memorial and Remonstrance," in William T. Hutchinson, et al., eds., *The Papers of James Madison* (Chicago & Charlottesville: Chicago Univ. Press, 1962-), vol. 8: 302 (Para. 11).

[27] Richard Hooker, *Of the Laws of Ecclesiastical Polity*, Preface, 9.1 (emphasis added); first published in 1593. Rpr. Richard Hooker, *Of the Laws of Ecclesiastical Polity: Preface, Book I, Book VIII*, ed. Arthur Stephen McGrade (Cambridge, England: Cambridge Univ. Press, 1989), 49.

fundamental core agreement about matters of first importance upon which free republican institutions finally depend (because resting upon consent of the people) be renewed and vivified without some authoritative orthodoxy of belief? Are the solutions of Lockean toleration or of Madisonian and Jeffersonian liberty of conscience merely seductive subterfuges, a dark calculus whereby radical secular Enlightenment propagating outright atheism is in time expected to claim the personal and social life of the country for itself, as long ago feared and lately reasserted?[28] Let us reflect upon these questions.

In discussing religious liberty it is important not to leave out the *religious* dimension of the subject, whatever one may conclude (or not conclude) about the spiritual interests and convictions of such luminaries as Washington, Adams, Jefferson, Madison, and Franklin. Such an impartial student as Alexis de Tocqueville makes the fundamental point that in America, perhaps uniquely in the world, "two perfectly distinct elements which elsewhere have often been at war with one another . . . somehow . . . incorporate into each other, forming a marvelous combination. I mean the *spirit of religion* and the *spirit of freedom*." This amazing feat is possible, Tocqueville believes, because the English colonists

> brought to the New World a Christianity which I can only describe as democratic and republican. . . . There is not a single religious doctrine hostile to democratic and republican institutions. . . . America is the place where the Christian religion has kept the greatest real power over men's souls; and nothing better demonstrates how useful and natural it is to man, since the country where it now has widest sway is both the most enlightened and the freest. . . . It was religion that gave birth to the English colonies in America. One must never forget that. In

---

[28] Cf. Thomas Lindsay, "James Madison on Religion and Politics: Rhetoric and Reality," *American Political Science Review* 85 (1991): 1321–37. This Spinozistic analysis of "Madison's deepest intentions," ibid., 1322, finds the Enlightenment subversion to be his true "project," ibid., 1329, 1330, 1332, and 1333, which is "hostile, in key respects, to religion," ibid., 1323, to the end that "religion would be gagged by its own liberty," ibid., 1334 (last phrase in the article). The most astonishing thing about this remarkable performance is that the main thesis *hangs* on the peg of Lindsay's reading, with *no* evidence to back him, of a single clause in *Federalist No. 10*, viz., "persons of other descriptions," ibid., 1324, as a code meaning "Moses, Christ, and Muhammed," ibid., 1324, "the world's great religious figures," ibid., 1325 and 1334. They are, thus, secretly and slyly condemned by Madison as the real villains of history, the culprits who are "destructive of their followers' abilities to 'cooperate for the common good,' " ibid., 1324, citing Clinton Rossiter, ed., *The Federalist* (New York: New American Library, 1961), 79. This is not merely reaching, even if in the customary spirit of deciphering esoteric writing. This is wildest surmise and sensationalism. Our leading founders (did Madison act alone or was there a conspiracy?) are portrayed as accomplices in a diabolical plot to dupe gullible religious Americans into surrendering their birthright! But perhaps this is merely an instance of hunch intoxication.

the United States religion is mingled with all the national customs and all those feelings which the word fatherland evokes. For that reason it has peculiar power. . . . Christianity itself is an established and irresistible fact which no one seeks to attack or to defend.[29]

If Tocqueville's status as founder or contemporary of the founders be questioned, a word from a famous Pennsylvanian can supplement these statements. Dr. Benjamin Rush, confidant of Jefferson, Franklin, Adams and signatory of the Declaration of Independence, subscribing as did most of his contemporaries to the proposition that liberty cannot be established without morality nor morality and a virtuous citizenry without religion, wrote:

The only foundation for a useful education in a republic is to be laid in RELIGION. Without this, there can be no virtue, and without virtue there can be no liberty, and liberty is the object and life of all republican governments. . . . The religion I mean to recommend in this place is the religion of JESUS CHRIST. . . . A Christian cannot fail of being a republican. . . . for every precept of the Gospel inculcates those degrees of humility, self-denial, and brotherly kindness which are directly opposed to the pride of monarchy and the pageantry of court. . . . his religion teacheth him that no man "liveth unto himself" . . . . [H]is religion teacheth him in all things to do to others what he would wish, in like circumstances, they should do to him.[30]

An evangelical Christian consensus that, whatever the diversity of creeds, generally marked America at the time of the Revolution was a fundamental of the society and recognized as such by leading figures.

The conventional understanding of religious toleration, religious liberty, or liberty of conscience reconciles it to one or the other of two models, one resting on political or rationalist principle the other on religious principle. The view was given succinct statement by Lord Bryce a century ago in his famous book on *The American Commonwealth*. The political principle, he wrote:

---

[29] Alexis de Tocqueville, *Democracy in America*, ed. J. P. Mayer, trans. George Lawrence (Garden City, N. Y.: Anchor Books, 1969), 1: 46–47, 288–91; 2: 432.

[30] Benjamin Rush, *A Plan for the Establishment of Public Schools and the Diffusion of Knowledge in Pennsylvania: to Which are Added Thoughts upon the Mode of Education, Proper in a Republic* (Philadelphia: Thomas Dobson, 1786), reprinted in Charles S. Hyneman and Donald S. Lutz, eds., *American Political Writing During the Founding Era, 1760–1805* (Indianapolis: Liberty Press, 1983), 1: 682. For discussion see Sandoz, *A Government of Laws*, 132–33 and passim; see also Barry Alan Shain, *The Myth of American Individualism: The Protestant Origins of American Political Thought* (Princeton: Princeton Univ. Press, 1994), 96–97 and passim.

sets out from the principles of liberty and equality. It holds any attempt at compulsion by the civil power to be an infringement on liberty of thought, as well as on liberty of action, which could be justified only when a practice claiming to be religious is so obviously anti-social or immoral as to threaten the well-being of the community. . . . The second principle . . . starts from the conception of the church as a spiritual body existing for spiritual purposes, and moving along spiritual paths. It is an assemblage of men who are united by their devotion to an unseen Being, their memory of a divine life, their belief in the possibility of imitating that life, so far as human frailty allows, their hopes for an illimitable future. Compulsion of any kind is contrary to the nature of such a body, which lives by love and reverence, not by law. It desires no state help, feeling that its strength comes from above, and that its kingdom is not of this world. . . . Least of all can it submit to be controlled by the state, for the state, in such a world as the present, means persons many or most of whom are alien to its beliefs and cold to its emotions. The conclusion follows that the church as a spiritual entity will be happiest and strongest when it is left absolutely to itself, not patronized by the civil power, not restrained by law except when and in so far as it may attempt to quit its proper sphere and intermeddle in secular affairs.

Lord Bryce concludes that "[t]he former much more than the later . . . has moved the American mind." As a consequence of this happy arrangement, "[t]here are no quarrels of churches and sects. Judah does not vex Ephraim, nor Ephraim envy Judah."[31]

---

[31] James Lord Bryce, *The American Commonwealth* (1888; new ed., New York: Macmillan, 1922), 2: 676–69, 874. A document published in observation of the centenary of the Constitution had this to say about religion, America's providential destiny, and the actual operation of separation of church and state:

[I]t has worked well in practice. It has stood the test of experience. It has the advantages of the union of church and state without its disadvantages. . . . The tendency to division and split is inherent in Protestantism, and it must be allowed free scope until every legitimate type of Christianity is developed and matured. The work of history is not in vain. But division is only a means to a higher unity than the world has yet seen. . . . God has great surprises in store. The Reformation is not by any means the last word He has spoken. We may confidently look and hope for something better than Romanism and Protestantism. And free America, where all the churches are commingling and rivalling with each other, may become the chief theater of such a reunion of Christendom as will preserve every truly Christian and valuable element. . . . The denominational discords will be solved at last in the concord of Christ, the Lord and Savior of all that love, worship, and follow Him.

Philip Schaff, *Church and State in the United States; Or, The American Idea of Religious Liberty and Its Practical Effects, With Official Documents,* Papers of the American Historical Association (New York & London: C. Scribner, 1888), 2: 389, 460–65 (also paged as a separate publication, quoting from pp. 78–83). The sentiments Schaff expressed in 1888 accord well with those Ezra Stiles expressed a century earlier in the Connecticut election sermon of 1783:

This is important testimony to the prudential success of the founders' approach to reconciling religion and politics in America, given a century after their work was done. These observations, however, do not quite do justice to the view of religious liberty held by many eighteenth-century Americans. Perry Miller has written, perhaps thinking mainly of the established churches, that the "Protestant churches did not so much achieve religious liberty as have liberty thrust upon them." Generally speaking, they did not so much contribute "to religious liberty, they stumbled into it, they were compelled into it, they accepted it at last because they had to, or because they saw its strategic value."[32] The situation was more complex and contradictory than either Bryce or Miller suggests and the direct role of the dissenting churches, perhaps the Baptists chief among them, in establishing religious liberty as it took shape in the generation of the founding is unquestionably great.

A leading historian of the subject, William G. McLoughlin, contradicts Lord Bryce's judgment that primarily the political or rationalistic justification of religious liberty has moved the American mind:

> neither of the two approaches delineated above has prevailed. The establishment of the principle of disestablishment in 1791 [through adoption of the federal Bill of Rights] was a temporary, fortuitous and unresolved alliance between the two. And what applied to the federal government did not apply to any of its constituent states. For the major part of our history the pietistic approach has been dominant, though since 1925 the rationalist approach (which underlies most of the decisions of the United States Supreme Court) has become so. Still, the tension exists today as powerfully as it did in 1791.[33]

> It may have been of the Lord that Christianity is to be found in such great purity in this church exiled into the wilderness of America; and that its purest body should be evidently advancing forward, by an augmented natural increase and spiritual edification, into a singular superiority—with the ultimate subserviency to the glory of God, in converting the world.

Stiles, *The United States Elevated to Glory and Honour*, quoted as given in excerpted form in Conrad Cherry, ed., *God's New Israel: Religious Interpretations of American Destiny* (Englewood Cliffs: Prentice-Hall, 1971), 92. The complete text is given in John Wingate Thornton, ed., *The Pulpit of the American Revolution: or, the Political Sermons of the Period of 1776* (New York: Sheldon & Co., 1860; rpr., New York: B. Franklin, 1970). Cf. Note 8, supra.

[32] Perry Miller, "The Contribution of the Protestant Churches to Religious Liberty in Colonial America," *Church History* 4 (March, 1935): 55–66.

[33] William G. McLoughlin, *New England Dissent, 1630–1833: The Baptists and the Separation of Church and State* (Cambridge, Mass.: Harvard Univ. Press, 1971), 1: xv. I rely upon McLoughlin in the next paragraph. See also his *Soul Liberty: The Baptists' Struggle in New England, 1630–1833* (Hanover and London: Univ. Press of New Englnad, 1991).

Related to and defining religious liberty are several distinct elements that impact both politics and religion. Much of the struggle for "soul liberty" in America, once toleration had been achieved (in 1691 in New England), was for disestablishment of the Standing Order Congregational church in New England and of the Anglican church in much of the remainder of America and the rise of separatism or voluntarism in its stead. But exactly what is meant by *establishment* varies. One thing it tended to mean was the payment of taxes to support a church and its ministers whether one was a member of that church or not, a "dissenter," subject to sometimes severe penalties including imprisonment and public whipping. A second element related to the quest for acceptance and equality by dissenting communions that suffered physically and psychologically from discrimination and disabilities, both social and legal, that branded them as inferior. Thus, the quest for liberty was also one for equality as well, for respectability and leadership in society on a common footing with the members of other sects. A third element that complements voluntarism and pluralism is pietistic-perfectionism, a major symbolism of America itself as a city on a hill with a world-historic providential destiny to fulfill in an eschatological triumph of spirit. Since both the established and the dissenting communities were pietistic in America, the spectrum of attitudes ranged along related forms of pietism. These included the search for moral order, the thirst for religious freedom, and the interaction with enlightenment philosophies that played an important role from the 1750s onward. In comparing attitudes of the Baptist leader Isaac Backus with those of Thomas Jefferson, McLoughlin remarks: "Both Jefferson and Backus wanted separation of church and state so that the truth would prevail, but for Backus truth came through the heart by grace, whereas for Jefferson it came through the head by reason."[34] In the fourth place, there is the relation of the progress of religious liberty to the process of democratization itself as, in the wake of the founding, that matured to shape the rise of Jeffersonian and Jacksonian democracy with its individualism and laissez-faire attitudes.[35] These attitudes were undergirded by the revivals or Great Awakenings that had first stirred, and then tended to universalize, American religious experience so as to insist upon personal conversion, to maintain the priesthood of all believers, to oppose public support of religion, and to organize individual churches on the principle of congregational autonomy—subject to no authority for their communicants' faith but God, scripture, and

---

[34] McLoughlin, *Soul Liberty*, 260.

[35] See the account in Hatch, *Democratization of American Christianity*, 49–192; also, Gordon S. Wood, *The Radicalism of the American Revolution* (New York: A. A. Knopf, 1993), 229–369.

conscience. These originally religious attitudes conditioned and indelibly schooled American citizenship itself in the rising democratic nation.

All in all, in the result the "old religious myth of the errand into the wilderness, the city upon a hill, the Bible Commonwealth which was an outpost looking backward toward Europe, was rejected for the new nationalist myth of divinely directed manifest destiny." McLoughlin is the historian of the New England Baptists, primarily, but the story can rightly be generalized. Nor is it all rhapsodic:

> The trend toward individualism ends in the tyranny of the majority; the ardor of pietism is cooled by the necessity of institutionalization; the courageous dissenters are often intolerant conformists; the advocates of religious liberty practice religious discrimination; the non-conformist becomes the status-seeker; the fight for disestablishment ends in the creation of a new kind of establishment—the White, Anglo-Saxon, Evangelical Protestant "establishment."

Still, the American quest for liberty through the belief that all men are created equal rose and fell but never completely subsided after 1776. Nor did conviction falter among the evangelical Christians in the nation's oft-proclaimed providential destiny "to play the crucial role in advancing the Kingdom of God on Earth."[36]

As nurtured especially (not exclusively, of course) from the religious impetus, then, liberty of conscience may be said to have moved through three phases of development. From *toleration* viewed as a reluctant but necessary concession to dissenters wrung from the established order for the sake of peace, to an assertion of *liberty of conscience* based on the conviction of human equality before God, to the claim of *perfect freedom of belief and practice* conceived as essential to truth itself and to a life lived in accordance with truth. These stages generally can be identified with the writings and work of John Locke, Roger Williams, and Isaac Backus, respectively, as representative.[37] And it will have been seen that, whatever the ambiguities and inconsistencies involved, American claims to religious liberty did not annul the proclamation of Christian truth, retard its propagation, or dim hope for the universal triumph of that truth in the end time. The drive toward religious freedom in the 1780s was part and parcel of the American

---

36 McLoughlin, *New England Dissent*, 1: xx–xxi. See also Isaac Backus, *An Appeal to the Public for Religious Liberty* (Boston: John Boyle, 1773), rpr. in Sandoz, ed., *Political Sermons of the American Founding Era*, 327–68. On America's providential destiny see Notes 8 and 29, supra, for Ezra Stiles' election sermon of 1783, *The United States Elevated to Glory and Honor*, analyzed in Sandoz, *A Government of Laws*, 109–111.

37 Cf. E. Benjamin Andrews' address of 1893 in Joseph M. Dawson, *Baptists and the American Republic* (Nashville: Broadman Press, 1956), 67.

evangelical movement itself. It was a fervent religious conviction of such Baptist leaders as Isaac Backus in Massachusetts and, between 1776 and 1791, of Elder John Leland in Virginia, where the latter became Madison's obstreperous constituent and political ally in Orange County. Simply said, establishment equated with political control of religion and stifled spiritual growth and initiative. Moreover, the dissenting sects had much to gain by breaking the monopoly of the old established churches. "The greatest support for disestablishment and free exercise therefore came from evangelical Protestant denominations, especially Baptists, Quakers, but also Presbyterians, Lutherans, and others."[38]

Prudential Justifications for Religious Liberty: Madison and Jefferson in Virginia.—If we turn attention from the primarily religious to the primarily political concern for religious liberty (to the extent that the dichotomy is serviceable), we come face to face with the handiwork of Virginians, especially Thomas Jefferson and James Madison. Both of these men championed religious liberty throughout their careers, and especially Madison reacted in anguish and anger as a young man to Virginia's harsh persecution of dissenters that intensified in 1768 against the Baptists. When twenty-two years old he wrote his college chum William Bradford expressing attitudes that never left him for the remainder of his long life:

> [I] have nothing to brag of as to the State and Liberty of my Country. Poverty and Luxury prevail among all sorts [here in Virginia]: Pride, ignorance, and Knavery among the Priesthood, and Vice and Wickedness among the Laity. This is bad enough. But it is not the worst I have to tell you. That diabolical Hell-conceived principle of persecution rages among some and to their eternal Infamy the Clergy can furnish their Quota of Imps for such business. This vexes me the most of any thing whatever. There are at this [time?] in the adjacent County [*Culpeper?*] not less than 5 or 6 well meaning men in close Gaol for publishing their religious Sentiments which in the main are very orthodox. I have neither patience to hear talk or think of any thing relative to this matter, for I have squabbled and scolded abused and ridiculed so long about it, [to so lit]tle purpose, that I am without common patience. So I [leave you] to pity me and pray for Liberty of Conscience [to revive among us.].

An editorial note to this letter adds: "Apparently it was religious issues, more than tax and trade regulation disputes with England, which were rapidly

---

[38] McConnell, "Origins . . . of Free Exercise of Religion," 1438–39. On John Leland see Sandoz, ed., *Political Sermons of the American Founding,* 1079–1100, which reprints his famous tract entitled *The Rights of Conscience Inalienable* (New London: T. Green & Son, 1791].

luring JM away from his beloved studies and arousing his interest in contemporary politics."[39]

Madison's activities in personally defending jailed Baptist ministers was the beginning of a public career that next saw him helping to frame the Virginia Declaration of Rights, defending his state against the advocates of religious establishment through authorship of the Memorial and Remonstrance Against Religious Assessments, securing passage of Jefferson's long dormant Bill/Statute for Religious Freedom (January 1786), playing a pivotal role in the Philadelphia Convention in framing the Constitution of 1787, leading the drafting and passage of the federal Bill of Rights in the First Congress under the Constitution in 1789, enforcing it as President, and never deviating throughout his long lifetime in devotion to liberty of conscience. Madison regarded securing the enactment of the Virginia Act for Establishing Religious Freedom (the official title) as his most gratifying legislative achievement. "We now give full credit to the contribution of James Madison, mediating with consummate skill among Baptists, Presbyterians, and liberal Anglicans, putting through the Statute while Jefferson was in Paris," Henry F. May writes. "The troops were Baptists and Presbyterians and the tactics were Madison's, but the words—with a few minor corrections made by the Assembly—were Jefferson's. These were and are wholly representative of the Revolutionary Enlightenment."[40]

"Religious liberty," Madison's biographer Ralph Ketcham observes, "stands out as the one subject upon which Madison took an extreme, absolute, undeviating position throughout his life." He continues:

> There is no evidence that Madison's defence of religious liberty reflected any hostility to religion itself or to its social effects. On the contrary, he argued repeatedly that freedom of religion enhanced *both* its intrinsic vitality and its contribution to the common weal. He believed that attitudes and habits nourished by the churches could and did help importantly to improve republican government. He believed just as strongly that complete separation of church and

---

[39] James Madison to William Bradford, January 24, 1774, in Hutchinson, ed., *The Papers of James Madison,* 1: 106–107. Madison was born March 16, 1751 [March 5, 1750 Old Style], and died June 28, 1836. See Ralph Ketcham, *James Madison: A Biography* (New York: Macmillan, 1971), 8–9n. (Great Britain's calendar reform adopting the Gregorian for the Julian calendar came in 1752 and required an 11-day addition to Old Style dates; it also changed the beginning of the year from March 25 to January 1. When JM was born, toward midnight, the calendar on the wall of the Madison home would have read March 5, 1750.) The standard account of the persecution of the Baptists in Virginia is Lewis Peyton Little, *Imprisoned Preachers and Religious Liberty in Virginia* (Lynchburg, Va.: J. P. Bell Co., Inc., 1938).

[40] Henry F. May, *The Divided Heart: Essays on Protestantism and the Enlightenment in America* (New York: Oxford Univ. Press, 1991), 172.

state saved the church from the inevitably corrupting influence of civil authority. . . . Throughout his long public career he received cordial support from Protestants, Catholics, and Jews who admired his forthright stand on religious liberty. . . . Madison bespoke fully and cogently what came to be the characteristically American attitude toward the relation between religion and politics.[41]

The Virginia Declaration/Bill of Rights of 1776 was drafted by George Mason, and it was especially Article 16 that was revised in one key phrase at young James Madison's suggestion, in his first legislative triumph. It reads in final form as follows:

> 16. That Religion, or the duty which we owe to our Creator, and the manner of discharging it, can be directed only by reason and conviction, not by force or violence; and, therefore, all men are equally entitled to the free exercise of religion, according to the dictates of conscience; and that it is the mutual duty of all to practice Christian forbearance, love, and charity, towards each other.[42]

A half-century later, Madison believed that the effect of his emendation was to substitute for the word *toleration,* "inadvertently adopted" by Mason, "phraseology which—declared the freedom of conscience to be a natural and absolute right."[43] This was certainly the drift of his convictions and intentions more generally. The distance of the pietism of Isaac Backus from the Virginians' version of religious liberty can be gauged from the following article which the former proposed for inclusion in the Massachusetts Constitution of 1780:

---

[41] Ketcham, *James Madison*, 165, 167–68. See also Ralph L. Ketcham, "James Madison and Religion: A New Hypothesis," in Robert S. Alley, ed., *James Madison on Religious Liberty* (1960; rpr. Buffalo: Prometheus Books, 1985), 175–96. Of pertinence also is Paul Finkelman, "James Madison and the Bill of Rights: A Reluctant Paternity," *The 1990 Supreme Court Review* (Chicago: Univ. of Chicago Press, 1991), 301–347. Also, Daniel L. Dreisbach, "A New Perspective on Jefferson's Views on Church-State Relations: The Virginia Statute for Establishing Religious Freedom in its Legislative Context," *American Journal of Legal History* 35 (1991): 172–204.

[42] Virginia Declaration of Rights of 1776 as given in Bernard Schwartz, ed., *The Bill of Rights: A Documentary History* (New York: Chelsea House Publishers, 1971), 1: 236. Mason's original draft read:

> . . . violence; and, therefore, *that* all men *should enjoy the fullest toleration in* [are equally entitled to] the [free] exercise of religion, according to the dictates of conscience, [;] *unpunished and unrestrained by the magistrate, unless, under color of religion, any man disturb the peace, the happiness or the safety of society.* [;] [a]nd. . . .

The original (italicized) words were deleted in the final draft and the bracketed words, punctuation and letters inserted. Ibid., 239.

[43] James Madison's *Autobiography*, quoted ibid., 250. Not dated precisely, but probably written after August 1833 according to Irving Brant (quoted ibid., 249n).

As God is the only worthy object of all religious worship, and nothing can be true religion but a voluntary obedience unto his revealed will, of which each rational soul has an equal right to judge for itself; every person has an inalienable right to act in all religious affairs according to the full persuasion of his own mind, where others are not injured thereby. And Civil rulers are so far from having any right to empower any person or persons to judge for others in such affairs, and to enforce their judgments with the sword, that their power ought to be exerted to protect all persons and societies within their jurisdiction from being injured or interrupted in the free enjoyment of this right under any presumption whatsoever.[44]

The more specifically Christian appeal in Backus's language is to be observed. The pattern of calculated vagueness displayed by Madison, to avoid any sectarian identification, persisted throughout his career.[45] It is "God" who alone deserves "worship," and "true religion" is nothing but a voluntary obedience to his "revealed will," in Backus's language. Of course, the final clause in the Virginia document counseling "Christian forbearance" remained unchanged from Mason's original draft, as did also the first clause with its appeal to "reason and conviction"—and cannot be attributed to Madison. The latter notion is reflected in Backus's text which claims for every rational soul the liberty to judge religious truth for itself, and makes explicit the

---

[44] Isaac Backus quoted from McLoughlin, "Isaac Backus and Thomas Jefferson," in *Soul Liberty*, 260. Elsewhere McLoughlin remarks that Backus "was the most forceful and effective writer America produced on behalf of the pietistic or evangelical theory of separation of church and state." William G. McLoughlin, *Isaac Backus on Church, State, and Calvinism: Pamphlets, 1754–1789* (Cambridge, Mass.: Belknap Press of Harvard Univ. Press, 1968), 1. Backus doubtless had in hand Mason's intermediate draft version that had been given preliminary emendation by the committee (printed on May 27, 1776) which his own language tracks to some degree. This preliminary text was republished far and wide, including in Massachusetts where John Adams made use of it in 1776 and 1780, and it was everywhere taken as the finished document. The final version, containing Madison's emendations, was "not published outside of Virginia for about a half-century" and he, therefore, received little credit for his important accomplishment until much later. "Editorial Note" in Hutchinson, ed., *Papers of James Madison*, 1: 171.

[45] Thus, Madison remarks of the Executive proclamations for days of fasting and thanksgiving that he issued (there were four of these during his presidency): "I was always careful to make the Proclamations absolutely indiscriminate, and merely recommendatory; or rather mere *designations* of a day, on which all who thought proper might *unite* in consecrating it to religious purposes, according to their own faith & forms." JM to Edward Livingston, July 10, 1822, Gaillard Hunt, ed., *The Writings of James Madison* (New York: G. P. Putnam's Sons, 1900–1910), 9: 101. In writing of these proclamations elsewhere Madison states: " . . . a form & language were employed, which were meant to deaden as much as possible any claim of political right to enjoin religious observances." Fleet, ed., "Madison's 'Detached Memoranda'," 562. Proclamations in response to Congress's requests were issued by President Madison on July 9, 1812; July 23, 1813; November 16, 1814; and on March 4, 1815. Ibid., 562 n.54.

inalienability of every person's "right to act in all religious affairs according to the full persuasion of his own mind."

The Memorial and Remonstrance Against Religious Assessments and Its Aftermath.—The great document outlining Madison's case for religious liberty came with the Memorial and Remonstrance Against Religious Assessments in 1785. Here an elaborate argument is advanced that clearly does do what Madison believed years later he had done by modifying the language of the Virginia Declaration of Rights in 1776. It takes the form of a listing of fifteen arguments against enactment of a bill to support teachers of the Christian religion, this being seen as a device for reestablishing religion in Virginia. The issue was so treacherous politically that Madison kept his authorship secret for forty years, only acknowledging it in 1826. After all, in a religious time, with Christianity understood as the very foundation of life and morals, why should not its teachers be at least partly compensated from public funds? Were opponents really opposed to Christianity itself? The way out, politically, was through alliance with the Baptists and Presbyterians who stoutly opposed all forms of civil support of religion.

The deluge of arguments given in the Memorial and Remonstrance touches every level of appeal. It begins and ends with the quotation of the Virginia Declaration of Rights which embraces all of the liberties most sacred to the society. It is, thus, both fundamental law and undeniable truth that religion cannot be coerced but is strictly a matter of reason, conviction, and of the conscience that is unalienable and subject only to each person's inner judgment. Religious duty is precedent to all claims of civil society, and thus derives from a natural right resting on higher law. "Before any man can be considered as a member of Civil Society, he must be considered as a subject of the Governour of the Universe"—Creator, Universal Sovereign, and Supreme Lawgiver as God is variously named. The absolute superiority and priority of the freedom of conscience is such "that in matters of Religion, no man's right is abridged by the institution of Civil Society and . . . Religion is wholly exempt from its cognizance." Compulsion by any majority in civil society in matters of religion is *ultra vires*—a trespass against the minority's rights, since these are strictly beyond the reach of any civil process whatever. To overstep this limit is to plunge the society into slavery and tyranny. In a passage reminiscent of *Federalist No. 51*, Madison argues that the

> preservation of a free Government requires not merely, that the metes and bounds which separate each department of power be invariably maintained; but more especially that neither of them be suffered to overleap the great Barrier [of

unalienable natural rights and higher law] which defends the rights of the people.

To do so exceeds the outer limits of legitimate authority.

Paragraph 3 subtly plays on the language of the hated Declaratory Act of 1766 which so galvanized the American colonies against Britain when it claimed the right to bind them in all cases whatsoever, including in matters religious by threatening to send a bishop to America to secure uniformity. And Madison recalls the three-pence tax on tea as well, conjuring the worst fears of an audience ready to believe that great monstrosities can grow from tiny afflictions. "Who does not see that the same authority which can establish Christianity, in exclusion of all other Religions, may establish with the same ease any particular sect of Christians, in exclusion of all other Sects?" a devastating line of argument from the perspective of Elder Leland and his Baptist communicants. In Paragraph 8 the contrast with tyranny is drawn and just government identified as one that protects every citizen's enjoyment of religion in exactly the same way that it protects his property and person. The horror of persecution with the Inquisition as its end-form is evoked, as is also the futility of attempting to torment believers into unanimity of belief by coercing orthodoxy, the "[t]orrents of blood" of the old world offered as conclusive evidence. Thus, as a pragmatic matter the cure has been discovered: equal and complete liberty, which has dawned at last in America. A further practical matter attaching to the unenforceability of such coerced support of religion is the enervation of all law. The consequent demonstration of impotent rule inevitably follows, undermining all public authority and pushing society toward the brink of anarchy and civil strife. If despite all reason, such a policy will be pursued, then it ought at least to have the support of a clear majority of the people, which it currently did not have. Madison concludes by pointing out that infringing religious liberty, as guaranteed in the Declaration of Rights, will at the same time weaken protection of and potentially violate *all* of the most precious rights of free men under the Constitution. Freedom of the press and trial by jury will fall; next the separation of powers itself will be obliterated by concentrating all power in the hands of the legislature, who can then end the suffrage itself and therewith establish a hereditary power so as to tyrannize without stint.[46]

Madison's comprehensive line of argument, ranging from divine and natural law to social and existential catastrophe, made all the more persuasive through living memories of tyranny and vivid present evidence of

---

[46] "Memorial and Remonstrance," Hutchinson, ed., *Papers of James Madison*, 8: 298–302.

persecution, supplies the frame of reference for understanding less articulate justifications of religious liberty. The defeat of the assessments bill followed. This paved the way for enactment six months later of Jefferson's Statute for Religious Freedom, which premises that *"Almighty God hath created the mind free."* Jefferson regarded it as one of the three great achievements of his life, ranking with writing the Declaration of Independence and founding the University of Virginia. Its enactment, Madison claimed, had "in this country extinguished for ever the ambitious hope of making laws for the human mind."[47] The framing of the First Amendment to the Constitution came less than four years later, but the battles over the meaning and extent of free exercise of religion and no establishment had largely been fought out in Virginia by the very personalities who would take the lead in devising the Constitution's Bill of Rights.[48]

What, then, is the solution proffered by freedom of conscience? Madison's tenacity in holding to the position of the 1780s is exemplified in many places, not least of all during old age when he and Jefferson collaborated in founding the University of Virginia, whose rectorship Madison then assumed after the latter's death in 1826. It was to Madison that Jefferson turned when it came to selecting theological books for the new library. But there would be no professor of theology, and no instruction in the subject would be provided. Madison crisply gave the reasons why not to Edward Everett in 1823:

> A University with sectarian professorships becomes, of course, a Sectarian Monopoly: with professorships of rival sects, it would be an Arena of Theological Gladiators. Without any such professorships, it may incur for a time at least, the imputation of irreligious tendencies, if not designs. The last difficulty was thought more manageable than either of the others. On this view of the subject, there seems to be no alternative but between a public University without a theological professorship, and sectarian Seminaries without a University. . . . The difficulty of reconciling the Xn mind to the absence of a religious tuition from a university established by law and at the common expense, is probably less with us than with you. The settled opinion here is that religion is essentially distinct from Civil Govt. and exempt from its cognizance; that a connection between them is injurious to both; that there are causes in the human breast, which insure the perpetuity of religion without the aid of the law; that rival sects, with equal rights, exercise mutual censorship in favor of good morals; and if new sects arise with absurd opinions or overheated imaginations, the proper remedies lie in time, forbearance, and example; that a legal establishment of religion without a

---

[47] James Madison to Thomas Jefferson, January 22, 1786, ibid., 474.

[48] See the account in Sandoz, *A Government of Laws*, 203–217; and Helen E. Veit et al., eds., *Creating the Bill of Rights: The Documentary Record from the First Federal Congress* (Baltimore and London: Johns Hopkins Univ. Press, 1991).

toleration could not be thought of, and with a toleration, is no security for public quiet & harmony, but rather a source itself of discord & animosity; and finally, that these opinions are supported by experience, which has shewn that every relaxation of the alliance between Law & religion, from the partial example of Holland, to its consummation in Pennsylvania Delaware N. J., &c, has been found as safe in practice as it is sound in theory. Prior to the Revolution, the Episcopal Church was established by law in this State. On the Declaration of independence it was left with all other sects, to a self-support. And no doubt exists that there is much more of religion among us now than there ever was before the change; and particularly in the Sect which enjoyed the legal patronage. This proves rather more than, that the law is not necessary to the support of religion.[49]

Religious Liberty, Constitutionalism and Higher Law.—From what we have considered, it can be concluded that the religious and the philosophic appeal go hand in hand in fashioning the basis for religious liberty in America. The axiom emerged (shall we say) that liberty of conscience stands above and apart from the power of the state to legislate as a God-given, inalienable natural right of every individual person. It is antecedent to citizenship and independent of it, woven into human nature as inseparable from man's very being or specific essence. This is the high ground theoretically claimed and politically won in the struggle for religious liberty, as the victory was conceived by Madison, his supporters, and associates. Jurisprudentially, such a view underlines the meaning of *limited* free government in America: certain individual rights are beyond the reach of majorities in just governance, and to violate them is tyrannical.

From this perspective, the free exercise clause of the First Amendment has been called the "most philosophically interesting and distinctive feature of the American Constitution ... [because it] represents a new and unprecedented conception of government and its relation to claims of higher truth and authority."[50] How such an argument will fare in the courts remains to be seen. But it asserts a claim readily and rightly linked with the historic lineage of higher law convictions fundamental to the consensus of the American communities that declared independence, fought the American Revolution, and framed the basic instruments of government in the states and nation at the time of the founding.[51]

---

[49] James Madison to Edward Everett, March 19, 1823, in Hunt, ed., *The Writings of James Madison*, 9: 126–27 (spelling, capitalization, and emphasis as in original).

[50] McConnell, "Origins ... of Free Exercise of Religion," 1513.

[51] This large subject is canvassed from related perspectives in Edward S. Corwin, *The "Higher Law" Background of American Constitutional Law* (1928, 1929; rpr. Ithaca: Cornell Univ. Press, 1955); Sandoz, *A Government of Laws*, 163–240; Ralph Ketcham, *Framed for Posterity: The Enduring Philosophy of the Constitution* (Lawrence, Kan.: Univ. Press of

Truth to say, this perspective is far from new or esoteric in American jurisprudence. As one scholar recently stated:

> the framers *were* seeking to promulgate fundamental, higher law, which legislators and judges in later ages would apply to their own, altered circumstances. . . . Unless one accepts the idea that "those who have framed written constitutions contemplate them as forming the fundamental and paramount law of the nation" . . . and also accepts the abiding vitality of the great principles of republicanism, liberty, the public good, and federalism, then the United States can scarcely regard itself as a constitutional polity. . . . What Justice Jackson called "legal principles and . . . fundamental rights," dependent on no majority votes or transient conditions, must be understood as higher law, to be used as enduring standards, if the United States is to be a constitutional polity. The Constitution makes little sense either as mere rules of thumb used to make decisions in an ever-changing world, or as a two-hundred-year-old repository of specific injunctions to resolve current problems. The proper middle ground is to see its persisting principles—republicanism, liberty, the public good, and federalism—as general guides for the present and the future. That is what the judges, if they are truly faithful to "original intent," should say the Constitution is.[52]

Another scholar supplements this argument by identifying *rule of law* itself, as developed in America, with an indispensable appeal to a trans-societal source of justice or higher law:

> The underlying philosophy of American constitutionalism rests not only on a historical jurisprudence, as in England, but also on an implicit theory of natural law. It is presupposed that certain kinds of moral principles, rooted in reason and conscience, have binding legal force. Their basic terms are expressed, to be sure, in written form in a legal document, the Constitution, and thus they are embodied in positive law, but they are ultimately derived (in the words of the Declaration of Independence) from "Nature and Nature's God," and their

---

Kansas, 1993), 6–10, and passim; and Ellis Sandoz, "Foundations of American Liberty and Rule of Law," *Presidential Studies Quarterly* 24 (1994): 607–610. The background in English jurisprudence and constitutional history from the Middle Ages to the American Revolution is explored in Ellis Sandoz, ed., *The Roots of Liberty*, esp. 1–21.

[52] Ketcham, *Framed for Posterity*, 163–64. This is the language of *The Federalist* as well when Publius [Alexander Hamilton] writes:

> A constitution is in fact, and must be, regarded by the judges as a fundamental law. . . . where the will of the legislature declared in its statutes, stands in opposition to that of the people declared in the constitution, the judges ought to be governed by the latter, rather than the former. They ought to regulate their decisions by the fundamental laws, rather than by those which are not fundamental.

Federalist No. 78, Cooke ed., 525.

meaning transcends their written form. This means that they can be consciously and deliberately adapted by the courts to new situations from generation to generation.[53]

There also is to be noticed the massive shift in constitutional law after the mid-1950s known as the "civil rights revolution" whose theoretical foundation and moral fervor lay—beyond mere positive law legalities or, even, express Constitutional provisions—in ancient higher law principles such as those invoked, for example, by Martin Luther King, Jr., in his *Letter from Birmingham Jail*:

> One has not only a legal but a moral responsibility to obey just laws. Conversely, one has a moral responsibility to disobey unjust laws. I would agree with St. Augustine that "an unjust law is no law at all." Now, what is the difference between the two? How does one determine whether a law is just or unjust? A just law is a man-made code that squares with the moral law or the law of God. An unjust law is a code that is out of harmony with the moral law. To put it in terms of St. Thomas Aquinas: An unjust law is a human law that is not rooted in eternal law and natural law. Any law that uplifts human personality is just. Any law that degrades human personality is unjust. All segregation statutes are unjust because segregation distorts the soul and damages the personality.[54]

---

[53] Harold J. Berman, "The Rule of Law and the Law-Based State (*Rechtsstaat*): With Special Reference to the Soviet Union," (1991), rpr. in Donald D. Barry, ed., *Toward the "Rule of Law" in Russia? Political and Legal Reform in the Transition Period* (Armonk, N.Y.: M. E. Sharpe, 1992), 45–46. The higher law appeal as given in the language of the Declaration of Independence also is echoed in *The Federalist* which finds James Madison (as Publius) affirming "the transcendent law of nature and of nature's God, which declares that the safety and happiness of society are the objects at which all political institutions aim, and to which all such institutions must be sacrificed." *Federalist No. 43* in Cooke, ed., *The Federalist*, 297.

[54] Martin Luther King, Jr., *Letter from Birmingham Jail*, April 16, 1963, rpr. in Cherry, ed., *God's New Israel*, 351–52. King's allusions to Augustine and Thomas Aquinas rest on passages in the latter's *Treatise on Law* in *Summa Theologica* pt. 1.2ae, quests. 90–108, esp. quest. 91, art. 2, where Thomas states:

> [A]ll things subject to divine providence are ruled and measured by the eternal law. . . . Now among all others the rational creature [Man] is subject to divine providence in the most excellent way,. . . . Wherefore it has a share of the eternal reason, whereby it has a natural inclination to its proper act and end: and this participation of the eternal law in the rational creature is called the natural law.

Quoted from Dino Bigongiari, ed., *The Political Ideas of St. Thomas Aquinas: Representative Selections* (New York: Hafner Press, 1969), 13. Further, pt. 1.2ae, quest. 95, art. 2:

> As Augustine says, "that which is not just seems to be no law at all" [*De. lib. arb.* i. 5*]; wherefore the force of a [human or positive] law depends on the extent of its justice. Now in human affairs a thing is said to be just from being right according to the rule of reason. But the first rule of reason is the law of nature, as

As policy, the freedom of conscience constitutionally protected under the religion clauses of the First Amendment aims at securing individual liberty, thereby fostering diversity and pluralism in pursuit of truth in the life of the mind and spirit of the people. However, this can only be done within limits imposed by the nature of the system itself and by the consensus of the general public whose security and well-being are the primary concerns of government, unless the Bill of Rights is to incline toward becoming the "suicide pact" Justice Jackson warned of in his *Terminiello* dissent. Such a sense of political moderation runs through American history as a standard that already was stated in the Federal Convention of 1787: "We must follow the example of Solon who gave the Athenians not the best Government he could devise; but the best they would receive."[55] Concretely, this means achieving most of what the Baptists, Presbyterians, Quakers and other dissenting sects intended to achieve when they supplied the political muscle to secure religious liberty in Virginia and elsewhere in the country during the founding: "To them, the freedom to follow religious dogma was one of this nation's foremost blessings, and the willingness of the nation to respect the claims of a higher authority than 'those whose business it is to make laws' was one of the surest signs of its liberality."[56]

---

is clear from what has been stated above (quest. 91, art. 2. ad 2). Consequently, every human law has just so much of the nature of law as it is derived from the law of nature. But if in any point it deflects from the law of nature, it is no longer a law but a perversion of law.

Ibid., 58. Also, pt. 1.2ae, quest. 96, art. 4:

Laws framed by man are either just or unjust. If they be just, they have the power of binding in conscience, from the eternal law whence they are derived, according to Proverbs 8: 15: "By Me kings reign, and lawgivers decree just things." . . . [A]s Augustine says, "A law that is not just, seems to be no law at all." Wherefore such laws do not bind in conscience, except perhaps in order to avoid scandal or disturbance. . . . [A]s stated in Acts 5: 29, "we ought to obey God rather than men."

Ibid., 71–72. For a discussion of the "civil rights revolution" which considers the higher law dimensions see Ellis Sandoz, *Conceived In Liberty: American Individual Rights Today* (North Scituate, Mass.: Duxbury Press, 1978), 222–28; also ibid., 28–30, 39, 49, 51, 56–58. Cf. Thomas C. Grey, "Do We have an Unwritten Constitution?", *Stanford Law Review* 27 (1975): 703; and Thomas C. Grey, "Origins of the Unwritten Constitution: Fundamental Law in American Revolutionary Thought," *Stanford Law Review* 30 (1978): 843.

[55] Madison attributes the statement to Pierce Butler of South Carolina in his *Debates* as given in Max Farrand, ed., *Records of the Federal Convention of 1787* (1911; rev. ed. 1937; rpr. New Haven: Yale Univ. Press, 1966), 1: 125.

[56] McConnell, "Origins . . . of Free Exercise of Religion," *ad fin.*

The overwhelming majority of Americans in the period under discussion, throughout the nineteenth century, and most of the twentieth century have assumed this is a Christian country and expected government to uphold the generally agreed upon Protestant ethos and morality.[57] And this fact lies at the root of some of our current difficulties:

> In many instances, [Americans] had not come to grips with the implications their belief in the powerlessness of government in religious matters held for a society in which the values, customs, and forms of Protestant Christianity thoroughly permeated civil and political life. The contradiction between their theory and their practice became evident . . . with the advent of a more religiously pluralistic society, when it became the subject of disputation that continues into the present.[58]

Conclusion: Problems and Prospects.—What James Madison might think today seems, at first glance, evident enough: truth is great and will triumph— with the help of sound institutions and laws. The historian of the American Enlightenment, however, has doubts. He reflects on the splendid Jeffersonian Moment that found an unlikely coalition of *philosophes*, statesmen, and enthusiasts achieving a work of millennial significance, and then part company. They became separated by a great cultural chasm after 1800

---

[57] The history of this view is concisely sketched from the standpoint of constitutional law and history by Leo Pfeffer, "The Deity in American Constitutional History," in James E. Wood, Jr., ed., *Religion and the State: Essays in Honor of Leo Pfeffer* (Waco, Tex.: Baylor Univ. Press, 1985), 119–144 and summarized as follows:

> From the initial landing of the Pilgrims on these shores, up to the time of the Declaration of Independence, invocation of the Deity in official governmental acts was a practically universal practice. Thereafter it continued and still continues to be acceptable in state constitutions; indeed it is to be found today in almost all state constitutions. Those who wrote and those who adopted our national Constitution and its Bill of Rights, however, made a deliberate determination not to invoke the Deity therein. The Supreme Court, however, for more than a century and half, showed no reticence in invoking the Deity in its own decisions. In the course of this period, however, it expanded the meaning of the term to encompass the nontrinitarian Deity of the Unitarians and Universalists and by using the term "Judeo–Christian," to include the Deity of the Jews. In its most recent relevant decisions it has employed the amorphous and almost boundaryless term "Supreme Being" as that term is interpreted by each individual for himself. Finally, while it will not exercise its judicial power to inhibit invocation of the Deity outside the arena of public education, it will not sanction denial of privileges such as governmental employment to those who deny the existence of a deity.

Ibid., 141–42.

[58] Thomas J. Curry, *The First Freedoms: Church and State in America to the Passage of the First Amendment* (New York: Oxford Univ. Press, 1986), 219.

through the acceleration of the Second Great Awakening in the back country and on the frontier and with the rise of the common man. "For the rest of the century," May writes,

> I think it is fair to say, most Americans believed at the same time that man was a sinner dependent on unmerited grace and that he was endowed with the right and ability to govern himself. Anybody who can understand this paradox . . . can claim to understand . . . America. . . . [It] could never have been predicted, approved, or under[stood] by any prophet of the eighteenth-century Enlightenment.[59]

There is room to worry on other grounds as well. On the one hand the substance of the American solution to religious liberty and prohibition of establishment is one of the triumphs of the constitutional founding. Not least of all, this is because it has served to thwart the worst tendencies of religious zealots to persecute minorities with whom they disagree about ultimate truths. No one who considers the carnage presently being inflicted over Ulster or over Palestine or over the territory of former Yugoslavia, among other hot spots in the world, can doubt the service to peace in America of our constitutional solution to the religion problem. No religion is acceptable in America unless it premises and practices toleration, even against its better judgment!

In addition to this wonderful success, and despite the possibilities for aggressiveness, the American civil theology—especially as it came into play in Manifest Destiny, the abolitionist movement, and the Civil War—has never metastasized as ethnic imperialism such as has engendered soteriological nationalism and ideological totalitarianism in much of the modern world since the French Revolution. Those developments depended upon atomizing the societies down to isolated individuals and, at the same time, eternalizing the nation with the aid of ideology. The fatherland thereby became the Absolute Good into which all other goods are collapsed and submerged. Only in such terms were personal and social identity meaningful.[60] There is, by

---

[59] May, *The Divided Heart*, 177.

[60] For civil theology see Cherry, ed., *God's New Israel*; Joshua Mitchell, *Not by Reason Alone: Religion, History, and Identity in Early Modern Political Thought* (Chicago: Univ. of Chicago Press, 1993); Juergen Gebhardt, *Americanism: Revolutionary Order and Societal Self-Interpretation in the American Republic*, trans. Ruth Hein (Baton Rouge and London: Louisiana State Univ. Press, 1993); Sandoz, *A Government of Laws*, 51–162; and Charles W. Calhoon, "Civil Religion and the Gilded Age Presidency; The Case of Benjamin Harrison," *Presidential Studies Quarterly* 23 (Fall 1993): 651–67, and the literature cited therein. Political messianism generally and soteriological nationalism specifically also has a large literature, including especially: Jacob L. Talmon, *The Origins of Totalitarian Democracy* (New York: Praeger, 1960); Jacob L. Talmon, *Political Messianism: The Romantic Phase* (New York: Praeger, 1960); Jacob L. Talmon, *Myth of the Nation and Vision of Revolution*

contrast, something of an Augustinian quality about the American solution that somewhat paradoxically, to be sure, has kept (and still keeps) apart the spiritual and the secular. This is a true legacy of the distinction drawn between the city of the world and the city of God as transmitted by the dissenting Protestant tradition central to American consciousness.[61] The relationship between society and religion has been symbiotic, ambiguously reciprocal, throughout American history and never, in fact, so absolute as the "wall of separation" metaphor implies.[62]

(London and Berkeley, 1981; rpr. New Brunswick, N. J.: Transaction Publishers, 1993); Norman Cohn, *The Pursuit of the Millennium: Revolutionary Millenarians and Mystical Anarchists of the Middle Ages* (Rev. & Expanded ed., New York: Harper, 1961); Ernst Gellner, *Nations and Nationalism* (London, 1983); and E. J. Hobsbawm, *Nation and Nationalism Since 1780* (Cambridge: Cambridge Univ. Press, 1990); K. R. Minogue, *Nationalism* (New York: Basic Books, 1967); Karl Löwith, *Meaning In History* (Chicago: Univ. of Chicago Press, 1949); Eric Voegelin, *New Science of Politics*, 107–61; Eric Voegelin, *Die politischen Religionen* (1938; rpr., Stockholm: Bermann–Fischer verlag, 1939); and Hannah Arendt, *Origins of Totalitarianism* (New York: Harcourt, Brace, 1951). The discussion herein is indebted to Juergen Gebhardt, "Religion and National Identity," unpublished MS (1994). A general analysis of political nationalism is provided in John Bruilly, *Nationalism and the State*, 2nd Ed. (Chicago and Manchester: Manchester Univ. Press, 1993), esp. 34–72, 382–403.

61 For the distinctions between the city of the world and the city of God see St. Augustine, *City of God*, esp. bks. 11–14; trans. Marcus Dods, intro. Thomas Merton (New York, Modern Library ed., 1950), 345–478. The distinction is commonplace in American sermons at the time of the Revolution. It can be glimpsed in John Witherspoon, *The Dominion of Providence over the Passions of Men* (May 17, 1776) rpr. in E. Sandoz, *Political Sermons of the American Founding Era*, 530–58. Witherspoon was president of the College of New Jersey (later Princeton), the teacher of eight of the fifty-five participants in the Federal Convention of 1787 who had studied there (including James Madison), and as a member of the Continental Congress the only clergyman to sign the Declaration of Independence. See the discussion in Sandoz, *A Government of Laws*, 146n213. In passing, John Gray writes of "the Augustinian vision that inspired the Founding Fathers." Gray, *Beyond the New Right: Markets, Government and the Common Environment* (London and New York: Routledge, 1993), 50. Witherspoon's sermon "was the most widely read Calvinist justification of the Revolution." Robert M. Calhoon, *Dominion and Liberty: Ideology in the Anglo-American World, 1660–1801* (Arlington Heights, Ill.: Harlan Davidson, Inc., 1994), 93.

62 As Dumas Malone explains Jefferson's use of the famous phrase:

His answer to the Danbury Baptist Association of Connecticut [dated Oct. 7, 1801, printed Jan. 1, 1802] was to be quoted long thereafter. In it he declared that by means of the prohibition in the first amendment to the Constitution, a "wall of separation" had been built between church and state. He was seeking to encourage the dissenting minority in Connecticut and to rebuke the politico-religious rulers of the commonwealth. . . . Others besides the Danbury Baptists, seeing in [Jefferson's] past services "a glow of philanthropy and good will shining forth in a course of more than thirty years," believed that God had raised him up to fill the chair of state. His enemies might castigate him as an unbeliever, but the devotion of his followers had a religious fervor.

The moral fervor nourished by Christian faith has marked every crisis faced by the country from the onset of the movement for independence in the 1760s down to World War Two, which took on the character of a crusade against iniquity incarnate; not to forget the Cold War of the past half-century which regularly conjured visions of Armageddon and found the President of the United States as late as 1983 describing the Soviet bloc as "an Evil Empire."[63] Thus, when the Rev. Thomas Coombe in 1775 quaintly exclaimed

---

Malone, *Jefferson the President,* 108–109.

The *"wall of separation"* phrase made its way into constitutional law in Reynolds v. United States, 98 U. S. 145, 164 (1878) and became famous through the dictum in the Establishment Clause case, Everson v. Board of Education, 330 U. S. 1 (1947), when Justice Hugo Black wrote for the majority:

> The "establishment of religion" clause of the First Amendment means at least this: Neither a state nor the Federal Government can set up a church. Neither can pass laws which aid one religion, aid all religions, or prefer one religion over another. Neither can force nor influence a person to go to or remain away from church against his will or force him to profess a belief or disbelief in any religion. No person can be punished for entertaining or professing religious beliefs or disbeliefs, for church attendance or non-attendance. No tax in any amount, large or small, can be levied to support any religious activities or institutions, whatever they may be called, or whatever form they may adopt to teach or practice religion. Neither a state nor the Federal Government can, openly or secretly, participate in the affairs of any religious organizations or groups and vice versa. In the words of Jefferson, the clause against establishment of religion by law was intended to erect "a wall of separation between church and State."

Ibid., 15–16. The Court nevertheless upheld the New Jersey statute challenged that had for its purpose helping school children get to and from school safely, whether public or private. Justice Black added that the First Amendment "requires the state to be a neutral in its relations with groups of religious believers and non-believers; *it does not require the state to be their adversary,*" ibid., 18 (emphasis added). See the analysis in A. E. Dick Howard, "The Wall of Separation: The Supreme Court as Uncertain Stonemason," in Wood, ed., *Religion and the State*, 85–118.

[63] Cf. Dwight David Eisenhower, *Crusade in Europe* (Garden City, N. Y.: Doubleday, 1948); Revelation 16: 14–16; James Burnham, *The War We Are In: The Last Decade and the Next* (New Rochelle, N. Y.: Arlington House, 1967); Barbara Kellerman and Ryan J. Barilleaux, *The President As World Leader* (New York: St. Martin's Press, 1991); "Ronald Reagan's Campaign for Military Superiority," 174–96; President Ronald Reagan, "Remarks at the Annual Convention of the National Association of Evangelicals," Orlando, Florida, March 8, 1983, *The Weekly Compilation of Presidential Documents* 19: 369:

> I urge you to beware of the temptation of pride—the temptation of blithely declaring yourselves above it all and label both sides equally at fault, to ignore the facts of history and the aggressive impulses of an *evil empire*, to simply call the arms race a giant misunderstanding and thereby remove yourself from the struggle between right and wrong and good and evil.

(Emphasis added.) Reagan's entire address is a good specimen of contemporary American civil theology. For an overview of the period of the Cold War from the perspective of

that "patriotism without piety is mere grimace," he unwittingly spoke for all generations to come, with God and country typically invoked in the same breath.[64] Yet a distance was and has been maintained between the two spheres.

In stark contrast, modern soteriological nationalism and ideological totalitarianism arise out of the vacuum of identity created by the "death of God"[65] and collapse of Christianity in Europe so that a substitute is found for social and personal identity solely in the nation, or in the transnational apocalypse of mankind through ideological totalitarianism, or in a conflation of the two: the mystical body of Christ is transmogrified into the mystical body of the nation with its head in some party elite and leader. The careers of such deformations of human reality are at least superficially clear to us from the political adventures of Robespierre, Napoleon, Lenin, Stalin, and Hitler, even when the underlying etiology remains obscure or is carelessly forgotten. Solzhenitsyn's lamentation drives home a central lesson: "The destruction of souls for three-quarters of a century is the most frightening thing."[66]

---

foreign affairs, see Amos Yoder, *The Conduct of American Foreign Policy Since World War II* (New York: Pergamon Press, 1986).

[64] Quoted from Sandoz, *A Government of Laws*, 121.

[65] The "death of God" in the eighteenth century sent many people in search of focusses for collective identity, quite dissociated from the church and the confraternity of Christian believers. Such a substitute was found in the nation. By the mid–nineteenth century

> [what] did those salvationist hopes not promise: the coming of eternal peace, the total unfolding of a self-knowing and self-willing Spirit (or Reason) incarnate, the triumph at last of a genuinely spiritual and authentically social New Christianity, the emancipation of the most numerous and poorest class in a classless society, and . . . —the liberation of all peoples, and the emergence of a brotherhood of regenerated nations.

Talmon, *Myth of the Nation and Vision of Revolution*, 1 and 542. For a philosophical analysis see Eric Voegelin, *Science, Politics and Gnosticism: Two Essays* (1959; Eng. trans., Chicago: H. Regnery Co., 1968):

> The death of God is the cardinal issue of gnosis, both ancient and modern. From Hegel to Nietzsche it is the great theme of gnostic speculation, and Protestant theology has been plagued by it ever since Hegel's time. In recent years, it has been taken up by American theologians who are faced with the pressing phenomena of urbanization and alienation. . . . The struggle against the consequences of gnosticism is being conducted in the very language of gnosticism.

Ibid., vi.; cf. Voegelin, *New Science of Politics*, 107–32: chap. 4, "Gnosticism—The Nature of Modernity."

[66] A. I. Solzhenitsyn, *How Are We to Structure Russia?—A Modest Contribution*, English trans. quoted from *Foreign Broadcast Information Service*, FBIS-SOV-90-187, 26 September 1990, 47.

So, on the other hand, our worry is with the "vacuum of identity," with the "hollow men"[67] and their proliferation through multiple sources of social disintegration, of which questions of free exercise of religion and no establishment are but elements of focus, but important elements. As we have seen, a major difficulty lies in the ostensible "neutrality" in the public schools which in fact often serves to shelter expanding beachheads or safe-havens for anti-religious ideology and attack on American society's moral convictions, radical doctrines ranging from political correctness to advocacy of homosexuality and of neo-Marxism parading as dispassionate science. Such a situation runs counter to any test that might be devised on the basis of community standards of acceptability. In effect, it verges on making the "state" precisely the "adversary" of religious believers in ways not envisaged by James Madison and at least implicitly rejected as incompatible with the Constitution by Justice Hugo Black and the majority of the Supreme Court he spoke for in the *Everson* case.[68] Indeed, one can surmise that Madison would have detected oppression of free conscience in the *de facto* inculcation of principles of various radically secular ideologies (understood to be species of *Ersatz* religion themselves)[69] in public schools under the rubric of religious neutrality. The crisis in public education in the United States is profound enough without this sort of abuse. The matter is likely to attract the public's attention, as is suggested by Congress's enactment in 1993 of the *Religious Freedom Restoration Act*,[70] a straw in the wind.

---

[67] T. S. Eliot's symbol of oblivion and modern man's deformation: "We are the hollow men/ We are the stuffed men/ Leaning together/ Headpiece filled with straw. Alas!" T. S. Eliot, *The Hollow Men* [1925], in Eliot, *The Complete Poems and Plays, 1909–1950* (New York: Harcourt, Brace, & World, 1971), 56.

[68] Everson v. Board of Education, 330 U. S. 1, 18 (quoted in Note 62, supra.) Cf. Stephen L. Carter, *The Culture of Disbelief: How American Law and Politics Trivialize Religious Devotion* (New York: Basic Books, 1993).

[69] For this analysis see Voegelin, "*Ersatz* Religion: The Gnostic Mass Movements of Our Time," in *Science, Politics and Gnosticism*, 81–114:[69]

The term "gnostic mass movements" is not in common use. . . . By gnostic movements we mean such [ideological] movements as progressivism, positivism, Marxism, psychoanalysis, communism, fascism, and national socialism. We are not dealing, therefore, in all of these cases with political mass movements. Some of them would more accurately be characterized as intellectual movements—for example, positivism, neo-positivism, and the variants of psychoanalysis. This draws attention to the fact that mass movements do not represent an autonomous phenomenon and that the difference between masses and intellectual elites is perhaps not so great as is conventionally assumed, if indeed it exists at all. At any rate, in social reality the two types merge.

Ibid., 83–84.

[70] Public Law 103–141. For the text of this statute in pertinent part see Note 13, supra.

Especially because of the rise of statism and of the expansive American positive administrative state, with more and more government at all levels—municipal, state, and national—there looms a related set of *potential* issues whose mention verges on thinking about the unthinkable.[71] To the degree

---

[71] Daniel J. Elazar writes: "This trend has often been viewed as a simple expansion of federal power at the expense of the states. In reality, it has meant an expansion of the realm of activities of both federal and state governments to generate an increase in the velocity of government (that is, the amount of governmental activity in relation to the total activity of society) in the nation as a whole." Elazar, *American Federalism: A View from the States*, 2nd ed. (New York: Crowell, 1972), 50. Elsewhere Elazar writes:

> Until very recently, the overall thrust of the twentieth century was toward centralization of power in most political systems, whether federal in character or not. . . . Beginning in the late 1960s, however, contrary tendencies began to be noted.

> For more than three hundred years—at least since the beginning of the modern epoch—almost the entire effort of European civilization, as well as that of those people and countries that were influenced by European civilization, has been directed to building reified, centralized, sovereign states that force the people in their respective territories into the procrustean bed of a single government. In other words, their goal has been one people, one government, and one territory.
> . . .
> The results of this situation have been challenged in the postmodern era. . . . One major characteristic of the postmodern era is the ethnic revival. . . . This development is reflected politically in the worldwide movement from class-based to ethnic-based politics.
> A greater immediate problem is the bureaucratic revolution that has engulfed us all. We have now reached a point at which bureaucracies are not simply instruments of service to other elements in the society but have become self-generating. They create their own tasks. . . . If we use our political structures to prevent the coalescence of bureaucracy, we may have a fighting chance. The movement away from understanding federalism as a political-constitutional device to looking at it as an administrative device—as a matter of intergovernmental relations—makes it easier for bureaucracies to manage the polity rather than vice versa. . . . In sum, the question is whether they rule us or we rule them. That is the struggle before us.

Daniel J. Elazar, *Exploring Federalism* (Tuscaloosa, Ala.: Univ. of Alabama Press, 1987), 201, 223–24, 264. Justice Robert H. Jackson pointed up one aspect of the problem by writing: "The rise of administrative bodies probably has been the most significant legal trend of the last century. . . . They have become a veritable fourth branch of Government, which has deranged our three-branch legal theories." Federal Trade Commission v. Ruberoid Co., 343 U. S. 470, 487 (1952) (Jackson, J. dissenting); cited in Immigration and Naturalization Service v. Chadha, 462 U. S.919, 985 (1983) (White, J. dissenting).

> For some time, the sheer amount of law—the substantive rules that regulate private conduct and direct the operations of government—made by the agencies has far outnumbered the lawmaking engaged in by Congress through the traditional process. There is no question but that agency rulemaking is lawmaking in any functional or realistic sense of the term.

that pseudo-science and radical privatization of traditional religion tend to disparage faith as merely subjective, irrational surmising, a matter of no more than personal "value-choices" (as positivists insist) without any objective validity—thus as scientifically unworthy and publicly irrelevant to education and to concerns that count in social existence—the crisis of identity is exacerbated. That the vacuum will be filled we have no doubt from familiar recent history. The experiential appeal to transcendent divine reality that underlies the Anglo-American higher law tradition and is the substance of Judeo-Christian faith becomes increasingly vulnerable. Indeed, such an appeal seems already to be a dead letter in much of the West, so this is hardly a far-fetched notion. It can be rooted out of public discourse, of language, and, consciousness itself, denigrated and effectively excluded so as to widen the gulf of estrangement between the exercise of religion and socially approved activities of public life. To the degree that this occurs, major disruption of the fragile processes forming individual character tends to dissolve personalities through conditioning into the emptiness of hollow men in a mass society increasingly bereft of effective competing authority centers which might be capable of countering the slide into ideological unreality. Just around the corner in this process of deculturation lie the deformations of human existence associated with the autonomous Man of atheistic humanism, a familiar figure whose twentieth century reign in Germany and Russia created an historically unprecedented chamber of horrors.[72] With this massive range of *empirical* evidence before us, shall we through inattention perhaps partly induced by our euphoria that the Cold War now is "over" invite some sort of repetition? Those who understand best, among them Václav Havel and his fellow countrymen, can tell us something about "*Real Socialism*," for instance.[73] Professor McConnell's nightmarish apparition of Nietzschean America begins to take on unanticipated plausibility.[74]

Ibid.

[72] Cf. Henri de Lubac, *The Drama of Atheist Humanism*, trans. E. M. Riley (London: Sheed & Ward, 1949). This important theme affirming higher Reality, and rejecting the notion of the autonomous Self or autonomous Man emblematic of egophanic revolt of which Nietzsche's is a variety, is common to Václav Havel, Aleksandr Solzhenitsyn, and Eric Voegelin as well. See Václav Havel, *Disturbing the Peace: A Conversation with Karel Hvízdala*, trans. Paul Wilson (New York: Knopf, 1990); Aleksandr I. Solzhenitsyn, *A World Split Apart* in *East and West* (New York: Harper & Row, 1980), 69–71; Eric Voegelin, *The Ecumenic Age* (Baton Rouge: Louisiana State Univ., 1974), vol. 4, *Order and History*, 4: 260–71: "The Egophanic Revolt." For analysis see Ellis Sandoz, "The Politics of Poetry," *Modern Age* 34 (Fall 1991): 16–23.

[73]

The advanced totalitarian system depends on manipulative devices so refined, complex, and powerful that it no longer needs murderers and victims. Even less does it need fiery Utopia builders spreading discontent with dreams of a better

The founders, for their part, were clear on the point: no good institutions without good human beings first. One famous political scientist summarized the message of his edition of *The Federalist Papers* in these words: "no happiness without liberty, no liberty without self-government, no self-government without constitutionalism, no constitutionalism without morality—and none of these great goods without stability and order."[75] The founders had added (Professor Rossiter neglects to tell us), "that there can be no morality without religion."[76] George Washington's valedictory to the

---

future. The epithet "Real Socialism," which this era has coined to describe itself, points a finger at those for whom it has no room: the dreamers.

Václav Havel, "Stories and Totalitarianism" (April 1989) in Havel, *Open Letters: Selected Writings 1965–1990*, ed. Paul Wilson (New York: Vintage Books, 1992), 332. The counterpoint won by the Czech dissidents from their oppression was expressed by their leading philosopher, Jan Patocka, a few weeks before he died under police interrogation:

> The idea of human rights is nothing other than the conviction that even states, even society as a whole, are subject to the sovereignty of moral sentiment: that they recognize something unconditional that is higher than they are, something that is binding even on them, sacred, inviolable, and that in their power to establish and maintain a rule of law they seek to express this recognition.

Jan Patocka, "The Obligation to Resist Injustice," in Patocka, *Philosophy and Selected Writings*, ed. Erazin Kohák (Chicago: Univ. of Chicago Press, 1989), 341. Cf. the discussion of "'really existing socialism'" in the incisive study by Sir Ralf Dahrendorf, *Reflections on the Revolution in Europe* (New York: Times Books, 1990), 44, "Nomenklatura socialism," 49, 67; ". . . the point has to be made unequivocally that socialism is dead, and that none of its variants can be revived for a world awakening from the double nightmare of Stalinism and Brezhnevism" (42); "Socialism was an intellectual invention, from Saint-Simon to Lassalle, from Marx to Gramsci, and through the hundreds of byways of Marxism that are now all ending in the sewers of discarded history" (73).

74 Michael W. McConnell, "'God Is Dead and We Have Killed Him!'," 163, 188.

75 Rossiter, ed., *The Federalist Papers*, xvi.

76 Writing in 1789, Dr. David Ramsay's words are: "Remember that there can be no political happiness without liberty; that there can be no liberty without morality; and that there can be no morality without religion." Ramsay, *History of the American Revolution*, 2: 667. The conviction of the nation's dependence upon divine Providence for its happiness is symbolically expressed on the reverse of the Great Seal of the United States (which dates from June, 1782, and now is most readily seen printed on the back of the one dollar bill in U. S. currency):

> The pyramid signifies Strength and Duration: The Eye over it and the motto [*Annuit Coeptis*: It (Providence) is Favorable to Our Undertakings] allude to the many signal interpositions of providence in favour of the American cause. The date underneath [MDCCLXXVI] is that of the Declaration of Independence and the words [*Novus Ordo Seclorum*: A New Order of Centuries] under it signify the beginning of the New American Era, which commences from that date.

country in 1796, his *Farewell Address*, resonates into the present on the very point:

> Of all the dispositions and habits which lead to political prosperity, Religion and morality are indispensable supports. In vain would that man claim the tribute of Patriotism, who should labour to subvert these great Pillars of human happiness, these firmest props of the duties of Men and citizens. . . . [W]here is the security for property, for reputation, for life, if the sense of religious obligation *desert* the oaths, which are the instruments of investigation in Courts of Justice? And let us with caution indulge the supposition, that morality can be maintained without religion. Whatever may be conceded to the influence of refined education on minds of peculiar structure, reason and experience both forbid us to expect that National morality can prevail in exclusion of religious principle. 'Tis substantially true, that virtue or morality is a necessary spring of popular government. The rule indeed extends with more or less force to every species of free Government. Who that is a sincere friend to it, can look with indifference upon attempts to shake the foundation of the fabric?[77]

It may be important to add that these convictions of George Washington and other of the founders are solidly affirmed by a leading legal scholar who lately wrote as follows:

> I start from the fact that every legal order requires for its vitality the support of a belief-system which links law not only with morality but also with fundamental convictions about human nature and human destiny. . . . In all societies religion and law, in the broad sense of those words, are interdependent and interact with each other. In all societies there are shared beliefs in transcendent values, shared commitments to an ultimate purpose, a shared sense of the holy: certain things are sacred. And in all societies, there are structures and processes of social ordering, established methods of allocating rights and duties, a shared sense of the just: certain things are lawful. The prophetic and mystical sides of religion challenge, and are challenged by, the structural and rational sides of law. Yet the two are interdependent: each is also a dimension of the other.[78]

The *virtue* of the people, *The Federalist* teaches, is the *primary* reliance in republican government, and such virtue is rooted in individual personalities

---

Gaillard Hunt's 1892 paper on the seal as quoted from Eugene Zieber, *Heraldry in America*, 2nd. ed. (Philadelphia: Dept. of Heraldry of the Bailey, Banks and Biddle Co., 1909), 103; also 101–102, where the history and authoritative translations of the mottos and their likely sources in Virgil are given.

[77] George Washington, *Farewell Address*, September 19, 1796, in William B. Allen, ed., *George Washington: A Collection* (Indianapolis: Liberty Classics, 1988), 521–22 (emphasis and capitalization as in original.) James Madison, Alexander Hamilton, and John Jay assisted in the preparation of this famous speech by our first president, ibid., 444.

[78] Harold J. Berman, "Law and Logos," *DePaul Law Review* 44 (1994): 143, 158–59.

of character and intelligence. Even so, while *necessary* human virtue is never *sufficient* of itself. The auxiliary precautions of sound institutions and adversarial checking are dictated by prudence and experience, the genius of the American system. As Publius remarks; "Had every Athenian citizen been a Socrates; every Athenian assembly would still have been a mob."[79] If, then, we acknowledge the institutions to be generally sound and sufficiently adaptable—a millennial achievement, one admirable in the history of civilization—the compelling questions remaining pertain to the substance of the human beings who will conduct the affairs of society: *Whence the requisite virtue?* And what of the American community itself as a force in history? If America historically has been above all an idea, a state of mind—one constituted by and consciously consecrating liberty on the pattern found self-evidently and abidingly *true* in the Declaration of Independence taken as a symbol, standard, and rallying point—*how will American truth fare during the next two hundred years?*

---

[79] *Federalist No. 55*, in Cooke,ed., *The Federalist*, 374; cf. *Federalist No. 51*, ibid. 349:

[W]hat is government itself but the greatest of all reflections on human nature? . . . A dependence on the people is no doubt the primary controul on the government; but experience has taught mankind the necessity of auxiliary precautions. This policy of supplying by opposite and rival interests, the defect of better motives, might be traced through the whole system of human affairs, private as well as public. . . . These inventions of prudence cannot be less requisite in the distribution of the supreme powers of the state.

Elsewhere in *Federalist No. 55*:

As there is a degree of depravity in mankind which requires a certain degree of circumspection and distrust: So there are other qualities in human nature, which justify a certain portion of esteem and confidence. Republican government presupposes the existence of these qualities in a higher degree than any other form. Were the pictures which have been drawn by the political jealousy of some among us, faithful likenesses of the human character, the inference would be that there is not sufficient virtue among men for self-government; and that nothing less than the chains of despotism can restrain them from destroying and devouring one another.

Ibid., 378.

— ❧ 10 ☙ —

THE ACCOMMODATION OF RELIGION:
A TOCQUEVILLIAN PERSPECTIVE

*Thomas L. Pangle**

There is perhaps no respect in which recent American and Canadian constitutional traditions differ so profoundly as in their posture toward the establishment of religion, or, more broadly expressed, the proper separation of church and state. And one can hardly imagine a more fundamental constitutional issue. Religion is that sphere of life in which human beings, as individuals and as societies, attempt to come to terms with the ultimate questions of existence, through the worship of, obedience to, and rumination upon divinity and the afterlife or eternity. It is difficult to avoid the conclusion that it is in its posture toward religion that a nation most fully and clearly defines itself.

Now a leading and well-known feature of the American Bill of Rights is the First Amendment prohibition on establishment of religion. That prohibition is stated in remarkably ambiguous language: "Congress shall make no law respecting an establishment of religion." The history and intended meaning of this sentence, and especially of the words "respecting" and "establishment," remain highly controversial and to some extent

---

* Professor of Political Science, University of Toronto. A.B. Cornell University (1968); Ph.D. University of Chicago (1993). An earlier version of this chapter was included in Marian C. McKenna, ed., *The Canadian and American Constitutions in Comparative Perspective* (Calgary: University of Calgary Press, 1993), and is reprinted herein with permission.

conjectural. It is plain from the evidence available to us that many of those in the First Congress who voted for these words did not for a moment intend them to outlaw existing, generally rather modest, forms of established religion in the various states; indeed, a plausible argument has been made that most Congressmen intended the language to *protect* the established religions in the states.[1] But what we may fairly term the "extreme left" on the establishment issue at the time of the Founding (Madison and Jefferson) has in the twentieth century carried the day. The Supreme Court, beginning with *Everson v. Board of Education* (1947), has read into the establishment clause Jefferson's "wall of separation between church and state."[2] In order to read this "wall" into the establishment clause, the Court has had to ignore much of what was said in the debates in the House of Representatives over the intended meaning of the First Amendment (15, 17, and 20 August 1789); in addition, the Court has had to pass over the explicit governmental support for religious education voted in the reenactment of the Northwest Ordinance by the same Congress that passed the Bill of Rights.[3] The Court has on the whole refused to be guided by George Washington's authoritative pronouncements, not only in his Farewell Address, but in his early Presidential Proclamation of 3 October 1789: "It is the duty of all nations to

---

[1] Michael Malbin, *Religion and the First Amendment: The Intentions of the Authors of the First Amendment* (Washington: American Enterprise Institute, 1978); see also Walter Berns, *The First Amendment and the Future of American Democracy* (New York: Basic Books, 1976), chap. 1. The crucial sections of the Congressional debates are to be found in *Annals of the Congress of the United States; 1789–1824,* (Washington, D.C.: Gales and Seaton, 1834–56), 1: 729-31, 755, 766 (hereinafter *Annals of Congress*). Especially revealing are the remarks of Congressmen Sylvester and Huntington as well as Madison on 15 August 1789.

[2] Everson v. Board of Education, 330 U. S. 1 (1947); on state aid to church schools, see also Lemon v. Kurtzman, 403 U. S. 602 (1971), and the opinions on both sides of the decision in Tilton v. Richardson, 403 U. S. 672 (1971); on the issue of the constitutionality of released time from public schooling for attending church classes, see Illinois ex rel. McCollum v. Board of Education, 333 U. S. 203 (1948), which seems to be at some tension with Zorach v. Clauson, 343 U. S. 306 (1952). On the unconstitutionality of school prayers, see Engel v. Vitale, 370 U. S. 421 (1962); on the unconstitutionality of Bible readings in school, see Abington School District v. Schempp, 374 U. S. 203 (1963). The "wall of separation" phrase comes from Jefferson's letter to the Danbury Baptist Association, 1 January 1802, in A. Lipscomb and A. Bergh, eds., *The Writings of Thomas Jefferson* (Washington: Thomas Jefferson Memorial Association, 1905), 16: 281.

[3] The text of the Northwest Ordinance may be found in Charles C. Tansill, ed., *Documents Illustrative of the Formation of the Union of the American States,* 69th Congress, 1st session, House Document No. 398 (Washington, D.C.: GPO, 1927), 47–54; see Art. 3: "religion, morality, and knowledge being necessary to good government and the happiness of mankind, schools and the means of education shall forever be encouraged."

acknowledge the providence of Almighty God, to obey His will, to be grateful for His benefits, and humbly to implore His protection and favor."[4]

The Court has preferred to be guided by the "Memorial and Remonstrance" of 1785, in which Madison (supported by Jefferson) attacked a bill proposed in the Virginia legislature (supported by John Marshall, George Washington, and Patrick Henry, among others) that would have provided state funds to support "Teachers of the Christian Religion."[5] The same Madison later castigated as unconstitutional the appointment of Congressional chaplains, and voiced his disapproval of the Thanksgiving holiday proclamations, tax exemption for churches, and the appointment of chaplains for the armed services.[6] Perhaps most revealing of all, Madison as President vetoed on constitutional grounds a bill incorporating the Episcopal Church in the District of Columbia, in part because the bill empowered the church to educate poor children.[7] In accordance with the Madisonian line, the United States Supreme Court has in the last two generations looked with grave reserve on any form of state aid for parochial schooling, and on any intrusion of "religious activity" into public schools.

In sharp contrast, the Canadian constitutional tradition, lacking of course an "establishment clause," has always made a legitimate place for state-supported and approved denominational schools. Moreover, the Canadian head of state remains the English monarch, who is entitled "Defender of the Faith." Most striking of all, the present Canadian constitution begins from the premise that "Canada is founded upon principles that recognize the supremacy of God." The American Constitution, of course, makes no reference whatsoever to such principles or to such a "supremacy." The American Constitution begins, not with a reference to God, but with a reference to "We the People" as supremely authoritative. On the other hand, throughout most of its history, and indeed until our lifetime, the American constitutional and political ethos remained much closer to the Canadian, as was somewhat reluctantly acknowledged by justice Douglas, speaking for the Court in *Zorach v. Clauson*: "We are a religious people whose institutions

---

[4] James D. Richardson, comp., *A Compilation of the Messages and Papers of the Presidents, 1789-1897*, (Washington, D.C.: GPO, 1896–99), 1: 64. See also Madison's very pious Presidential proclamation of 16 November 1814, ibid., 1: 558.

[5] The text and historical background may be found in Marvin Meyers, ed., *The Mind of the Founder* (Indianapolis: Bobbs-Merrill, 1973), 8–16.

[6] Madison to Edward Livingston, 10 July 1822, in G. Hune, ed., *The Writings of James Madison*, (New York: G.P. Putnam's Sons, 1900–1910), 9: 100–103; Madison, "Detached Memoranda ca. 1817," *William and Mary Quarterly*, 3d series, 3 (1946): 554–60.

[7] The veto message, and the fierce debate it stirred in Congress as to the intended meaning of the establishment clause, may be found in *Annals of Congress* 22: 982–87 (21 and 23 February 1811).

presuppose a Supreme Being." But in the last two generations, especially at the level of the legal elite, the traditional American ethos, lacking any explicit grounding in the text of the Constitution, has eroded, not to say evaporated. When leading legal scholars today speak of "Constitutional Faith," they have in mind postmodernist Heideggerianism or Rortyism, not the faith of the Founding Fathers.[8]

We must hasten to add that the predominant view we have just limned, in each country, is now under challenge. In Canada, there is a strong tendency amongst the legal elite to adopt or adapt what is presumed to be the superior American consensus in almost all aspects of legal theory; and this tendency is likely to become steadily more evident in the legal elite's posture toward church-state relations. At the same time, the recent American consensus, at least as regards the establishment clause, is being increasingly shaken by a minority of scholars, judges and activists who doubt both the civic wisdom and the historical or legal legitimacy of the Madisonian-Jeffersonian doctrine.

In this situation of flux and reconsideration of fundamentals, we are prodded to ruminate, in the broadest possible context, on the relative merits of these two rather different contemporary constitutional attitudes toward the proper relation between church and state. I propose to contribute to this rumination by viewing the question from what I believe to be a most illuminating vantage point, transcending both the American and the Canadian perspectives: the vantage point afforded by Tocqueville's democratic theory. It is not my purpose to investigate which of the two contemporary constitutional outlooks Tocqueville would favor were he to be resurrected—though I am inclined to surmise he would prefer the Canadian. My aim is rather to enrich our understanding of what it is we should be thinking about, what it is we should see to be at stake, when we consider the merits and demerits of these two contrasting constitutional postures toward religion.

The Basic Issues.—Tocqueville's meditation on the relation between religion and politics in modern democracy prompts, and helps us to come to grips with, the most important question which must be addressed in any thorough consideration of the relation: why are religious liberty, and the separation of church and state, good? Or to put the question another way, what ends ought we to have in view as we formulate, interpret, and

---

[8] See Sanford Levinson, *Constitutional Faith* (Princeton: Princeton University Press, 1988), and my discussion in *The Ennobling of Democracy: The Challenge of the Postmodern Era* (Baltimore: Johns Hopkins University Press, 1992).

administer laws and policies that foster and that limit religious liberty and the separation of church and state? Tocqueville thus allows us to shake free of the complacent illusion that separation of church and state, and religious liberty, may be treated as ends in themselves. He compels us to seek the more fundamental, principled basis for our attachment to religious liberty.

In the societies with which we and Tocqueville are most immediately concerned, religion means principally the Christian religion (Protestant and Roman Catholic), and secondarily the Judaic religion. While these religions conflict in important secondary teachings, they agree on still more important fundamentals: it suffices to mention the Ten Commandments, the commandments to love God and to love one's neighbor, and the afterlife in which judgment is rendered which sanctions these commandments. Every individual and every society must take a stand, one way or another, implicitly if not explicitly, toward these or kindred claims of religion to afford the decisive, authoritative guidance for life. We may then say, at the cost of leaving in the background many sorts of ambiguous compromise positions, but in order to clarify the basic issues, that religious liberty is supported, and defined or interpreted by its supporters, with a view either to: a) the opinion that such liberty, properly defined, will maintain or strengthen a certain degree of religious authority, which is seen as a good thing; or b) the opinion that such liberty will check or weaken religious authority, which is seen as a bad thing. The converse reasons are in play when religious liberty is opposed.

The Cause of Religious Liberty in the French Revolution.—In his study of the French Revolution as it emerged out of the "Old Regime," Tocqueville analyzes a great political and intellectual movement which espoused religious liberty, the disestablishment of religion, and the separation of church and state in the name of the destruction of religion. The "philosophy of the eighteenth century," which was "one of the principal causes of the Revolution," was "profoundly irreligious"; "the philosophers of the eighteenth century opposed the church with a sort of fury; they attacked its clergy, its hierarchy, its institutions, its dogmas, and, so as to better overthrow these, they wished to rip up the very foundations of Christianity."[9] A few "searching and intrepid geniuses," carrying to an extreme the "examining spirit" induced by the Reformation, came to the conclusion that "not just some, but all" the Christian traditions were false: "the same spirit which, at the time of Luther, made several million Catholics leave

---

[9] Alexis de Tocqueville, *L'Ancien regime et la revolution*, ed. J.-P. Mayer (Paris: Gailimard, 1967; revised ed. 1984), bk. 1, chap. 2, 63. Subsequent references will be to this edition; all translations are my own.

Catholicism, pushed several isolated Christians each year out of Christianity itself."[10] But unlike their freethinking philosophic ancestors, the philosophers who accepted the premises of the modern Enlightenment did not remain "isolated." They spread their skepticism among masses of revolutionary followers with whom they appeared to share "a sort of new religion": a "faith" in the "perfectibility" and the "power" of mankind guiding itself by individual, autonomous reason.[11] The church "leaned principally on tradition," while the revolutionary writers "professed a great contempt for all institutions which founded themselves on respect for the past"; the church "recognized an authority superior to the individual reason," while the promoters of the revolution "appealed to nothing but that reason itself.[12]

The philosophers of the Enlightenment opposed religion not only because they thought it to be false, but thought life guided by scientific truth to be precious for mankind at large, as well as for individual philosophers. They launched an attack on all existing political institutions in the name of more specific new doctrines of justice, including "the natural equality of men; the consequent abolition of all the privileges of castes, classes, professions; the sovereignty of the people; the onmipotence of the social power; the uniformity of rules, etc."[13] They saw the Christian church and its doctrines to be diametrically opposed to these new conceptions of justice. The church "founded itself on a hierarchy," but the new way of thinking "tended toward the confusion of ranks."[14]

> In order to come to terms with one another, there would have been required on both sides a recognition that political society and religious society, being by nature essentially different, cannot govern themselves by similar principles; but at that time they were far from such recognition, and it appeared that, in order to mount the attack on the institutions of the state, it was necessary to destroy those of the church, which served the former as foundation and model.[15]

Besides, the church "was itself then the first of political powers, and the most detested of all, even though it was not the most oppressive."[16]

Last but not least, the *philosophes* confronted in the church "precisely that part of the government that was the closest and the most directly opposed to them." The church, "being specially charged with surveillance over thought

---

[10] Ibid., bk. 3, chap. 2, 242

[11] Ibid., 251.

[12] Ibid., 245.

[13] Ibid., bk. 1, chap. 2, 63.

[14] Ibid., bk. 3, chap. 2, 245

[15] Ibid.

[16] Ibid., 245–46.

and censorship of writings, troubled them every day."[17] The philosophers of the French Enlightenment championed religious liberty against church authority as part of their crusade against censorship in all its forms. They were convinced that censorship, even of the limited sort that prevailed in France prior to the Revolution, was a grave obstacle to radical, independent writing and speaking, which they identified as the core of "the general liberties of the human spirit."[18]

Now Tocqueville argues that the *philosophes* were wrong in almost every aspect of this understanding of the relation between religion and democracy, and hence in their understanding of the value of religious liberty. Their errors come into sight, according to Tocqueville, not only in the subsequent history of the French Revolution and its aftermath, but even more clearly when one undertakes a comparative study of democracy as it has emerged in America, in contrast to the democratic movement as it emerged in France.

To begin with, religious liberty understood as entailing the abolition of censorship, does not in fact promote radical and independent writing as well as does a censorship of the sort that prevailed in France prior to the Revolution. Those who, like Tocqueville himself, espouse religious liberty entailing the abolition of censorship must resign themselves to this melancholy truth. The constriction of true religious, political, literary, and philosophic diversity and the diminution of radical independence of thought are severe costs of such religious liberty. The historical evidence proves that true intrepidity of thought and boldness of expression flourish where a limited degree of repression challenges and tests intellectual courage:

> There are times when the oppression of writers can arrest the movement of thought, others when it animates that movement; but it has never been the case that a sort of policing such as that which was exercised in the eighteenth century has not multiplied a hundredfold the power of thought.

The authors of the eighteenth century "suffered that species of check which animates the struggle, and not the heavy yoke that breaks it." Tocqueville appeals here to the authority of David Hume, who astonished Diderot by writing him in 1768 to the effect that French intolerance "was more favorable to the progress of the spirit" than the liberty of the English: "The Scotchman was right. Inhabiting a free country, he had experience; Diderot judged the thing as an intellectual, Hume judged it as a political man."[19]

---

[17] Ibid., 246.

[18] Ibid.

[19] Ibid., 247–48. One may analogously compare the relative vitality of literary and spiritual life behind the Iron Curtain in the last twenty years and in the Free World; as

The utter failure of the French intellectuals to understand the relation between freedom of the spirit and toleration, especially the toleration characteristic of modern democratic society, is for Tocqueville the most acute symptom of their general failure to understand the specific dangers to freedom and spirituality presented by modern democracy. Only if one grasps those dangers with full clarity will one begin to think hard and seriously about remedies or ameliorations, and only then will one begin to appreciate the enormous value religious faith and authority have for modern democracy. At that point, Tocqueville teaches, one is in a position to recognize that religious liberty can and must be properly conceived as the means to the strengthening, within modern democracy, of politically responsible religious authority.

The Dangers of Democracy as Seen in America.—Tocqueville identifies the "tyranny of the majority" as the gravest threat to the human spirit in the age of democracy. Majority rule is basic to democracy.[20] Majority domination is directly entailed in the fundamental democratic principles of equality and individual liberty: one man, one vote. But human beings hardly become more wise or virtuous simply by being gathered together in large groupings, or by discovering their collective political power. A majority can be at least as oppressive as any individual or minority. In a democracy, majoritarianism is therefore desperately in need of a moral education that humbles majority arrogance. In democracies, the dominant majority needs to be taught or induced to listen to, and even in some measure to respect, dissenting minorities or individuals. But education is not a sufficiently reliable limit on democratic majoritarianism. The majority also needs social, political, and

---

Itato Calvino concluded, in a comparison of the life of the mind in Eastern and Western Europe, "this is the paradox of the power of literature: it seems that only when it is persecuted does it show its true powers, challenging authority, whereas in our permissive society it feels that it is being used merely to create the pleasing contrast to the general ballooning of verbiage"; or as Philip Roth put it after returning from eastern Europe in the 1980s, "in my situation, everything goes and nothing matters; in their situation, nothing goes and everything matters" (both authors quoted in *New York Times,* 8 February 1990, B1). Isaiah Berlin observed more generally that "integrity, love of truth, and fiery individualism grow at least as often in severely disciplined communities or under military discipline, as in more tolerant or indifferent societies": see *Two Concepts of Liberty* (Oxford: Oxford University Press, 1958), 13–15 and 48.

[20] Alexis de Tocqueville, *De la Democratie en Amerique,* ed. J.-P. Mayer (Paris: Gallimard, 1951), vol. 1, pt. 2, chap. 7. In quotations, I have used the translation by George Lawrence, edited by J.-P. Mayer (Garden City, N.Y.: Doubleday Anchor, 1969), frequently altering the translation to make it more literal; specific page references will be to this translation, to be cited as *Democracy in America.*

economic competitors, whose power is not dependent on winning majority approval.

It is not easy to see where such education and such competition may come from in modern democracy. Citing the authority of Madison and Jefferson, Tocqueville expresses grave doubts as to whether the chiefly institutional checks and balances in the American Constitution effectively limit majoritarian tyranny at the political level.[21] The first volume of *Democracy in America* develops a complex and subtle diagnosis of the majoritarian ills of the democratic political process in America. Yet the most serious danger lies at a deeper level. The worst and fullest tyranny to which mankind tends to be enslaved is the tyranny over the mind, the tyranny over opinion, and above all the tyranny over *moral* opinion, opinion as to what is right and wrong. It is the *moral authority* of the majority in democracies that is most inescapable and overwhelming. The symptoms, in America, of this tyranny Tocqueville vividly describes in part 2, volume 1 *of Democracy in America* (chapter 7, in the section titled "The Power Exercised by the Majority in America Over Thought"). But I believe that he succeeds in fully plumbing the psychological roots and mechanism of democratic slavery only in his analysis of intellectual life in part 1, volume 2 of *Democracy in America.*

Tocqueville begins from the observation that the modern democratic spirit exemplified in America is decisively formed by a popularized, individualistic, and materialistic or down-to-earth philosophic outlook that is profoundly skeptical towards all authority, be it traditional or contemporary. This rationalist doubt of authority, though genuine and thoroughgoing in the hands of the rare geniuses who spawned it (e.g., Descartes and Bacon), became inevitably vulgarized as it was translated by the eighteenth century Enlightenment into a mass phenomenon. In modern democracy, the egalitarian rejection of authority is itself a new, authoritative moralism in disguise—and hence all the more insidious in its despotism. Americans are indoctrinated from early youth with the dogmas that they have a moral duty to think for themselves, that their dignity consists in their regarding themselves as intellectually equal individuals, and that they ought to be ashamed at appearing to bow to anyone's authority. Americans are certainly not taught to think skeptically about the social commitment to intellectual autonomy, or to examine the great premodern philosophic arguments against such a commitment. They are not induced to comprehend sympathetically the great virtues of, and arguments for, premodern, hierarchic, and more authoritarian societies. More generally, inhabitants of modern democracy

---

[21] Ibid., 260–61: Tocqueville quotes Madison's *The Federalist,* No. 51 and Jefferson's letter to Madison of 15 March 1789.

tend not to understand democracy because they have no firm comparative basis for critical moral self-assessment. Even the intellectual elites of modern democracy simply assume, without demonstration or even argument, that democracy is superior and aristocracy inferior. Modern democrats tend to be deplorably ignorant of the distinctive virtues and vices, the characteristic strengths and weaknesses, the peculiar forms of freedom and slavery, that define, respectively, democratic and aristocratic societies. As a result of this massive moral prejudice, citizens of democracy tend to be woefully unaware of the herdlike limits on their pretended independence of opinion.

For the fact is, Tocqueville insists, that there is no such thing as a non-authoritarian society. "It can never happen that there are no dogmatic beliefs, that is to say, opinions which men take on trust and without discussion," because "without ideas in common, there is no common action, and, without common action, there may still exist human beings, but not a social entity."[22] The "spirits of all the citizens" have to be "held together by certain leading ideas." The question, then, "is not to ascertain whether there exists an intellectual authority in the democratic centuries, but only where it is lodged and what its limits are." In *aristocratic* ages, people are "naturally inclined to take as the guide for their opinions the superior reason of a man or a class, while they are very little disposed to recognize any infallibility in the mass of men." Precisely "the contrary holds in centuries of equality." The "disposition to believe in the mass of men augments, and it is more and more public opinion that rules the world." When the person who inhabits democratic countries compares himself to all those who surround him, "he feels with pride that he is equal to each of them"; but, "when he comes to contemplate the *collectivity* of his fellows, and to place himself alongside this great body, he is overwhelmed by his own insignificance and weakness." In other words, "the *same* equality that renders him independent of each of his fellow citizens taken one by one leaves him isolated and defenseless in the face of the majority." "The public therefore," Tocqueville concludes, "has among democratic peoples a singular power, of which the aristocratic nations could not conceive."

Democratic public opinion does not typically achieve its sway by persuasion, but rather by a kind of moral imposition, "an immense pressure of the spirit of all on the intelligence of each." Public opinion holds sway in such a way as to dampen and even to morally condemn daring dissent. The tolerance of democratic public opinion exhibits an unhealthy, despotically egalitarian proclivity to degenerate, first, into the easygoing belief that all

---

[22] Quotations in this paragraph are taken from *Democracy in America*, vol. 2, pt. 1, chap. 2, "On the Principal Source of Beliefs Among Democratic Peoples."

points of view are equally valid (or invalid)—and hence none is in need of searching critical argument or stalwart defense;[23] and then further into the strident belief that anyone who does insist on making judgments about others, or who argues passionately for the superiority of specific character traits, ways of life, conceptions of human nature and justice, etc., is somehow (as we hear nowadays) "exclusivist," "elitist," "intolerant," "antidemocratic," and hence immoral.

The sapping of the individual mind's capacity to think in genuine independence from a molasses-like public opinion goes hand in hand with a shrinking of the individual citizen's belief in and inclination toward meaningful civic action or significant involvement in public life. Tocqueville describes in the democratic way of life a specific new behavioral and emotional syndrome for which he invents a word: "individualism."

To understand what Tocqueville means, we must follow him in sharply distinguishing "individualism" from selfishness or egoism. Passionate, excessive self-love is a vice coeval with human nature. It manifests itself in all societies, in various ways, and most vividly in active, ambitious competition with others. Individualism, on the other hand, "is a quiet and considered sentiment which disposes each citizen to isolate himself from the mass of his fellows and retire into the circle of family and friends."[24] Modern democratic society, with its antitraditionalism, its opening of opportunity, its restless mobility, its stress on individual initiative and autonomy grounded in the moral principles of universal rights, uproots and detaches citizens one from another, steadily constricting the avenues and possibilities for any one person to shape or care for the lives of others. Modern democracy makes "the duties of each individual to the species much clearer, the devotion to another individual much rarer: the bond of human affection widens but weakens." "To the extent that conditions are equalized," Tocqueville points out, "there are more individuals who, not being rich enough or strong enough to exercise a great influence on the fate of their fellows, have nevertheless acquired or conserved enough enlightenment and wealth to be able to be self-sufficient." These individuals "owe nothing to anyone, they expect nothing, so to speak, from anyone; they habituate themselves to thinking of themselves always in isolation; they gladly imagine that their whole destiny is in their own hands." Thus, "democracy doesn't just make each person forget his ancestors, it hides from him his descendants and separates him from his contemporaries."

---

[23] Cf. ibid., vol. 2, pt. 1, chap. 5, 444: "Opinions are ill-defended or abandoned, and in despair of solving unaided the greatest problems of human destiny, men ignobly give up thinking about them."

[24] Quotations in this paragraph are from ibid., vol. 2, pt. 2, chap. 2., "On Individualism in Democratic Countries."

The powerful tendency of the democratic personality to withdraw into the narrow circle of immediate acquaintances is intensified by the inordinate taste for physical comfort that is yet another dangerous proclivity of modern democratic society. To grasp the peculiar character and intensity of this passion in modern democracy, Tocqueville again appeals to the contrast with aristocratic society. He states his basic premise as follows: "What most vividly seizes the human heart is not by any means the quiet possession of a precious object, it is the imperfectly satisfied desire to possess it accompanied by the incessant fear of losing it."[25] Now in aristocracy the few who are well off enjoy their hereditary comforts without having had to acquire them and without fear of losing them; while the vast majority who are poor lack the comforts of life without hope of acquiring them. In modern democracy, "when on the contrary, the ranks are blurred and privileges destroyed, when patrimonies are divided and enlightenment and liberty spread, the longing to acquire well-being presents itself to the imagination of the poor and the fear of losing it haunts the spirit of the rich." What is more, "a multitude of middling fortunes are established, whose possessors have enough material enjoyments to acquire a taste for them, but not enough to be contented; they never procure the material enjoyments without effort and do not indulge in them without anxiety." Accordingly, "they ceaselessly attach themselves to pursuing or to retaining these material enjoyments that are so precious, so incomplete, and so fugitive." The "passion for material well-being," Tocqueville contends, is thus "essentially a passion of the middle class," with which it grows and extends itself and finally becomes preponderant. The objects of this passion are "petty, but the soul cleaves to them: it dwells on them, every day and very closely, until finally they hide from it the rest of existence."

The democratic soul tends to be characterized by an unprecedented truncation of its conception of the future. "When each strives ceaselessly to change his station, when an immense competition is open to all, when riches are accumulated and dissipated in a few instants amidst the tumult of democracy, the idea of a quick and easy fortune, the image of Luck, in all its forms, presents itself to the human spirit."[26] "The present bulks large; it hides the future, which is eclipsed, and men no longer think beyond tomorrow." The result is not only spiritual barrenness and moral irresponsibility, but also an economically unhealthy disregard for long-range consequences.

---

[25] Quotations in this paragraph are from ibid., vol. 2, pt. 2, chaps. 10 and 11, "On the Taste for Material Well-Being in America," and "Particular Effects Produced by the Love of Material Enjoyments in Democratic Centuries."

[26] Quotations in this paragraph are from ibid., vol. 2, pt. 2, chap. 17, "How in Times of Equality and Doubt it is Important to Distance the Goal of Human Actions."

From the strange force of democratic man's passionate attachment to the petty and evanescent grows what Tocqueville calls "the secret anxiety which reveals itself in the actions of Americans."[27] "He who has constricted his heart to the sole quest for the goods of this world is always in a hurry"; "the recollection of the brevity of life goads him on continually"; "apart from the goods he already possesses, he imagines at every moment a thousand others that death will prevent him from enjoying, if he doesn't hurry." Yet the passion for physical pleasure is by nature easily discouraged: since the goal is enjoyment, the means must be pretty prompt and easy or they contradict the goal. As a consequence, in modern democracy "most of the souls are at one and the same time ardent and soft, violent and enervated." To this must be added the peculiarly depressing effects of the equality of opportunity. For this equality arouses in the imagination the ultimately delusive prospect of a boundless, preeminent success, if only one works hard enough and has a bit of luck; but in fact, "when men are more or less equal and following the same course, it is very difficult for any of them to move quickly and get through the uniform crowd surrounding and hemming them in." The equality democratic citizens find among themselves is then never quite the equality they seek; it is always disappointing. They always think themselves on the verge of being in a social station where they wish to be: they never find a station in which they can be content. "It is to these causes," Tocqueville says in summation, "that it is necessary to attribute the singular melancholy which the inhabitants of democratic countries often exhibit in the midst of their abundance."

The Remedy of Religion.—The preceding resume does not by any means exhaust Tocqueville's diagnosis, but it circumscribes some of the most important ills of modern democracy to which religious belief and authority may provide remedies.

Religion counteracts in manifold ways the "secret anxiety" to which democratic man is prey. "Most religions," Tocqueville submits, "are only general, simple, and practical means for teaching to men the immortality of the soul."[28] This is "the greatest advantage that a democratic people draws from the faiths, and one which makes those faiths more necessary to such a people than to all the others." In worship that inspires and is inspired by belief in the immortality of one's soul, the inhabitant of democracy is momentarily liberated "from the petty passions which agitate his life and

---

[27] Quotations in this paragraph are from ibid., vol. 2, pt. 2, chap. 13, "Why the Americans Show Themselves to be so Anxious in the Midst of their Well-Being."

[28] This and the preceding quotations in this paragraph are from ibid., vol. 2, pt. 2, chap. 15, "How Religious Faiths from Time to Time Turn the Soul of Americans Toward Spiritual Enjoyments."

from the evanescent interests which preoccupy it." "Religions instill a general habit of behaving with the future in view"; "in this respect," Tocqueville adds, "they work as much in favor of happiness in this world as of felicity in the next."[29]

Besides, no human being can avoid some obsession with the question of man's fate after death. Drawing on his studies of, and firsthand experiences in, the successive French Revolutions, Tocqueville argues that in the absence of authoritative religious answers to metaphysical questions, the anxiety which is in any case endemic in democracy grows to the point of a paralyzing enervation that prepares a people for bondage. Worried and exhausted by the "perpetual agitation of things," by the total mutability of the spiritual world, "they wish, at least, that everything would be firm and stable in the material realm, and, not being able to recover their old beliefs, they give themselves a master."[30]

Religion does not only counter in a direct way the anxiety peculiar to democratic man; it goes to the root causes of that anxiety, by opposing both materialism and individualism. It is this, Tocqueville judges, that is "the greatest advantage of religions" for democracy:

> There is no religion that does not place the goal of the desires of the human being beyond and above earthly goods, and that does not naturally elevate his soul toward regions far superior to those of the senses. Nor is there any that does not impose on each certain duties toward the human species, or in common with it, and that does not thus draw one, from time to time, away from the contemplation of oneself.
>
> Religious peoples are then naturally strong precisely where democratic peoples are weak; this shows clearly how important it is that men preserve their religion in becoming equal.[31]

One of Tocqueville's great themes is the way in which Americans combat the effects of individualism through "the doctrine of self-interest rightly understood" (la doctrine de l'interet bien entendu). This enlightened utilitarianism or egoism "does not inspire great sacrifices, but every day it prompts some small ones; by itself it cannot make a man virtuous, but its discipline shapes a lot of orderly, temperate, moderate, careful, and self-controlled citizens."[32] But if this doctrine "had in view this world only, it would be far from sufficient; because there are a great number of sacrifices

---

[29] Ibid., vol. 2, pt. 2, chap. 17.
[30] Ibid.
[31] Ibid., vol. 2, pt. 1, chap. 5.
[32] Ibid., vol. 2, pt. 2, chap. 8.

which cannot find their recompense except in the other world."[33] Religion provides this crucial additional dimension to the doctrine.

Still, Tocqueville cannot avoid drawing attention to a grave difficulty. It is, to say the least, far from clear that Christianity, or perhaps any refined religion, maintains itself as a matter of calculation of future rewards. Christianity teaches, Tocqueville reminds us, that "one ought to do good to one's fellows out of love of God." Christianity at its purest teaches the "magnificent" doctrine that a human being can "enter, through his intelligence, the divine thought," and, "in sacrificing his individual interests to that admirable order of all things, awaits no other recompense except the pleasure of contemplation." Tocqueville thus leaves his readers in some doubt as to whether he believes, in the final analysis, that Christianity, or any religion of truly sublime power, is altogether compatible with the central moral doctrine of modern democracy. In this very chapter, Tocqueville reminds us that for him *the* guide and model for Christian faith at its peak is Pascal; and in an earlier chapter Tocqueville "confessed" that he could "hardly believe" that passions such as are exhibited in Pascal "can emerge and develop as easily in the midst of democratic societies as they can in the bosom of aristocracies."[34]

Yet if truly profound religious faith is at some tension with modern democratic morality, Tocqueville insists that religion is to a much more massive degree supportive of and even essential to the morality democracy needs. Precisely because the private sphere assumes such importance in the lives of modern democrats, it is crucial, Tocqueville argues, that in their domestic lives Americans experience an oasis of order, tranquility, love, decency, and trust. The role of women in America—their piety, chastity, and fidelity, their voluntary submission to the non-despotic authority of their husbands, their often nigh heroic devotion to the nurture and education of their children—Tocqueville regards as perhaps the single most important factor in the success of the democratic experiment in America, as contrasted with France or Europe more generally. "In Europe, almost all the disorders of society are born around the domestic hearth and not far from the nuptial bed." In America, "religion reigns supreme over the soul of woman, and it is woman who makes the mores." Piety at once expresses and strengthens the mores and influence on mores of American women. It is at the hearth and in the home, under the influence of mothers and wives, that Americans learn to

---

[33] This and the following quotations are from ibid., vol. 2, pt. 2, chap. 9, "How the Americans Apply the Doctrine of Self-Interest Rightly Understood as Regards Religion."

[34] Ibid., vol. 2, pt. 1, chap. 10, 461–62.

surmount selfishness, appreciate order and stability, control sensual appetites, and enjoy pleasures that cannot be purchased.[35]

This means to say that American women, largely through and because of their piety, decisively influence political life. The Americans' religion, though it does not directly intervene in politics, must nevertheless "be considered as the first of their political institutions."[36] The various denominations and priesthoods make no claim to participate in earthly legislation, but they remind citizens of supramundane limits that the citizens, even when gathered together in the majority, are obliged to heed, in thought as well as in action. "Thus the human spirit never sees an unlimited field before itself; however great its audacity, it feels from time to time that it must arrest itself before insurmountable barriers." "Up until now," Tocqueville adds with some caution, "no one has ever been found, in the United States, who has dared to advance this maxim: that everything is permitted in the interests of society— an impious maxim, which seems to have been invented in a century of liberty in order to legitimate all the tyrants to come." For "what can be done with a people that is master of itself, if it is not subject to God?"

The philosophic method popularized by the eighteenth-century phil- osophers does not reign unchallenged in America, as it does in France, principally because Christianity has "preserved a great empire over the spirit of the Americans, and—this is the point I wish to emphasize—it does not at all reign only as a philosophy adopted after examination, but as a religion that is believed without discussion."[37] The Christian religion, with its authoritative and unquestioned dogmas, thus provides a powerful counterweight to that sway of public opinion that, combined with the inescapable need for authoritative guidance, is the outcome of the dogmatic distrust of all authority.

On the strictly political level, Tocqueville helps us to appreciate the advantages derived from the fact that the churches or religious denominations in modern democracy, and especially the Roman Catholic Church, are institutions whose authority and structure are neither dictated by, nor intermingled with, nor simply subordinate to, the constituted political authorities. The churches do not directly compete with democratic political

---

[35] Quotations are from ibid., vol. 1, pt. 2, chap. 9, "On the Principal Causes Which Tend to Maintain the Democratic Republic in the United States," subsection entitled, "Indirect Influence Which Religious Faiths Exercise on Political Society in the United States"; for Tocqueville's analysis of the role of women, see also ibid., vol. 2, pt. 3, chaps. 8–12.

[36] Quotations in this paragraph are from ibid., vol. 1, pt. 2, chap. 9, 292–94.

[37] Ibid., vol. 2, pt. 1, chap. 1.

authority, but they do stand apart, reminding all citizens of a higher law and a higher legal authority.

Tocqueville argues fervently and repeatedly that the strict but friendly separation of church and state in American democracy, so far from representing a compromise of religion's influence and strength, in fact creates the condition under which religion's true strength and influence can flourish. "Considering religions from a purely human point of view," their real strength lies in the overwhelming natural human desire for immortality. When a religion founds itself on this, "it can aspire to universality"; "it can draw to itself the heart of the human species." But when it allies itself to political powers or governments, religion mortgages its universal and permanent appeal to the limited and temporary prop of a specific regime. "It augments its strength over some but forfeits the hope of reigning over all." In addition, "it is sometimes constrained to defend allies who are such from interest rather than love; and it has to repulse as adversaries men who still love religion, although they are fighting religion's allies." In the long run, religion allied with any specific political authority is compelled to share in some measure the mortality and ultimate fragility of any such specific regime. These general considerations take on heightened significance in democracy, where the struggle of parties, factions, and individuals produces a natural agitation and restless instability in political life.[38]

Moreover, since "in times of enlightenment and of equality, the human spirit is loath to receive dogmatic beliefs, and senses vividly the need for them only in religion," it follows that "in these centuries, religions ought to restrict themselves more discretely than in other ages to the limits which are proper to them"; "for, in wishing to extend their power beyond religious matters, they risk not being believed in any matter."[39]

The Difficulties in Toqueville's Presentation.—Tocqueville's argument for the essential harmony between religion and modern democracy is not free from ambiguities and even grave problems. He admits, nay, he calls attention to, the implication that the Catholic religion and modern democracy are incompatible.[40] Reminding us that he speaks "as a practising Catholic," Tocqueville further concedes that, in the case of Roman Catholicism, the at first sight felicitous situation of religion in America is paradoxical; he confesses, indeed, that this situation is contrary to the historical practice and,

---

[38] The preceding quotations are from ibid., vol. 1, pt. 2, chap. 9, "On the Principal Causes that Render Religion Powerful in America."

[39] Ibid., vol. 2, pt. 1, chap. 5.

[40] Ibid., 445.

what is more, the traditional spirit of Roman Catholicism. But "I think," he wavers, with uncustomary hesitation, that the experience of American Catholicism shows that "one is mistaken in regarding the Catholic religion as a natural enemy of democracy."[41]

To be sure, "every religion has some political opinion linked to it by affinity"; the human spirit "seeks, I daresay, to *harmonize* earth with heaven"; and "Catholicism is like an absolute monarchy": "among Catholics, religious society is composed of just two elements—the priest and the people." This means that Catholicism is eminently compatible with equality, though less so with liberty or independence: "Catholicism places all intelligence on the same level," and "in applying to each human being the same measure, it loves to confound all the classes of society at the foot of the same altar." So how exactly does such a religion sympathize with democracy? Catholicism "disposes the faithful to obedience"; but does it dispose them to active private enterprise and republican citizenship? If American Catholics "are not strongly drawn by the nature of their beliefs toward democratic and republican opinions, at least they aren't naturally opposed, and their social position, as well as their being in a minority, make it a law for them to embrace those opinions." In America, Catholics, because they tend to be poor and few in number, "are led, perhaps in spite of themselves, toward political doctrines which, perhaps, they would adopt with less zeal were they rich and predominant."

The deep roots of the fruitful American partnership between religion and politics lie in the anti-Catholic New England Protestantism that is the fertile soil of the American experiment: "most of English America was peopled by men who, having shaken off the pope's authority, submitted to no other supremacy in religion; they thus carried into the New World a Christianity which I cannot describe better than in calling it democratic and republican: this fact singularly favored the establishment of the republic and of democracy in the conduct of business"; Protestantism "directs men much less towards equality than towards independence."[42] The Protestantism of New England saw "in civil liberty a noble exercise of the human faculties, the world of politics being a field opened up by the Creator to the efforts of intelligence."[43]

But Tocqueville's detailed study of New England Protestantism does not confirm the purported symbiosis between even this religion and modern

---

[41] Quotations in this paragraph are from ibid., vol. 1, pt. 2, chap. 9, "On Religion Considered as a Political Institution, How it Powerfully Contributes to Maintaining the Democratic Republic Among the Americans."

[42] Ibid., 288.

[43] Ibid., vol. 1, pt. 1, chap. 2, 47.

democracy. The founders of New England were "ardent sectarians."[44] They were "held within the narrowest bounds by certain religious beliefs"; not merely in the religious, but "in the moral world, everything was classified, coordinated, foreseen, and decided in advance." Their moral rigidity was balanced, however, by their political flexibility: "In the world of politics," everything was "in turmoil, contested, and uncertain." "In the one case obedience is passive, though voluntary; in the other there is independence, contempt of experience, and jealousy of all authority."

Tocqueville insists that "far from harming each other, these two apparently opposed tendencies work in harmony and seem to lend mutual support. Religion, he contends, "being free and powerful within its own sphere and content with the position reserved for it, realizes that its sway is all the better established because it relies only on its own powers and rules men's hearts without external support."

Yet Tocqueville is compelled to take note of the fact that Puritanism "was almost as much a political theory as a religious doctrine." The framers of the early New England penal laws "were especially concerned with the maintenance of good behavior and sound mores in society, so framers of the early New England penal laws "were especially concerned they constantly invaded the sphere of conscience, and there was hardly a sin not subject to the magistrate's censure." They took their inspiration from the Bible, and "conceived," as Tocqueville puts it, "the strange idea of borrowing their provisions from the text of the Holy Writ." Tocqueville deplores the "ridiculous and tyrannical laws" which resulted, although he stresses that "we must not forget" that these laws "were not imposed from outside—they were voted by the free agreement of all the interested parties themselves." He adds a reminder that Puritan "mores were even more austere and puritanical than their laws." In short, Tocqueville has to admit that the democratic spirit of the New England Protestants was neither modern nor liberal, but at best a contradictory, uneasy, and untenable compromise between premodern and modern, between closed and open, conceptions of society.

It may be doubted whether Tocqueville succeeds in sustaining his thesis that the steady progress of a more liberal outlook strengthens or even in the long run maintains religious faith and authority of a healthy sort. He concedes that "the spirit of individual independence" is religion's "most dangerous enemy," even while insisting that "religion succeeds in struggling

---

[44] Quotations in this paragraph are from ibid., vol. 1, pt. 1, chap. 2, "On the Point of Departure of the Anglo-Americans and its Importance for their Future."

successfully" against this spirit, by "respecting all democratic instincts which are not contrary to religion and making use of many of them."[45]

On the very next page he remarks that men who live in democratic centuries "are strongly inclined to shake off all religious authority."[46] When they do submit to such authority, he continues, "they want it at least to be single and uniform," because the democratic spirit is one which gives men "the taste for and the idea of a power in society that is unique, simple, and the same for all." The prospects for Protestantism, and the support it provides for a spirit of independence, are therefore not sanguine: "our contemporaries are naturally little disposed to belief, but once they have a religion, they encounter immediately within themselves a hidden instinct which unconsciously urges them toward Catholicism." This "instinct" draws strength from the fact that it is not illogical:

> One of the most familiar weaknesses of the human intelligence is to want to reconcile contrary principles and to purchase peace at the price of logic. There have therefore always been and always will be men who, after having submitted in some of their religious beliefs to an authority, still seek to exempt some of their other religious beliefs, and allow their spirits to float at random between obedience and liberty. But I am led to believe that the number of these types will be smaller in democratic centuries than in other centuries, and that our grandchildren will tend more and more to divide themselves between those who abandon Christianity completely and others who enter into the bosom of the Church of Rome.[47]

Even more disturbing than this prediction of the inanition of Protestantism is Tocqueville's warning about the future vigor and effects of pantheistic religious beliefs. The strength of pantheism is the predictable outcome of the fact that "as conditions become more equal, each individual becomes more like his fellows, weaker, and smaller, and the habit grows of ceasing to think about the citizens and considering only the people; individuals are forgotten, and the species alone counts." In this democratic age, "the concept of unity becomes an obsession for the human spirit; it searches for unity everywhere." Precisely because pantheism "destroys human individuality," it will "have secret charms for the men who inhabit democracy": "it fosters the pride and soothes the laziness of their minds." "It

---

[45] Ibid., vol. 2, pt. 2, chap. 5, 449.
[46] Ibid., vol. 2, pt. 1, chap. 6, 450.
[47] Ibid.

is against this that all those who still appreciate the true grandeur of man ought to unite and fight."[48]

All of these observations, Tocqueville notes, are perfectly compatible with the further observation that Americans are and will increasingly be given to feverish outbreaks of short-lived religious enthusiasms and madnesses of all sorts, manipulated by wild or cunning preachers "hawking the word of God from place to place": "if ever the thoughts of the great majority of mankind came to be concentrated solely on the search for material goods, one can anticipate that there would be a colossal reaction in the souls of some; they would distractedly launch out into the world of spirits."[49]

At the bottom of Tocqueville's richly ambiguous and thought-provoking reflection on the place of religion in American democracy, one discerns the following fundamental difficulty. The spirit of Tocqueville's analysis is that of an enlightened and prudent supporter of modern democracy. Religion, properly conceived in terms of this spirit, is valued not for its truth, but for its usefulness in remedying or limiting the secular ills of a secular society. But the overwhelming stress on the utility of religion does not establish, and indeed it may contribute to undermining, its credibility. To esteem religion above all for its usefulness in serving worldly ends entails denying what is, from the religious point of view, the necessarily supreme value of the essentially otherworldly ends of religion itself.

As Tocqueville repeatedly remarks, he is viewing religion "from a purely human point of view," and in that perspective, "what is most important for society is not that all citizens should profess the true religion but that they should prove religion."[50] "The main business of religion is to purify, to regulate and to restrain the overly ardent and too excessive taste for well-being that is felt by men in ages of equality."[51] Insofar as the democratic citizenry come more and more to share this perspective, Tocqueville argues, "religion is loved, supported, and honored, and only by looking into the depths of men's souls will one see what wounds it has suffered."[52]

But what if anything can heal or even staunch these wounds? "I do not know," confesses Tocqueville, "what is to be done to give back to European Christianity the energy of youth: God alone could do that."[53] Yet Tocqueville cannot shirk the duty of attempting to discern how government might foster

---

[48] Quotations in this paragraph are from ibid., vol. 2, pt. 1, chap. 7, "What it is that Inclines the Spirit of Democratic Peoples Toward Pantheism."

[49] Ibid., vol. 2, pt. 2, chap. 12.

[50] Ibid., 290.

[51] Ibid., 448.

[52] Ibid., 300.

[53] Ibid., 301.

religious faith without violating religious liberty. "I think that the only effective means which governments can use to make the doctrine of the immortality of the soul respected is daily to act as if they believed it themselves. I think that it is only by conforming scrupulously to religious morality in great affairs that they can flatter themselves that they are teaching the citizens to understand it and to love and respect it in little matters.[54]

Tocqueville knows that this is not enough. "Governments must study means to give men back that interest in the future which neither religion nor social conditions any longer inspire"; "in accustoming the citizens to think of the future in this world, they will gradually be led without noticing it themselves toward religious beliefs. Thus the same means that, up to a certain point, enable men to manage without religion are perhaps after all the only means we still possess for bringing mankind back, by a long and roundabout path, to a state of faith."[55]

It is hard to believe that this thought satisfied Tocqueville. Tocqueville's defense of religious liberty and the separation of church and state, and his defense of modern democracy as resting essentially, for its stability as well as its dignity, on such liberty and separation, is not as reassuring as one might hope. If Tocqueville is largely correct in his analysis, then our situation and our difficulties are grave indeed.

Returning to the comparative considerations with which we introduced this Tocquevillian reflection on the role of religion in modern democracy, we may close with the following observations. If or to the extent that we decide Tocqueville is right in his analysis of the specific ways religion—especially organized religion—can contribute to saving modern democracy from some of its worst proclivities, we will be inclined to prefer the more moderate Canadian constitutional approach to the establishment of religion. We will surely be led to recommend that Canadian jurists think twice before rushing to incorporate into Canadian constitutional law any approximation to the recent American (and original Madisonian) view of the radical constitutional separation of church and state, especially at the levels of provincial and local government, and in the administration of the nation's schools.

---

[54] Ibid., vol. 2, pt. 2, chap. 15, end.
[55] bid., vol. 2, pt. 2, chap. 17, end.